Rereading
Jack London

Jack London, ca. 1904.

REREADING JACK LONDON

EDITED BY LEONARD CASSUTO
AND JEANNE CAMPBELL REESMAN

With an Afterword
by Earle Labor

STANFORD UNIVERSITY PRESS
Stanford, California
1996

Stanford University Press,
Stanford, California
© 1996 by the Board of Trustees of the
Leland Stanford Junior University

Printed in the United States of America

Frontispiece reprinted by permission of the Henry E. Huntington Library, San Marino, California, and the Trust of Irving
Shepard.

CIP data appear at the end of the book

Stanford University Press publications are
distributed exclusively by Stanford University Press
within the United States, Canada, Mexico, and
Central America; they are distributed exclusively by
Cambridge University Press throughout
the rest of the world.

For Milo Shepard

ACKNOWLEDGMENTS

As editors we have enjoyed generous advice and assistance during the preparation of this volume. First we wish to thank all of the scholars who participated in the First and Second Biennial Jack London Society Symposia, held in 1992 in Sonoma and in 1994 at the Henry E. Huntington Library in San Marino. Their additions to London scholarship have dramatically expanded and deepened the field, and many of these new views are collected here. For their enduring friendship and support we warmly thank I. Milo Shepard, Trustee, the Trust of Irving Shepard, and Sara S. Hodson, Curator of Literary Manuscripts at the Huntington Library. We also thank Wayne Furman of the Office of Special Collections at the New York Public Library; Earle Labor of Centenary College of Louisiana; Babette Babich of Fordham University; Cathy N. Davidson, editor of *American Literature*; Gerald A. Kirk, editor, *Studies in the Novel*; Jacqueline Tavernier-Courbin, editor, *Thalia: Studies in Literary Humor*; and Gary Scharnhorst, Robert Fleming, and James Barbour, editors of *American Literary Realism, 1870–1910*, for their assistance.

We are grateful to Norris Pope, Helen Tartar, Ellen F. Smith, and Barbara Phillips of Stanford University Press for their enthusiasm for the book and for their careful assistance in its preparation. And the exacting efforts of Mieko Greening, Gail Jones, Mark Juelg, Jan Lowe, and Jennifer Myers enabled manuscript preparation to move forward smoothly.

Quotations from London's typescript of *Cherry* in Andrew Furer's " 'Zone Conquerors' and 'White Devils': The Contradictions of Race in the Works of Jack London," as well as those from London's notes for _Adventure_ cited in Clarice Stasz's "Social Darwinism, Gender, and Humor in _Adventure_," are used by permission of I. Milo Shepard. The notes from _Adventure_ (Acquisition #1624) in Clarice Stasz's essay, the quotations from Luther Burbank's June 2, 1906, letter to Jack London (JL 3445) in Andrew Furer's essay, and the letters from S. S. McClure (JL 14201, 14211) and John Phillips (JL 16482, 16485, 16486, 16487, 16489, 16491) in James Williams's "Commitment and Practice: The Authorship of Jack London," are reproduced by permission of the Huntington Library, San Marino, California. The letters of George Brett to Jack London in James Williams's essay, located in Macmillan Company, Records, Rare Books and Manuscripts Division of the New York Public Library, are reproduced by permission of the Astor, Lenox, and Tilden Foundations.

Jonathan Auerbach's "Congested Mails: Buck and Jack's Call" first appeared in _American Literature_ 67 (March 1995): 51–76 and is reprinted here by permission of Duke University Press. Sam S. Baskett's "Sea-Change in _The Sea-Wolf_" is reprinted by permission from _American Literary Realism, 1870–1910_ 24 (Winter 1992): 5–22, © 1992 McFarland & Co., Inc., Publishers, Jefferson, North Carolina 28640. Clarice Stasz's "Social Darwinism, Gender, and Humor in _Adventure_" was originally published as "Sarcasm, Irony, and Social Darwinism in Jack London's _Adventure_," in _Thalia: Studies in Literary Humor_, Special Issue, _The Humor of Jack London_, ed. Jacqueline Tavernier-Courbin, 1–2 (1992): 83–90. Christopher Hugh Gair's " 'The Way Our People Came': Citizenship, Capitalism, and Racial Differences in _The Valley of the Moon_" first appeared in _Studies in the Novel_ 25 (Winter 1993): 418–35. Copyright 1993 by the University of North Texas. Reprinted by permission of the publisher.

CONTENTS

CONTRIBUTORS

JONATHAN AUERBACH is associate professor of English at the University of Maryland. His publications include *The Romance of Failure: First-Person Fictions of Poe, Hawthorne, and James* and *Male Call: Becoming Jack London*.

SAM S. BASKETT is Professor Emeritus of Michigan State University and was the first president of the Jack London Society. His publications include the 1956 Rinehart edition of *Martin Eden* and pioneering essays on London in *American Literature, American Quarterly, Modern Fiction Studies*, and *Western American Literature*.

LAWRENCE I. BERKOVE is professor of English at the University of Michigan-Dearborn. He is the editor of *The Fighting Horse of the Stanislaus: Stories and Essays by Dan De Quille* and De Quille's *The Gnomes of the Dead Rivers*, as well as De Quille's *Dives and Lazarus* and a collection of Ambrose Bierce's work, *Skepticism and Dissent: Selected Journalism, 1898–1901*.

LEONARD CASSUTO is associate professor of English at Fordham University. He is the author of *The Inhuman Race: The Racial Grotesque in American Literature and Culture* as well as articles on naturalist writers.

CHARLES L. CROW is professor of English at Bowling Green State University. He is co-editor of *The Occult in America: New Historical Perspectives* and *The Haunted Dusk: American Supernatural Fiction, 1820–1920*, as well as *Itinerary Seven: Essays on California Writers*. He is the author of the critical study *Janet Lewis* and many articles on Western and California writers.

SCOTT DERRICK is assistant professor of English at Rice University. He is the author of several articles on James, Mary Shelley, Hawthorne, and other writers and focuses his work on the construction of masculinity in narrative.

ANDREW J. FURER is visiting assistant professor at the University of Connecticut. He is the author of articles on Jack London, Theodore Dreiser, and other naturalist writers, and is working on a book on the relationship between self reform and social reform in the early twentieth century.

CHRISTOPHER HUGH GAIR is lecturer in English at the College of St. Mark and St. John, Plymouth. He has published essays on London in *Arizona Quarterly*, *Essays in Literature*, *Over Here*, the *Magazine of Cultural Studies*, *Studies in the Novel*, and *Works and Days*.

EARLE LABOR is the Wilson Professor of American Literature at Centenary College of Louisiana. He is the author of the first major critical book on London, *Jack London* (Twayne U.S. Authors series, 1974). In addition to numerous articles on London and other American writers, he is also the editor of several editions of the writer's work, including those from Macmillan, Oxford, and Harper and Row, and a is co-editor of the Stanford *Letters of Jack London* (1988) and the *Complete Stories* (1993). He is now working on a major biography of London for Farrar, Straus and Giroux.

ROBERT PELUSO has taught at the University of Pittsburgh. He is at work on a book entitled *Incorporating Cultural Practice: The Origin and Meaning of a National Institute and an American Academy of Arts and Letters*.

JEANNE CAMPBELL REESMAN is director of the Division of English, Classics, and Philosophy and professor of English at the University of Texas at San Antonio; she is also Executive Coordinator of the Jack London Society. She is the author of *American Designs: The Late Novels of James and Faulkner* and co-author of *A Handbook of Critical Approaches to Literature* and, with Earle Labor, the Twayne U.S. Authors series volume *Jack London: Revised Edition* (1994). She has published articles on Jack London and other American writers in *American Literary Realism*, the *Jack London Newsletter*, *The Kenyon Review*, *Renascence*, *Western American Literature*, and elsewhere. She is presently at work on a book on London's short fiction.

FRANCIS R. SHOR is associate professor of humanities in the Interdisciplinary Studies Program at Wayne State University. He has two books in progress on the history of American radical and reformist politics and has published widely on these topics, as well as on literary figures such as London.

JAMES SLAGEL is on the faculty at the all-Hawaiian Kamehameha School in Honolulu.

CLARICE STASZ is professor of history at Sonoma State University.

She is the author of seven books and numerous scholarly articles, including *Sexism: Scientific Debates*, *The American Nightmare: Why Inequality Persists*, *American Dreamers: Charmian and Jack London*, and *The Vanderbilt Women: Dynasty of Wealth, Glamour and Power*.

TANYA WALSH is a Ph.D. candidate in English at the University of Kansas, where her major fields are modern fiction and critical theory.

JAMES WILLIAMS is managing editor of *Critical Inquiry* and the author of articles on Jack London in *American Literary Realism* and *The Jack London Newsletter*. He is the editor and founder of the *Jack London Journal*.

THE WORKS OF JACK LONDON

The Son of The Wolf (stories). Boston: Houghton Mifflin, 1900.
The God of His Fathers (stories). New York: Century, 1901.
Children of the Frost (stories). New York: Century, 1902.
The Cruise of the Dazzler (juvenilia). New York: Century, 1902.
A Daughter of the Snows (novel). Philadelphia: J. B. Lippincott, 1902.
The Kempton-Wace Letters (with Anna Strunsky). New York: Macmillan, 1903.
The Call of the Wild (novella). New York: Macmillan, 1903.
The People of the Abyss (sociological study). New York: Macmillan, 1903.
The Faith of Men (stories). New York: Macmillan, 1904.
The Sea-Wolf (novel). New York: Macmillan, 1904.
War of the Classes (essays). New York: Macmillan, 1905.
The Game (novella). New York: Macmillan, 1905.
Tales of the Fish Patrol. New York: Macmillan, 1905.
Moon-Face and Other Stories. New York: Macmillan, 1906.
White Fang (novel). New York: Macmillan, 1906.
Scorn of Women (play). New York: Macmillan, 1906.
Before Adam (novel). New York: Macmillan, 1907.
Love of Life and Other Stories. New York: Macmillan, 1907.
The Road (tramping reminiscences). New York: Macmillan, 1907.
The Iron Heel (novel). New York: Macmillan, 1908.
Martin Eden (novel). New York: Macmillan, 1909.
Lost Face (stories). New York: Macmillan, 1910.

Revolution and Other Essays. New York: Macmillan, 1910.

Burning Daylight (novel). New York: Macmillan, 1910.

Theft: A Play in Four Acts. New York: Macmillan, 1910.

When God Laughs and Other Stories. New York: Macmillan, 1910.

Adventure (novel). New York: Macmillan, 1911.

The Cruise of the Snark (travel sketches). New York: Macmillan, 1911.

South Sea Tales. New York: Macmillan, 1911.

The House of Pride and Other Tales of Hawaii. New York: Macmillan, 1912.

A Son of the Sun (stories). Garden City, N.Y.: Doubleday, Page, 1912.

Smoke Bellew (stories). New York: Century, 1912.

The Night-Born (stories). New York: Century, 1913.

The Abysmal Brute (novella). New York: Century, 1913.

John Barleycorn (semi-autobiographical prohibition treatise). New York: Century, 1913.

The Valley of the Moon (novel). New York: Macmillan, 1913.

The Strength of the Strong (stories). New York: Macmillan, 1914.

The Mutiny of the Elsinore (novel). New York: Macmillan, 1914.

The Scarlet Plague (novella). New York: Macmillan, 1915.

The Star Rover (novel). New York: Macmillan, 1915.

The Acorn-Planter: A California Forest Play. New York: Macmillan, 1916.

The Little Lady of the Big House (novel). New York: Macmillan, 1916.

The Turtles of Tasman (stories). New York: Macmillan, 1916.

The Human Drift (miscellany). New York: Macmillan, 1917.

Jerry of the Islands (novel). New York: Macmillan, 1917.

Michael Brother of Jerry (novel). New York: Macmillan, 1917.

The Red One (stories). New York: Macmillan, 1918.

On the Makaloa Mat (stories). New York: Macmillan, 1919.

Hearts of Three (novel). New York: Macmillan, 1920.

Dutch Courage and Other Stories. New York: Macmillan, 1922.

The Assassination Bureau, Ltd. (novel completed by Robert L. Fish). New York: McGraw-Hill, 1963.

Letters from Jack London, edited by King Hendricks and Irving Shepard. New York: Odyssey Press, 1965.

Jack London Reports (essays and newspaper articles), edited by King Hendricks and Irving Shepard. New York: Doubleday, 1970.

Daughters of the Rich (curtain raiser written by Hilda Gilbert but published under London's name with his permission), edited by James E. Sisson. Oakland, Calif.: Holmes Book Co., 1971.

Gold (three-act play written by Herbert Heron, based upon two London stories, "A Day's Lodging" and "The Man on the Other Bank," published under the names of Heron and London as joint authors), edited by James E. Sisson. Oakland, Calif.: Holmes Book Co., 1972.

Jack London on the Road: The Tramp Diary and Other Hobo Writings, edited by Richard W. Etulain. Logan: Utah State University Press, 1979.

No Mentor But Myself: A Collection of Articles, Essays, Reviews, and Letters, by Jack London, on Writing and Writers, edited by Dale L. Walker. Port Washington, N.Y.: Kennikat Press, 1979.

A Klondike Trilogy: Three Uncollected Stories, edited by Earle Labor. Santa Barbara, Calif.: Neville, 1983.

Dearest Greek: Jack and Charmian London's Presentation Inscriptions to George Sterling, edited by Stanley Wertheim and Sal Noto. Cupertino, Calif.: Eureka, 1983.

With a Heart Full of Love: Jack London's Presentation Inscriptions to the Women in His Life [Eliza London Shepard, Charmian London, Flora Wellman London, and Mabel Applegarth], edited by Sal Noto. Berkeley, Calif.: Twowindows Press, 1986.

The Letters of Jack London, edited by Earle Labor, Robert C. Leitz, III, and I. Milo Shepard, 3 vols. Stanford, Calif.: Stanford University Press, 1988.

The Complete Short Stories of Jack London, edited by Earle Labor, Robert C. Leitz, III, and I. Milo Shepard, 3 vols. Stanford, Calif.: Stanford University Press, 1993.

Parts of Books

Umbstaetter, H. D. *The Red Hot Dollar and Other Stories from The Black Cat*, with an Introduction by Jack London. Boston: Page, 1911.

Sinclair, Upton. *The Cry for Justice: An Anthology of the Literature of Social Protest*, with an Introduction by Jack London. Philadelphia: John C. Winston, 1915.

Cox, Francis A. *What Do You Know About a Horse?*, with a Foreword by Jack London (Foreword written by Cox but published under London's name with his permission). London: G. Bell and Sons, 1915.

Schwarz, Osias L. *General Types of Superior Men: A Philosophical-Psychological Study of Genius, Talent, and Philistinism in Their Bearings upon Human Society and Its Struggles for a Better Social Order*, with a Preface by Jack London (Preface written by Schwarz but published under London's name with his permission). Boston: R. G. Badger, 1916.

The world,—this shadow of the soul, or other me,—lies wide around. Its attractions are the keys which unlock my thoughts and make me acquainted with myself. I run eagerly into this resounding tumult. I grasp the hands of those next me, and take my place in the ring to suffer and to work, taught by an instinct that so shall the dumb abyss be vocal with speech. I pierce its order; I dissipate its fear; I dispose of it within the circuit of my expanding life. So much only of life as I know by experience, so much of the wilderness have I vanquished and planted, or so far have I extended my being, my dominion. I do not see how any man can afford, for the sake of his nerves and his nap, to spare any action in which he can partake. It is pearls and rubies to his discourse. . . . A strange process too, this by which experience is converted into thought, as a mulberry leaf is converted into satin. The manufacture goes forward at all hours.

—Ralph Waldo Emerson
"The American Scholar"
(1837)

Introduction

Jack London, a Representative Man

LEONARD CASSUTO AND

JEANNE CAMPBELL REESMAN

Jack London's autobiographical hero, Martin Eden, finds himself early in his writing career "engaged continually in tracing the relationship between all things under the sun and on the other side of the sun," drawing up lists of "the most incongruous things," and looking for kinship among "love, poetry, earthquake, fire, rattlesnakes, rainbows, precious gems, monstrosities, sunsets, the roaring of lions, illuminating gas, cannibalism, beauty, murder, lovers, fulcrums, and tobacco." As an artist Martin travels this universe, wandering "through its byways and alleys and jungles, not as a terrified traveler in the thick of mysteries seeking an unknown goal, but observing and charting and becoming familiar with all there was to know." The more he knew, "the more passionately he admired the universe, life, and his own life in the midst of it all."[1] Jack London was by no means identical to Martin Eden, but artist and character share a desire to know and to believe. The art of impassioned realism that London developed as a response to this desire reflects his own immersion in a unified diversity of forms. Throughout his life he seemed determined to enter into culture after culture and community after community and to describe them from within. Working out his epistemological and artistic desires in one of the most volatile periods in American cultural history, London voiced his curiosity about the world through an astonishing array of characters: American Indians, South Sea Islanders, sourdoughs, scientists, socialists, sea-wives, prizefighters, murderers, the mentally retarded—even poets and literary critics. His list of 50-odd books is led by the titles that made him the most famous American author in the world:

The Call of the Wild and the other Klondike stories, *The Sea-Wolf*, and *Martin Eden*. These works continue to find their readers today, but in addition some lesser-known works are being reprinted, including *The Valley of the Moon*, "Samuel," "The Night-Born," and "The Red One," access to which allows us to go beyond the naturalist, adventurer-writer, and racialist categories that have kept us dwelling in only a few of Jack London's worlds.

The breadth and depth of new critical study of London's work since the 1970's attest to his newfound respectability among critics. During the last decade, London has received unprecedented attention, from the publication of the Stanford *Letters* (1988) and *Complete Stories* (1993) to the many important critical books, articles, and special issues of journals that have appeared. There has been new initiative not only to move beyond traditional versions of realism and naturalism in addressing London but also to replace biographical treatments of his works with new and diverse theoretical approaches. This book brings together the most current and exciting of these new voices.

As a way of entering the volume through an illustration of London's multiplicity, let us consider James Slagel's and Robert Peluso's contributions. Both these writers apply critical insights from cultural studies—specifically, the pioneering views of Edward Said—to texts by Jack London, but their conclusions contrast sharply. Slagel argues that London's sympathetic treatment of native Hawaiians in "Koolau the Leper" speaks for a deep, and at that time rarely seen, consciousness of the integrity of native cultures, and that by rendering the struggles of Koolau and his countrymen in fictional form, London brings a dignity to their fight against colonialism that is absent from the "official" historical account. Peluso uses the same critical apparatus to examine London's *People of the Abyss*, but he concludes that London's political radicalism has a profoundly establishmentarian cast, that his exposé of England's urban poverty is a textual springboard for an imperialistic nationalism that is far more conservative than has been supposed of an author who declared that his intellectual and emotional home was with the Left. If we accept the arguments of both Slagel and Peluso, how are we to account for their disparate views? What does the contrast between them say about the thought and work of Jack London?

Answers to these two questions underlie the thesis of this book. We might turn to Whitman's "Do I contradict myself? / Very well then I contradict myself, / (I am large, I contain multitudes)"; but to explain London's own kosmos, with all its attendant contradictions, we should look to Whitman's self-declared inspiration, Ralph Waldo Emerson. Like Whitman, Emerson was no stranger to contradictions. In 1850 he published a collection of essay-length portraits that he had written during the preceding two years. In *Representative Men*, he described not so much "greatness" (though that theme was a preoccupation of his), but something more complicated, more limited, and finally more concrete in place and time. Emerson's great men are "partial men,"[2] containing, as Jerome Loving says, only certain qualities of the ideal. They "put their limitations to best use in an imperfect world. They make allowances."[3] "Representativeness" is, to Emerson, a condition of partial embodiment, of the self's idealism within a society that both constrains and enables it.

As Maurice Gonnaud has observed, Emersonian "representativeness" is best understood within the context of the individual's relation to the group. This is true by definition (to be "representative" assumes the existence of that larger group for which one stands) and in practice as well. We may consider, for example, the difference between Thomas Carlyle's and Emerson's visions of human greatness: Carlyle's hero is aloof from humanity, while Emerson believes that "the function of representative men is to comfort and reassure" by proximity. In perhaps the best single instance of this distinction, Emerson calls Plato "a great average man."[4] Such renderings are part of what Gonnaud calls "an equalization at the top." In Emerson's words, "The constituency determines the vote of the representative. He is not only representative, but participant. Like can only be known by like. The reason why he knows about them is that he is of them; he has just come out of nature, or from being a part of that thing." The representative man is decisively of his time, an ineradicable part of whatever he produces and whomever he affects. As Emerson says of Shakespeare: The great man "finds himself in the river of thoughts and events, forced onward by the ideas and necessities of his contemporaries."[5]

Emerson's democratic vision may be contrasted with the pessimistic, frustrated elitism of one of London's acknowledged influences, Friedrich Nietzsche. Nietzsche called Emerson "a man as instinctively feeds on pure ambrosia and leaves alone the indigestible in things."[6] Emerson spotlighted representativeness rather than "greatness" as such, with the representative man inspired by (as well as inspiring) the larger group, but Nietzsche saw a more oppositional relationship, with greatness always undermined by mediocrity and the "virtue of the herd" inevitably triumphing. Of the "great man," Nietzsche wrote that "when not speaking to himself, he wears a mask. . . . He rather lies than tells the truth: it requires more spirit and *will*."[7]

Though London saw value and challenge in Nietzsche's ideas (first available, it should be noted, in inaccurate translations), we suggest that his un-systematic, often self-contradictory worldview, buttressed by his eccentric vision of "individualistic socialism," may be better described by Emersonian representativeness than by Nietzschean greatness and its accompanying dis-contents. (Indeed, London lamented what he saw as a critical misunder-standing of *The Sea-Wolf* according to which he himself endorsed Nietz-schean ideas.) The point here is not to trace literary influence—there is no evidence that Emerson made any significant impression on London. Instead, Emerson's metaphor is a helpful navigational tool to get through London's tangled ideas and—as will become clear—a way of emphasizing the impor-tance of London to American literary studies.

The passage from *Martin Eden* with which we began sounds remark-ably like Emerson's delineation of the world of representative men and re-inforces Emerson's notion that the representative man is really a heightened version of any man:

> A man is a centre for nature, running out threads of relation through every thing, fluid and solid, material and elemental. The earth rolls; every clod and stone comes to the meridian: so every organ, function, acid, crystal, grain of dust, has its relation to the brain. It waits long, but its turn comes. Each plant has its parasite, and each created thing its lover and poet. Justice has already been done to steam, to iron, to wood, to coal, to lodestone, to io-dine, to corn and cotton; but how few materials are yet used by our arts! The mass of creatures and of qualities are still hid and expectant. It would seem as if each waited, like the enchanted princess in fairy tales, for a destined human deliverer. Each must be disenchanted and walk forth to the day in human shape.

The young Martin would have agreed with Emerson's excited vision of Ge-nius as "the naturalist or geographer of the supersensible regions," and of humanity "as elastic as the gas of gunpowder," for "a sentence in a book, or a word dropped in conversation, sets free our fancy, and instantly our heads are bathed in galaxies, and our feet tread the floor of the Pit." "As to what we call the masses, and common men,—there are no common men," Emer-son averred, but because of caste and custom most never find their great-ness.[8] None of the men he profiles (Plato, Swedenborg, Montaigne, Shake-speare, Napoleon, Goethe) is a social reformer. But they all affect the world in their own ways; they all shape and are shaped by their surroundings so as to create the world that can accommodate and in turn generate their pow-erful visions of new realities.

Jack London is one of American literature's representative men, a figure of singular importance in our national tradition, even as his work occupies a unique place within the specific time and place in which he lived.[9] By this we do not mean to recycle Charles Child Walcutt's pioneering but now familiar argument that American naturalist literature descends from the Transcendentalist impulse. Rather, we propose that Emerson's "man in his place" metaphor of representativeness—encompassing the dynamic between self and society at a particular moment—is especially useful for understanding Jack London today.

"A man in his place," says Emerson, "is constructive, fertile, magnetic, inundating armies with his purpose, which is thus executed." The phrase is crucial, but what does it mean for a writer to be "in his place"? For London, the answer has many facets. As a fictionist, journalist, political theorist, and pamphleteer, London carved out a place of unprecedented breadth in the early-twentieth-century American literary landscape. Yet because London has received far more biographical than critical attention, his "place" as a writer looking within his own culture has yet to be examined in enough detail. Emerson writes in "The American Scholar" that the American man of letters should be a student of nature and man of action as well as a reader of books, that "only so much do I know, as I have lived. Instantly we know whose words are loaded with life, and whose not." Similarly, in "Literary Ethics" he insists that "the new man must feel that he is new, and has not come into the world mortgaged to the opinions and usages of Europe, and Asia, and Egypt"; he must strive for the "sense of spiritual independence" that is like "the lovely varnish of the dew, whereby the old, hard, peaked earth and its old self-same productions are made new every morning, and shining with the last touch of the artist's hand." But Emerson's emphasis upon action is followed by his observation that "the final value of action," through what he calls the "great principle of Undulation" in nature, is that it propels the mind: "Thinking is the function. Living is the functionary."[10] Scholarly emphasis on the events of Jack London's life has drawn attention away from the writing, which was always the central activity within that life. If London fits Emerson's mold of an artist engaged with the world, then it follows that having in the past focused more on London's "world," we should now look more closely at his art and the numerous worlds it uncovers. This book is the first collection primarily composed of original critical essays on London; we hope and expect it will not be the last.

American naturalist criticism has been moving beyond its previous locus of determinist ideas to embrace more complex, less dogmatic visions of turn-of-the-century United States culture. Jack London's work provides a rich ground for the probing examination naturalism has undergone as its boundaries have become more permeable, and the study of London's writing enriches both humanistic and deterministic reevaluations of naturalism.[11] In each case, the connecting thread is London's deeply felt need to believe—a need shared with Emerson—accompanied by his avowed materialism. Joel Porte has noted Emerson's great preoccupation with "the universal impulse to believe,"[12] and if any thematic thread can be followed through Jack London's vast corpus of work, it is perhaps that of belief. But belief was always a conflicted struggle for London—as it was for many of his literary contemporaries—in significant part because the verities of his world were changing so fast. London's fiction often features unresolved clashes between systems of belief: in *The Sea-Wolf,* for example, Wolf Larsen's harsh Darwinian materialism opposes the postlapsarian but re-sexualized version of Genesis that American Victorians Humphrey Van Weyden and Maud Brewster enact on Endeavor Island at the end of the book. Similarly, in *Martin Eden,* Martin's newly adopted Spencerian doctrine is at perpetual war with his native sympathy for the unfortunate. Daniel Borus has described how systemic changes in material culture—typewriters, for example—exerted a formative pressure on writers during the post–World War I era; it is clear that London anticipated these changes.[13] From the Northland stories, which wrestle with the question of whether a larger force watches or guides the icy struggle, to the self-conscious mythmaking of his final South Seas fiction, London confronts the reality of being a writer in a world that was changing physically and spiritually, technologically and economically. Though an eventful half-century separates them, Emerson the New England Unitarian and London the western materialist share a desire to confront the world whole, rejecting the dualism of matter and spirit, as well as the possibility of approaching these separately.

London struggled mightily as a writer and thinker to understand his world and to change it. As with Emerson—and his representative men—the constant in London's intellectual life was movement. His politics displayed a notorious inconsistency, and the range of his works defies intellectual or generic categorization. Though readers have never had trouble approaching it, London's work is hard to read critically because of its diversity. Early in his career he successfully opposed the popular magazines' prevailing literary modes of overheated sentimentality with the frigid blast of his radical reconstruction of nature in the Northland. Then came the stories of New Women, racial others, alien cultures, cavemen, and dystopians as chosen centers of consciousness. Throughout, London strives for an ineffable spiritual reality, which he sought most explicitly in his last year, following his reading of C. G. Jung. The primordial vision of the Northland stories is transmuted into his California agrarian dream and then finds its final, but still dynamic, form in the psychological and archetypal Oceanic Paradise Lost with which he ended his career. His only consistency may seem to lie in the volume and power of his barbaric yawp, his effort to know and to be heard, to make himself a force in the world in which he lived. But his consistent appeal is in the artistry he employs to convey this force, in his craftsmanship with language.

London was a writer of his time then, but we continue to read him today because he is more than ever a writer for our time as well. Our present theoretical focus on context as a way of studying literature helps to bring his time and ours together. Peluso and Slagel show us how a similar lens can be used to view London in different ways, but their findings are only representative of the possibilities offered by London studies in today's varied critical laboratory, where the author's richness is just beginning to be understood.

In these pages, James Williams and Jonathan Auerbach see London largely as an exemplum of market forces in American literature. Focusing on London's relationship with his editor at *McClure's*, Williams relies on theories of authorship and authenticity to view London's works as a dialectic formed by his process of subject-formation and contemporaneous cultural activity. Auerbach examines the construction of author that underlies *The Call of the Wild*, allowing London to reveal "unnatural" cultural issues that demystify the book's concept of nature: "vocational training, the quest for social approval via diligent work, the material conditions of literary production, the meaning of fame."

In "Ishi and Jack London's Primitives," a study of the loss of culture as "history," Charles L. Crow demonstrates London's relevance to the study of ecology in London's own day. The conflicting versions of "wildness" throughout his career, his racist stereotypes, and his visionary quest for an "abiding place" in which to live in harmony with the landscape all receive attention in this comparison of the life of California's last "wild man" and the author whose career furnishes a history of the California landscape. Crow offers analyses of *Before Adam* and *The Scarlet Plague* as well as *The Call of the Wild* and *White Fang*.

Questions of race and gender occupy the center of the volume in essays by Francis Shor, Sam S. Baskett, Scott Derrick, Clarice Stasz, Christopher

Hugh Gair, and Andrew Furer. Shor's essay on *The Iron Heel* widens and deepens the view of London's apocalyptic social novel as a version of the class struggle, discussing an engendered language that creates male and female narrative frames which contextualize the political and intellectual conflicts of the novel. Baskett readdresses the social dimension of *The Sea-Wolf*, which comes to light only through reassessment of how the role of Maud Brewster promotes androgyny as the novel's central value. Derrick surveys gender and sexuality in several of London's works, concentrating on *Martin Eden* and *The Sea-Wolf*. He approaches *The Sea-Wolf* and its cast of characters by reexamining naturalism's construction of heterosexual masculinity, emphasizing how the body poses a threat to the autonomous self, initially for the anxious Humphrey Van Weyden, but finally for the impossibly detached Wolf Larsen. This anxiety is ultimately contained within the bounds of teleological narrative.

Stasz concentrates on social history through the nearly forgotten *Adventure*; gender and London's unpredictable radicalism frame the discussion. One of the first critics to examine gender in London's works, Stasz sees in *Adventure* how the racial ideologies of the changing roles of women are interwoven in a tale of unstable colonialism. Gair reexamines the social and political conventions of naturalism, in this case in *The Valley of the Moon*. Gair's discussion of sentimentality, storytelling, and race anxiety in the face of the Progressive "Melting Pot" of California adopts—and at the same time challenges—Walter Benn Michaels's investigation of race and cultural identity, concluding that the apparent triumph of Saxon Brown Roberts's feminine voice in the novel represents an abandonment of London's socialist tendencies and an embrace of the middle-class culture rejected in *Martin Eden*. Furer offers an answer to the nagging question of why London at times seems comfortable with collisions of race and cultures, as in Hawaii, but at other times, as in Alaska, he is not, and why he champions the virtues of non-white people in some works, such as "Chun Ah Chun" and "Koolau the Leper," but not in others, including *A Daughter of the Snows* and *The Mutiny of the Elsinore*. Furer situates London's racial attitudes in the social and political contexts of his times as well as in the thought of Herbert Spencer.

Tanya Walsh also places the focus on London as a commentator on the politics and history of his time. In her study of one of London's Hawaiian stories, "Shin Bones," Walsh notes a radical shift in London's narrative concerns and a growing modernity of style that connects him with later writers, especially with James Joyce. In this tale of a Hawaiian prince who has internalized the conflict between his native ancestry and his Anglocentrism and modernization, London's dialogic structure concerns itself with the control of history through narration, as Walsh reveals via the insights of Stephen Greenblatt and others.

Finally, for Lawrence I. Berkove, the psychology of London's narrator as storyteller is the crucial issue. Examining "The Red One," perhaps London's most mysterious story, written only a few months before he died in 1916, Berkove finds that instead of an overarching unity to be supplied by Jungian archetypes, the tale's psychological suggestiveness and literary allusiveness in fact create a profound skepticism. The story offers an extraordinarily comprehensive impression of London's inner world at a pivotal historical moment, combining the powerful stimuli of Freudian as well as Jungian theory, mythology, and Darwinism with thoughts on World War I, skepticism, and mysticism. Berkove argues that "The Red One" represents London's apprehension that human intelligence divorced from other humane qualities leads to "a pitiless process of random natural selection" that subverts human wholeness.

London was a naturalist, a romantic, a primitivist, and a visionary. He was a self-conscious and self-promoting writer, and an ideologue, a social critic, a theorist on race and gender and class, a satirist, a historian, and a fabulist. He was both a pessimist *and* a humanist. The broad conclusion is that London is indeed one of American literature's representative men. Jonathan Bishop says of Emerson's "Representative Men" that "Genius is defined by its utter receptivity to the 'spirit of the hour.' "[14] London was nothing if not engaged with that spirit. Like Montaigne, London as skeptic lived in the worlds of the ideal and the practical without committing himself fully to either. Though he insisted throughout his career that he was a materialistic monist, his work is filled with spiritual and humanistic ideas, and though he was the most successful of the naturalist writers, his work has undeniable romantic elements as well. London is best understood not as a dogmatist (as he has so often been seen) but as a dynamic artist and intellect in the Emersonian tradition: a human creative force of his own "hour" who has something to offer our own. At a time when critics are beginning to appreciate London as the author of much more than dog stories and autobiographical fiction, we offer this book as a collection of trailheads.

Commitment and Practice

The Authorship of Jack London

JAMES WILLIAMS

"What can be said in defense of a writer who proclaimed defiantly that he would rather win a water fight than write the great American novel?"[1] So begins Charles N. Watson, Jr.'s *The Novels of Jack London: A Reappraisal* (1983), a central work in London studies. That this work was motivated by a desire, even a necessity, to defend Jack London's professional status speaks to the strength and pervasiveness of the accepted, derogatory narrative that Watson faced. One of Watson's accomplishments was to make the "accepted" unacceptable, and it is now possible to examine the identity of London as author without, so to speak, looking over one's shoulder.[2] Continuing the work of definition, I want to outline in all their complexity the multifaceted models of authorship that London was creating for himself and that were being created for him up to the moment he died. Every poem, piece of journalism, novel, autobiography, story, essay, and peculiar, unclassifiable hybrid was produced out of the dialectic formed by London's process of subject-formation and by contemporaneous cultural activity.

I would like to begin with a rough distinction between the identity of the author and the office of the author. The first is a matter, though not exclusively, of personal construction. The second is a matter, though again not exclusively, of socioeconomic, cultural, and textual construction. When we look at the relation of the subject-author to its text, we have to take into account the exchange between the individual act of subject-formation and the socioeconomic and cultural forces exerting their pressures on the individual and the texts at the same moment. Or, to put it a different way, identity-formation goes to and comes from models of authorship. Just as authors are able to some extent to create and maintain themselves, so too do texts and others create and maintain them.

To assert the importance, or even the operation, of such a dialectic is to presume that the figure of the author—the living, historical author—somehow matters in the conduct of literary analysis. The living figure of Jack London does matter, but not in the way described by traditional author criticism and its most recent incarnations. We will never be able to retrieve a pure London presence from the creation of Martin Eden—or, for that matter, from the words of the narrators of *People of the Abyss, John Barleycorn,* and the other semi-, quasi-, or "straightforward" autobiographical works.[3] As Roland Barthes rightfully asserts, "In the multiplicity of writing, everything is to be *disentangled,* nothing *deciphered.*"[4]

Jack London as author has been limited to a writer of short, vigorous stories in the naturalistic mode set in Alaska. Or he has been constructed as the author of vigorous, overblown propaganda marked by idiosyncratic interpretations of Marx and Engels as influenced by certain key socialistic events in turn-of-the-century America. His function as an author, in critics' attempts to construct a unified subject, always remains an incomplete and inadequate projection. In addition, by tracking the selections of London's work in American literature anthologies, one gets an idea of how critics construct a fictional unified subject and how that subject shifts despite anthologists' attempts to fix it. In 1937, *War of the Classes* was excerpted; these days, "Law of Life" or "To Build a Fire" is collected. The Library of America approaches London's status as author differently—it includes only two novels, *The Sea-Wolf* and *Martin Eden,* in 2,500 pages of text.[5]

Given that a residue of authorial identity makes itself known in the text, and given a different understanding of individualism and subjectivity, what can we find about the author in the text? We do not have to limit ourselves to a finished product—the published and marketed text—because we can expand our notion of what a work is. We can locate authorial identity in the correspondence between author and editor, in marginalia in books the author read, even in certain works by others that seem to parallel the author's own. To speak of an author is not to speak of a person who writes and publishes; it is to speak of a writer who is. This writer has no identity apart from writing, but the writing is not separate from the world. Authorship makes itself known in material activity, and the process of the formation of the subject-author is made known to us only in texts: fictional, contractual, nonfictional, fragmentary, and so on. As Michel Foucault writes, "Suspicions arise concerning the absolute nature and creative role of the subject. *But the subject should not be entirely abandoned.* It should be reconsidered, not to restore the theme of an originating subject, but to seize its functions, its intervention in discourse, and its systems of dependencies."[6] The key words for this methodology or path of study are *practice, authenticity*, and *fundamental commitment*. These concepts can help us locate London's authorial identity in the world of his texts. I will be focusing on subject-formation; the other term in the dialectic—cultural activity as a constructive force—will recur and be recuperated in the "system of dependency" I describe.[7]

The philosopher Akeel Bilgrami reminds us that in some profound sense we are what we practice. *Practice* means, for example, in the sphere of religion, that Muslims know that they are Muslims because they make pilgrimages, give alms, pray, and participate in the activities of the mosque. These practices sustain identity.[8] They underlie what Bernard Williams has called "fundamental commitments." Bilgrami, in his important critique of this concept, gets to its heart by asking what would happen if he were to abandon a fundamental commitment: "I would have felt a deep and *integrated* destruction of my self, which is missing from the more ordinary, though undoubtedly genuine and severe, bad feelings induced in me by my having failed to act on . . . other values. It is not merely that I would have had *more* such bad feelings or worse feelings. It is rather that I would have felt . . . that I had lost something much more defining of what held my self-conception together."[9] A fundamental commitment, then, is not simply something that one pledges oneself to. It is reinforced internally by practice and made external in practice—to give it up would entail a change of self.

Bilgrami is somewhat reluctant to name exactly what is given up, but he comes close to deciding upon *authenticity*: "The existentialists described the source of this integrity of the self [or what holds self-conception together] as *authenticity*, an obscure term no doubt."[10] He says that Williams's vagaries concerning fundamental commitments allow us "to infer that they lead up to the existentialist idea (and even perhaps ideal) of authenticity. And it is this connection between a person's fundamental commitments and the idea of the authentic self that explains the persistence of questions about identity despite an acknowledgment of the radical negotiability of the concept of identity."[11] This statement refers exactly to the debate over reconstructing the individual in the face of the loss of autonomy.[12]

Bilgrami is attempting to resuscitate the notion of authenticity as long as it is connected to fundamental commitments that are determined by historical circumstances.[13] As Bilgrami explains, given a conflict between two fundamental commitments, one might be led to "settle down with the idea of being locked helplessly in a conflict, a sort of tragic stasis; and that would make things too easy for oneself in another way—something akin to the familiar intellectual laziness that accompanies existential anguish."[14] Bilgrami does not explicitly say so, but I take it he believes that authenticity is negotiable too, just as are fundamental commitments. In other words, the concept of authenticity, in the face of post-structuralist theories, works only if it is inseparable from the concept of fundamental commitment. We do not look under or below fundamental commitments for real identity; in author criticism, this would only turn us away from texts and back to biography.

My interest in authenticity as a concept to help us understand both the author-subject in general and London as an author centers on a key word that London himself uses to describe what I take as his authentic authorial self: *sincerity*. In a crucial letter to George Brett, president of Macmillan, London writes, "I have always insisted that the cardinal literary virtue is sincerity, and I have striven to live up to this belief. If I am wrong in the foregoing, if the world downs me on it, I'll say 'Good bye, proud world,' retire to the ranch, and plant potatoes and raise chickens."[15] Here is a near-complete statement of what I take to be a fundamental commitment. Sincerity is such a deep value for London that it is synonymous with his idea of his entire writerly self. To live as an author—and not just to make a living as an author—London must be sincere in his own eyes. In the same letter he writes, "In *The Road*, and in all my work, in all that I have said and written and done, I have been true. This is the character I have built up; it constitutes my biggest asset. . . . I am willing to grant the chance that I am wholly wrong in believing that sincerity and truthfulness constitute my big asset" (*Letters*, 2: 675). Putting aside conjectures about self-deception, I take London at his word—truthfulness and sincerity constitute his very authorial self—"all that I have written."

Further, he asserts that people buy his books because "this is the character I have built up"—a truthful, sincere persona. He does not say that he constructed this persona so that he can sell books. If his books actually do not sell, then he does not offer to change his writerly persona. Instead, London imagines himself earning money in a new way, living a new life, being a farmer. That is, to give up on sincerity or truthfulness as a writer would mean to give up as a writer. In fact, because of the similar meaning of *sincerity* and *authenticity*, the latter functions for London in the same way that Bilgrami seems to want it to describe the integrated self. Without a belief in sincerity, London concludes that he could no longer be authentic as a writer. He would lose a sense of integrated self and be forced to refashion himself. By looking at his career as a whole, then, as London encourages Brett (and us) to do, I believe that there are at least six ways in which London practiced this fundamental commitment: *locale, mobility, documentation, continuous production, dual publication,* and *publicity.* To give any one of these up would have been to be insincere, that is, unauthentic. These are the nonnegotiable details of his authorial identity.[16]

From London's point of view, the totality of these practices did not fit one preexisting model of authorship.[17] The contemporary models that confronted London have the most bearing on his career. He read *The Writer, The Editor,* and various manual-writers—L. A. Sherman and Herbert Spencer, among others—in order to learn these models. The writers' magazines themselves promoted that of the neophyte author, with such rules as "write from personal experience," "keep an eye on the markets," and "don't begin a story with landscape description."[18] They also promoted a craftsman model, "a skilled manipulator of predefined strategies for achieving goals dictated by his audience."[19] London borrowed from another contemporary model, that of the journalist-author, and it acted upon him powerfully, though for short, concentrated periods. The model of the solitary genius as exemplified by the British aesthetes, however, greatly influenced London, and though he early on rejected it in favor of a more materially inflected model, his strategy of dual publication allowed him the integrity that he believed was a primary characteristic of the identity of Swinburne, Pater, and Wilde.

None of these models were sufficient for London, for he came to each of them with more (and less) than they offered. He encountered them not just in books and magazines but in letters from and meetings with editors and publishers. In these encounters, a conflict would ensue, based not on financial matters, but on questions of status, power, and identity. At times, when London felt that he was being forced to write in a way he wished not to, he experienced an identity crisis; foreign practices clashed with his sense of self. I will move to a narrative of such a crisis, but first and briefly I want to describe these six practices that give shape to London's authorial identity.

Locale is a defining characteristic, a formative practice, in that by choosing to be a Western author London consciously rejected European and East Coast models. That is, a Western writer was expected to graduate from local color, journalism, humor, and/or small magazine publication and proceed to mature novel and magazine writing in the East. This was the path that Mark Twain, Frank Norris, Gelett Burgess, Bret Harte, and Condy Rivers followed. Rivers, the hero of Norris's *Blix* (which climaxes with the hero's departure for New York and an editorial job with the Centennial Publishing Company), most emphatically wanted to "arrive": "Of all the ambitions of the Great Unpublished, the one that is strongest, the most abiding, is the ambition to get to New York. For these, New York is the *point de depart*, the pedestal, the niche, the indispensable vantage ground."[20] As a matter of fact, S. S. McClure offered both Norris and London the same kind of job in the same time period at almost exactly the same moment in their careers. Norris took it, and London emphatically rejected it. The physical frontier may have closed, but London re-created it in the psychological space of the author's identity.

Second, *travel*, which had helped him escape poverty and jail, became synonymous with observation, thought, and ultimately writing. Further, faced with dilemmas of choice—for example, McClure's offer of a guaranteed income coupled with the requirement to work in an office in New York—he chose mobility. George Brett understood how writing and travel worked together for London:

> You are the most energetic man with whom I have ever had to do: not content with the execution of a programme the life of which the world has seldom seen in the way of navigation and exploration [he is referring to the *Snark* voyage], you are in addition able to keep your mental faculties constantly at work on your books, and now you tell me of the beginning of a new novel of a hundred thousand words. Personally I have always found travel most inimical to the prosecution of any sort of continued mental effort. Apparently your own faculties are merely stimulated thereby.[21]

This choice of mobility worked into his writerly way of life in another manner: as physical activity, especially sailing, camping, and traveling of all kinds. The many photographs of London writing outdoors testify not so much to his "naturalness" but rather to his decision to be a writer on the move.

Tied into mobility is *documentation*. Much of London's work originated in what he called "human documents," a complex term used principally by the staff of *McClure's Magazine* to designate sometimes photographic, more often textual re-creations of the past. London himself used "human documents" (as Lewis Hine did much later)[22] to explain the photographic veracity of the sources for his fiction. In doing so, he was using writing as a kind of photography and photography—literally, "writing with light"—as a kind of writing. The phrase "human documents" was another, more complete way of expressing Martin Eden's "impassioned realism" or his own "idealized realism."[23] The idealization or passion came out of the real, and, however slippery these terms were—and he was quite conscious of their ambiguity and tendency to overlap—he nonetheless insisted that the real was known only when it was documented.

Fourth and fifth, London chose to sell his work to magazines first and then had the work republished in book form. In this sense *dual publication*— I mean the phrase to work in two distinct ways—is one indicator of London's conflation of roles, that is, author and agent, and allowed him *continuous production*. This was not simply a good business maneuver but a choice London made that guaranteed an income without a sacrifice of artistic integrity. First, Brett agreed to publish him as he wished, and Macmillan published at least one book a year from 1902 to 1916. London was assured that his writings had a permanent home in book form, and this security allowed him to defer to magazine editors who invariably wanted to cut and rewrite his work to fit a more limited audience and format. Without Brett's backing, London would have been forced to choose between the lucrative contracts magazines offered and the felt necessity of publishing exactly what he wrote. Dual publication has another meaning as well. It is one of the peculiarities of London's oeuvre that his books seem to repeat themselves at least once, the second version an attempt at a deeper, more fulfilling version of the first. Not every work is doubled, it is true, but most are, and it seems to have been London's intent to work out ideas and characters over the course of a number of stories or novels to get them just right. *The Call of the Wild* pairs with *White Fang*; "To Build a Fire" (1902) with "To Build a Fire" (1908); *The Iron Heel* with *A Farthest Distant*, one of his uncompleted projects; *Before Adam* with *The Star Rover*, and so on.[24]

Sixth, to understand the *public nature* of his authorial identity, one might profitably turn to Jürgen Habermas and others and theories of the public sphere. Or one might go to Earle Labor's thesis of London as American Adam, a neo-Jungian archetype that works best, I believe, as an explication of the publicness of London's identity.[25] Another way to look at his effect on the American public sphere would be to analyze his appearances in advertisements, on the lecture circuit, in scandalous newspaper stories, and in the guise of London imitators/doubles, as well as the wide impact of his catch-phrases—"the call of the wild" and "the iron heel." For now, it is enough to point out that so much of London's work was meant to instigate and provoke discussion that he can be called a principal figure in the public sphere of early-twentieth-century America.

Finally, his so-called overproduction may be seen not as a sign of egotistical domination of the external world but as a ritual to maintain his authorial identity. He had to produce so much because he constantly experimented with form. This particular practice brought a challenge from Brett, which prompted London to write the "sincerity" letter quoted above, the letter that so clearly documents a crisis of identity. That is, Brett had asked London to postpone the publication of *The Road*, which was nearing completion. Brett's request, which does not survive, was preceded by his January 23, 1907, letter, wherein Brett wrote apropos of a major change he suggested for *The Iron Heel*: "You must bear in mind always that any suggestions that I take the liberty of making to you are made always from the commercial standpoint and that I say it with a view to your commercial interest as much as to our own."[26] In this spirit, he suggested that the near-simultaneous publication of *The Road* and *The Iron Heel* would overburden London's readers; in fact, Brett later sent London a clipping from the *New York Times* that ostensibly supported his case. London, in turn, upped the stakes, for it was a question of authorial identity: "No," London emphatically wrote in his "sincerity" letter, "if you put before me good evidence that the publication of *The Road* would be likely to damage the sale of my other books, it would not affect the question of my desire for you to go ahead and publish it. . . . And while it is possible that just immediately the sale of my other books might be slightly damaged, I believe ultimately there would be no damaging effect at all." And then London made his larger claim about truth, sincerity, and authorial self. In other words, if Brett wanted to publish the person of Jack London, he had to take the chance of market saturation. The action and its risks could not be separated.

Market saturation may seem like a risky business practice (thus Brett questioned it), but to London conducting business in this way gave him the freedom to write as he was moved to, and to publish a work as soon as it was completed. He told Brett that "I look back on my life and draw one great generalization: IT WAS MY REFUSAL TO TAKE CAUTIOUS ADVICE THAT MADE ME," and of course the idea of making oneself is not limited to monetary success; authorial identity is the subject in this and every sentence of the letter.[27] He chose to write according to his fundamental commitment to sincerity, and overproduction was an essential practice or manifestation of it. He next recounted for Brett one instance when he had refused to be persuaded to be conservative by a publisher—S. S. McClure, in 1900. This story is important as a formative moment in his process of authorial subject-formation and as a narrative to be related during moments of identity crisis (like this one with Brett in 1907). It is more than the story of his first book contract. It is one of the many stories of how he chose to be an author.

After six months of correspondence with S. S. McClure, John Phillips, and other editors at *McClure's Magazine*, London received an offer of $100 per month for five months, beginning August 1, 1900, as advance money against the sales of London's first novel, as yet unwritten, but which turned out to be *A Daughter of the Snows*. London bumped it to $125, and the deal was made.[28] In December 1900, on the strength of one, possibly two offers from rival publishers, London and Phillips agreed to extend the advance money for another six months at the beginning of 1901; payments were extended again in July, and then ended in October 1901.[29] The reasons for the end of their contract are complicated, and neither party was satisfied. London was without a publisher, and according to Phillips's calculations, by the end of 1901 London owed nearly $2,000.[30]

"At the very beginning," London told Brett, meaning the beginning of his career, "had I taken the advice of the magazine editors, I'd have been swiftly made into a failure." One notes London's acute sensitivity to the dialectic of subject and world; authors make choices from a world of options that editors and publishers construct. He continued: "*McClure's Magazine* gave me $125 per month, and held the bread-and-butter lash over me. [John] Phillips said, 'Write such and such stories for our magazine. Quit writing the stories you are writing.' . . . It was because I refused his advice that I broke with *McClure's*. In fact, Phillips fired me and took away the $125 per month."[31]

It is true that Phillips insisted that London write a particular kind of story for him and so in yet another way conform to a foreign (that is, to London) model of authorship. What, though, happened in 1901 that led London in 1906 to vacillate between two versions of the event? Did Phillips use a "lash" or did he advise? Was London fired, or did he quit? It is not surprising, given the dynamic of author/world relations, that London gives a conflicted version. From the point of view of McClure and Phillips, in May 1901, when they had read the novel they had granted London the time to write, they were left in a quandary. The novel, they felt, was too awful to publish. What sort of contractual arrangement should then exist between the author and the company? How would London pay off his debt of a year's worth of advances? Phillips's solution was to persuade London to write short stories: "Steady, concentrated, intelligent work is required, and a man must do it day after day," he told London, thus becoming the first and the last person to accuse London of failing to work hard at creating fiction. "It is a question of the command of your intellectual and artistic powers," Phillips said, deepening the wound, "self-domination of your own ability: that comes by hard work, by keeping at it, keeping at a long piece of work, not according to whim, sentiment or feeling, or anything else, but under self-discipline, control and self-direction."

Phillips's emphasis on the word *self* is noteworthy. Phillips was creating for London an identity of an author that he hoped London would accept. Then, to help London complicate this construct—the novice writer, a carefree, spontaneous sort of fellow who wrote off the top of his head and was unable to sustain a large project—Phillips offered this advice: "If it were possible for you to take up your sea adventures and use them in short fiction it would give you fresh inspiration, I should think, because it is material you have perhaps not handled as fully as you have the Klondike material."[32]

Though London and Phillips agreed that dedicated daily work was a desirable, nonnegotiable professional practice, Phillips had failed to see it in *Daughter*. This failure then led to his false characterization of London's authorial identity and ultimately to the end of their relationship. London himself had admitted to friends that he felt the novel was bad; if Phillips had judged his performance differently, their relationship would perhaps have continued. But it was not so much the quality and politics of the novel that drove publisher and author apart; it was the author's "failure" to conform to the publisher's ideal model for him.

When London replied to Phillips, he was conciliatory, and though he did defend his practice as an author, he led Phillips to believe, consciously or not, that he would conform. Phillips, in turn, expressed relief that London seemed ready to comply with his request for short stories. All depended on the next submission.

One would think, then, that he would have sent a short story, preferably a sea story, to Phillips. London knew full well what Phillips wanted and what was at stake. He was determined, however, to frustrate publishers' expectations in order to publish material on his own terms, hoping to convert, without antipathy, a publisher's desires to his own. This was the higher stake. At this crucial, sensitive moment in his career, in the spring of 1901, London sent McClure and Phillips a newly written, firebrand essay, "Wanted: A New Law of Development."[33] The submission may have seemed a calculated move to aggravate Phillips, but it was also the outcome of a deep, personal enthusiasm for the subject, an enthusiasm lately ignited by a visit by Frank Strawn-Hamilton, the hobo-philosopher whose talk would so greatly influence London.

Phillips, for his part, was less happy with the essay than he had been with the novel. He did not even bother to write the rejection letter himself. Stunned by his new author's naivete or ignorance or bullheadedness, he tried to be polite, again: "We never attempt this sort of thing," he dictated to London. "There is no doubt that you have handled with considerable freshness, a very old question"—so old, that is, that it doesn't deserve resurrection—"and I felt my hump of combativeness warming as I read your article."[34] Of course Phillips was not in favor of starving the bairns of poor people; but he was neither a trade unionist nor a socialist. He was also an impatient publisher who was waiting with growing anger for some short stories.

He decided that if London would not come to him, he would send a *Mc-Clure's* staffer to discover the value of this young author. He sent Ray Stannard Baker, who was then an editor and not yet the nationally famous muckraker, and who was planning a vacation to California. Baker, like London, had marched in Coxey's army; he had been present at the Pullman strike, had interviewed Debs. His credentials as an experienced man, as far as London was concerned, were impeccable, though he was no socialist. He was 31 to London's 25, and Phillips hoped Baker could talk sense to him. London was living at Villa La Capriccioso, Felix Peano's bizarrely constructed house (its staircase was built outside), and told Baker that when he arrived London expected that he and five or six friends would be engaged in their weekly entertainment—"a little group which read old English plays now and again. Gelett Burgess will be among them in the bad company of two or three good socialists," including Anna Strunsky and Cameron King. Baker recalled,

Jack had secured from the libraries in Oakland and San Francisco several ancient editions of Elizabethan plays, some of them printed in miserably small type and illustrated with old-fashioned engravings. After considerable jolly conversations we calmed down to the serious business of the evening. . . . We took up one of Ben Jonson's plays, I think *The Silent Woman*, and having chosen parts began reading it. Some of us had several parts and often lost our places, had to be reminded that it was our turn, found it difficult to master the archaic English. We got sleepy. I have never, anyway, been able to make sense out of a book thus read, turn by turn. . . . We became steadily more earnest, more serious. We concealed our yawns and waked up quickly when we missed our cues. . . . I don't know how long we should have persisted, if Gelett Burgess, with his God-given sense of humor, had not suddenly closed his book with a bang. "I don't know how it goes with the rest of you," he said, "but I can't make a damn thing out of this play." We all roared with laughter, Jack as much as any, and banged our books.

The next day, Baker and London went sailing, and Baker undoubtedly repeated the experience to Phillips when he returned to New York:

> I understood him better, there with the wind in the sails and his hand on the
> tiller, than I had the night before when he and all of us were lumbering through
> the dry wastes of Ben Jonson. How beautifully deft he was, and what joy he
> had in it! His head was bare and his loose shirt open at the throat, a pattern
> of physical perfection. He told me innumerable stories full of sweat and blood,
> and brutal poverty, and profanity and rum, some of which I saw afterward
> in his stories and novels. I remember especially his account of a wild night in
> Japan, after too much hot *sake*, when he and his friends ran through the pa-
> per partitions in the house where they were staying and wound up by arous-
> ing the village and fighting the entire Japanese population while they backed
> away to their ship.

Baker ended his trip, as he told Phillips, insisting that London send *McClure's*
more short stories.[35]

Partly because the visit had been friendly and partly because he still felt
loyal to the publisher who gave him his first chance at a novel, London gen-
uinely desired to remain with Phillips and McClure. In July, he told Anna
Strunsky, "I find I must do something for *McClure's* at once, or they will be
shutting off on me. So I am springing at once into a short story, which will
be finished by end of week."[36] This sounds like capitulation. London completed his first short story since October 1900, "Nam-Bok the Unveracious,"
and sent it to Phillips. It was one of his liar tales.[37] Nam-Bok, an Indian from
a Yukon Delta tribe who has never been out of their immediate area, returns
to his village after a long absence in the United States; he had been blown
off-course while canoeing on the sea. His stories of white men—their enormous ships, houses, and numbers—so startle the villagers that they become
convinced he is lying and is a "shadow" that must return to the land of shadows—the land of white people—before he causes them all to die. For his
part, Nam-Bok wishes to leave as well because he discovers that he can no
longer stomach their fish and oil diet nor tolerate the bleak landscape of their
lives.

Because the figure of the liar or tall-tale teller is so often linked in London's work to the artist, we can take this story as a fable of manuscript rejection. In fact, the villagers are people who crave stories. Doubting Nam-
Bok's physical presence as he first stood before them, they grudgingly admit
him to their camp when he assures them that he has tales to tell. They are
London's figures for his magazine readership. "And Opee-Kwan," the head

of the village, "knew that his people were eager, and further, he was aware himself of an itching curiosity concerning those untold tales."[38] But like Opee-Kwan, Phillips could not take the story. "I am very sorry that it does not seem to me the thing for *McClure's* but as it does not, there is nothing for me to do but to return it promptly to you. I feel sure that you can dispose of it without any trouble." (Five months later *Ainselee's* paid $100 for it.) "I regret the more that we cannot take the story, because we should like very much to have something from you to advertise in our prospectus for the coming year."[39]

Phillips had now reached the end of his patience, and though London told Anna in mid-September that "*McClure's* have dropped me so I am free lance again," the break Phillips proposed did not have to be permanent.[40] It was not, however, a proposal made out of mutual desire: If London could write again the kind of stories Phillips wanted to see, their relationship could be more financially regular. But, Phillips observed obliquely, "your work seems to have taken a turn which makes it impractical for the most part for the magazine." Rather than restart his strategy of remaking London's self-conception as an author, he chose a less subtle, more complimentary approach: "Of course I appreciate that you must follow the lead of your genius, that you must do the things which you see to do. Probably there would be neither satisfaction nor growth in any other course. . . . It is rather a question with me, however, whether it is wise for either you or us, to continue indefinitely the monthly salary. . . . We wanted to give you a chance to write your novel unhampered by any bread and butter worries." The letter closed gently, but now it seemed less sincere, because the company no longer wanted to place friendship over money: "I have written quite frankly, my dear Mr. London, because I feel convinced that you know that we are your friends, and that we want always to be fair and kind with you. Will you not write me at once how you feel about the matter?"[41]

He wrote the day he received the letter, in a "manly" spirit, said Phillips afterward. That is, he neither complained nor bargained; he simply asked for an extension to October (Phillips agreed), promised some short stories, and inquired after the success of *The God of His Fathers*. He then wrote five short stories and sent them; none were accepted. London had suspected the publisher's antagonism and had responded in kind. His recounting of this crisis in 1907 to Brett exaggerates what Phillips wanted, but it does poignantly describe how far apart the author and the publisher were: Phillips "wanted me to write petty, smug, complacent bourgeois stories."[42] The five stories he sent after "Nam-Bok"—"The Sunlanders," "Li Wan, the Fair," "The Master

of Mystery," "One Thousand Dozen," and "In the Forests of the North"—
were not overtly political. They were, though, motivated by the same enthusiasm behind "Wanted" and were unified by a socialist view of the gold
rush in Alaska as a massive exploitation of indigenous people. London had
in past stories sufficiently worked out various and complex meanings for the
white man of the wilderness and newborn Alaskan society. Now, without
abandoning his socialism, he reversed the narrative viewpoint 180 degrees
and captured the white men and women as if in photographs taken by Native Americans.

London was not such a believer in the Anglo-Saxon that he could ignore the extreme cost in human life that came in conquering other people's lands. His repudiation of the white point of view made these Alaskan
stories foreign and unacceptable, and Phillips, as we have seen, was already
predisposed against the Klondike as a setting and socialism as an ideology.
The stories were not romantic tales of "Indianness" in which one could find
authentic Indians and alien whites. In one sense the Native Americans are
represented mythologically, as the title of the collection in which he eventually published them indicates—*Children of the Frost*. In another sense, they
are represented photographically as struggling against the whites and losing. But to Phillips their characterization was unrecognizable, thereby making the photographic realism seem fake. (In reverse, Edward Curtis's faked
photographs of Native Americans, at the turn of the century, had seemed
real.) London's photographs of whites, however, were like so many "wanted"
posters, and they provoked denial. London's whites are rapacious imperialists, consciously destroying the land and the peoples who lived on it.

London's five stories are not so much about Indian life in the North as
they are about the new dissolution of Indian life brought about by the invasion of the whites. The resentment between the two cultures that London
touches on in *Daughter of the Snows* gets full treatment. Where *A Son of the
Wolf* and *God of His Fathers* defined the new community of whites, new in
the extreme sense of the creation of an order where there had been none before, *The Children of the Frost* tells the story of the destruction of centuries-
old communities and what becomes of them. Thus we do not find anything
about the brotherhood of the trail, an ethos that binds men and women
together when faced with natural disaster or extremity. If London's first two
volumes are about nation building and the American empire, the third
volume is about nation destruction.

Phillips and the other readers at *McClure's*, however, thought it utopian
to write of and lament the manifold destruction of the northern tribes. Lon-

don, in repudiating the whites, advocated the "impossible" scenario of whites and Indians working in socioeconomic harmony. To the magazine, this vision was simply not reasonable and therefore not realistic. This turnaround of viewpoint was consistent with London's practice of experimentation, but Phillips and McClure were not the sort of publishers to tolerate such practices. This unreconcilable difference, over what an author should be and do, ended the contractual arrangement.[43]

Cloudesley Johns had once asserted that London wrote fiction to attain "the assurance of being able some day to sell any sort of work on the strength of a name." London replied, "O no. . . . Every year we have writers, old writers, crowded out—men, who once had names, but who had gained them wrongfully, or had not done the work necessary to maintain them. In its way, the struggle for a man with a name to maintain the standard by which he gained that name, is as severe as the struggle for the unknown to make a name."[44] This realization of the fragility of his position as subject-author never left him. Even as late as 1913, when he was in the midst of writing *The Star Rover* under contract to Macmillan, free from writing short stories, he confessed to an acquaintance that he had no confidence that what he was writing would be accepted for publication, even though he was under contract.[45] If one applies, say, the genius model or any kind of teleological model of authorship to London's career—that it was natural, or inevitable, or divinely ordained that London would become a writer, that he had a natural gift, or talent—then one loses sight of London's own recognition of the dialectic between the author and the world in which he or she works. To become an author or, as London called it, "to make a name," is not a simple matter of a historical figure arriving within a cultural scene. The creation of an authorial identity requires the practice of fundamental commitments by the historical figure of the author and the acknowledgment of those practices by the historical figures of the circumambient cultural realm. Those who wish to reexamine the professional status of an author must keep the dialectic of practice and acknowledgment alive.

"Congested Mails"

Buck and Jack's "Call"

JONATHAN AUERBACH

Frustrated by a recalcitrant Congress, President Theodore Roosevelt in 1907 sought to divert himself by playing the role of literary critic. He took as his texts—no surprise—animal tales, among them the dog stories by Jack London. Lumping London together with popular boys' writers such as W. J. Long, Roosevelt dismissed these authors as mystifying "nature-fakers." If London and the others really understood nature, Roosevelt charged, they would not humanize animals in such preposterous and unbelievable ways. Taking on Roosevelt in an essay published the next year, London accused the president of being "homocentric," a rank "amateur" unschooled in the principles of evolution that insist on an intimate "kinship" or strict continuity between animals and humans. Early in the article London does admit some crucial difference—that his "dog-heroes" were "not directed by abstract reasoning." But he points out that he "clogged his narrative" and violated his "artistic canons" with such phrases as "He did not think these things; he merely did them" in order to emphasize this difference, rather than cover it up, as Roosevelt implied.[1]

Teddy and Jack challenging each other's authority about (and over) nature. My aim here is not to settle this rivalry between one of America's most flamboyant and virile presidents and one of its most flamboyant and virile writers, a dispute still being waged today in more sophisticated ways among sociobiologists, cultural constructivists, animal rights activists, and others.[2] Although it is difficult to imagine the representation of nature that could avoid being "homocentric," it seems equally naive to attempt to measure

London's "dog-heroes" against some absolute standard of verisimilitude, as Roosevelt would have it. More important is the narrative self-consciousness alluded to by London that attends the plotting of his animal-protagonists. Reviving the dispute the following year (1909), the critic Frederic Taber Cooper makes the point nicely:

> There is a vast difference between thinking of man as a healthy human animal and thinking of him as an unhealthy human beast—and the Call-of-the-Wild school of fiction is tending toward precisely this exaggerated and mistaken point of view. The chief trouble with all the so-called Back-to-Nature books is that they suggest an abnormal self-consciousness, a constant preoccupation regarding the measure of our animalism. Now, it is a sort of axiom that so long as we are healthy and normal, we do not give much thought to our physical machinery. . . . But this, in a certain way, is precisely what the characters in the average Call-of-the-Wild novel seem to be doing, or at least what the authors are constantly doing for them. They seem, so to speak, to keep their fingers insistently upon the pulse of their baser animal emotions— and this is precisely what the primitive, healthy savage is furtherest removed from doing.[3]

Deftly conventionalizing London's narratives as already part of a literary "school" by means of those three hyphens, Cooper raises the key issue of self-consciousness, but mistakes a cause for an effect. Introspection in London is not some abnormal, degenerate end-stage alternative to "healthy savage" human animalism; it is, rather, a logical prerequisite for such natural primitivism, manifesting itself most starkly (as Cooper's wording suggests) in the confusion between what his characters seem to be doing and what London as narrator does *for* them. In this sense the entire concept of nature that underwrites London's literary naturalism is fundamentally "faked," to borrow TR's memorable phrase.

Tracing the reversion of a domesticated dog to a savage wolf-beast in the primitive Yukon, London addresses a set of "unnatural" cultural issues in *The Call of the Wild* (1903): vocational training, the quest for social approval via diligent work, the material conditions of literary production, the meaning of fame. These complex concerns all center on the practice of writing, I will argue, following the lead of several recent studies that seek to revise the still prevailing understanding of American literary naturalism as a mode grounded in environmental and biological determinism. Christopher Wilson, for example, makes a compelling case for Progressive Era writers, including London, as participating in an emerging culture of professionalism that treated writing as a discipline and a business. Wilson does not, however, discuss in any detail how such vocational concerns are enacted in the fiction itself—my emphasis throughout this essay.[4]

Written at a crucial juncture in London's career, just as his apprenticeship work in magazines was beginning to attract a wider national audience, *The Call of the Wild* dramatizes London's own struggle to gain recognition as a writer. Reading the dog Buck's "calling" as a mail carrier in light of his author's aspirations, I further hope to show how London's narrative renders literal what a trio of influential critics (Walter Benn Michaels, Michael Fried, and Mark Seltzer) have recently identified as a particular thematics of naturalist writing—texts that tend to draw attention to their status as material marks. Although these critics treat such writing strictly in terms of its production, I believe that London is more interested in how writing gets published, how the artist/dog makes a name for himself once letters are circulated and delivered in the wild.[5]

To analyze London's constructing of nature in *The Call of the Wild*, we need to begin by examining more closely Buck's double status as "dog-hero," as well as the related vexed doubling between character and narrator. Most critics rely on terms such as "anthropomorphism," "beast fable," and/or "allegory" to explain Buck, but the technical representation of an animal center of consciousness and the rhetorical *effects* of such a center are more complicated (and interesting) than these terms generally allow. London's verbs, for instance, show that it is easy enough to compile a list of mental actions attributed to Buck that seem problematic, to say the least: at various points in the narrative, Buck "imagines" (7), "decides" (9), "realizes" (9), "knows" (9), "divines" (10), "wonders" (12), and so on, over and against London's catchall convenient verb phrases "dimly aware" (7) and "feels vaguely" (50).[6] These relatively innocent epistemological quirks centering on matters of cognition are presumably inevitable, to invoke London's own accusation about TR's "homocentrism." But early in the narrative these verbs are crucial to the reader's being able to identify with Buck as a thinking presence who is on occasion disturbed by dreams and memories, as when the "scene" of Curly's death returns to trouble his sleep (16), or when he stares into a fire and "thought of Judge Miller's big house" (41) and then reviews other scenes of his recent past.

London usually is scrupulous in avoiding such unmediated access to Buck, achieving in the process a far more ambiguous and complex representation of his dog-hero. When Buck is initially caged, for instance, London writes, "He could not understand what it all meant" (8), followed by two interrogatives. As in the case of Norris's *McTeague*, it is uncertain whether

these free-floating questions belong to the character or to the narrator thinking for him; the result is a mental state that belongs exclusively neither to
Buck nor to Jack, but seems shared. London's use of the modal "could" in
the sentence above reinforces this ambiguity: is Buck's lack of understanding a structural incapacity stemming from his nature as dog, or only a temporary limitation, to be overcome by the greater force of insight or knowledge, when the "meaning" of his experience would become available to him?
As we shall see, this sort of question is most important, once we move
from the static representation of Buck to consider how he is directed as "hero,"
how he and his mind grow and change as London plots for him.

It will be useful briefly to consider some precursor texts before we look
at *The Call*'s plotting, the better to zero in on the peculiarities of London's
animal tale. Two popular stories are pertinent here: Kipling's *Jungle Book*
(1893) and Ernest Thompson Seton's *Wild Animals I Have Known* (1898).[7]
Drawing on a literary tradition that extends back to Chaucer and beyond,
Kipling's Mowgli stories are beast fables, filled with Mother Wolves and Father Wolves commenting wisely about complex social rules and regulations—
"The Law of the Jungle." Clearly, the effect of having animals speak in their
own (human) voices is different from London's narrating for his mute hero.
As is true in most beast fables, Kipling's talking animals serve to defamiliar-
ize the human world (babies are "naked cubs"). When London on occasion tries such an effect—for example, he refers to gold in his opening paragraph as "yellow metal" (5)—the results are feeble, for he is not really interested in using his dog to make humans seem strange; if anything, the
natural realm, not the cultural, gets progressively defamiliarized during the
narration.

Seton wrote beast fables for children as well, often substituting a Native
American mythos for Kipling's Orientalism. Seton also wrote about animals
in a naturalist vein closer to London than London perhaps cared to admit
in his 1908 defense against Roosevelt's accusations. Like Buck and his sledmates, Seton's "wild animals I have known" are heavily invested with various character traits—sullenness, courage, fidelity, and pride. A fierce wolf
dies of a broken heart at the loss of his freedom and the loss of a beloved
mate. An abandoned sheepdog spends years waiting patiently for his unde-
serving master, and so on. But since Seton's narration depends on string-
ing together anecdotes, we never really see the origins or the development
of these humanized personalities, nor do we see how these animals socially
interact with one another (a strong feature of Kipling's tales). And since he
sees himself as a naturalist rather than a novelist, Seton tells his shaggy-dog

stories by attributing personality without presuming to register any of the animals' internal mental states.

Neither exactly beast fable nor sentimentalized anthropomorphism, London's careful plotting of and for the mute Buck might suggest that allegory would be a more accurate critical category. Mark Seltzer has recently made such a case by dubbing London and his animals "men in furs."[8] But it is *The Call of the Wild*'s very resistance to transparent allegory that is remarkable, insofar as we continue to imagine London's hero as a dog despite all his complex mental attributes. London's surprise that his contemporaries regarded his tale as an allegorical treatment of the human jungle may well have been feigned.[9] Yet he does make Buck look and act like a dog-hero until the very end of his narrative, even if at times Buck's nature as a beast needs to be reinforced by simile. When we read that Buck enters camp so exhausted that he "lay down like a dead dog" (28), we are forced into making a series of negotiations that prevent us from resting easily in either the human or the animal realm.

How does London manage this effect? First, Buck is powerfully gendered in ways that cut across species lines, so his maleness allows London to keep the animal a "he." Second, and more complex, is the pattern London sets up in the first half of the narrative. Buck is in a situation beyond his control, and then is invested with a human mentality and morality to evaluate the situation. Thus the *values* that coincide with London's own as narrator. Buck is then represented as reacting to that situation by way of "instinct," a kind of black-box biological explanation that enables London to maintain the doctrinaire survival-of-the-fittest logic that ostensibly drives his plot.

I say "ostensibly" because there are really *two* plots driving London and Buck, and the more important one (neglected by most critics, who have been blinded by the text's dog-matic Darwinism) has to do with values rather than instincts. The central paradox informing the narrative is that Buck must learn to be wild. Wildness in this book is not a state of nature to be gained or regained by a reversion to type, as the naturalist plot of primordial atavism would have it. Attaining wildness, rather, entails disciplined education— technical and moral, a distinction collapsed by the representation of work/writing. The famous "call" that Buck heeds thus has more to do with a vocation or professional calling than some mysterious instinctual pull toward nature. *White Fang*, the companion piece to *The Call* that seems to reverse direction by tracing the taming of a wild wolf, is in this sense less a sequel to Buck's experience than a replay, making explicit what is only more covert in the earlier tale. There is a massive set of contradictions about Buck at the heart of the narrative, which moves in two seemingly opposite directions: toward nature from culture (the standard naturalist plot of decivilization), and a more troubled but also more passionate movement toward self-transcendence, which cannot be fully contained by the conventional naturalist model.[10]

For one thing, the naturalist plot of decline depends on some clear demarcation between nature and culture, however much a continuum exists between them (as London argued in his reply to Roosevelt). Without this distinction, no linear plotting can make much sense.[11] London tries to keep the two distinct yet linked by three mediations, all centering on the vague notion of the "primitive" (12): the "law of club and fang" (15); the representations of Buck's inherited racial memory during which the dog reverts to a savage state of attendance on now "hairy" (41) masters (examples of London's "men in furs"); and the curious introduction at a key juncture late in the narrative of a tribe of Indians, the Yeehats, who presumably operate somewhere in between Buck's world and Jack's world. In all three mediations, London draws attention to the very "faking" of nature that he would gloss over. By eliding club and fang under a single primitive "law," for example, London confuses the means of human instrumentality with its ends—in this case, training by negative conditioning. Although it might be argued that both club and fang seek to establish dominance, London carefully insists that the man in the red sweater beats Buck to gain obedience, not conciliation. Similarly, why should masters, hairy or otherwise, be dwelling in Buck's racial unconscious, as if human mastery over nature were somehow natural in itself?[12] Such questions point to the cross-purposes throughout the novel as London tries to negotiate or navigate his dog-hero between the animal world and the human world.

Taking stock of his hero at one point during his narration, London himself nicely captures this doubleness: "His development (or retrogression) was rapid" (22). Trying to have it both ways and still avoid commitment (by using "or" rather than "and"), this assertion follows close on a more extended bit of commentary, a good example of London's self-conscious protesting, or narrative clogging, which he used in his own defense:

> This first theft [of a slice of bacon] marked Buck as fit to survive in the hostile Northland environment. It marked his adaptability, his capacity to adjust himself to changing conditions. . . . It marked, further, the decay or going to pieces of his moral nature, a vain thing and a handicap in the ruthless struggle for existence. . . .

Not that Buck reasoned it out. He was fit, that was all, and unconsciously he accommodated himself to the new mode of life. (21)

Unlike a typical character in a realist novel who possesses a highly developed moral nature subject to decay, Buck is a dog from the start; London's fixation on morality immediately triggers his anxiety about Buck's reasoning, or lack thereof. Precisely when moral considerations are introduced, considerations well beyond the issue of Buck's adaptation to his environment, London feels compelled to register some sharp distinction between beasts and men while he goes on to insist that "civilized" Buck "could have died for a moral consideration, say the defence of Judge Miller's riding-whip" (21). That Buck "civilized" begins life under a judge is no coincidence, especially since the judge's "moral consideration" and not the dog's presumably would motivate the animal's defense of the whip—a symbolically resonant piece of his master's private property and a sleeker version of the club that disciplined Buck in the wild.

Focusing on the programmatic aspects of the story's naturalism, Charles Walcutt surmises that London makes his hero a dog because "if Buck were a man there would have to be some kind of ethical responsibility."[13] The decay of his "moral nature" can thus be tossed aside without the reader's losing respect for Buck. But London is obsessed with his dog-hero's moral nature and the question of "justice" (13). It is precisely Buck's sense of value, especially his own worth in the eyes of others, that wins our respect, as a quick glance at the early chapters demonstrates. The emotions Buck experiences in the opening scenes, cast as a captivity narrative, are striking: "a fine pride in himself" ruling over the judge's ranch as a "sated aristocrat" (6); "rage" once his "quiet dignity" (7) is repeatedly affronted by his captors; "obeying" (12) the law of the club (obedience explicitly distinguished from "conciliation"); feeling "ashamed" (anger turned inward by others' disapproval) when "onlookers" (14) laugh at him; "hatred" (16) of his immediately recognized rival Spitz.

Pride, dignity, anger, obedience, shame, and hatred culminate in "imagination," a "quality that made for greatness" (35), which finally allows Buck, perversely enough, to kill his dreaded rival. Animals may have "a logic of feelings,"[14] but these emotions are not necessarily structured by a coherent narrative leading to self-fulfillment. Buck's character develops along the lines of a traditional nineteenth-century bildungsroman, in which identity is a process of becoming via moral education: a portrait of the dog as a young artist, if you will. Compared to the figures inhabiting, say, Crane's *Maggie* or Norris's *McTeague*, Buck is not only smarter but has a clearer sense of right and wrong, is *more* human.

Such acquired humanity casts doubt on a key argument underpinning June Howard's ideological analysis of naturalism. Demonstrating how the genre's preoccupations with force and fate express middle-class Americans' fear of proletarianization, Howard insists that turn-of-the-century naturalist texts polarize the categories of helpless brute (character) and privileged spectator (narrator). But Buck's education, by work, suggests that for London these class-based antinomies are not as rigid and absolute as Howard suggests, that an upwardly mobile working dog (and his narrator double) can be a humanized beast without necessarily becoming a brute.[15]

Learning his many "lessons" (12, 15, 18), knowing his proper place, disciplining his body, and struggling for approval, Buck fulfills a higher calling. This calling has less to do with the wild than with the dignity of labor. *The Call of the Wild* thus strictly follows the dictates of the bildungsroman plot: transforming nature by work leads to self-transformation, leads up from slavery to freedom. For Buck and Jack, work initially becomes the source for identity, the means to make a name for themselves. Functioning as a path to self-transcendence, labor in London's narrative thus carries enormous philosophical import—Hegelian import, to be more specific.

Hegel, not Darwin, offers the common ground for the oft-noted split between London's Marxist socialist side and his preoccupation with Nietzschean supermen. Marking a division between nature and culture, Hegel posits self-consciousness as separating humans from animals—the sort of crucial distinction that London evoked in his response to Roosevelt's "nature-faking" charge. Self-consciousness can be gained, according to Hegel, only when animal desire negates itself, that is, moves outside itself to desire something beyond self-preservation. Beyond the instinct to survive is the desire to desire itself, manifested as a desire for recognition. This struggle to be valued, to be found worthy by others, demands the dominance of one man over another; hence the origins of a master/slave dialectic, whereby the conquered slave ("having subordinated his human desire for recognition to the biological desire to preserve his life"), by working, becomes master over nature and, in doing so, frees himself from nature as well as from himself, from his nature as a slave. Quite simply, work humanizes, freeing the slave from the master, whose idleness marks his identity as static.[16]

This may be a fairy tale, as Marx's historical-materialist explanation of subjugation makes clear, but it is Buck and Jack's fairy tale nonetheless. Dog recognition, not dog cognition, becomes the central issue in the narrative, in terms of how Buck is evaluated by humans, then by the dogs, and most problematically by his adored master, John Thornton. Initially valued strictly for his potential for work (size, strength, and ferocity), Buck's "worth" is measured in money in the marketplace (as is true in many slave narratives), and by other means of rational calculation: "One in ten t'ousand," his new owner Perrault "comments mentally" (13) during the moment of exchange.

Once Buck enters into social relations with his sledmates—also the precise moment he enters into work—his "worth" takes on a new meaning. As London introduces his crew of dogs, he gives them each a distinct personality—introspective, appeasing, fair, wise, lazy, and so on—largely in relation to how Buck values them and how they value Buck. More to the point, perhaps, these evaluations become intimately linked to Buck's "calling," his learning to pull the sled with his mates. The ability of Sol-leks, for example, to "command respect" is limited by his lack of "apparent ambition," until Buck later sees him at work with his partner Dave and "learns" to value their "even more vital ambition" (17). Like the two "new kind of men" (13) driving them, Dave and Sol-leks on the job suddenly become "new dogs, utterly transformed by the harness. All passiveness and unconcern had dropped from them. . . . The toil of the traces seemed the supreme expression of their being, and all that they lived for and the only thing in which they took delight" (19).

When London tries to give this Hegelian self-transcendence via labor a Darwinian slant, the results are peculiar, as in the famous "ecstasy" passage that London inserts right before he has Buck kill Spitz:

> There is an ecstasy that marks the summit of life, and beyond which life cannot rise. And such is the paradox of living, this ecstasy comes when one is most alive, and it comes as a complete forgetfulness that one is alive. This ecstasy, this forgetfulness of living, comes to the artist, caught up and out of himself in a sheet of flame; it comes to the soldier, war-mad on a stricken field and refusing quarter; and it came to Buck, leading the pack, sounding the old wolf-cry, straining after the food [a rabbit] that was alive and that fled swiftly before him through the moonlight. He was sounding the deeps of his nature, and the parts of his nature that were deeper than he, going back into the Womb of Time. (33–34)

Buck's ambition to lead the pack, otherwise always expressed in terms of work, suddenly is manifested as hunting a wild rabbit in the heat of the kill. London matches this primal thirst for blood by moving spatially inward ("deeps") and temporally backward ("Womb of Time"), so that transcen-

dence can be converted into, or *repressed*, as instinct—"the deeps of his nature." But the first half of the passage undermines the latter half, insofar as
London needs to keep reminding us of our forgetfulness, illustrated by examples of an artist and a soldier at work producing, or at least willfully acting, not unconsciously tearing into raw flesh.

In an interesting footnote to his influential reading of Hegel, Alexandre
Kojève remarks that animals do have "techniques" (a spider's web), but that
for the world to change "essentially" and become "human," work must realize a "project" or, as he says a bit later, be activated by an "idea."[17] Through
a regimen of service and self-discipline, Buck's "idea" embodied in work is
to become leader of the pack by conquering "the disciplining" (17) Spitz, his
rival for mastery. Once he defeats Spitz in this "war" (29) and gains from
both dogs and humans the recognition and respect that he has struggled for,
what is left for him to do? Since Buck is part of Jack's plot, since London in
the act of narrating is himself working *for* Buck, we are able to see glimpses
of a larger project informing the labor of narration. That idea or ambition
is writing itself.

Buck has been associated with writing, from the very first sentence of
the story: "Buck did not read the newspapers, or he would have known that
trouble was brewing" (5). This is certainly a strange way to introduce a dog-
hero, making Buck's (not) reading seem a matter of preference, rather than
possibility (using "did" instead of "could"), and establishing a kind of subjectivity, by a reference to the materiality of writing, which fades away by the
end of this opening paragraph. Before it is clearly fixed that his protagonist
is an animal, London's little joke here is to make us imagine the act of reading, and then immediately negate it by embodying the reader as a dog. The
result is a trace of Buck's understanding print, as if the news of the Klondike
gold strike that occasions his subsequent captivity is somehow available to
him, as if he verges on knowing what he cannot know. Literalizing in this
way the operations of the unconscious, London positions Buck midway between a passive sign to be read and a reader of signs himself.[18]

The most important link between Buck and writing concerns his work
itself, his toiling in the traces to deliver letters. It is quite extraordinary, though
hardly ever noticed by critics, that in a tale ostensibly devoted to representing the howling blank frozen white wilderness of the Yukon, men and dogs
have a noble civilizing function, bringing mail to the remotest outposts of
progress, "carrying word from the world" (40). More pointedly, these "new
men" François and Perrault act as official agents of the state, "couriers" car-

rying various "government" (Canadian) "dispatches" (16, 19). These "important" (19) and "urgent" (32) dispatches, moreover, account for the urgency of London's own labor as writer, the need to get his message out, be recognized by others for his work, and make a name for himself. As in the case of Poe's purloined letter, we never see the contents of the dispatches, for London emphasizes the delivery of mail, how writing gets circulated, distributed, and published after it is initially composed. But toiling in the traces that leave their own marks on the white landscape, both Buck and Jack fulfill their calling.

In a long footnote to his discussion of London, Mark Seltzer anticipates my claim about the inscription of writing on landscape, only to reject this interpretation by insisting that a mechanics of literary production under what he calls naturalism's "body-machine complex" forecloses such a "traditional" notion of writing as a means to self-identity.[19] Here Seltzer is implicitly interrogating the work of Walter Benn Michaels, who has argued that for the naturalist writer self-possession via the work of writing entails a self-consumption, leading to a thematics of writing, which can neither be reduced to its material marks nor transcend its materiality, just as the writer's person is neither identical with body nor independent of it. Seeking to challenge Michaels's positing of self (and totalized market) as a closed circuit of exchange, Seltzer tends to overemphasize the role of technology in literary production, at least in the instance of London, whose understanding of writing is less mechanistic than organic, drawn from the animal realm, as Seltzer's own powerful reading of "men in furs" shows. As my reliance on Hegel indicates, I would argue that London in fact holds very traditional assumptions about work and writing; in response to Michaels's thesis, however, it seems to me that London's modernity suggests that he understands how an author's circulated name can sometimes carry more weight than the production of marks themselves.

Working like a dog finally is not enough, then, and by implication neither is writing like one. Once Buck vanquishes Spitz to achieve his highest ambition as top dog, he is soon sold off—by "official orders" (40)—to a new (nameless) master, also a mailman but not ostensibly a government courier. London's plotting here begins to grow less urgent. The disenchanting of work actually begins shortly before Buck becomes leader of the pack. In a long, self-consciously overheated passage celebrating "that nameless, incomprehensible pride of the trail and trace" (30), London conflates Buck's "desire for mastery" (30) over Spitz with the pride that all these dogs take "in the toil to the last gasp," the "ordained order that dogs should work" (31). For

Buck to gain supremacy over the pack, however, he must *disrupt* work, must break down "discipline" (32) and "destroy the solidarity of the team" (32). Describing this "challenging [of Spitz's] authority" (32) as an "open mutiny" (30) or "revolt" (32), London points to a gratification beyond work: "He [Buck] worked faithfully in the harness, for the toil had become a delight to him; yet it was a greater delight slyly to precipitate a fight amongst his mates and tangle the traces" (33). It is surely no coincidence that in the next paragraph London allows Buck and his fellows to go off chasing that wild rabbit. Working gives way to hunting, an activity more akin to play or sport that celebrates blood lust (desire) more than eating for survival (need).

Although London does his best to offer the spirit of defiance as a means of transcendence that surpasses discipline and servitude, Buck is finally no demonically driven Ahab. The problem seems to be more mundane: sheer disgust and exhaustion with work itself. With Buck now at the lead, London suddenly remarks that "it was a monotonous life, operating with machine-like regularity. One day was very like another" (40). A page later his last desperate effort to restore the nobility of work has precisely the opposite effect. In London's most extended treatment of another dog, something goes "wrong" with that wonderful worker Dave, who becomes "sick unto death," suffering a mysterious "inward hurt" that would not go away, despite his overwhelming "pride of trace and trail" (43). London settles this existential crisis the best he can, consecrating the fact that "a dog could break its heart through being denied the work that killed it" (44), and then finally putting Dave out of his misery with a pistol shot, whose meaning Buck "knew" (44). So much for Hegel.

Speaking for Buck, why should Jack in the end also find that "his heart was not in the work" (50), even as this "heart" can still remain "unbreakable" (54)? A significant clue to answering this question can be found in a curious essay entitled "How I Became a Socialist," which London first published in March 1903, just as he was negotiating the book publication rights to *The Call of the Wild*.[20] The most productive and important year of his life, 1903, also saw, among other personal matters, the publication of London's book *The People of the Abyss*, an account of his journalistic foray the previous summer into the East End of London, where he poignantly charted the conditions of the British underclass.[21] In both essay and book his central metaphor for this underclass is an abyss or bottomless pit; he makes clear in his essay that "socialism" primarily serves to keep him from falling into such a pit. London begins autobiographically by remarking that as a young "MAN" he used to be "one of Nietzsche's *blond beasts*," "one of Nature's strong-armed noblemen" who proudly believed that "the dignity of labor was to me the most impressive thing in the world." Associating such "orthodox bourgeois ethics" with "rampant individualism," he claims that this "joyous individualism" was "hammered out of me" as soon as he began to come in close contact with "what sociologists love to call the 'submerged tenth'"—the underclass that industrial capitalism uses up and discards. Conveniently forgetting his own (illegitimate) birth *in* the pit of the working class, London ends his story with a striking vow: "*All my days I have worked hard with my body, and according to the number of days I have worked, by just that much am I nearer the bottom of the Pit. I shall climb out of the Pit, but not by the muscles of my body shall I climb out. I shall do no more hard work, and may God strike me dead if I do another day's hard work with my body more than I absolutely have to do*" (1119). This oath is remarkable for at least three reasons. First, in disavowing his own beginnings in the pit, London "confesses" that his primary motivation is the "terror" of joining the underclass. He expresses absolutely no solidarity, the working-class consciousness that Marx and Engels saw as necessary for revolution. Second, given his terror of the pit, work itself becomes terrifying; the object is not to struggle to make work less alienating and thereby rehumanize it, but merely to "run away" from it altogether. Third, London simply equates manual labor with "hard work." I take "hard" here also to mean "difficult," so he is by implication suggesting that brain work would somehow necessarily be easy. But then trying actually to imagine his "reborn" life without such deadening hard work, London is forced to admit, "I was running around to find out what manner of thing I was," a state of being that he rather optimistically labels "socialist."

London's essay might more accurately have been titled "How I Became a Successful Author," for it carries enormous implications for a discussion of the presence of writing throughout *The Call of the Wild*. Earlier I emphasized the physicality of writing for both Buck and Jack: hauling the heavy letters inch by inch through a blank white wilderness. Writing's materiality thus renders nature immaterial. But London's distinction between hard work and easy work suggests a second, more abstract notion of writing whereby the author controls and manages the deployment of letters but does not actually carry them himself. In the scene of writing that informs the narration up to this point, London is both slave, figured as Buck toiling in the traces, and *simultaneously* master, the plotter who directs the course of the sled and the beasts he uses (buys and sells) to pull it. The writing master thus hopes to gain some control within a potentially degrading capitalist market. But once hard work is fundamentally called into question, starting with the death of the dog Dave, how can letters be moved at all? That is, how can writing be strictly easy? Commenting on Hegel, Kojève notes that the bourgeois worker under capitalism has no master, but nonetheless freely accepts his enslavement by the idea of private property, of capital itself.[22] London turns this fear on its head by imagining "socialism" as a state of mastery without slavery, without any hard work, so the writer is now free to roam in search of "what manner of thing" he has suddenly become. In the end London is left looking for a kind of easy work to replace the hard work that he has given up.

In this disenchanting of hard work and hard writing, London seems to be abandoning his dog-hero's project for self-transcendence as well—it is difficult to imagine how Buck's education can proceed. With the sacrifice of Dave, the plot threatens to stop. One clear possibility is to fall back on the Darwinian model of instinctual regression, which, we have seen, has so far consisted mainly in Buck and the other dogs chasing rabbits. I am perhaps being flippant here, since there are clearly key moments in the narrative when London powerfully evokes a sense of a "dominant primordial" (24)—manifested as "ancient song" (22–23), "wild fathers" (32), "blood-longing" (77)—pulling the beast Buck back into his primitive past. But these passages are literally *lyric* in that they are almost always detachable from the plot, neither closely following from prior events nor leading to others. The relationship between chasing rabbits and the "ecstasy of living," for example, is tenuous at best. Such ecstasy is powerful, in fact, precisely when it can effectively escape London's plotting.

Powerful and dazzling, such intermittent evocations of nature most importantly keep Buck an animal and therefore are precisely the points of resistance that prevent the type of transparent allegorizing that I earlier rejected but now might seem to be bordering on: Hegel in furs. Insofar as London depends on his role as plotter deploying and delivering letters to give him his status as writing/publishing master, such ecstatic moments threaten to sever the ties between Jack and Buck. At the risk of slighting the dog's ostensible return to the wild, I want to pursue for the remainder of this essay the problem of authorial mastery—a growing concern for London that manifests itself in his partial disengagement from Buck the dog as a primary source of identity in the later stages of the novel and his increasing identification with human characters.

What remains for London then, before letting go of his plot, letting humans "pass out of Buck's life for good" (40), is to comment on the writing of the story itself, via a series of cautionary tales with interesting consequences. Instead of development or reversion we get a kind of stasis or holding pattern as London presents a pair of moral lessons about bad masters and good masters. This structure of alternating bad and good closely resembles many animal tales for children (such as *Black Beauty*), as well as episodic slave narratives.[23] More important, from this point on in London's narrative, morality will no longer be rooted in Buck's nature, or even in his masters', as the plot begins to take on decidedly theological overtones.

First, the bad masters, an unlikely trio of husband, wife, and wife's brother. They appear on the scene immediately after London alludes to "congested mail" (46)—a striking homonym punning on the impasse in his plot and along with it the thwarting of Buck's manhood. New "official orders" (46), from nowhere, suddenly demand the sale of the dogs, who are now said to "count for little against dollars" (46). Up to this juncture in the narrative, Buck's continuity of identity depends on carrying letters, but Charles, Mercedes, and Hal are not couriers with urgent dispatches. What they are doing venturing through the North, in fact, remains to the end a "mystery of things that passes understanding" (46)—a faint New Testament echo (Philippians 4:7) referring apparently to London's own uncertainty about their motives as much as to Buck's uncertainty, just as the subsequent paragraph's narrative commentary on "a nice family party" seems to capture Buck's own ironic disgust as well as London's.

Here, then, is Buck and Jack's worst "nightmare" (53), toil without writing, without project, without meaning. Not only are their motives uncertain, but these new masters are technically incompetent: "They were slack in all things, without order or discipline" (51). In the most prolonged departure from Buck as a center of consciousness for the narrative, London unsubtly satirizes the dangers of domesticated irrational feminine disorganization (the sin of "dishes unwashed," mentioned twice). Confronted with an alien environment, the overcivilized family registers chaos, whereas the state of wildness clearly depends on strict regimentation, again only possible through regulated work. Given the absence of such service, at once ennobling and enabling, nature can be represented only by what it is not. The two men unwisely overburden the dogs, the family quarrels, Mercedes gives in to "the chaotic abandonment of hysteria" (57), and they finally and foolishly fall through thin ice, taking with them all their dogs, except for the presciently stubborn Buck. A kind of providential punishment for their poor mastery, the "yawning hole" (58) that they leave in their downward wake serves brilliantly to literalize London's fable of negative transcendence. Hal and Charles and Mercedes have truly become the people of the abyss.[24]

Once the bad masters drop out of the picture, we might expect Buck to attend immediately to the beckoning call of the wild. But before he can be free of all encumbrance he owes a debt of gratitude to his savior, John Thornton, which he will repay in spectacular fashion. Entitled "For the Love of a Man," the John Thornton chapter seems totally out of place, contributing neither to Buck's working education nor to his instinctual regression. The episode instead functions as a religious parable of sorts in which Love as a single unifying transcendental signifier is meant to subsume—in effect cancel out—both the dignity of labor and the law of club and fang. And what a love it is: "feverish and burning, that was adoration, that was madness" (60), that emerges intense and full-blown, out of nowhere, and strains, if not absolutely bursts, the boundaries of London's plot.

As the repetition of "adoration" makes clear, Buck's passion is religious and therefore ostensibly not a form of slavery; perhaps the dog-hero will find his true "calling" as a disciple. London seems to be working on the analogy that Buck is to other dogs as Thornton is to other men. Buck thus can meet his match only by worshiping a god, an "ideal master" (60). As perfect master, however, Thornton grants Buck an all too perfect freedom, letting him do nothing and consequently, in Hegelian terms, forcing him to be nothing. Even though Buck cannot overcome bad masters without providential aid, at least his passive resistance to the family trio allows him to maintain his dignity. But dignity becomes a problem for both Jack and Buck, once Love dissolves all such resistance, freeing them *from* work instead of freeing them *to* work. Trying to sustain an impossible oxymoron (ideal mastery) by an imposed religious analogy (Christ incarnate), London ends up operating at cross purposes, oscillating as Buck does between elevating Thornton and ignoring him so he can then heed his call.

Thornton's progressive diminishment manifests itself in two connected ways: his odd assumptions of various gender roles and his equally strange simulations of work. In keeping with his status as ideal master, he is initially figured as a benevolent father, seeing to "the welfare of his [dogs] as if they were his own children" (60). The problem is that Buck is no ordinary pet but a special being, closer to his master, closer to humans (if other dogs are dogs), closer to a god (if other dogs are just human). Portraying the intense intimacy between Buck and Thornton, London is compelled to level the difference between man and beast, to make them share the same ontology. First London equalizes their respective powers of verbalization: the moment he rescues Buck, Thornton is said to utter "a cry that was inarticulate and more like the cry of an animal" (57), whereas a few pages later Thornton sees Buck's "throat vibrant with unuttered sound" and gushes, "God! you can all but speak!" (60). When letters disappear, "with the mail behind them" (42), then sounds will have to do.[25] The communion between them grows more problematic, once London gives their mutual love a physical basis; in addition to Buck's religious "adoration" by way of his respectfully distant "gaze" (61), we are privy to a more corporeal sort of love play where the two males "embrace" (60) and caress each other until Buck's "heart would be shaken out of his body so great was its ecstasy" (60).

From god the father to male lover, Thornton more and more plays the part of wife, and a badly treated one at that. London first introduces Thornton in this chapter as "limping" (59) and home-bound, a condition that reinforces Buck's growing sense that his love for John "seemed to bespeak the soft civilizing influence" (61). After the bad masters satirized in the previous chapter, this influence is clearly feminine and domestic, "born of fire and roof" (61), and therefore to be avoided at all costs. Lest I seem unduly harsh about London's opinion of the feminine here, a brief review of the four female "shes" in the novel should set things straight: Curly, who is savagely ripped to shreds by the other dogs, thereby conveniently becoming the source for Buck's hatred of his (male) rival Spitz; Dolly, "who had never been conspicuous for anything" (28), suddenly goes "mad" (dog hysteria?); Mercedes, who "nurses the grievance of sex" (53); and finally Skeet, Thornton's "little Irish setter" who "as a mother cat" nurtures the wounded Buck, whose "dying condition" prevents him from "resenting her first advances" (59). He is saved from the threat of a same-species, heterosexual relationship only by finding a higher love in John. Once Buck starts to feel the pull of the primitive, Thornton's own feminine domesticity becomes a nuisance, as the dog more and more takes to being with his wolf companions, "sleeping out at night, staying away from camp for days at a time" (76). Prone to sentiment and tears (56, 70, among others), the wronged Thornton meanwhile can only wait at home for the straying, unfaithful lover now "seized" by "irresistible impulses" and "wild yearnings" (74). A vulnerable victim finally unable to defend himself in the wilderness, Thornton is anything but lord and master by the time he meets his fate.

Thornton's "calling" as a worker follows a similar trajectory. Like the previous bad masters, this good one does not deliver letters either. Nor does he do much of anything. A wounded god, he lazily waits, as Buck does, to heal himself. Love is the means of healing for both, but this mutual passion soon begins suspiciously to resemble a curious kind of work whereby Buck must prove himself all over again. Their love turns into a series of perverse tests (edited from the story's first serialized version); although defending his master against a legendary desperado and then saving his life (tests 2 and 3) can be explained in terms of Buck's gratitude, a payback, how do we explain Thornton's command that Buck jump off a cliff (test 1)? Fortunately unconsummated, this "experiment," which Thornton calls "splendid" and "terrible" (63), may strike the reader as not simply "thoughtless" (63) but downright sadistic, especially once we imagine for a moment (as we have been invited to do) that Thornton and Buck are human lovers.

Perhaps even stranger is Buck's final test, yet another "heroic" "exploit" (66) that explicitly takes the place of work. Boasting like a proud lover about the prowess of a mate, Thornton borrows money to bet heavily against a famous "Bonanza King" (67) on Buck's ability to haul a heavy sled. Here the hard work of Buck as sled dog delivering letters is mocked as a kind of "free play" (69), especially when Thornton actually wins the bet, which is made for cash ($1,600), rationally calculated, not for honor or dignity. By means of an empty gesture (the sled goes nowhere and is filled with dummy weight), Buck's worth thus gets converted into market speculation. We have come full circle, since London's plot is initially triggered by betting as well: recall that Buck was sold to pay off the lottery debts of the Mexican gardener whose "faith in a [gambling] system . . . made his damnation certain" (7). For both Manuel and Thornton, Buck equals bucks.

"When Buck earned sixteen hundred dollars in five minutes for John Thornton, he made it possible for his master to pay off certain debts and to journey with his partners into the East after a fabled lost mine, the history of which was as old as the history of the country" (71). So begins the final chapter of the novel. Given the narrative's prior emphasis on work, the devastating irony of that term "earned" is troubling, as is the perfunctory nature of the rest of the rambling sentence, as if Jack simply wanted to get his story over with, swiftly make his *own* Big Buck, and go home to enjoy the fruits of his labor, now that those "certain debts" have been discharged, thanks to Buck's five minutes of love.

Here the autobiographical and vocational dimensions of the narrative become most apparent, for John Thornton clearly doubles for John "Jack/Buck" London, as the recent Stanford edition of London's letters helps us to see. Linked by London's obsessive concern with the material conditions of his craft, the writer's life and fiction tend to merge. The $1,600 that Thornton wins by gambling on Buck, for example, virtually matches the $1,800 that London sought (and got) as an advance from his book publisher, Macmillan. In two letters to his editor George Brett (dated November 21 and December 11, 1902), London lays out an absurdly ambitious scheme to write six books in *one* year, plans preoccupied with word counts, dollar amounts, debts, profits, market values, financial risk, and production timetables—the stuff of rationalized capitalism. London (like Thornton) at this time also enjoyed "doing credit on a larger and Napoleonic scale" (London to Cloudesley Johns, January 27, 1903), in effect trading on the promise of his name.[26]

Despite London's heavy investment in the writer's market, the heroic deeds that Buck has performed for his master suggest another sort of economy operating in the end, an economy that depends less on Buck's work as a mail carrier and more on the spreading of his "reputation" and "name . . . through every camp in Alaska" (64). That is, the sign that Buck finally produces for himself is not the mark of writing, but the mark of fame—a difference that entails a shift in the narration from work to adventure. Heroism now suddenly leads to a "wandering" (72) search for that "fabled lost mine"; although the Lost Cabin remains a mystery, Thornton's fabulous get-rich-quick scheme of course succeeds, London curtly narrating how "like giants they toiled, days flashing on the heels of days like dreams as they heaped the treasure up," while "there was nothing for the dogs to do" (73). This self-conscious modulation into legendary fame and fortune looks forward to Buck's eventual apotheosis as immortal "Ghost Dog" (85), a kind of concluding emblem for London's career aspirations as a writer.

If this novel is an allegory at all, in fact, it should be read as an uncanny anticipation of the course of London's professional "calling," his great popularity—starting with the publication of *The Call of the Wild*—as well as his subsequent struggles to maintain and manage his success in the literary marketplace. Striking it rich, London takes revenge on his public—he does not stop writing, as Buck stops working; instead, the disenchanted London is driven, drives himself, to write more, to write about himself, about his own fame, over and over again until he eventually breaks down. In this respect his fate as a writer closely resembles the fate of the workaholic dog Dave, whose chronic "inward hurt"—"something wrong inside" (43) that cannot be fixed—eventually kills him. Imagining the career of Buck, London traces a more satisfying path. As totemic leader of the (wolf) pack, Buck is obliged only to "muse" (86) dutifully at the final resting place of his beloved master, nature's own altar of the dead, sometimes bringing his wolf companions along with him. In this way we are reminded that from start to finish, Buck has never lost touch with civilization.

During the novel's concluding wish-fulfillment of permanent celebrity, London tries to sustain moral tension in his narration by representing Buck as torn between his allegiance to his adored human master and his increasing kinship for his wild wolf "brother" (76, 85). But this growing dilemma within Buck between devoted domesticity and wild "restlessness" (76) is conveniently cut short by the sudden introduction of a band of Indians—the Yeehats—who render the question of the dog-hero's moral choice rather moot. Without a "trace" (83), Thornton's exit in the narrative as sacrificial victim (courtesy of the Yeehats) is as surprising as his entrance as perfect master and lover. Although Thornton's abrupt departure allows London and his readers to return in the end to Buck as a primary source of identification, such a reaffirmation of the wild's call exacts its own price.

A kind of parody of the primal horde of sons whom Freud imagines as slaying the father in *Totem and Taboo*, the Yeehats kill Thornton and his mining partners while Buck is off fulfilling his nature as primordial beast by tenaciously stalking an old "great" (81) bull moose. London thus offers an astonishing series of displaced murders: while Buck is killing moose, mediatory primitive Indians kill his white master; said Indians are in turn killed in a rage by Buck, who must avenge the master's murder, London explains, "because of his great love for John Thornton"—a love, London adds, by which Buck "lost his head" (82). With "reason" (82) now firmly entrenched as instinct and "passion" (82) conversely located in civilization, London's booby-trapped naturalism finally explodes, forcing us to scramble for other sorts of supernatural explanations. Having tasted men's blood, "the noblest game of all" (83), the dog-hero is finally free to become top wolf, leaving both the human world *and* nature behind for good (or at least until he reappears as White Fang).

The difficulty is that in Freud's version of this sacred myth Buck (the son) must kill Thornton (the father) directly, to resolve the problem of authority by and for himself. Nietzsche's retelling similarly demands that Buck (the human) directly kill Thornton (the god). But by introducing middlemen, London chooses for his animal-hero a weaker resolution that seems to beg the fundamental question of Buck's moral self-transcendence. Slaying for Buck, the savage Yeehats in effect allow the dog to remain civilized, but thereby drain Thornton's sacrificial murder of its sacred power. Although he may be a "Fiend incarnate" (82, see also 10, 37, 58) when it comes to killing the Indians, Buck does not appear man enough to do the real job himself.

Buck's masculinity has been a central issue throughout the entire narrative, on Judge Miller's ranch, in captivity, at work transmitting messages, and finally as a "killer" in the wild (77). In the end, then, perhaps Buck's true calling depends less on whom he murders than the spectacular way he does it, given the crucial transformation in the novel from toiling in the traces to instant success that culminates during the staged sled pull. London's progressive disenchantment with work in the story registers the growing fear felt by many turn-of-the-century American men that the market, increasingly abstract and rationalized, could no longer offer the grounds to define manhood, particularly those ideals of self-reliance, diligence, and mastery at the heart of nineteenth-century liberal individualism.[27] Once the workplace diminishes in significance in the new century, masculinity threatens to become primarily a performance or pose displayed for its own sake, like the theatrical shows of passion that characterize the Thornton-Buck relation ("as you love me, Buck"), and the dog-hero's equally melodramatic final conquests of bull moose, Yeehats, and wolf pack (just prior to which Buck is said to stand "motionless like a statue" [84]). Buck's toil as a letter carrier gains him respect and recognition, but his intense killing ultimately grants him the iconographic status of Ghost Dog, an awe-inspiring totem far more powerful and lasting than civilized man's paler version, fame.

Seeking to test manhood in non-economic arenas (the wilderness, war, sports), turn-of-the-century Americans such as Teddy Roosevelt struggled to combat a mounting spiritual crisis in masculinity by trying to naturalize dominance. In one of his earlier excursions into literary criticism, an 1892 review of Kipling and other writers praising war, Roosevelt remarks that "every man who has in him any real power of joy in battle knows that he feels it when the wolf begins to rise in his heart."[28] London's own quest for power is a bit more subtle than Roosevelt's, less patently "homocentric," to invoke again his counterattack against TR's "nature-faking" charge. Taking Roosevelt's glib metaphor literally, London in his naturalist masterpiece imagines himself becoming—through captivity, delivering letters, and ritual slaying—the male-creature that Roosevelt can only superficially conceive of as a man in wolf's clothing. In contrast to TR's imposed metaphoric pretense, Buck under London's direction does work as a high-charged cultural carrier. For this reason *The Call of the Wild* continues to merit critical attention. Simultaneously on extravagant display and buried deep, like a bone, within his animal-hero, Jack London's mail manages to affirm his own public calling—to make his bold mark for all to admire.

Ishi and Jack London's Primitives

CHARLES L. CROW

Jack London's short, intense career was dominated by a single quest: to find a way of living in harmony with the landscape. He understood, with considerable accuracy, that progress had somehow gone awry, and the promise of the westering experience was yet unfulfilled. He wanted to find a way to live that would make the California countryside home to him, an "Abiding Place," in some emotionally satisfying way he sensed but never quite found. The quest took many forms: in a critique of capitalism, and a career as a socialist propagandist; in pioneering work as an ecologist and model rancher; and in many fictions, some didactic, some visionary, some written frankly for a quick dollar. Even at his best, his fiction was warped by misguided ideology, often of the most embarrassing racist kind. His notion of the "primitive" in humanity was filled with unchallenged stereotypes, and it hindered him at every turn when he tried to imagine a simpler life. Still, there was a visionary artist in London striving with the ideologue. In flashes of insight, he fashioned a series of fables that ask his key questions over and over: How to live in this new land? What would it be like to discover home here, or to fail to discover it and be alienated forever? These issues can be seen most obviously in his California novels, *Burning Daylight* (1909), *The Valley of the Moon* (1912), and *The Little Lady of the Big House* (1914), closely linked narratives that portray ranch life in the Sonoma Valley. *The Valley of the Moon*, I have argued elsewhere, is among the most ambitious of London's works and has more complexity and unity than critics thus far have credited—a unity best seen in terms of California themes.[1] But also relevant, among other works, are the seldom-considered science-fiction novels *Before Adam* (1906) and *The Scarlet Plague* (1910), and the novella that launched his career and remains his most read and admired, *The Call of the Wild* (1903), along with its sequel, *White Fang* (1906). These four works, written during a short period in London's life, form a kind of parable history of California.

As we put these fables together, we see an ideal vision emerge—dim but distinct—of a being at once simple and fully civilized, living in the landscape in deep communion with it, with instincts and intelligence completely united, with needs so satisfied that history—that record of our discontent—is irrelevant. This person we might call, after the dog Buck's lupine alter-ego, London's "wild brother."

One of the great ironies of London's life is that such a man did exist: his California contemporary, the Yahi Indian we know as Ishi. Called "the last wild man in North America," Ishi lived most of his life dispossessed, hunted, among a dwindling handful of the survivors of the massacre of his village, until he was at last alone, and, half-crazed, he surrendered to the white men who had destroyed his people. In his attempts to imagine a person at home in the landscape, London produced uncanny echoes of Ishi's own life, as we will see. The men seem shadows of each other, and they literally drew closer together, to within a few miles or even, sometimes, city blocks of each other, in their last years, probably without ever meeting, though London did have some knowledge of the celebrated California "wild man." Ishi's life provides a reality check on London's vision, showing us the failures of ideology and racism, which London shared with his time, and those instances when the artist's imagination triumphantly broke free of them.

The Call of the Wild seems a purely naturalistic beast-fable, yet the work is close to myth and dream. It is difficult to believe that London was not influenced even at this stage in his career by Jungian thought, since clearly he was drawing on the kind of substrata he would subsequently find explained in the writings of the great psychologist.[2] Much of London's later career as a writer can be viewed as an attempt to work out in human characters the fable that was so coherent and compelling in the story of Buck, and in particular to reconcile that work's two visions of home.

The Call of the Wild begins with a sketch of the good life: Judge Miller's home in the Santa Clara Valley is recognizable as one version of prosperous ranch life, a particular theme of California in the late nineteenth and early twentieth centuries, and one to which London would return in his Sonoma Valley novels a few years later. It is important to stress that nothing ever refutes the judge's ranch as a vision of pastoral abundance. It is a home

Buck loses, a somewhat idealized home, but anchored in real time and history in California, in exchange for another home, one approached through the hard facts of naturalistic initiation, but located in the realm of dream and myth.

Buck's initiation, his response to a call "to mature selfhood and triumphant life," as Charles N. Watson, Jr., aptly puts it, is also a homecoming.[3] His heeding of this call is a return not so much through time as out of time, to a prehistory of perfect harmony with nature. He edges away from John Thornton's campfire toward the Younger World of the hairy man, and finally touches noses with the Wild Brother, who is certainly a long-submerged level of himself. Successfully crossing the threshold, severing ties with civilization after John Thornton's death, he enters the Abiding Place— that particularly resonant term London used here, I believe, for the first time. There Buck is subsumed into myth and becomes the Ghost Dog, father of a new tribe.

Buck's is the most convincing success story in London's fiction—indeed, one could argue, in the entire tradition of American masculine literature. Looking back along that tradition and viewing the pairs of male characters— Natty and Chingachgook, Ishmael and Queequeg, Huck and Jim—we see that London has sensed and clarified its underlying logic. Those bondings of white males and supposedly primitive sidekicks represented a desire to recover an element of self, a lost harmony with nature and instinct, a condition recalled in dream and in myth. Put another way, Buck's life is triumphant because he draws on both ends of the evolutionary scale: his strength and intelligence come from the evolved breeding of his St. Bernard and Scotch Shepherd parents; his cunning from the buried life of his wolf ancestors, which he recovers.

London's sequel *White Fang* is often dismissed as a potboiler, yet the apparently mechanical reversal of *The Call of the Wild* may help focus London's larger themes. White Fang begins his life in the Yukon and, after kidnaping and adversity, becomes a watchdog in the Santa Clara Valley, rewards his benefactor by saving his family from a killer, and at the end he has fathered a litter of pups. Combining the two stories as a single fable, we have a nearly perfect equivalent of Joseph Campbell's monomyth pattern: the call to adventure, crossing the threshold, descent into the underworld or forest, struggle with an antagonist, and return home, transformed, with new vision or saving power.[4]

In his later California novels, London tried to locate the human equivalent of these canine parables. Then the problem was to find a way to transform human life through some initiation during which people could safely encounter their buried instincts, overcome whatever demons they might meet in themselves or without in this quest, regain a unity of personality and a close kinship with nature, and bring this vision back, to retain it, to incorporate it in a new kind of life in California.[5] Without the initiation, the promise of the landscape was empty—one could never discover the homeland there. Pieces of this problem appear in several works, and London puzzled out the solution in different ways. At times he seemed to despair of it, and at others—most notably in *The Valley of the Moon*—he believed for a time that he had found the key. *Before Adam* and *The Scarlet Plague* were essential explorations within this program.

In his dreams Buck remembered his wolf ancestor and "the hairy man" of those Younger Days of prehistory. In *Before Adam*, which began magazine serialization the month *White Fang* concluded (October 1906), London returns to the Younger World to tell the story of the hairy man. As in *The Call of the Wild*, the way into the dim past is through racial memory. The unnamed narrator of *Before Adam* discovers in his dreams the fragments he fits together to form the story of his remote ancestor Big Tooth, his mate the Swift One, his enemy Red Eye, and the destruction of the village of the Folk by the Fire People. As in London's California-Yukon dog stories, this caveman narrative (one of the earliest of its kind) is a fable about home.

Indeed, loss of home and search for home constitute almost the entire plot of *Before Adam*. We witness a literal fall from home of the child Big Tooth—he is shaken from his treetop nest by his jealous stepfather; his brief wandering until he discovers the main Abiding Place of the Folk, his own species of pre-people; his flight into the forest with his companion Lop Ear, a kind of initiation journey in which he encounters the Tree People, an earlier arboreal species, and the more evolved and dangerous Fire People; his wedding journey with the Swift One. These trips of the young Big Tooth always circle back to the Abiding Place, which might be a perfect home, were it not for the murderous, gorilla-like Red Eye, "the atavism," as London frequently labels him.

The Abiding Place is lost when it is attacked by the Fire People. With most of his tribe fallen to the invaders' arrows, like fire an unknown technology to the Folk, Big Tooth, the Swift One, Lop Ear, and a few others begin a long, confused journey westward through an unknown swampland, to emerge by a cold sea. After a few seasons they are spied out again by the Fire People, flee again, and find a final Abiding Place south of the swamp, in a sheltered valley, where, presumably, Big Tooth lives out his days and has the children who pass on his racial memories, ages later, to the narrator. The novella ends with an enigmatic glimpse of Red Eye, another survivor, ruling over a terrified community of Tree People.

As is always the case with London's best work, *Before Adam*, despite some crudities, stirs us because of its kinship with dream and myth, and it contains troubling ambiguities. These deeper levels of London's imagination often seem to struggle with the ideologies imposed on its surface. We would expect, for example, that the sympathies of Jack London, notorious Social Darwinist and apologist for white man's rule, would be with the Fire People, so obviously destined to conquer with their advanced language, reason, and weaponry, so obviously more evolved toward future humanity, toward us. Yet London is drawn to the more primitive Folk, who resemble, in their defeat, American Indians and other peoples who have fallen before Western "progress": "And all day hunting parties of the Fire People ranged the forest, killing us wherever they found us. It must have been a deliberately executed plan. Increasing beyond the limits of their own territory, they had decided on making a conquest of ours. Sorry the conquest! We had no chance against them. It was slaughter, indiscriminate slaughter, for they spared none, killing old and young, effectively ridding the land of our presence."[6] Anthropologist Loren Eiseley, who was haunted by this novel as a boy, is certainly right in seeing the flight of the Folk through the swampland as "the symbol of man's everlasting displacement from his natural home in nature." As we read London's book, Eiseley continues, "the more perceptive among us turn its pages and by some haunting, inescapable compulsion find that we are not the Fire People after all. We are, for all our modern skins, the lost, eternally lost, but still safe-hidden remnant of the Folk."[7]

As Ursula Le Guin and other later writers would do, London evokes anthropology and our own dreams to uncover human qualities lost in our "progress," qualities that might lead us back to our natural home in the Abiding Place. What that home would be like, in present California, London still had difficulty envisioning. And as we respond to London's mythic vision, we must also note the irony of what he missed. The attack of the Fire People upon the Folk had its perfect parallels throughout the nineteenth century in London's own region. The first attack on Ishi's village—one such tragedy among many—had occurred in 1865, eleven years before London's birth; and as London wrote *Before Adam*, Ishi was still in hiding, like Big Tooth at the end of the novel, though without Big Tooth's consoling mate and children.

London's *The Scarlet Plague* (serialized in 1913 but written in 1910) is another ambiguous work of science fiction, with its questions about humanity this time pushed into the future. *The Scarlet Plague* is one of the first works in a now-recognizable regional tradition, the vision of a post-apocalypse or post-industrial life in California. London's fable is narrated by one James Howard Smith, a professor of English literature at Berkeley, who, in the early twenty-first century, lived through what seemed to him "the end of the world": a fast-spreading, incurable disease that destroyed all human life except a few scattered individuals who were unaccountably immune to the plague. Now, decades later, Smith, on the beach near what was San Francisco, tells the story of the plague to a rabble of skin-clad young savages who are his grandsons. The life of the surviving Californians, cut off from whatever other humans may live elsewhere, has become tribal, mimicking the earlier life of California Indians. Bears and wolves roam the landscape.

The meaning of London's fable is murky—one intelligent reader finds the closing images "horrifyingly apocalyptic," while another sees them as "a lyrical celebration of the cycle of life."[8] Smith's narrative voice is the source of this ambiguity. Although a framing narrator describes the scene, Smith alone speaks of the plague time, and he is unreliable. A creature of the leisure class, a Berkeley English professor (that enduring figure of satire), Smith could never be a spokesman for London's own values. The civilization he regrets was corrupt, ruled overtly by an industrial oligarchy, as London elsewhere predicted in *The Iron Heel*, and ready to be swept away by some oncoming social storm, if not by plague.

Yet Smith's voice has some authority, because he is the only survivor of the early days and the only living human with a sense of history. Smith foresees a slow climb toward civilization again, a growth of population and of knowledge, and the rediscovery of lost arts such as the making of gunpowder. His view of history is cyclical, like that of Spengler or of Thomas Cole in his *Course of Empire* paintings. The vision was shared by London in some moods, and it casts a melancholy over the last pages of the novella.

These last pages of *The Scarlet Plague*, however, are in the voice of the framing narrator, and they present images of nature. A herd of wild horses, "led by a beautiful stallion," stands at the edge of the surf. Then there is this concluding picture of a sunset:

> The low sun shot red shafts of light, fan-shaped, up from a cloud-tumbled horizon. And close at hand, in the white waste of short-lashed waters, the sea-lions, bellowing their old primeval chant, hauled up out of the sea on the black rocks and fought and loved.
>
> "Come on, Granser," Edwin prompted.
>
> And old man and boy, skin-clad and barbaric, turned and went along the right of way into the forest in the wake of the goats.[9]

The images are of beauty and renewal. The reader may be reminded of Robinson Jeffers's stern but beautiful pictures of the California coast, and his longing for a landscape emptied of the crowds and debris of modern society. We are left to reflect upon the failure of the old professor to see the beauty of this sunset, and to judge for ourselves whether or not a skin-clad boy, caring for his grandfather, might not after all be worthy of it.

We read *The Scarlet Plague* today with the knowledge that a real-life drama was being played out in California, even as London wrote, which ironically mirrored the events of the novella. London imagined Smith living for a time in the Sierras, believing himself the last human on earth, until, crazed and lonely, he descended to find a few other survivors. In August 1911, between the writing and the serial publication of *The Scarlet Plague*, Ishi, the last of his tribe, emerged from the foothills near Oroville. Strangely enough, this was three days after George Santayana's famous speech at Berkeley, entitled "The Genteel Tradition in American Philosophy," which ended with an appeal that Californians form a new culture in harmony with their landscape. Ishi met, not the violent death that his experience with white men had led him to expect, but warmth and friendship. He lived the remaining five years of his life at the San Francisco museum of the University of California, sometimes visiting the campus at Berkeley—where London's imaginary Professor Smith was to teach. One of his closest friends was Alfred Kroeber, whose future wife, Theodora, would write *Ishi in Two Worlds*; their daughter, Ursula K. Le Guin, would use insights from her father's legendary friend, along with much art and wisdom, in writing her novel, *Always Coming Home*, which would in many ways fulfill the tradition of California speculative fiction London had invented.[10]

What would London have learned from Ishi, had he met his Wild Brother? It is appealing to imagine such a meeting, since the parallels between Ishi and London's characters become stronger the more one learns of the Yahi's life. Ishi, indeed, seems the man in harmony with the landscape whom London had envisioned, whom he had longed to become. Like most northern California Indians, Ishi was probably a direct lineal descendant of the first human beings to enter the valley where he was born. The Yahi had found their Abiding Place thousands of years ago. Nothing was foreign or nameless to them in their environment. According to Theodora Kroeber, that fact allowed the handful of Yahi, and finally Ishi alone, to survive so long: although denied much of their land for hunting and food gathering, forced for years to crawl through the brush for concealment during daylight hours, they were still, finally and fundamentally, *at home* in a way no European American has ever been.[11]

No such encounter, as far as I can learn, ever took place; there was no moment of London's life as compelling as Buck's meeting with his Wild Brother, no moment of epiphany to confirm London's deepest insights and sweep away the dross of inherited confusion about primitive peoples. And we must not judge London for failing to know the Ishi of Theodora Kroeber's reconstruction, to be written some 60 years later. Instead, we have only hints of what London knew and felt about Ishi, and we can speculate, with the perspective of eight decades, on how Ishi may have interacted with London's imagination.

That London did know of Ishi we can be certain. (It would be surprising, indeed, given the publicity around the "wild man," if London had not heard of him.) Some time between 1911 and 1915, reading his copy of Stephen Powers's *Tribes of California*, London made a notation: "Ishi's tribe." The passage describes the Mill Creek Indians (as the Yahi were called by settlers) and gives a sympathetic portrait of them as victims of persecution.[12] Something in the Ishi story struck fire with London, for near the end of *The Star Rover* (1915), amid the swirling images of previous lives of his hero, Darrell Standing, there is "Ushu the archer," who was "lost from [his] own people" and was "taken in by a strange people."[13] Standing had led this life, but he does not have time to tell us about it: perhaps this implies Ishi's place in London's imagination. He sensed an identity with Ishi, or at least saw potential in his story, but had not worked out its implications. Thus leaving the last trace that Ishi left in a text, we conjecture how London's beliefs enabled and hindered him as he tried to fit Ishi into the larger fable of California he had for many years been evolving in his imagination.

London's own quest for an Abiding Place in the California countryside had much that was noble and farsighted in it, involving a clear-headed critique of American notions of progress and exploitation of the landscape. Earle Labor's arguments here (and his refutation of Kevin Starr's reading of London's last years) are persuasive.[14] Yet, as Edward Said's analysis of Rudyard Kipling and Joseph Conrad shows, even the criticism of a culture by its most enlightened members (and surely London was one such) cannot climb outside that culture and will inevitably carry its assumptions. Conrad, for example, can denounce colonial oppression of subject peoples, but he is unable to envision them *except* as subjects and victims.[15] For London, his attempt to reconnect with the landscape carries a similar flaw, as perhaps all such attempts must. Anthropologist James Clifford asserts that "questionable acts of purification are involved in any attainment of a promised land, return to 'original' sources, or gathering up of a true tradition." For London, this purification involved an "almost automatic reflex," again described by

Clifford as typical of Western cultures, "to relegate exotic peoples and objects to the collective past."[16]

London, typical of his age and of our own, had little difficulty granting value and dignity to native peoples, as long as they were placed in the legendary past or transposed into exhibits or texts.[17] He had more difficulty envisioning them as living people interacting with others in present-day California. *The Valley of the Moon* shows this reflex. Native Americans are the antagonists of the Great Plains, which Saxon's ancestors crossed, who have left the bullet hole in the family's chest of drawers—which Saxon once kisses as though it were a holy relic.[18] Native Californians likewise gave the legendary name to the valley, whose putative translation gives the book its name; they do not exist in the present. London's own act of purification in search of the Abiding Place required that the landscape be nearly empty, a blank page, on which the story of Billy and Saxon is written. The original inhabitants have no way of *writing back* and can leave only their single word, Sonoma.

So the emergence of a real landscape dweller into present time may have been a disruption, a dissonance for London, even though Ishi was quickly framed (in Said's sense) by Alfred Kroeber and Thomas Waterman as a living exhibit of an exotic past. Since London was a genuine artist, however, the dissonance may have been stimulating. Perhaps the story of Ishi/Ushu, the exiled archer, worked in London's psyche, helping to fuel his interest in other indigenous peoples, as revealed by the remarkable stories of Hawaii in his last months.

At the end, having discovered Jung, London felt that he was at the brink of a new world, his imagination fertile with many untold stories. We cannot know what part Ishi might have had in them. Jack London and Ishi died in the same year, 1916, the strange parallels holding true to the last.

Gazing at Royalty

Jack London's 'The People of the Abyss' and the Emergence of American Imperialism

ROBERT PELUSO

In the summer of 1902, Jack London spent seven weeks living in and writing about the slums of London's East End. The book he produced gives a view of urban poverty that remains a significant document in the history of writing about the city. "Things are terrible here in London," he wrote a friend as his book *The People of the Abyss* neared completion, "& yet they tell me times are good and all are employed save the unemployable. If these are good times, I wonder what bad times are like?" He concludes, "There's no place like California, & I long to be back."[1] In certain ways, throughout his stay in the East End, Jack London never left California and the "good times" that it stood for.

Of course, it would be foolish to claim that he traveled from California to London simply to write a book glorifying the United States. However, written as a series of vignettes in a style that interweaves statistical information from British sociological studies and excerpts from newspaper or police-court reports with highly impressionistic renderings of people, dialogue, and scene, his book about the East End also reveals a production of knowledge deeply indebted to a number of fundamental American values and meanings. And, more to the point, London's deployment of these values and meanings converges with and legitimizes a rapidly developing American imperialism.

With the closing of the domestic frontier and the growth of industrial capitalism in the 1890's, many Americans were beginning to imagine their country as a major actor in the international scene. Announcing the United

States as a world power at the 1893 Columbian Exposition, those eager for worldwide recognition would have to wait until after the panic of 1893 to realize their objectives. But with the economic recovery and the quick victory over Spain in the late 1890's, impediments to global stature began to seem, if not less formidable, at least worth the risk: with the details of a coherent foreign policy still to be worked out, the United States became involved in colonial encounters in Cuba, the Pacific, China, and elsewhere.[2]

That a writer's attitudes toward larger social-political objectives have a constitutive role in writing about the country and the city Raymond Williams has amply demonstrated. "For what is knowable," he says, "is not only a function of objects—of what is there to be known. It is also a function of subjects, of observers—*of what is desired and what needs to be known*."[3] Consequently, Williams explains, even though a real-world community may seem "wholly known" in relation to the value system of a given text, its representation is "very precisely selective."[4]

Although many cities had become sites for "knowing" urban poverty, the East End of London emerged during the 1880's and 1890's as a key location for British writers who wanted to construct or "prove" either flaws in industrial capitalism or problems with democratic politics. What is important in terms of Williams's argument and Jack London's book, is that in order to articulate what were fundamentally class-based fears, these accounts used a dualistic mapping of the city that derived its images and values from the notion of empire. Arraying an impoverished East End, whose inhabitants were likened to colonial subjects, against a wealthy West End, whose inhabitants stood for order and civilization, British writers produced a knowledge about urban poverty that would have been impossible without the discursive formations arising from imperialist activity.[5]

Because of their reliance on the strategies and rationales of imperialism, these representations of the East End might be seen as forming what Edward Said calls in regard to Orientalism an "imaginative geography and history." In a way that extends Williams's insights, Said shows that the creation of such "imaginative" conditions actually functions as self-definition, "help[ing] the mind to intensify its own sense of itself by dramatizing the distance and difference between what is close to it and what is far away." That is, by exploiting distance (temporal, spatial, emotional) and difference (racial, cultural, economic), this "imaginative" knowledge marks off the object of study (here, the East End dweller) as exotic Other in order to reaffirm an already privileged self-understanding.[6]

Complicated under any circumstances, the use of these strategies in Jack

London's case is more complex because mingling with the East End inhabitants was a direct provocation to his own self-understanding. Having himself barely escaped a life of poverty and exploitation, London developed a
strong fear of falling back into, in his words, "the Social Pit."[7] If this contact
with the people of the East End drew from London a powerful reaction that
marked his estrangement from the working class and a growing, if uneasy,
commitment to middle-class life, it also stirred in him a compassion for the
unparalleled "mass of misery" (*Letters*, 1: 305) he discovered at the bottom
of society.[8] Such a complicated reaction to urban poverty obviously raises
important questions about where *The People of the Abyss* fits into London's
own politics.[9]

Chronologically, his experiences in the East End took place between his
early socialist phase of the 1890's, which was typified by a reformist and par-
liamentarian view, and the more confrontational version of 1905–11 in which,
at least in theory, London's stance was more revolutionary.[10] Viewed against
this turn toward an outspoken radicalism, the experiences recorded in *The
People of the Abyss* seem to announce the pivotal middle moment in Jack
London's political philosophy. The "conversion" to socialism that London
spells out in "How I Became a Socialist," although apparently the result of
events prior to his trip to the East End, was more likely caused by the head-
on confrontation, which he had already described in *People*, with the urban underclass there.[11]

It seems, then, that by clarifying once and for all his distance from those
in "the Social Pit," his East End experiences reinforced his commitment to
socialism and were perhaps even instrumental in pushing him toward his
radical stage. Although this scenario is enticingly complete, the shift it outlines elides a second pole in London's politics, namely, the equally strong
pull of an evolutionary view of Anglo-Saxon dominance, which, developing
from simple nationalism to strenuous imperialism, reveals a second important direction in London's mature political philosophy. *People of the Abyss*,
in other words, marks a formative moment in Jack London's mature politics because with it he discovered a discursive formation to discuss urban
poverty that could tie together his long-standing belief in Anglo-Saxon supremacy and his growing interest in imperialism as a way of actualizing it.[12]

In the years leading up to his East End book, London shared with many
socialists the seemingly antithetical commitments to nationalism and in-
ternationalism, to class equality and racial superiority. In this context London's dual allegiance both to a nationally grounded view of Anglo-Saxon superiority and to international socialism is rather unremarkable. So, for ex-

ample, even though his support of the Spanish-American War deviated from
the uncompromising internationalist perspective of De Leon's Socialist Labor Party, his views were in sympathy with those of other, more moderate
factions such as the Christian Socialists or Victor Berger's Social Democrats.
The result of such compromises for London, as for a number of American
socialists, was that by 1900 when they were not actually ignoring imperialist activities, they were supporting them.[13] However, London departs from
these other socialists in the reasons behind his support for imperialism.
Whereas they believed that introducing capitalism into so-called backward
areas would create class conflict and thereby accelerate the socialist revolution,[14] London held a strong belief in evolutionary development. Accordingly, evolution would produce Anglo-Saxon leaders who would direct workers toward a socialist state, and, once in power, these workers would spread
socialism throughout the world. Thus London, perhaps influenced by the
stronger racialism in the California wing of the movement or perhaps because of his own intellectual interests, seems to have compromised somewhat more on the matter of imperialism. He actively used evolutionary doctrine to support interventionism on the grounds of racial supremacy as much
as, if not more than, international socialism.[15]

The attitudes and assumptions behind such racially charged views of
evolutionary development were relatively unproblematic for London when
he dealt with Innuit, Japanese, Koreans, Mexicans, and Hawaiians; and in
situations involving these groups he could readily—though he did not always—invoke an evolutionary epistemology to affirm Anglo-Saxon dominance.[16] But when the two races were the same, as are East Enders and Americans, London was forced into a more vocal cultural chauvinism, not unlike
that of, say, Josiah Strong, which privileged his "own" America of "spacious"
skies and vibrant men and women.[17] And just as Strong had deftly woven
strands of America's national narrative into his message of Anglo-Saxon superiority in order to promote imperial activity, so London would use traditional American meanings and values to enable the same cause.[18] Indeed,
on this issue London's self-understanding converges with the national self-
understanding to produce that "imaginative geography and history" needed
to advance American imperialism at the turn of the century.

In a decisive move that exploits the imperialist framing of the East End
in British urban writings, Jack London was able to resolve the tensions between his sympathy for and his revulsion against the urban poor—that is,
to reconcile his impulses toward socialism and his commitment to Anglo-
Saxon superiority—by adopting the subject position of colonizer.[19] London

develops this stance throughout *People* by continually and carefully asserting his Americanness and by repeatedly deploying a recognizably American
value system as his means of confirming his distance—and difference—from
the urban poor of the East End.[20] The consequences of this maneuver are
twofold. First, assertions of Americanness secure for Jack London a kind of
safe haven from which to "know" the East End poor: he can view their
misery, comment on its horror, and at the same time remain uncontami-
nated by it. Second, these self-conscious claims to Americanness converge
with a fascination from childhood with American versions of Anglo-Saxon
superiority and narratives of sturdy self-reliance.[21] In regard to this second
point, his narrative offers in a broader cultural arena precisely "what is desired and what needs to be known" for an emerging American imperialism.
Effectively marginalizing Great Britain via an epistemological-ideological
colonization, which uses narratives of America as a land of opportunity and
abundance to understand the extreme urban poverty existing, by all accounts,
in the very center of empire, Jack London's *The People of the Abyss* replaces
narratives of empire dominated by British agency with a version grounded
in American agency.[22] Performing an act of colonization in its own right, his
book thus participates in a contest of what Said calls "positional superiority."[23]
    Jack London's book was not alone in pointing the way toward, in Colin
Mercer's words, "the future of new significations" ("Baudelaire and the City,"
30) that would enable American imperialism. Brooks Adams, for instance,
had only the year before positioned the United States in "a war to the death"
with other countries, asserting, "There is not room in the economy of the
world for two centres of wealth and empire"; and no doubt Jack London's
representation of the coronation of Edward VII reassured alarmists like
Adams that the United States was indeed destined for the dominance it de-
served.[24] Occupying a full chapter almost exactly in the middle of his narrative, the coronation stands out amid descriptions of the doss lines, workhouses, and missions that pervade the book as a conceptual landmark ori-
enting Jack London's entire urban exploration toward a critique of British
imperial supremacy.[25]
    In this regard, Mercer's observations about Baudelaire's encounter with
Paris are also true of Jack London's contact with the East End. Having arrived in London for the crowning of a new king, Jack London could be said
to have discovered the city, as Baudelaire did Paris after the 1848 revolution, precisely during a critical moment in its cultural hegemony. And, like
Baudelaire, he used a change in political power to signal a rupture in the
continuity of legitimizing narratives (that is, those used to uphold the hege-

mony of British imperialism). He invented a new subjectivity for himself and a new "structure of discourse" that would win consent for a new set of actualities (namely, American imperialism).[26]

Standing in Trafalgar Square, which he describes in his book as " 'the most splendid site in Europe' and the very uttermost heart of the empire" (*People*, 139–40), London watches the vast military procession, noting that such imperial "force, overpowering force" with its "ships to hurl them to the ends of the earth" (*People*, 140) occurs while "the East End of London, and the 'East End' of all England, toils and rots and dies" (*People*, 140–41). By repeatedly linking the coronation to imperial activity (*People*, 140–41, 144–45, 146) and then by infecting its splendor with hints of industrial exploitation and overt scenes of violence, degradation, and brutality (see esp. *People*, 147–57), London effectively challenges its role in the continuation of British empire. That is, by underscoring the brutality and degradation embedded within the official ceremony, London in effect refuses to mark the coronation as an extension of the civilizing mission that had underwritten imperialist activities during Victoria's reign.[27] Jack London's representations of the underside of the coronation as a transvalued imperialism thus convert the event into a certification of England's declining world stature, enabling him to claim, "I never saw anything to compare with the pageant, except for Yankee circuses and Alhambra ballets; nor did I ever see anything so hopeless and so tragic" (*People*, 138). As he has staged the event, the greater the coronation spectacle, the greater the English decline.

If new discursive formations celebrating U.S. superiority were needed to legitimize and actualize American expansionism, then Jack London's willingness to provide them could only have been reinforced by his complex relation to the marketplace.[28] "Let us have an eye to the ills of the world and its need," he declared shortly after writing *The People of the Abyss*, "and if we find messages, let us deliver them. Ah, pardon me, purely for materialistic reasons. We shall weave them about with our fictions and make them beautiful, and sell them for goodly sums."[29] Given the subject matter of his East End book, it is not surprising that London was often troubled about its reception. Claiming that "it is written first for money; second, in its own small way, for the human good" (*Letters*, 1: 309), London from beginning to end of the project was never free from worries about the demands of the market (*Letters*, 1: 306, 312). But perhaps his attitude is best revealed in a letter to Cloudesley Johns a few days before the manuscript was completed. Here London refers Johns to his new essay, "Again the Literary Aspirant," which had just appeared in the *Critic* (*Letters*, 1: 311–12) and in which London speaks of the "howling paradox" of trying to be truthful to one's perceptions without violating the good will of one's audience (see Hedrick, *Solitary Comrade*, 151–68). Infiltrating his entire East End project, London's persistent concern about the tortuous relationship between speaking the truth and appealing to middle-class readers who were to consume that truth had telling ramifications. As Theodor Adorno has remarked, "Not only does the mind mould itself for the sake of its marketability and thus reproduce the socially prevalent categories. It also grows to resemble ever more closely the status quo even where it subjectively refrains from making a commodity of itself."[30]

In one sense, then, it might be possible to predict that Jack London's self-conscious commodification of his intellect (see his 1906 comment about wishing to become "a vender of brains"), during a time when many Americans, boasting of renewed economic prosperity, were beginning to position their country as an imperial power in its own right, would bring out even more strongly his own attraction to narratives of American superiority and self-reliance.[31] The nationalist structuring can go far toward explaining the periodic appearance of harsh outbursts against the poor, as, for example, during the coronation when he says of a crowd of well-heeled revelers, "I confess I began to grow incensed at this happy crowd streaming by, and to extract *a sort of satisfaction* from the London statistics which demonstrate that one in every four adults is destined to die on public charity" (*People*, 150, emphasis added). The recurrence of these attitudes signals not London's callousness toward suffering human beings but their role in his imaginative history. That is, although his book confirms conventional views of the East End as a human wasteland, it does so only in certain ways. And where it deviates from the habitual representations, it changes from simple urban exploration narrative to complex national anthem, one that could, at times, even overwhelm or compromise the book's radical-reformist message. As one reader angrily penciled on the final page, "Remember 7.000.000 people People who live in glass houses should not trow stones. Conditions in the United States are no better Housing and hand to mouth poverty."[32]

For someone as sensitive about his relations to poverty as was Jack London, the desire to "dramatize" (as Said would say) his distance from the actual people he confronted in the East End would also prove important to his conceptualizations of himself as an American. Reacting against the possible identity between himself and the East Enders, London produces them as different (as Other) by invoking a narrative that makes them known by their distance from the very source of their redemption, America. The procedure begins immediately in chapter 1 when London stages his descent by focus-

ing on his change of clothes, "my costume," he calls it (*People*, 13). Moving
from his personal feelings about dressing like the urban poor, his *former*
class, London arrives quickly at his message, the socioeconomic comparison between Great Britain and the United States. In a chapter dominated by
sartorial matters, London's articulation of his transformation from well-
heeled American to impoverished East Ender (see *People*, 10–15) is surely required as much by the conventions of urban exploration narratives (Keating, *Into Unknown England*, 17) as by his personal self-consciousness (Hedrick,
Solitary Comrade, 59–71) and the need to stage the conditions for his imaginative history.[33] Thus, in the recurrent phrase "rags and tatters," which London uses to describe his East End clothing, the play on Alger's rags-to-riches
formula hints repeatedly at the American narrative of success. At one point,
London comments in language indebted to Alger that his underclothes
and socks were "of the sort that any American waif, down in his luck, could
acquire in the ordinary course of events" (*People*, 10–11). In America, London seems to be saying, even the poorest of the poor have more than the
very best East Enders can expect in the heart of empire.

What is implicit in these early scenes, London makes explicit in later
ones. In the second chapter, for instance, he opens with a discussion of the
detective's house he was using as "a port of refuge" (*People*, 19). There was
nothing unusual about this decision. Of course, from the 1820's until at least
the 1860's, thrill-seeking West Enders had been going into the poorer sections of the city in quest of excitement, often in the company of a detective.[34]
Although Jack London's use of a detective's house as his home base may not
be unusual, his description of this commonplace event reveals his nationalist agenda. "Let it suffice that he lives on the most respectable street in the
East End—a street," London continues, "that would be considered very mean
in America, but a veritable oasis in the desert of East London" (*People*, 16;
and see 23). Against the best that the East End can offer, which is "mean" in
the sense of being poor and of being harsh and unfeeling, America comes
out in this simple comparison as far richer and kinder. Conceptually, the
meanness of the East End had been important for urban writing for many
years, reaching something of a classic formulation in 1894 with Arthur Mor-
rison's *Tales of Mean Streets*.[35] But by establishing the (grammatically and
logically) faulty comparison between a section of the city, "East London,"
and an entire country, "America," Jack London subverts the habitual conception of urban poverty for purposes of domestic social and political reform (as had, for example, Walter Besant) and underscores that virtually *any*
street in the United States is superior to this "most respectable" of streets

in the imperial capital of the world. The tactic appears throughout London's book: in one late scene, for instance, he compares the coffeehouse fare of East End workers and the food he ate while serving time in a California prison for vagrancy (*People*, 234–35). And not only do East Enders come out worse than American convicts in this comparison, but London moves quickly to a consideration of workers: "an American laborer," he says, eats food that "the British laborer would not dream of eating" and, as a result, the better-fed American will "put to shame the amount of work [the British laborer] turned out" (*People*, 234–35).

If Brooks Adams had had any doubts in 1901 about which empire would dominate after the "New Industrial Revolution," Jack London must have allayed them when he asserted that a British worker brought to the United States would work to American standards of productivity and with a "standard of living" that would be "rising all the time" (*People*, 235). As David Potter has shown in his classic account of U.S. politics,[36] not only did a commitment to abundance precede a commitment to democracy in America (*People of Plenty*, 126) but also—a point as central to London's own politics as it is to the play on Adams's phrasing—the American mission of world redemption was a "revolutionary message" predicated on the spread of such abundance (134). London thus prepares for America as the new center for a post-Victorian world order by privileging both the American Way and the American Mission when he represents the urban poor as suffering individuals who need only to be transplanted to America in order to be healthy, well-paid productive citizens. London puts a fine edge to this narrative of upward mobility, abundance, and productivity: a British worker, after fourteen years in America, where he had been jobless for just twelve hours, "had saved his money, grown too prosperous, and returned to the mother country" (*People*, 95) only to become hopelessly impoverished. Providing a structural principle for the entire book, such comparisons are not so much "objective" differences, as Joan Hedrick claims (*Solitary Comrade*, 59), as they are elements in an "imaginative history" that celebrates both American abundance *and* American productivity and thereby underwrites a strong bid for superiority in international politics.

London certifies the Americanness of his project in another way as well when he goes to the American consul-general, "a man with whom I could 'do business' " (*People*, 5), before making his descent. In this scene, London develops the first of many opportunities to dramatize a variety of English governmental, economic, enforcement, and relief agencies as inefficient, apprehensive, and timid both in theory and in practice. Focusing on the police, London juxtaposes the American official's knowledge and decisiveness—one might even say, his Yankee "know-how"—to the fussy demurrals of the British Chief Office. After a noticeably brisk, productive encounter, London departs with a handshake as the American official remarks, "All right, Jack. I'll remember you and keep track" (*People*, 5). The handshake having confirmed London's affiliation with American officialdom, the American consul in many ways stands for Jack London's entire enterprise; that is, the exchange certifies London's Americanness, testifies to the practical competence of the American official, and, perhaps most important in terms of the remainder of the book, represents American national character in action. As London concludes, "I breathed a sigh of relief. Having built my ships behind me, I was now free to plunge into that human wilderness of which nobody seemed to know anything" (*People*, 5). Grounding the narrative on a credentialed Americanness secures for Jack London a "strategic position" (Said, *Orientalism*, 20) just to the side of English urban discourse and allows him to produce a specific knowledge about this "wilderness."

It is worth recalling that the trope of a descent into unknown territory had been familiar at least since James Greenwood's book *A Night in a Workhouse* (1866) and, furthermore, that even though it was still in use by the late 1890's the East End itself had become so intensely "known," one international study declared flatly in 1896, "Awakening is not needed. Every thinking man has thoughts upon this matter. And along with this realisation has come practical experiment, in many places and on an immense scale, towards a solution."[37] By intentionally stressing within his text the "unknown" quality of this "wilderness" and by ignoring the actual solutions then in effect, London systematically—and strategically—prepares the way for his own imaginative geography.[38]

In one powerful scene, London subverts an ongoing tradition of writing about the East End by exploiting this "unknown" quality when he goes to the famous Thomas Cook & Son travel bureau and apostrophizes, "O Cook, O Thomas Cook & Son, pathfinders and trail-clearers, living signposts to all the world . . . with ease and celerity, could you send me to Darkest Africa or Innermost Thibet, but to the East End of London, barely a stone's throw distant from Ludgate Circus, you know not the way!" (*People*, 3). First, by referring to the East End as a foreign nation next to, and just out of sight of, the more civilized and respectable districts, Jack London again seems to follow the conventional ideology that frames it as an equivalent of "darkest Africa."[39] Although he seems to validate this conventional way of imagining the East End (Keating, *Into Unknown England*, 14), the apostrophe—

a form that draws attention to a dead or absent (or inadequate?) figure by a literal "turning away" from the central action—actually sounds a death knell to British imperialist activities: standing quite literally within the agency, London denies its active presence in the narrative of imperialism by his apostrophe to it. We can gauge the audacity of this move by comparing it to Sims's framing of a similar exploration into the East End, which he claimed "lies at our own doors . . . , a dark continent that is within easy walking distance of the General Post Office."[40] Whereas writers like Sims or William Booth or Henry Mayhew had used exoticism to advance domestic political agendas, Jack London confirms the exoticization to clear a space for his own project. That is, he exploits the imperialist "doubling" (to borrow from Nord) of the East End and Africa only as a way of canceling out the centrality of British agencies like Thomas Cook & Son. He renders them as incapable of providing the information and expertise required for exploring a place already claimed by a major discursive tradition as within reach.

By using the apostrophe, a device especially appropriate for elegy,[41] Jack London can turn away from (and in effect annul) the active and ongoing tradition of urban writing that presents the journey into the East End as just such an exercise in adventurism, and he can suggest that this preeminent emblem of British imperialism is no longer an active agent in that process. Significantly, it was Thomas Cook & Son that London chose: as Patrick Brantlinger has shown, by the late Victorian period imperialism had become invested with "an elegiac quality" and one of the central symptoms of this problematic status was an increase in tourism as a kind of transmuted exploration.[42] Put another way, Jack London returns to English imperialism its own worst fear, which, as Brantlinger notes, is "the decline of Britain's position in the world as an industrial, military, and imperial power."[43] His apostrophe thus acknowledges imperialism and denies English domination over it.[44]

London further empowers an American national narrative after the apostrophe when he stages a verbal exchange between himself and a clerk at the travel agency who, London says, refers to him as "the insane American who *would* see the East End" (*People*, 4). By representing himself as an unambiguously *American* explorer, London simultaneously acknowledges the discourse of imperial exploration and adds a clear new accent to it. Unlike Sims, Mayhew, or William Booth, London (the insane *American*) places himself firmly outside this tradition by refusing to consider imperialist parallels that enable domestic policy. From a British perspective, then, it *is* insane for an American to claim to know the East End because the production of this entity had traditionally been the work of English writers whose use of it was circumscribed in specific ways. By stressing his distance from this tradition, London in effect refuses to endorse either their concern for domestic social reform or their underwriting of British imperialism via the two-nation theory (with its representations of the poor as colonial subjects). Instead, London uses the apostrophe to rupture the circuit of urban writing and imperialism by using tropes of exploration in service of *American* imperial activities, thereby menacing the structure of politics, power, and knowledge both domestically and internationally construed: his was truly an unsound, irrational—"insane"—position when viewed from within the established "regime of truth."[45]

Certainly Jack London's descent was filled with "psychic peril" (Hedrick, *Solitary Comrade*, 59; and see 63–67); and in the complicated psychodrama that results from this situation, he appropriates the urban poor into a nationalist-imperialist vision that transmutes them into moments within his— and America's—narrative of success. Musing at one point on the constricted conditions of those East Enders who were hard-working and frugal, London writes, "And I thought of my own spacious West, with room under its sky and unlimited air for a thousand Londons; and here was this man, a steady and reliable man, never missing a night's work, frugal and honest, lodging in one room with two other men, paying two dollars and a half per month for it, and out of his experience adjudging it to be the best he could do" (*People*, 32). Since London's "imaginative history and geography" are governed by the repeated circulation of images and metaphors drawn from American superiority, he can reinscribe the beliefs of some of the nation's most reactionary imperialists, who saw in expansionism an opportunity to reassert traditional values against nagging domestic problems as well as a means of refuting the small, short-lived anti-imperialist movement that had formed in opposition to Philippine annexation and grounded its resistance in similar appeals to traditional American values.[46]

Given that a central issue of imperialism was the acquisition of new territory, London suggestively confirms the nation's readiness to proceed with colonization when he alludes to room for "a thousand Londons" in a "spacious" United States. Indeed, the figurative annexation of a city he continually identifies as the symbol of the British empire recalls his entire project of positional superiority. But if announcements of America's ability to add new territories and to displace British dominance confirmed imperialist visions, they would do little to appease staunch anti-imperialists. In fact, as London continues he provides a strong retort to their opposition. By understanding the East End dwellers through values such as honesty, thrift, frugality, and reward for hard work, what Robert Wiebe calls "village values" that undergird the American conservative narrative of sturdy self-reliance, Jack London answers the anti-imperialists with their own ammunition.[47] As if creating a character in response to the list, London has a "steady," "reliable," "frugal," and "honest" worker who expects a just reward for his hard work and is not simply a victim of a corrupt system, but he is victimized by his distance from the United States. The point is clear. If this man were in America, he would be well-respected and rich. And, what is more, to exclude him from the source of such well-being is by implication to deny the divine mission of the American Anglo-Saxon race and its inevitable drive toward world redemption. Here, as elsewhere in *People*, London produces a knowledge of East End poverty through metaphorical relations that confirm the correctness of these fundamental American values, meanings, and ideals—indeed, the rightness of America itself.

The overdetermined quality of images and metaphors that is constitutive of producing new discursive formations illuminates my point about the qualified radicalism of London's book.[48] That is, even while he is expressing a sympathy for the conditions endured by those in deep poverty, London makes this knowledge possible through a figural device that takes us *away* from their stunted lives and into the mind ("And I thought") of the *American* ("my own . . . West") Jack London, who is, not surprisingly, contemplating a part of the country whose spaciousness is more than geographical. As a potent symbol of abundance and opportunity, the western United States is vital to the American grammar of manifest destiny: as it does in London's book, so in the national discourse, it is the place where fulfillment and moral virtue converge.[49]

If on the one hand these "new significations" for knowing the urban poor coincide with London's gradual embrace of the country and agrarian ideals, which began in 1901 and preoccupied him throughout his life, then on the other they intersect with several important moments in the construction of turn-of-the-century American imperialism as well. Written out when Americans were busy dividing the world into civilized and uncivilized parts and then further dividing the civilized part into a vibrant, young America and an old, tired Europe (Wiebe, *Search for Order*, 225–26), the values embedded in London's representations support American prowess in two additional ways. First, they implicitly posit an America poised for action by alluding to the idea of converting the desert into the garden of the world, which, with its reference either to redeeming the world or to individual self-realization, had long been constitutive of manifest destiny. Second, the tropes summon what had been another major component of manifest destiny, namely, the idea of a distinct "American race."[50]

Devised initially to explain and justify intercontinental expansion, manifest destiny enabled the expansionism of the late 1890's and early 1900's by allowing claims to American racial and materialistic superiority to reinforce one another.[51] Josiah Strong, for instance, had deployed manifest destiny to locate "the seat of Anglo-Saxondom" in the United States, a formulation he used to advance American imperialism. Similarly, both America's redemptive mission and its racial distinctness would become important later in London's book when he declared the shift in empire from Britain to the United States. In fact, pursuing ideological directions similar to Strong's, London provided a powerful antidote to anxieties about the decline of American Anglo-Saxonism then running beneath American imperialist thought: in one of many such inversions, he indicts Great Britain the colonizer on grounds of racial degeneracy.

Opening an early chapter with a comparison that would recall William Booth's analogy between pygmies and the urban underclass (*In Darkest England and the Way Out*, 1890), London initiates his own ethnological comparison that once again depends on a fantasy of the American West, "And I, walking a head and shoulders above my two companions, remembered my own husky West, and the stalwart men it had been my custom, in turn, to envy there" (*People*, 55). As he walks further into the East End, the inhabitants' designations become more dubious. They are human, but they are also subhuman: "a spawn of children," for example, wriggles on "the slimy pavement, for all the world like tadpoles just turned frogs on the bottom of a dry pond" (*People*, 56), and there is "a young babe, nursing at breasts grossly naked and libelling all the sacredness of motherhood" (*People*, 57). Accompanied by a native "guide" (*People*, 64), London pushes on through the "black and narrow" (*People*, 57) tenement where he voyeuristically tabulates room sizes, occupants, and jobs before emerging into the sooty streets and Spitalfields Garden, where his exploration temporarily ends.

Through these representations, the East Enders are allowed faint traces of humanity even as the language forbids that humanity from assuming any dignity or decency. By giving his readers images of arrested development in the history of the race, a moment that by implication he and they had fortunately surpassed (after all, they require a "guide" into this foreign land), London in effect has tribalized the urban poor.[52] Bearing "multiple and contradictory" identifications that enable both "official" and "secret" knowledge (Bhabha, "The Other Question," 164, 168), these representations engage the "fetishistic" element of colonial discourse (ibid., 159–66) *and* urban writing about the East End. That is, even as colonial discourse constructs the colonized "as an object of surveillance, tabulation, enumeration" it also represents them as an object of "paranoia and fantasy" (ibid., 156). Colonizers, in other words, represent their colonial subjects simultaneously as Other and "as entirely knowable and visible" (ibid.). By filling his book with precisely such surveillance, tabulation, and so on, London produces significations of the East End inhabitants through identical procedures. Offered as both "knowable" and "other," these scenes are not, then, simply images of urban degradation; they are carefully constructed markers of London's—and his middle-class American readers'—fascination with depictions of their own displaced origin: as they glimpse the humanness of the East Ender they recognize themselves by strategies of differentiation that block full identification.[53]

Hedrick comes close to recognizing the power of these representations when she discusses London's chapter "The Ghetto," in which he writes about the "short and stunted" East Enders as "a breed" apart, but she fails to develop this insight, insisting that "London's application of animal language to the poor *reflects only their* degraded circumstances" (*Solitary Comrade*, 61–62, emphasis added).[54] As I have been suggesting, the significance of these representations is that they "reflect" *Jack London*'s position perhaps even more than those of the urban poor. That is, the East End inhabitants are designated a "race" or "breed" apart by virtue of their difference from sturdy Americans. Beginning as a comment on "class supremacy" (*People*, 220), London's chapter 19 turns directly to imperial matters. The East End, he says, teems with "a deteriorated stock" continually weakened as "the strong men, the men of pluck, initiative, and ambition, have been faring forth to the fresher and freer portions of the globe, to make new lands and nations" (*People*, 221). Having alluded to the Alger formula of pluck and luck, London concludes the chapter with a drama of passing empire that confirms the brightest expectations of people like Strong and Adams. He writes: "It is absurd to think for an instant that they can compete with the workers of the New World. Brutalized, degraded, and dull, the Ghetto folk will be unable to render efficient service to England in the world struggle for industrial supremacy which economists declare has already begun" (*People*, 231).

A graphic instance of this transvaluation is in the opening sequence of London's sustained and revealing "dramatizations," which literally reoccupy a discursive tradition valorizing British imperialism by co-opting and exploiting—one might say, colonizing—the images and representations of a major piece of British urban writing, Booth's *In Darkest England and the Way Out*. In Booth's classic depiction, the East End gets confirmed as a doubling of "darkest Africa." Musing on the "terrible picture" H. M. Stanley has recently given of the continent with its "human beings dwarfed into pygmies and brutalised into cannibals" (quoted in Keating, *Into Unknown England*, 142), Booth finds that this "awful presentation of life . . . in the vast African forest" is "only too vivid a picture of many parts of our own land." And he asks his famous question, "As there is a darkest Africa is there not also a darkest England?" (quoted ibid., 145). Using precisely these tropes of exploration and wilderness, Jack London readily assents to this darkest England; however, he just as readily refuses to accept Booth's view that " 'Greater England' " could "minister to" darkest England's (the East End's) "social regeneration" (quoted ibid., 151). Agreeing with the British writer that urban-industrial reform was needed, London does so by placing American political and economic superiority at the center of his narrative. As he shows again and again, America, with *its* greater wealth, will minister to and regenerate all of England. So sanguine was Jack London about American supremacy that when in 1902 his publisher George Brett sent him a copy of Jacob Riis's newly published urban exposé, *The Battle with the Slum*, London wrote back: "I was especially pleased when Riis pointed out the deadness & hopelessness that characterize the East-London slum, and added that there was life & promise in our American slum" (*Letters*, 1: 331). The remarks become more striking when one realizes that London, while thanking Brett for Riis's book, was also commenting on his suggestion to add a final "optimistic chapter . . . pointing out the possibilities of amelioration of the terrible conditions that you set forth" (*Letters*, 1: 331 n. 2). London found this suggestion "excellent" and promised to write "a final & hopeful chapter" (*Letters*, 1: 331). It is a chapter in which the "amelioration" Brett called for acts as a genuine closure to the book's nationalist-imperialist agenda.[55]

London called this chapter "The Management," and he took as his central question, "*Has Civilization bettered the lot of the average man?*" (*People*, 311). Given London's rewriting of the narratives that had legitimized British imperialism, his declaration that inefficiency and mismanagement portend Britain's collapse makes the message of this chapter more complicated than a simple warning, as Andrew Sinclair ("View of The Abyss," 236) claims, to get Britain back on track. As a concept underwriting colonial activity, civilization had always been tightly woven with the idea of natural selection. Now, through a brilliant series of displacements that use natural selection to make the case against Great Britain's dominance, Jack London radically redistributes the meanings of imperialism's civilizing function in order to position America as the new dominant power. Using the concept of management to orient his question about civilization and abundance, he produces a view of the efficient, industrial-bureaucratic American state as the answer to a decaying British imperialism that coincided perfectly with the new-middle-class framing of American foreign policy.[56] He reappropriates the very procedures and discourse of English colonialism with an extended comparison of the conditions of British citizens and of the Innuit Indians of Alaska. Having made the East End stand for all of Britain and having further systematically converted the East Enders into a race apart, London makes it unmistakable that the center of empire has indeed passed to the United States: "Civilization has failed to give the average Englishman food and shelter equal to that enjoyed by the Innuit" (*People*, 313). By privileging a conventionally marginalized group, London was making a decisive point: in effect, he says, these people at the outermost reaches of American life are better off than English men and women in the heart of the heart of civilization and empire.

What is important here is that despite a scathing critique of the "incapable management" of "the United Kingdom" (*People*, 316), neither imperialism nor Anglo-Saxon superiority per se is critiqued in this final chapter. As he had done with his elegiac apostrophe to Cook & Son, where he preserved the circuit of urban-imperial doubling but radically redistributed the political economy of its meanings, here, too, he preserves the notion of empire and of Anglo-Saxon control but decisively shifts the emphasis to the United States. "Blood empire is greater than political empire," London writes, and the point of his chapter is to confirm that in the United States such "blood" is still "strong and vigorous as ever." He concludes solemnly, "The political machine known as the British Empire is running down. In the hands of its management it is losing momentum every day" (*People*, 316).

This final chapter thus signals a specific brand of American "optimism." First, its focus on management dovetails with an emerging narrative of world industrial hegemony as embodied in the 1893 Exposition and all that it symbolized. Second, it couples this industrial-bureaucratic hegemony to racial issues, which supplied an imperialist rationale for market expansion and cultural domination. Thus, if in London's remarks on inadequate management, one can hear the discourse of industrial efficiency later codified in Frederick Winslow Taylor's *Principles of Scientific Management* (1911), then in his racial comments about the Innuits, one can hear no less distinctly those of politicians like Theodore Roosevelt, John Hay, Henry Cabot Lodge, and John T. Morgan or those of intellectuals like Brooks Adams, Josiah Strong, and Abbott Lawrence Lowell.[57]

London's *People of the Abyss* thus offers a justification for an emerging imperialist *policy* that deployed both efficiency and racism as central values. Although American imperialist ventures had certainly occurred prior to 1902, these were mainly *ad hoc* engagements. It was not until the early 1900's that the need for a genuine policy led to a more systematic elaboration of American imperialism (see Wiebe, *Search for Order*, 224–55), an expansionism that Jack London's book drew from and helped develop and support. Senator Albert Beveridge marked this turning point when he addressed the United States Senate in 1899: "God has not been preparing the English-speaking and Teutonic peoples for a thousand years for nothing but vain and idle self-admiration. No! He has made us the master organizers of the world to establish system where chaos reigns. . . . He has made us adepts in government that we may administer government among savages and senile peoples."[58]

If Jack London's discussion of the Innuit in the final chapter converts East Enders into one of the subjects of Beveridge's imperialist fantasy (that is, his "savages"), then another thematically central scene, this time from chapter 15, gives them over as Beveridge's second group, namely, "senile peoples"—or, in London's own words, the "enfeebled" "stay-at-home folk" (*People*, 316). London recalls his earlier staging of the East Enders as embodiments of Englishness, which he stressed was a racially and nationally distinct category, by opening the chapter with a sustained musing of Thomas Mugridge and his wife. Continuing his pose as explorer, he tells how he is penetrating into the very essence of Englishness: "And as I talked to them, all the subtleties and complexities of this tremendous machine civilization vanished away. It seemed that I went down through the skin and the flesh to the naked soul of it, and in Thomas Mugridge and his old woman gripped hold of the essence of this remarkable English breed" (*People*, 180–81). But this "essence," like the empire itself, is tainted, dying. An elegiac quality hovers in the room as London discovers the racial core of empire: "I found there the spirit of the wander-lust which has lured Albion's sons across the zones" (*People*, 181). But this urge to roam and conquer has been a dubious blessing, leading to "foolish squabblings and preposterous fights" as well as to sacrificing "the best of its sons to fight and colonize to the ends of the earth" (*People*, 181). These are hardly images of glory. Indeed, the calculus that requires offering up "the best" of a nation's youth for such trivial "squabblings," only to stumble "blindly through to empire and greatness" (*People*, 181), seems, to put it mildly, flawed.

The logic of these musings culminates in a key section at the end of the chapter where the worn-out East End couple who embody "the essence of this remarkable English breed" sit in a quiet, empty house. In language rich in Darwinian allusions, London observes that they themselves are past the age of reproducing and that even those city-dwellers who are less jejune will "not be breeding very much of anything save an anaemic and sickly progeny" (*People*, 184). As for the offspring who "may carry on the breed," they have already left Britain and such reproducing will only happen elsewhere, in Australia, Africa, America (*People*, 184). "The strength of the English-speaking race to-day," London concludes, has passed to "the New World overseas" (*People*, 184–85).

Significantly, London prepares for this pronouncement of "the succession of empires"[59] with an image of mute and ineffectual spectatorship centered on the absent queen. Remembering when he had seen two pictures of Victoria in the old couple's house, one of a young girl with the caption "Our Future Queen" and the other of an old woman with the words "Our Queen—Diamond Jubilee," London stages the issue as a vision of the future, a kind of prophecy: "England has sent forth 'the best she breeds' for so long, and has destroyed those that remained so fiercely, that little remains for her to do but to sit down through the long nights and gaze at royalty on the wall" (*People*, 184). Played off against the full chapter on Edward's coronation, the gazing scene exploits the ideological crisis in British imperialism engendered by Victoria's death not by announcing a new phase in British world domination, but by certifying the imperial power of Victorian England as literal memory. This is "imaginative history" at its best. Or as Senator Beveridge said, while the English indulge in vain and idle self-admiration, the United States will be taking over the world.

It was no coincidence, then, that an American writer chose to imagine the city of London as emblematic of industrial chaos and imperial decline at a time when his own country was beginning to imagine itself as a quintessentially industrial, progressive nation-state as well as a force of international order and civilization. That is, in Jack London's hands, the horrifying conditions in the English world capital certify the success of a politics of abundance in a United States recently emerged from severe economic depression and, more important, attest to the correctness of a newly emerging U.S. foreign policy that had at its core colonizing activities of its own. All of this is not to say that London felt no sympathy for the East End poor. Rather, it is to claim that his sympathy was expressed in and through discursive procedures that affirmed American supremacy. Jack London, by exploiting colonial structures, advances a personal and national fantasy of American cultural supremacy that imagines the English capital less as a place for actualizing a radical political program of urban industrial reform than as a symbolic territory for articulating American expansionism. In this way, his book attempts to curtail the perpetuation of the very idea of Victorian England and the grand narrative that places it at the center of empire and civilization even as he tries to acknowledge the difficult lives of the impoverished East Enders. Given a book of such ambition, it is no wonder that Jack London claimed to have "put more of my heart into *The People of the Abyss* than into any other book" (*Letters,* 3: 1590).

Power, Gender, and Ideological Discourse in 'The Iron Heel'

FRANCIS SHOR

Seven years after the publication of *The Iron Heel*, Jack London wrote to a friend that he would not consider "writing another book of that sort. It was a labor of love and a dead failure as a book. The book buying public would have nothing to do with it and I got nothing but knocks from the socialists."[1] Although *The Iron Heel* was scorned by most contemporary socialist critics and readers of fiction, London's visionary and cataclysmic tale of abortive revolution and counterrevolution captured the attention of later critics and generations schooled in the actualities of post–World War I revolutions and the fascist counterrevolutions that followed in the 1920's and 1930's. That *The Iron Heel* would be resurrected from its "dead failure as a book" precisely because of what a later generation would see as its prophetic power seems to contradict Jack London's own assessment that he "didn't write the thing as a prophecy at all."[2] It is clear, however, that in the immediate aftermath of an exhaustive year of lecturing as president of the Intercollegiate Socialist Society, he was preoccupied with spreading the gospel of revolutionary socialism. In addressing a potentially hostile audience at Yale on January 26, 1906, Jack London hurled the following challenge: "We will be content with nothing less than all power, with the possession of the whole world. We Socialists will wrest power from the present rulers. By war, if necessary. Stop us if you can."[3]

This challenge is repeated by Ernest Everhard, London's fictional alter ego in *The Iron Heel*, during his address before the upper-class California Philomath Club. Speaking of the "army of revolution" composed of "twenty-

five millions strong" worldwide, Everhard declares that the "cry of this army
is: 'No quarter! We want all that you possess. We will be content with nothing less than all that you possess. We want in our hands the reins of power
and the destiny of mankind.' "[4]

The description of Everhard's body language during this inflammatory
passage and the immediate response to his discourse and demeanor are noted:

> And as he spoke he extended from his splendid shoulders his two great
> arms, and the horseshoer's hands were clutching the air like eagle's talons. He
> was the spirit of regnant labour as he stood there, his hands outreaching to
> rend and crush his audience. I was aware of a faintly perceptible shrinking on
> the part of the listeners before this figure of revolution, concrete, potential,
> and menacing. That is, the women shrank, and the fear was in their faces. Not
> so with the men. They were of the active rich, and not the idle, and they
> were fighters. A low, throaty rumble arose, lingered on the air a moment, and
> ceased. It was the forerunner of the snarl, and I was to hear it many times that
> night—the token of the brute in man, the earnest of his primitive passions.
> (55–56)

Such commentary is particularly revealing of and consistent with the approach to power and gender found throughout *The Iron Heel*. That is, power
is demarcated by London's mediation of the dynamics of class struggle and
his symbolic evocation of Social Darwinism, and it is portrayed in gender
images and language endemic to London's writings, naturalist literature, and
the ideological temper of the times.

The above description of Ernest Everhard and the Philomath audience,
as well as everything else in the main body of *The Iron Heel*, is presented as
the personal recollections of Avis Everhard, dutiful wife and comrade of
Ernest. This narrative is framed and annotated by Anthony Meredith, a resident of a utopian society seven centuries into the future. While critics
have commented upon the appropriateness of the asymmetry of this double point of view, reflecting on London's sensibility that emphasizes present
realities over an idealized future,[5] little has been made of the way Meredith's
annotations locate a utopian critique of power and gender in the present.
Such a critique also provides insight into the contradictions of Jack London
and his age.

Many of the biographies of Jack London highlight his contradictory personality, or what one study calls his "divided consciousness."[6] Biographical
studies often overpsychologize London the writer and, in the process, reduce the text to a reflection of the personal demons and drives that constituted London's identity. Although there are important psychological con-

nections that any critical reading of London's writings can illuminate, I believe the key to the meaning of any one text is an analysis of the "context in the text."[7] In other words, situating *The Iron Heel* in the context of Jack London's mediation of the intellectual and political currents of the time should provide some insight into how this text embodies those currents and the contradictions that run through them.[8] Moreover, by deconstructing the ideological discourse embedded in the novel, one can better gauge London's mediations of power and gender.

In order to conceptualize how that discourse is placed in the language and images of power and gender in *The Iron Heel*, I want to identify two interrelated constructs—discursive chains and ideological icons. These constructs overlap the functions of manifesto and fable, identified as key components of the utopian fiction in *The Iron Heel*.[9] Discursive chains operate as linked markers in a whole field of discourse, and they in turn demarcate the ideological terrain of that field.[10] I will follow these discursive chains between the character and arguments of Ernest Everhard and the ideological discourse of power and gender. Ideological icons represent the metaphorical enactment of what Fredric Jameson calls the "ideologeme"—the "historically determinate conceptual or semic complex which can project itself variously in the form of a 'value system' or 'philosophical concept,' or in the form of a protonarrative, a private or collective narrative fantasy."[11] The ideological icons of "Jackson's arm" and the "Chicago Commune" in *The Iron Heel* suggest how the metaphorical enactment of the ideologeme in the novel reflects and refracts London's presentation of power and gender.

The character of Ernest Everhard is a vehicle not only for the articulation of Jack London's political manifestos but also for a mediation of the ideological discourse of the age, especially as it relates to power and gender. According to Joan London, "Ernest Everhard was the revolutionist Jack would have liked to be if he had not, unfortunately, also desired to be several other kinds of men."[12] Although Everhard's embodiment of masculine power and virile radicalism represents certain historically validated social and cultural characteristics, those characteristics also demarcate a discursive force field out of which power and gender operate. By tracing the discursive chains London uses to describe Everhard, to identify his demeanor, and to qualify his message, we may evaluate the power and gender codes embedded in the various masculinities London projects.[13]

In both physical and psychological makeup, London and Everhard seem to share certain attributes. Especially in the articulation of an ideological discourse of socialism, much of what motivates London seems to run through

Everhard's message. In describing the emotional roots of socialism for London as "a cry for justice, a fear of degradation, a loathing of the waste of human potential," Andrew Sinclair could also be outlining the passionate appeals of Ernest Everhard.[14] In noting that "socialism was Jack London's holy war . . . , [giving] him the psychic release of a religion and the physical release of a fight," Joan Hedrick could also be describing the framing of Everhard's demeanor.[15]

In portraying those physical and psychological characteristics of Everhard, London does more than provide some insight into his own psyche; he presents the reader with an opening to deconstruct how power and gender are linked in discursive chains that open up the context in the text. When Avis refers to her "Eagle, beating with tireless wings the void, soaring towards what was ever his sun, the flaming ideal of human freedom" (5), she deploys an image that recurs of this fierce, proud, and American bird of prey. Linking that bird to Ernest's devotion to the cause for which he gave his "manhood," London reveals part of the struggle by American socialists like Eugene Debs (also often referred to as an eagle)—to rescue their manhood through an American application of socialism.[16]

In describing the physical characteristics of Everhard, London generates a discursive chain that fixes him as a masculine hero of the working class and allows that portrait to be subverted by the seemingly androgynous editor, Meredith. In characterizing his ill-fitting suits, Avis notes that "the cloth bulged with his muscles, while the coat between the shoulders, what of the heavy shoulder-development, was a maze of wrinkles. His neck was the neck of a prize-fighter, thick and strong" (7). This allusion allows Meredith to remark in the footnotes that "it was the custom of men to compete for purses of money. They fought with their hands. When one was beaten into insensibility or killed, the survivor took the money" (7). London's distancing of this masculinist characteristic may have something to do with his own effort to transcend a "manhood" that is associated with "the lower-class values of the Oakland street culture" out of which he emerged and from which, according to Joan Hedrick and others, he was trying to escape.[17] It may also have to do with what Clarice Stasz calls London's "visionary conception of masculinity and femininity," which although "no feminist's dream, is a male chauvinist's nightmare."[18]

Elsewhere, in the depiction of Everhard's argumentative style, there is further evidence of the masculinist and class basis for the character and his message. Referring to the "war-note in his voice," Avis contends that in such arguments Ernest "took no quarter and gave none" (16). The reference to taking no quarter allows Meredith to comment that the expression "arises from the customs of the times. When, among men fighting to the death in their wild-animal way, a beaten man threw down his weapons, it was at the option of the victor to slay or spare him" (16). Beyond the obvious distancing from such barbaric times, Meredith speaks of animal-like behavior, a formulation that London was noted for and that was part of the discourse of naturalism, particularly related to issues of class struggle. As one interpreter of naturalism pointed out, "The fear of class warfare that is part of the material worked by naturalism must be recognized as a powerful element of the ideology of the period."[19]

London's discourse throughout *The Iron Heel* on class warfare is replete with references to irrational male behavior and atavistic social ethics, especially in Meredith's annotations. In Everhard's debate with the bishop he demonstrates what was bedrock in London's Social Darwinist beliefs about the innate selfishness of all classes. Reflecting a tenet of revolutionary socialism about the "irreconcilable conflict" (23) between labor and capital, which he took from *The Communist Manifesto*, London nonetheless allows Meredith to denounce such conflicts as strikes:

> These quarrels were very common in those irrational and anarchic times. Sometimes the labourers refused to work. Sometimes the capitalists refused to let the labourers work.
>
> In the violence and turbulence of such disagreements much property was destroyed and many lives lost. All this is inconceivable to us—as inconceivable as another custom of that time, namely, the habit the men of the lower classes had of breaking the furniture when they quarrelled with their wives. (23)

In this instance the double point of view captures what in another instance Joan Hedrick refers to as "sympathy for the manhood that inspired [such revolts] and fear of consequences it provoked."[20]

Yet London, when he wrote *The Iron Heel*, was too immersed in the ideological discourse of revolutionary socialism to shy away from embracing the logic of class confrontation and conflict. In setting the confrontation in chapter 5 between Ernest Everhard and the representatives of the California ruling class, London repeats the political arguments that he had been delivering in his speeches and writings during 1906. Moreover, the chapter follows a moral indictment of capitalism as a system through Avis's investigation of the responsibility for one worker's having lost an arm. Thus, before considering further the discursive chains in chapter 5 that illuminate questions of power and gender, I want to turn to the iconic significance of "Jackson's arm" for the ideological discourse of *The Iron Heel*.

"Jackson's arm" becomes the metonymical vehicle for educating both Avis and the reader about the dynamics of power; it reveals as well how gender informs the discourse of the novel.[21] The interconnection here of ideological discourse, images, and language is illuminated by French sociolinguist Michel Pecheux's contention: "The meaning of a word, an expression, a proposition, etc. doesn't exist 'in itself', but is determined by the ideological positions brought into play in the socio-historical process in which words, expressions, and propositions are produced."[22] Thus, by identifying how London's ideological discourse emerges out of the context, one can better discern the sociohistorical meanings of power and gender in *The Iron Heel*.

"Jackson's arm" manifestly exposes the inherent exploitative and unjust operation of corporations and the courts and the biases of the press precisely because of London's ideological commitment to presenting how such interlocking corruption has robbed workingmen of their capacity to be productive members of society. Building on an actual story that London had read in a muckraking journal—a worker named Jackson had been maimed in an industrial accident—London traces the unraveling of the conspiracy through Avis's investigation.[23] By personalizing the tragedy of one worker and the innocent Avis's disillusionment with the lack of fairness toward this man, London may have hoped to arouse the conscience of his middle-class readers against the scandals of industrial capitalism and the institutions that supported and legitimized it. In "A Curious Fragment" (1908), a short story set in a dystopian future and published soon after *The Iron Heel*, London again uses the severing of an arm in an industrial accident to condemn the brutishness of capitalism and to appeal to the conscience of his readers.

Through the ideological icon "Jackson's arm" London excoriated the brutal, arrogant, and uncaring power of the industrial machine while further testifying to the ways in which that industrial system emasculated and made slaves of workingmen. Thus, London could incorporate an anticapitalist critique found in progressive journals and socialist tracts of the times. He represented through "Jackson's arm" what historian Nell Irvin Painter has noted of the period: "During the early years of the century working men, women, and children had no effective statutory protection to limit working hours, set minimum wages, provide compensation for accidents on the job, old-age pensions, unemployment compensation, or occupational safety. At the same time the incidence of industrial accidents in the United

States was the highest in the world. About half a million workers were injured and 30,000 killed at work every year."[24] London's emphasis on Jackson's being reduced to a peddler and his attendant loss of income suggests not merely symbolic but an iconic representation of the loss of manhood in a era when making a decent living was the measure of true masculinity, especially for men in the working class.[25]

In the chapter entitled "Jackson's Arm," London takes the naive Avis through a series of meetings with those men associated with the fictitious Sierra Mills, where Jackson lost his arm in an industrial accident, and with those involved in the court case when Jackson sought compensation. London allows her outraged innocence to indict the men and the positions they represent. Moreover, Meredith's annotations help to reinforce the ideological critique of the exploitative and irrational economic practices of the day:

> In those days thievery was incredibly prevalent. Everybody stole property from everybody else. The lords of society stole legally or else legalized their stealing, while the poorer classes stole illegally. Nothing was safe unless enormous numbers of men were employed as watchmen to protect property. The houses of the well-to-do were a combination of safe deposit, vault, and fortress. The appropriation of the personal belongings of others by our own children of today is looked upon as a rudimentary survival of the theft-characteristic that in those early times was universal. (31)

Although this critique is a predictable indictment by London of the cozy ruling circles that include Colonel Ingram, corporate lawyer for Sierra Mills, and Judge Caldwell, lodge buddy of Ingram and the trial judge who dismissed Jackson's claims, Avis and the reader are confronted with the duplicity of a fellow worker, Peter Donnelly, who justifies his siding with the company on the grounds of protecting his livelihood so he can feed his family. When Avis reports her findings to Ernest, whom she calls, in an obvious nod to patriarchal authority, her "father confessor" (38), Ernest retorts that "not one of them was a free agent. . . . They were all tied to the merciless industrial machine. And the pathos of it and the tragedy is that they are tied by their heart-strings" (38). This sets up London's ideological denunciation of a class system that rewards the wealthy with dividends made from the tragedies of workingmen like Jackson and that makes wage slaves out of men like Donnelly.

Another ideological icon that links Jackson's arm to the larger indictment of industrial civilization is the image of blood. In fact, one interpreter of *The Iron Heel* says that the "central unifying image throughout the novel is blood."[26] From Ernest's charge that "our boasted civilisation is based upon blood" (38) to Avis's acknowledgment that she "saw the blood of Jackson upon my gown as well" (41), the "scarlet stain" (38) seems to affect everyone and every incident in the novel. (London's apocalyptic short story, "The Scarlet Plague" [1912], transforms this indictment of civilization's bloodshed into a disease that destroys so-called advanced civilization and returns the remnants of humanity to "cave-man" existence.) In immersing the novel in the image of blood, London telescopes a manifest ideological critique of power through several lenses—socialist (the bloodshed caused by capitalism and the red revolution embraced by Ernest), Christian (Ernest as the potential Christlike blood sacrifice), and naturalist (the animal-like bloodletting of contending forces).

On another level, the image of blood exemplifies the gender contradictions that London and the culture embodied. Such contradictions are evident in the phallocentric violation that Ernest imposed on Avis by accusing her of having a "gown . . . stained with blood" (28), which caused Avis to remark that she "had never been so brutally treated in my life" (28). Ernest's aggressive indictment of Avis's blood-stained complicity with destructive capitalism and her naivete about the roots of Jackson's tragedy not only reveal Everhard's masculinist inclinations but also underscore the patriarchal politics of an age when men welcomed public bloodletting and conflict. Thus, "Jackson's arm" and the image of blood reflect and refract the ideological discourse about power and gender that made London both a spokesman for socialism and a symbol of the contradictions of the age's gender prerogatives.[27]

In turning to other discursive elements in *The Iron Heel*, one can begin to see more clearly the ideological terrain upon which London and other revolutionary socialists stood. London's own need to demonstrate his intellectual superiority and the superiority of the ideological discourse articulated through Everhard attempts to move the novel's structure from a didactic to a dramatic moment in the Philomath Club confrontation, foreshadowing the violent confrontation described in "The Chicago Commune" chapter. Nonetheless, much of what transpires in the Philomath Club and the follow-up chapters aims at convincing Avis and other members of the middle class through ideological set-pieces that they will have to "awaken to the inescapable choice between a past and future, between capitalism and socialism."[28]

Everhard revels in pugnaciously challenging the denizens of the upper-class Philomath Club on their failed economic leadership, repeating London's amalgamation of socialist and progressive tracts and previous utopian treatises on the inefficiencies and immorality of capitalism. What sets London's language apart from that of Bellamy in *Looking Backward* or that of Debs in speeches is the naturalist tone of the discursive chains. For example, Ernest says to Avis: "I shall menace their money bags. That will shake them to the roots of their primitive natures. If you can come, you will see the cave-man, in evening dress, snarling and snapping over a bone. I promise you a great caterwauling and an illuminating insight into the nature of the beast" (50). As June Howard points out in her study of naturalism, "in the rhetoric of the period, the powerful as well as the powerless can be brutes."[29]

Everhard's excoriation of the ruling class focuses not only on their brutishness but also on their "intellectual stupidity" (53). In denouncing the selfishness and materialism of the master class, Everhard links their lack of Christian morality to their class hatred and hypocrisy. Talking about his involvement with members of the upper class, Everhard avers: "I met men . . . who invoked the name of the Prince of Peace in their diatribes against war and who put rifles in the hands of Pinkertons with which to shoot down strikers in their own factories. I met men incoherent with indignation at the brutality of prize-fighting, and who, at the same time, were parties to the adulteration of food that killed each year more babes than even red-handed Herod had killed" (53–54).

In this passage London manages to hold up to ridicule a ruling class that decries the vices of a lower class, such as prize-fighting (a vice from which he had previously distanced himself), and perpetrates even greater crimes of violence on the working and lower class. By alluding to the adulteration of food, London reiterates the muckraking charges made by Upton Sinclair in *The Jungle* while focusing, as did Sinclair, on the heinous disregard by men of wealth for the well-being of innocent children. Such criticism allows London to deplore the flawed manhood of upper-class males who look down their noses at the vices of the poor without recognizing their own responsibility for the suffering of the less well-off. Furthermore, by connecting the crimes of a ruling class to Herod and the neglect of the message of the "Prince of Peace," London recalls the social gospel and Christian Socialist discourse of the time, as well as propagating his own brand of evangelical socialism.[30]

As one critic notes, *The Iron Heel* is "framed by the Marxist dialect . . . , the apocalyptic vision of Christianity, and the naturalistic imagery of social Darwinism."[31] There are, as we have seen, traces of all three ideologies in the discursive chains enunciated by Everhard. However, when the focus shifts to a debate over power, a form of crude but poetic Marxism takes precedence. For instance, as part of the challenge to expropriate the wealth and possessions of the ruling class, Everhard remonstrates: "Here are our hands. They are strong hands. We are going to take your government, your palaces, and all your purpled ease away from you, and in that day you shall work for your bread even as the peasant in the field or the starved and runty clerk in your metropolises. Here are our hands. They are strong hands!" (55). This Marxist vision of workers' expropriating society's wealth and power and the attendant ruling-class destitution is also at the core of London's futuristic short story, "The Dream of Debs" (1909). The repetition of hands as the metaphorical equivalent of labor power here conveys the discursive code of class struggle, anticipating and perhaps inspiring the last stanza and chorus of "The Preacher and the Slave," written by Wobbly balladeer and martyr Joe Hill:

> Workingmen of all countries unite,
> Side by side we for freedom will fight;
> When the world and its wealth we have gained
> To the grafters we'll sing this refrain:

> You will eat, bye and bye,
> When you've learned how to cook and to fry;
> Chop some wood, 'twill do you good,
> And you'll eat in the sweet bye and bye.[32]

In fact, there was an overlap in the ideological discourse between Jack London and the Wobblies, especially those itinerant members from the western United States whose own background mirrored some experiences that London had had as a young man. Wobblies like Joe Hill and "Big Bill" Haywood (a leader of the Industrial Workers of the World after their founding convention in Chicago in 1905) were marginalized members of a working class and self-taught alienated intellectuals whose uncompromising vision of class struggle and revolutionary millennialism challenged the ruling elites and labor and socialist reformers as well. Indeed, London's short story, "South of the Slot," features a Haywood-like character called "Big" Bill Totts, the schizoid virile radical half of the effete academic Freddie Drummond. This story concludes with Drummond/Totts abandoning his comfortable bourgeois life and delicate fiancée Catherine Van Vorst for the robust life of a labor leader, resident of a working-class ghetto, and husband of the firebrand president of the International Glove Workers Union No. 974, Mary Condon.

The Wobblies and London experienced contradictory currents of Nietzschean, Darwinist, and syndicalist thought. A clear common thread, however, was the matter of power. When George Speed, an early friend and comrade of London's in Oakland and an IWW organizer, asserted that "power is the thing that determines everything today," he expressed the Wobblies' sentiments and echoed Everhard's assertion: "Power will be the arbiter, as it always has been the arbiter" (64).[33]

Of course, Everhard's challenge to the Philomath Club does not go unanswered. However, the answer is not a philosophical refutation but is phrased in the language of power, which reflects a curious symmetry between Everhard's challenge and the ruling-class response.[34] "Our reply," says Wickson, an outraged member of the Philomath audience, "will be couched in terms of lead. We are in power. Nobody will deny it. By virtue of that power we shall remain in power" (63). To try to heighten the drama of an otherwise static screed, Avis comments: "He turned suddenly upon Ernest. The moment was dramatic" (63). This rather heavy-handed reinforcement of the confrontation is a prelude to the overly aggressive language: "When you reach out your vaunted strong hands for our palaces and purpled ease, we will show you what strength is. In roar of shell and shrapnel and in whine of machine-guns will our answer be couched" (63). Meredith's annotation here fixes the political conflict embedded in the language of the speaker: "To show the tenor of thought, the following definition is quoted from 'The Cynic's Word Book' (A.D. 1906), written by one Ambrose Bierce, an avowed and confirmed misanthrope of the period: 'Grape shot, n. *An argument which the future is preparing to the demands of American socialism*'" (63).

The future these passages presage and the seven centuries that Meredith looks back upon certainly attest to London's orthodox Marxist sensibility that overcoming capitalism will take a long time and that capitalism must pass through several stages. In fact, at the beginning of his involvement with socialism and after his resignation from the Socialist Party near the end of his life, London expressed a Darwin-tinged vision of class struggle in which socialism was at best a distant albeit inevitable goal. In a letter to Cloudesley Johns in 1901, London wrote:

> I should like to have socialism yet I know that socialism is not the very next step; I know that capitalism must live its life first. That the world must be exploited to the utmost first; that first must intervene a struggle for life among the nations, severer, intenser, more widespread, than ever before. I should much more prefer to wake tomorrow in a smoothly-running socialistic state; but I know I shall not; I know that a child must go through its child's

sicknesses ere it becomes a man. So, always remember that I speak of the things that are: not of the things that should be.[35]

This letter, which reveals London's pessimism about an easy and bloodless transition to socialism, also indicates the morbidity that would plague London and his times. Reflecting on the struggle for socialism in Italy, the more dialectical Marxist Antonio Gramsci commented: "The crisis consists in the fact that the old is dying and the new cannot be born; and in this interregnum a great variety of morbid symptoms appears."[36]

Beyond these morbid symptoms, London's letter also helps to frame the dystopic utopian structure and ideological discourse found in *The Iron Heel*. Furthermore, it provides additional evidence of the seemingly anomalous connections of the socialist, naturalistic, and masculinist orientations of much of London's writings. Although any anomalies in *The Iron Heel* can likely be explained by the "antinomies of [London's] own protean mind and character,"[37] such antinomies belong to the naturalist project and the social contradictions of the time.[38] A sense of crisis and cataclysm in the United States and the West in general promised both reform and repression, elements that are evident in the discourse and narrative of *The Iron Heel*.[39] Furthermore, in the character and language of Ernest *Everhard*, the continuous masculinist posturing reflects London's own concern with his manhood, the ethos of naturalism, and the strong emphasis on virile power, especially for important segments of the radical working class.[40]

The confrontation between Everhard, the revolutionary spokesman of the working class, and Mr. Wickson, the leader of the Philomath elite, reflects the class and gender dynamics evident throughout *The Iron Heel* and refracts London's own emotional and ideological orientation. In London's article "How I Became a Socialist" (1903), he highlights that orientation: "And I looked ahead into long vistas of a hazy and interminable future into which playing what I conceived to be a MAN'S game. I should continue to travel with unfailing health without accidents, and with muscles ever vigorous. As I say, this future was interminable. I could see myself only raging through life without end like one of Nietzsche's blond beasts, lustfully roving and conquering by sheer superiority and strength."[41] Given London's attraction to *Übermensch* socialism, it should be no surprise that Ernest Everhard is described as "a natural aristocrat—and this in spite of the fact that he was in the camp of the non-aristocrats. He was a superman, a blond beast such as Nietzsche has described, and in addition he was aflame with democracy" (8).[42]

The irony is that Everhard and London had little faith in democracy or, for that matter, the avoidance of bloodshed. When London contended that he looked "to the strong man, the man on horseback to save the state from its own rotten futility,"[43] he was reflecting his infatuation with Nietzsche and his part in the trajectory of authoritarian socialists from Bellamy to De Leon.[44] In "Goliah," a utopian short story published soon after *The Iron Heel*, London's protagonist changed from a working-class superman to a scientist superman while retaining the authoritarian socialist cast. Finally, London's own assessment of the future reiterated the pessimistic tone in the discourse over power and the obsession with the endless violence that marked the fable-like latter half of *The Iron Heel*: "Everything appears almost hopeless; after long years of labor and development, the people are as bad off as ever. There is a mighty ruling class that intends to hold fast to its possessions. I see years and years of bloodshed. I see the master class hiring armies of murderers to keep the workers in subjection, to beat them back should they attempt to dispossess the capitalists. That's why I am a pessimist. I see things in light of history and the laws of nature."[45]

Such pessimism is deeply embedded in the lead-up to the cataclysmic events of "The Chicago Commune" denouement of *The Iron Heel*. Halfway through the novel, Everhard realizes that even with the socialist advances in the electoral arena, the counterrevolution has begun to seal the fate of those seeking immediate radical change. Everhard reflects: "I had hoped for a peaceable victory at the ballot-box. I was wrong. Wickson was right. We shall be robbed of our few remaining liberties; the Iron Heel will walk upon our faces; nothing remains but a bloody revolution of the working class. Of course we will win, but I shudder to think of it" (112). Even with the obligatory nod to a deterministic reading of history and revolution, London betrays a well-earned fear of the repressive apparatus of the state. From his own experiences in Coxey's army and the continual intervention of police, military, and paramilitary forces to repress working-class struggles, London was keenly aware that the entrenched capitalists could call upon such forces to retain their privileges and prevent social change.[46]

On the other hand, London's understanding of the workings of capitalism and the lure of its contradictory powers compels him in *The Iron Heel* to focus on something other than repression—namely, co-optation—as undermining an easy and bloodless transition to socialism. Retaining his orthodox Marxist and De Leon–tinged distrust of mainstream unions, London allows Everhard prophetic denunciations of co-opted unions:

In the favoured unions are the flower of American workingmen. They are
strong, efficient men. They have become members of those unions through
competition in place. Every fit workman in the United States will be possessed
by the ambition to become a member of the favoured unions. The Oligarchy
will encourage such ambition and the consequent competition. Thus will the
strong men, who might else be revolutionists, be won away and their strength
used to bolster the Oligarchy. (141)

It is also clear from this passage that such co-optation plays off of the lure of
competition for workingmen whose manhood is defined by their achieving
recognition for their skills as efficient workers. In an era when efficiency and
ambition are measures of manhood, London is particularly attuned to the
ways the message of revolutionary change for workingmen is undermined.[47]

From the criticism of the "aristocracy of labour" to the establishment
of the clandestine cadre of revolutionists, London's *The Iron Heel* recalls
Lenin's "What Is to Be Done?" (1902). In the emergence of the "Fighting
Groups," the underground revolutionary organization that was to exact revenge and wreak mayhem on the Iron Heel, the Oligarchy's counterrevolu-
tionary organization, London demonstrates a characteristic emphasis on the
efficacy of violence.[48] Although admittedly brutal in their treatment of their
enemies and traitors within their own ranks, the "comrades of the Fighting
Groups were heroes all," as Avis says in her memoirs, "and the peculiar thing
about it was that they were opposed to the taking of life. They violated their
own natures, yet they loved liberty and knew of no sacrifice too great to make
for the Cause" (155–56). Meredith's long commentary on the Fighting Groups
acknowledges the inspiring influence of Russian revolutionists and the history of Fighting Groups' martyrs, men and women, leading to the Brotherhood of Man. He concludes his commentary: "We, who by personal experience know nothing of bloodshed, must not judge harshly the heroes of the
Fighting Groups. They gave up their lives for humanity, no sacrifice was too
great for them to accomplish, while inexorable necessity compelled them to
bloody expression in an age of blood" (157).

If the "inexorable necessity" of revolution led London to cast the power
struggle as bloody class warfare, then those who embraced revolutionary
conflict would have to become class warriors. In the chapter "Transformations," London's revolutionaries become estranged from their previous way
of life, taking on those gender codes that defined London's own ideological
discourse. Avis is required to alter her looks and demeanor so that she can
infiltrate the Oligarchy. In transforming herself, she will not only inure herself to the coming violence but also take on the role of an independent New

Woman. In effect, at Ernest's demand, Avis the naive and helpless middle-class maiden must become a strong comrade-mate, not unlike London's real-life "mate-woman," Charmian Kittredge.[49]

Like Avis, the other men and women who were inexorably pulled into the orbit of the revolution had to throw off any bourgeois sentimentality in order to harden themselves for battle. In describing their transformations, London also demonstrates his gendered readings of what constitutes weakness and failure of nerve. No longer responsible for feeding their families, the characters Jackson and Peter Donnelly seek class and gender revenge through the revolution. As Donnelly says when joining the "Frisco Reds": " 'Tis revenge for my blasted manhood I'm after" (178). In the character of Anna Roylston, dubbed the "Red Virgin" (179), London reveals once more how, in the words of Joan Hedrick, "the bourgeois virtues [are associated] with a narrow, effeminate way of seeing"[50] and how women, in transcending such bourgeois values, must to some extent de-sex and harden themselves. Thus, Anna Roylston and the other revolutionaries of the Fighting Groups must avoid the snares and sentiments of family life.[51] In the case of Anna Roylston, this means eschewing any maternal role in favor of becoming "an executioner for the Fighting Groups" (168). Many critics have identified the character Anna Roylston with the real-life Jane Roylston, secretary of a local IWW chapter, but Charles N. Watson, Jr., has suggested that a clipping and notes for an article on anarchy and Louise Michel, heroine of the Paris Commune, provide more insight: "Louise Michel, the Red Virgin. Describe her life, and, after pointing out how illogical, unscientific and impossible is anarchy, hold Louise Michel up as a better type of human than a woman of the bourgeoisie, fat and selfish and dead."[52]

If London had Louise Michel and the Paris Commune in mind as models for the revolutionaries of the Fighting Groups in cataclysmic conflict with the counterrevolutionaries of the Iron Heel, the location of the climax of the novel in the Chicago Commune is a testament to that city's iconic hold on radicals of the time. From Haymarket (1886) to the Pullman strike (1894), Chicago was seen as the locus of a firestorm of radical activity and repression. Avis notes in her journal: "There the revolutionary spirit was strong. Too many bitter strikes had been curbed there in the days of capitalism for the workers to forget and forgive. Even the labour castes of the city were alive with revolt" (197). The Everhard Manuscript points out that "Chicago had always been the storm-centre of the conflict between labour and capital, a city of street battles and violent death . . . [which would] become the storm-centre of the premature First Revolt" (197).

Why the "Chicago Commune" would produce a premature revolt has as much to do with resonances of apocalyptic utopian novels like Ignatius Donnelly's *Caesar's Column* (1890) as with London's own loss of faith in the redemptive and efficacious power of mass movements for radical change.[53] The climaxes in *Caesar's Column* and *The Iron Heel*, although in different cities, see the massive lumpen and even proletarian elements of urban America in a rage that can only explode into mindless and vengeful violence.[54] For London, who prided himself on his superior intelligence and the need for disciplined understanding of the workings of nature and society, such an outburst would be doomed to failure precisely because it lacked a directing intelligence. Moreover, the "people of the abyss" that London wrote about and feared were themselves icons for the predispositions of naturalism, according to which the proletariat was unthinking and lacked all traits necessary for its own redemption.[55]

In the class war that engulfs the "Chicago Commune," primitive cries amid modern weaponry conclude in a futile effort at revolution. The final image in the chapter recalls an earlier century's failed utopian image of Liberty and the people and the difficulty of regeneration and redemption that London would recognize in socialism and in his own life.

> Turning a corner, we [Avis and a male comrade named, appropriately, Hartman] came upon a woman. She was lying on the pavement in a pool of blood. Hartman bent over and examined her. As for myself, I turned deathly sick. I was to see many dead that day, but the total carnage was not to affect me as did this first forlorn body lying there at my feet abandoned on the pavement. "Shot in the breast," was Hartman's report. Clasped in the hollow of her arm, as a child might be clasped, was a bundle of printed matter. Even in death she seemed loath to part with that which had caused her death; for when Hartman had succeeded in withdrawing the bundle, we found that it consisted of large printed sheets, the proclamations of the revolutionists. (205)

Just as Delacroix's 1831 painting foregrounded the bare-breasted figure of Liberty, waving the tricolor while leading revolutionaries to the barricades, London's emphasis on this anonymous dead women's breast wound could be read as the appropriate symbol of a stillborn revolution. Although it is tempting to read this image through psychobiography—London's estrangement from his mother and frustration over his and Charmian's inability to have a male offspring—the gender and power dimensions of the paragraph and, indeed, the whole chapter suggest instead the difficulty of defending and sustaining revolutionary socialism against the well-armed and ruthless minions of the capitalists, or, in the case of Jack London, of sustaining his ideological fervor in the face of both personal and political limitations.

The failure to give birth to a successful revolution and the effort to render abortive any attempts to do so, as captured in the image above, further reinforce the sense that *The Iron Heel* is about London's focus on dystopian realities rather than utopian possibilities and emotional limitations rather than political liberation.[56] Yet, perhaps the final meaning of the novel is that the power and gender relationships unveiled in *The Iron Heel* cannot persist if utopia and political liberation are to be realized. If fact, in all of Meredith's annotations cited above it is evident that such power and gender relationships have been superseded in the utopian society of the future. The key to that supersession and to London's own despondency about the future is the Nietzschean idea of the "transvaluation of values." Avis refers to the "passionless transvaluation of values" (208), and London often referred directly and indirectly to the concept.[57] Moreover, the transfigurative politics that are integral to the "transvaluation of values" are crucial to the utopian project and those ideologies promoting such a politics and a project.[58]

That London saw in revolutionary socialism an ideology that promised a transvaluation of values is apparent in much of what he wrote and lectured about until nearly the end of his life. However, London's appropriation of the ideological discourse of revolutionary socialism contained those contradictions that marked his life, the socialist movement, and the era of the late nineteenth and early twentieth centuries. As one critic of London's work points out: "His Socialism was always interpenetrated by his individualism, a condition which explains how both he and his writings could at once combine racism, the glorification of the superior individual over the mass, a fascination with brute force, and a warm-hearted sense of the brotherhood of man."[59] The socialist movement contained any number of tendencies and a variety of factions, and it was riddled by tensions over ethnicity and class and plagued by debates over evolution versus revolution, organizational alignments, and political versus direct action strategies and tactics.[60] In exposing those contradictions and tensions through the ideological discourse of *The Iron Heel*, Jack London provides the reader with some insight into the icons, images, and language of a socialism mediated by a man who, "probably more than any other writer of his generation, was profoundly and consciously affected by his times."[61]

Sea Change in 'The Sea-Wolf'

SAM S. BASKETT

Many readers of Jack London's *The Sea-Wolf* have found themselves in agreement with Ambrose Bierce's dismissal of the last half of the book. "The 'love' element," Bierce pronounced, "with its absurd suppressions and impossible proprieties, is awful. I confess to an overwhelming contempt for both the sexless lovers."[1] The undeniable achievement of the novel has been widely recognized, but it has been seen to lie principally in the characterization of Wolf Larsen as an embodiment of the Spencerian-Darwinian-Nietzschean complex of ideas at the turn of the century, with the sentimentality of "the love element" a major flaw. The publication of *The Letters of Jack London*, however, provides the impetus for reconsidering this generally accepted assessment. For the letters from the time of the gestation and writing of the novel throw considerable light on what London was attempting.

These are attractive early letters—Jack's impulsive first marriage, his star-crossed love of Anna Strunsky, his intense yearning toward the ideal "mate" he was determined to find in Charmian—just while he was writing *The Sea-Wolf.* Two phrases from the letters are particularly striking in relation to the theme of the novel: "the woman in me" (written to Anna) and "the man concealed in woman" (written to Mabel Applegarth).[2] When these and other similar statements in the letters are kept in mind, *The Sea-Wolf* can be seen in a different perspective. Undeniably mawkish at times, "the love element" is neither contemptible nor irrelevant, actually no more sexually outrageous than the "Wolf Larsen element"; and, moreover, the lovers, at first expressing the attitudes of a sexually bifurcated society, eventu-

92

ally rebel against such attitudes. *The Sea-Wolf* is far ahead of its time in anticipating late-twentieth-century views of an ideal androgynous relation between women and men.

Carolyn Heilbrun has written that androgyny "defines a condition under which the characteristics of the sexes, and the human impulses expressed by men and women, are not rigidly assigned. Androgyny seeks to liberate the individual from the confines of the appropriate."[3] This is the liberation that London seeks to embody in his developing characters; and this theme is the insistent unifying motif of the novel, to which even the vivid characterization of the Sea Wolf himself is, it becomes apparent, clearly subordinated.

London's grappling with the ideal of androgyny, although not in that terminology, is evident early on, the Mabel Applegarth letter concerning "the man concealed in woman" being dated December 1898. This theoretical interest in the characteristics of the sexes continues in many other letters to both female and male correspondents. That his ideas are not always consistent—London is rarely to be accused of consistency—is consonant with Heilbrun's reference to the "unbounded and hence fundamentally indefinable nature of androgyny" (xi). At times London does seem to express the conventional sexual attitudes of his age. Even in the letter written to Anna Strunsky in February 1902, he is on the verge of mutually exclusive distinctions: "the woman in me pleads, but my manhood reasons" (*Letters*, 1: 278). The important thing to note, however, is that London is wrestling with sexist issues, as he was with racist issues throughout his career, when most of his contemporaries considered these issues resolved.

One aspect of his musings about gender relations is expressed in an April 1899 letter to Cloudesley Johns: "All my life I have sought an ideal chum. . . . I never found the man in whom the elements were so mixed that he could satisfy, or come anywhere near satisfying my ideal" (*Letters*, 1: 63). What he values most is a "brilliant brain" and "no physical cowardice." The latter he could "forgive" in a woman, never in a man. Such statements and, to anticipate, Humphrey Van Weyden's appreciation of Wolf Larsen's masculine beauty have made London the subject of conjectures about possible latent homosexuality. Again, Heilbrun has written tellingly: "Androgyny appears to threaten men and women even more profoundly in their sexual than their social roles. There has been a fear . . . of homosexuality, or the appearance of homosexuality . . . as the consequences of less rigid patterns of social behavior" (xi–xii).

Another letter, to Mabel in January 1899, touches on two other aspects of sexual definition: he praises Ella Wheeler Wilcox's description of the passionately good woman as one who, distinguished from "the sweetly good woman," has the capacity to sympathize with the full range of human emotions. And he cites Spinoza to the effect that "the love both of husband and wife" should be based on "chiefly liberty of mind" (*Letters*, 1: 44).

These and many other comments are indicative of London's continuing, thoughtful interest in defining sexual identity freed from the "appropriate." This intellectual aspect should be recalled as we read his more emotional and personal writing about the topic to Anna and Charmian, lest his expressions be regarded as the overwrought lover's typically romantic idealization of the beloved. In his first letter, in December 1899, to "My Dear Miss Strunsky," although London had just met her, it seemed as if he had known her "for an age." He, as a published author addressing a "literary aspirant," believes that she "is given to feel the deeps and the heights of emotion in an extraordinary degree," that she "can grasp the intensity of transcendental feeling, the dramatic force of situation, as few women or men either, can" (*Letters*, 1: 133–34). The following May, London having married Bessie Maddern in April, Anna's letters make "it seem as though some new energy had been projected into the world and that I cannot fail gathering part of it to myself" (*Letters*, 1: 183). Two months later, he tells "Dear Anna," after a theoretical disagreement, that he feels "there was no inner conflict; that we were attuned, somehow; that a real unity underlaid everything. The ship, new-launched, rushed to the sea; the sliding-ways rebel in weaking creaks and groans; but sea and ship hear them not; so with us when we rushed into each other's lives—we, the real we, were undisturbed. Comrades! Ay, world without end!" (*Letters*, 1: 198). By the end of 1900, he can write "Comrade Mine," "A white beautiful friendship?—between a man and a woman?—the world cannot imagine such a thing, would deem it as inconceivable as infinity or non-infinity" (*Letters*, 1: 228–29). And in April 1901, "Large temperamentally—that is it. It is the one thing that brings us at all in touch. We have, flashed through us, you and I, each a bit of the universal, and so we draw together. And yet we are so different" (*Letters*, 1: 244). Obviously, these are love letters, whether consciously or not on the part of the young husband, but they are from a man who is radically questioning the rigidly defined sexual roles of men and women. The collaborative debate with Anna in writing *The Kempton-Wace Letters*, beginning in August 1900, pursues this questioning on a literary level. Ostensibly, the debate is between romantic love, in the character written by Anna, and love considered from the standpoint of scientific materialism, in the character written by Jack. But there is a firmness to Anna's letters and a romantic flair to Jack's that blur their respective stances.

The two issues, the "white beautiful friendship between a man and a woman" unimaginable to the world at large and Jack's by-now avowed love for Anna, converged when he received a letter in England from her, written after she had learned of Bessie's second pregnancy. Jack, completing the experience that led to *The People of the Abyss*, was crushed by Anna's understandable withdrawal. Distraught, almost incoherent, chastened, he faced the fact that he would not recognize his ideal with Anna: "And now it is all over and done with. So be it. Henceforth I shall dream romances for other people and transmute them into bread & butter" (*Letters*, 1: 313). As a married father, he had to accept the end of the ideal relationship he had envisaged. As a writer, however, and as a person, he clung to the ideal he would express in fiction.

By January 1903, he could write George Brett, his publisher,

> I am on the track of a sea story . . . which shall have adventure, storm, struggle, tragedy, and love. The love-element will run throughout, as the man & woman will occupy the center of the stage pretty much of all the time. . . . The motif, however, the human motif underlying all, will be what I may call mastery. My idea is to take a cultured, refined super-civilized man and woman, (whom the subtleties of artificial, civilized life have blinded to the real facts of life), and throw them into a primitive sea-environment. . . . The superficial reader will get the love story & the adventure; while the deeper reader will get all this, plus the bigger thing underneath. . . . I intend to take plenty of time over it. (*Letters*, 1: 337–38)

As the book progressed, and the anguish over the rupture with Anna abated, Jack, considering his marriage "eminently unsatisfactory," was on the prowl, "preparing to go to pieces" as a stage toward his separation from Bessie. He was going "to have a hell of a time, with any woman I could get a hold of. I had my eyes on a dozen women," one of whom was Charmian Kittredge (*Letters*, 1: 521). By June, however, Jack was in love with her, as intensely as he had been with Anna the summer before. Hardly an attractive picture: married only three years, father of two girls, and passionately declaring himself the soul mate of two other women within a period of months, unknown to his trusting wife.

Another view can be entertained, however: Jack, by his own impulsiveness, trapped in a marriage based on stereotypic sexual roles, despite his theoretical and, indeed, emotional concept of androgyny as a necessary condition for human fulfillment. Defending his action, doubtless primarily to himself, in marrying Bessie, he slides into writing *The Kempton-Wace Letters* with the highly attractive Anna Strunsky, who clearly was a fresh and more compatible love object, with whom he might achieve his androgynous ideal. Herself attracted to Jack, Anna could write many years later, after his death, "He was youth, adventure, romance. . . . He had a genius for friendship. He loved greatly and was greatly beloved."[4] As their relationship intensified she, cognizant of what was involved, withdrew; Charmian, older, experienced, did not. The androgynous relationship between an androgynous man and an androgynous woman he had envisioned for himself and Anna, which could never be possible with Bessie, would now be fulfilled with Charmian.

Or so they wrote to each other in June and July 1903. He loves her beautiful body and the "beautiful mind that goes with it," rejoicing in the frankness of that mind, that she had not been "coy and fluttering." And then follows his highest praise: "You are more kin to me than any woman I have ever known" (*Letters*, 1: 369–70). In a subsequent letter, in early July, he refers to "a wonderful moment," when apparently Charmian "repeated" to him, "You are more kin to me than any woman I have ever known." This expression was, to Charmian, the "one really great thought" in that late June letter. Jack continued, this thought, "most vital to me and to my love for you, stamped our kinship irrevocably. Surely we are very One, you and I!" Then he describes his dream of the "great Man-Comrade." What he had briskly sketched to Johns four years earlier, he now expands to five paragraphs, more than 500 impassioned words, to Charmian. The writer is unmistakably pouring out his soul to the woman with whom he has just fallen in love, but, strangely, his subject is his dream of a man-comrade. In addition to typical masculine qualities, this individual should be fanciful, imaginative, sentimental, delicate, tender, warm—the evocation of the perfect blending of masculine and feminine qualities goes on. Earlier, London says, he had told his dream in the arms of a woman he loved and who loved him, but she grew "passionately angry." The implication is that Charmian will understand that this blending in each of them is the basis of their "kinship." "Do you see, my dear one," he begins his fifth paragraph on this theme, "the man I am trying to picture for you?—an all-around man, who could weep over a strain of music, a bit of verse, and who could grapple with the fiercest life and fight good-naturedly or like a fiend as the case might be. Don't you see, dear love, the all-around man I mean?—the man who could live at the same time in the realms of fancy and of fact" (*Letters*, 1: 370–71).

It is just at this time, of course, that London was working intensively on

The Sea-Wolf. On July 24, he wrote George Brett that it was "about half-done" and that "it will be utterly different in theme and treatment from the stereotypical sea novel" (*Letters*, 1: 376). On September 2, he writes soothingly to Brett that Richard Gilder, editor of *Century Magazine*, where the novel was to appear first, need not worry about a man and a woman alone on a deserted island: "The American prudes will not be shocked by the last half of the book." He gives Gilder permission to blue pencil, but the nature "of the characters themselves, will not permit of anything offensive. . . . I elected to exploit brutality with my eyes open, preferring to do it through the first half and to save the second half for something better" (*Letters*, 1: 383).

The "something better" is the ideal androgynous relationship that develops between Maud and Humphrey, in contrast to the male brutality embodied in Wolf Larsen and highlighted by the effeminate timidity and cowardice of Mugridge and Humphrey Van Weyden himself. This theme and the treatment of it, referred to proudly by London in the July letter to Brett, had persisted in London's letters to his intimate correspondents over a period of years prior to his writing *The Sea-Wolf*, as the passages I have excerpted make unmistakable. The quest for an ideal androgynous relationship, if impossible in life, was to be realized in this fiction, as his despairing letter to Anna had prophesied. But then Charmian had come into his life, and, as in the writing of *The Kempton-Wace Letters*, London's quest in his fiction, in his letters, in his life became virtually indistinguishable.

With these revealing letters in mind, now let us reconsider *The Sea-Wolf*. Three distinct but related aspects of Humphrey Van Weyden's characterization stand out: initially, he is deficient in "masculine" qualities; he is a philosophical idealist; and he is a highly regarded literary critic, "Dean of American Letters the Second," as Maud terms him.[5] Had London entitled the novel "The Rise of Humphrey Van Weyden," the complexity of his characterization might have received the considered attention it requires. As it is, the title and the vivid uniqueness of the Sea Wolf himself have made him loom large in the novel, overshadowing Humphrey, relatively vapid, but nonetheless the character whose transformation is central to the unifying theme adumbrated in London's letters.

At the age of 35, Humphrey says that his mother and sisters have been "always about me." His complete "innocence of the realities of life" had caused him to be nicknamed "Sissy." He has never been in love, his interest in women having been "aesthetic and nothing more." Somewhat dissatisfied with this self-image, he has "vaguely" thought of escape from "the atmosphere of women," but he has not had enough strength of will. Similarly, although he has a good physical constitution, he has never developed his body as doctors advised. He cannot swim: his muscles are "small and soft, like a woman's." On the *Ghost*, even the offensively effeminate ship's cook calls him a "mama's darlin'." Trying to recover the $185 the cook has stolen from him, and "unused to violence of any sort," he cowers before the threatened blows, shamefully recognizing that his cowardice has "smirched and sullied his manhood."

In the coarse, savage, all-male world of the *Ghost*, the crew appears to Humphrey as "a half-brute, half-human species, a race apart, wherein there is no such thing as sex; that they are hatched out by the sun like turtle-eggs, or receive life in some similar sordid fashion." It dawns on him that he has never "placed a proper valuation upon woman kind." If these men had wives, sisters, daughters, "they would then be capable of softness, and tenderness and sympathy. As it is . . . not one of them has been in contact with a good woman, or within the influence, or redemption, which irresistibly radiates from such a creature" (128–29). This passage has been cited to show that London, despite his disavowals, holds to the stereotypical view of "good" women as redeemers of the male, further proof that the novel, the "Larsen element" apart, is a conventional sentimental romance. It should be remembered, however, that the sexually discredited Humphrey—not the Jack London who distinguished between the "sweetly" and the "passionately" good woman— utters these thoughts, and that he is confused about his own feminization, having tried to "escape" from his mother and sisters. In other words, the "over-civilized" Humphrey can envisage redeeming falseness only by falseness—brute masculinity by sentimentalized femininity. But he does not really believe in such a redemption, as is evident in his contempt for the half-world of sentimental femininity expressed as the ferry is sinking. A "preternaturally calm" passenger, a former sailor who has artificial legs, comments, " 'Listen to the women scream,' he said grimly—almost bitterly, I thought, as though he had been through the experience before." In contrast, the women are "hysterical" as the "calm" man fastens their life jackets for them. The fear of death upon them, they made sounds that remind Humphrey, by now "becoming hysterical myself," "of the squealing of pigs under the knife of the butcher, and I was struck with horror at the vividness of the analogy" (6–7). Neither a strictly feminine approach, historically susceptible to reductive sentimentalization in a male-controlled society, nor a strictly masculine approach, historically susceptible to brutalization in that society, is adequate, and Humphrey intermittently recognizes this. But his insufficient realization of either genuine femininity or genuine masculinity is a mark of his Prufrockian incapacity in both thought and action.

Before he can understand true femininity and make it part of his total androgynous sexual being, Humphrey must first "escape" his effeminacy; and a step in that direction is his realization that Larsen will not help him recover the stolen money: "Whatever was to be done I must do for myself" (90). He does overcome the effeminate Mugridge, but only "out of the courage of fear." In this weaklings' *pas de deux*, Humphrey learns to see himself more accurately.

His next tutor is Wolf Larsen, to whom Hump, as Larsen renames him, is attracted, and many have seen latent homosexuality in the character—and in his creator. As Heilbrun observed, to a man with an impulse toward androgyny, the label of homosexuality is always a threat. In context, however, the label is invalid. Hump does recognize Wolf's "elemental" strength, "a thing apart from his physical semblance." But this strength is the "potency of motion," which "lingers in a shapeless lump of turtle-meat and recoils and quivers from the prod of a finger" (18–19). The echo of the turtle imagery should be remarked—the description of the crew in the womanless world of the *Ghost*—a world in which "there is no such thing as sex." In effect, London gives the newly rechristened Hump the dawning realization that masculinity with no admixture of feminine qualities is asexual. The same point is repeatedly made regarding sentimentalized femininity in the face of physical danger or the raw realities of life. If such men are like turtles hatched by the sun, such women are like squealing pigs under the knife. Hump's own "hysteria" and his effeminacy suggest that he, too, initially is sexless.

On the *Ghost*, Hump slowly claims an androgynous sexuality partly through his appreciation of Larsen. Acting effectively in the stereotypically feminine role of "nurse," tending Larsen's wounds after the forecastle fight, Hump describes him as the "man-type, the masculine, and almost a god in his perfectness." This seemingly "aesthetic" appreciation is undercut by the immediately following description of "the great muscles [that] leapt and moved under the satiny skin. . . . His body, thanks to his Scandinavian stock, was as fair as the fairest woman's. . . . I could not take my eyes off him," "watching his biceps move like a living thing under its white sheath." Much has been made of this passage, but to reduce it simplistically to homoeroticism is to ignore London's careful treatment. Shortly before this scene, a crew member has stated that Hump is "all right. . . . He don't like the old man no more than you or me." Immediately prior to the description just quoted,

Hump refers to the "powerfully muscled" but physically flawed crew. There is "only one whose lines were at all pleasing, while in so far as they pleased, that far had they been what I should call feminine." Then begins the description of Larsen's "masculine" physique. But in the midst of this, a different note is sounded. These are the biceps "that had nearly crushed out my life once, that I had seen strike so many killing blows." And immediately after the passage, when Hump tries to relate Larsen's well-made body to "purpose," Larsen dismisses the idea: "Purpose? Utility is the better word." Hump's conclusion makes clear that he considers physical masculine perfection, Larsen's stark manhood, to be insufficient. Hump backs away from arguing teleologically, but he does dehumanize the Sea Wolf's masculinity: "I had seen the mechanism of the primitive fighting beast, and I was strongly impressed as if I has seen the engines of a great battleship" (141–44). To achieve full manhood, Hump, reductively feminized by his society, must grow beyond Thomas Mugridge; he cannot accept the crew in their brutishness, signified by their actions and physical malformations; and even the physically magnificent Wolf Larsen is ultimately an inadequate model. Developing a better understanding of manhood, he can see raw masculinity for what it is. He is appreciative of Larsen's "godlike" physique and strength of mind, but he is repelled by his brutish actions and his militant philosophical materialism.

Larsen's explanation of the "purpose" of his beautiful, muscled body is "stability, equilibrium"—he has "legs to stand on," in specific contrast to Humphrey. "You stand on dead man's legs," he had taunted on learning of an inherited income. Hump does learn to function effectively as the "mate" of the *Ghost*. But he must also stand on his own legs philosophically, and this he does in pitting his idealism against the other's radical materialism. Larsen envisages life as like yeast, "a ferment, a thing that moves . . . but that in the end will cease to move . . . something which devour[s] life that it might live"; and living is "merely successful piggishness" (50–52). Hump finds Larsen's materialism "compelling." " 'Not that I,' he protests to himself, 'a confirmed . . . idealist,—was to be compelled: but that Wolf Larsen stormed the last strongholds of my faith with a vigor that received respect, while not accorded conviction'" (83).

Reiterated rebirth imagery emphasizes that Hump's change is nothing less than a complete transformation, physically, psychologically, and philosophically from the hollow man he had essentially been, though he presented a facade of superficial achievement and conventional understanding. His rebirth could scarcely be stated explicitly: The story begins on a January morning, Monday, a new year, a new day. The "Dean of American Letters the Second" is "pulled from the water" (he had been unable to "cry out") and, gradually regaining consciousness, becomes aware of a "mighty rhythm . . . the lift and plunge of the ship." He catches his breath "painfully," opens his eyes, sees his body bloody from attempts to force air into his lungs. He is on the *Ghost*—the name emphasizes that he is indeed in another world. Humphrey Van Weyden, literary critic, is given a new name; he learns "to walk" on the ship; he receives repeated "impresses from the die which had stamped the crew"; he loses his "innocence," seeming to find in Wolf Larsen's forbidding philosophy "a more adequate explanation of life than I found in my own." He finds it remarkable that he the former literary specialist can function as a sailor. But his change is more fundamental. He begins to feel

> that I could never be quite that same man I had been. While my hope and faith in human life still survived Wolf Larsen's destructive criticism . . . he had opened up for me the world of the real, of which I had known practically nothing and from which I had always shrunk. I had learned to look more closely at life as it was lived, to recognize that there were such things as facts in the world, to emerge from the realm of the mind and idea and to place certain values on the concrete and objective phases of existence. (156)

Recently, Joseph Boone has compared *The Sea-Wolf* with *Moby-Dick*, *Huckleberry Finn*, and *Billy Budd*.[6] He notes that the texts of Melville and Twain explore the realization within men themselves of emotions and values traditionally associated with women, that the union of the androgynous attributes takes place internally, but that in *The Sea-Wolf* it is external, with Maud Brewster representing the feminine component of the androgynous union. It seems clear, however, that Hump has, to a considerable extent, achieved such a union before Maud appears, having shed his superficial, and essentially false, effeminacy and having become more "manly" in the transformation detailed through the course of the novel.

And so, as one might expect from London's letters expressing his desire for an ideal female and male comrades as essential for a full life, Maud Brewster appears in the middle of the Darwinian sea. Charles N. Watson, Jr., has observed that the novel's central action "involves a crisis of sexual as well as intellectual identity. In this crisis, 'masculinity' implies heterosexuality and nihilism (the creed of brute strength), while 'femininity' implies heterosexuality and ethical idealism. . . . Humphrey must pass through the intermediate stage of masculine exclusivity before arriving at a final stage of sexual and psychological adulthood."[7] This is an admirably succinct abstraction of some of the major issues, as well as the cultural, sexual, and psychological undertones of those issues. But such reductions take too little notice of the careful and convincing way in which London has sketched Hump's development as a person, not as an abstract idea. Recall that London's letters about ideal male and female roles alert the reader not to slight this personal element. Hump must be seen as a person, whatever the author's shortcomings in making him believable; on the other hand, the Sea Wolf, whatever the author's success in having him embody powerful contemporary ideas, is never faintly credible as a person. Moreover, it seems to me that Watson takes too little account of Maud Brewster's role in this connection. He does state that Maud, although unconvincing, enables London to preserve "a certain theoretical consistency in choosing a sexual and philosophical equilibrium for the woman as well as the man" (76). But she is more significant in the resolution of the novel than this "theoretical" nod suggests. Admittedly, at times she is unconvincing and painfully conventional, which indicates London's problem in presenting her and what he does to resolve it. London had to create not the female persona implicit in his letters to Anna and Charmian, but one that editor Gilder and "American prudes" would accept. As she is delineated, Maud is central in Hump's crisis of identity which involves a social identity.

The three opening paragraphs of the chapter immediately preceding the one in which Maud appears give the only detailed description of the mission of the *Ghost*—killing seals for their pelts. By now, Hump is "mate," "handling and directing" the crew in their bloody tasks on the decks "covered with hides and bodies," although his soul and stomach are "revolted." And yet "Sissy" Van Weyden considers his position "wholesome" as he improves his "executive" abilities. In the same passage he comments that this "wanton slaughter" would provide the skins that "might later adorn the fair shoulders of the women of the cities" (155).

On first reading, these paragraphs seem unlike anything else in the book, and yet in them London skillfully brings three strands of the novel together. Hump, now capable of dealing with "the world of the real," contrasts sharply with the effete litterateur of the opening chapter who relished his role as a specialist, smug in his ignorance of the objective world. Moreover, he is now able to offer social criticism. In the opening scene he complacently accepted "the division of labor"—he could publish in the *Atlantic*, the officers could sail the ferry across San Francisco Bay, and a passenger could read the article. But now he sees the division of labor differently. Hump, before the *Ghost*, could not have perceived so much. This social criticism relates to another apparently incongruous passage, in which Wolf Larsen uncharacteristically explains himself in social terms. Unlike Hump, with an inherited income, he had only his own legs to stand on. Hump has strengthened his physical legs, but he can now understand Larsen's social criticism—and this is central to the novel—in sexual terms: brutish men kill to survive in a social scheme in which hypocritically "civilized" men buy the results of their "wanton slaughter" to bedeck their women's "fair shoulders," and this economically inequitable and sexually bifurcated society keeps women in parasitic dependence.

In the next chapter Maud enters the novel, however unbelievably. Hump's conventional idealization of her as he falls in love is often embarrassingly evident in his vocabulary and his attitudes, seeming to support Boone's assertion that a "model shift from quest format to erotic-seduction narrative accompanying Maud's arrival serves to underscore London's vision of 'correct' male behavior" (206). Care must be taken, however, to distinguish the character, even as he has been transformed in his masculinity, from the author. The point has been insistently made that all his life Hump has been "surrounded" by women in a feminized culture, but also apart from them—viewing them stereotypically. There has been no basis for a complete transformation of his understanding in the all-male world of the *Ghost,* although the social-sexual criticism cited above provides hints of his awakening. That London is attempting to create a character undergoing change rather than representing his own views of women is suggested by the contrast between Hump's mawkish effusions and even London's most passionate letters to Anna and Charmian. Moreover, under this mawkishness, due to whatever complex of failures—personal, artistic, and cultural—different notes are sounded as London develops the relation between the characters in terms of their mutual androgyny.

As the *Ghost* approaches the small boat carrying Maud, some think it the craft two crew members used to flee Larsen's persecution, and Hump, surely for the first time in his life, takes a loaded shotgun in his hands, intending to confront Larsen. Yet this scene also indicates that Hump has still to grow. As the *Ghost* comes closer, one of the crew gives a curious exclamation: "May I never shoot a seal again if it ain't a woman!" (176)—a remark that, along with Hump's action, ties women and the male seal-shooting world together in their distinct separation. But even as they are yoked in this exotic scene, the sexual bifurcation is emphasized—a version of the sexual attitudes characteristic of the society, the society that shaped Humphrey Van Weyden, literary critic. After four months at sea, "We," Hump thus includes himself with the crew, "were agog with excitement" at a woman in their midst. But to the crew she is simply a sexual object, as is to be enacted in Larsen's subsequent attempted rape. To Hump, she is "like a being from another world," the world he had previously known—and yet not really known. He forgets his "mate's duties," so enraptured is he by her conventionally ethereal femininity: "It seemed to me that I was realizing for the first time what a delicate, fragile creature a woman is" (178). This is only one of a host of his conventional rhapsodic effusions.

Thus neither the crew nor Hump sees Maud accurately. The crew sees her ultimately in terms of lust. And Hump's transformation has not included his conventionally sentimental attitude toward women. But looking back on his first reaction to Maud's presence, he reflects, "All this, in frankness, to show my first impression, after long denial, of women in general and of Maud Brewster in particular" (178). The sentence is far from clear, but it may be read that Hump is self-critically recalling his first impression of Maud, "in frankness." He offers as the reason that it was inaccurate "the long denial" of women, which could refer to the womanless life on the *Ghost*—or his conventional, "aesthetic" consideration of women, in effect a lifelong "denial" of women as they really are. Further, since there had been no long denial of Maud, his first impression of her is the same as his conventional impression of women in general, which he now must admit—"in frankness"—is wrong. As he has been wrong in his feelings about what constituted manhood, so he had been wrong about womanhood.

In part, the development toward androgyny after Maud enters the novel is in terms of Hump's better understanding of her; in part, it is in changes in Maud herself. Their backgrounds are the same. She is a highly civilized, well-regarded writer in the sexually bifurcated society that the two have shared. She has published several "thin" volumes of poetry, which Humphrey had read appreciatively, including a "perfect sonnet," "A Kiss Endured." Like him, she is an unreflecting idealist. However, she is more than merely conventional, expressing confidence and courage in stark circumstances, even though she is "unaccustomed to the vagrant, careless life" of the *Ghost*. At first, naively, she is "perturbed . . . but not frightened" when she learns that her "simple faith" that "shipwrecked people are always shown every consideration" is a "misconception" (178). When she learns of Larsen's "man-play," during which a shark bites off the cook's leg, she does not faint as Hump expects, but "controls herself." She can understand that this may have been "largely an accident." But she cannot condone Hump's failure to try to prevent the murder of the two crew members through "moral courage [which] is never without effect," even as she rejects the idea of killing Larsen. Hump responds that moral courage is "worthless . . . on this little floating world," as is all her previous experience. He advises her to dissemble, but Larsen approaches and Hump turns the conversation to the literary world and the lack of "moral courage" of editors "afraid" of publishing a certain writer—perhaps London's concealed swipe at editor Gilder, albeit on another floating world. In any event, despite her previous "faith," her unwillingness to lie "by speech and action," she follows his advice and does dissemble.

As Larsen's sexual intentions become increasingly obvious, Maud is "terrified" but not "hysterical," and Hump admiringly notes that there is a considerable amount of "robust clay in her constitution." When the *Ghost* is attacked by Death Larsen, she calmly states that she intends to show Wolf that "we are as brave as he," bringing forth his appreciative and pointedly sexual comment: "Books, and brains, and bravery. You are well rounded . . . fit to be the wife of a pirate chief" (233). Hump, having realized his love for her and the danger she is in with Larsen, observes them together: "Each was nothing that the other was, everything that the other was not . . . and I likened them to the extreme ends of the human ladder of evolution—the one the culmination of all savagery, the other the finished product of the finest civilization" (213). It is easy to read in this and similar outpourings the elements of the conventional sentimental romance, and many have. The fair maiden is threatened with violation by the villain; unalloyed femininity by brutal masculinity; idealism by unprincipled materialism—with Hump as hero to save all. But the complex implications of these oppositions go beyond melodrama. Even London's bald but skillful metaphor—"A Kiss Endured" versus rape—suggests the ambivalence. Maud is not yet, the novel makes clear, "a finished product" when she comes aboard. The "finest civilization," where Maud and Hump have both earned their laurels, where "a kiss" is sentimentalized, is a pallid world, as Hump is coming to realize. Given his transformation, on his return he will be unable to live in that world on the same basis as before, as London's letters and the novel suggest. And given his ability to function in Larsen's world, he will be unable to deny what he has achieved on the *Ghost*. Maud is hardly likely to write another "Kiss Endured," but she will write of love given in honesty rather than sentimentality. This is explicit in the closing sentence of the book, Maud's frank expression of sexual desire. These are the strands of masculinity and femininity that London seeks to bring together in androgynous resolution of the love story and the novel.

In terms of the action of the novel, Hump is able to rescue Maud—they escape to Endeavor Island, where they will "try" together to make, as man and woman, the best of the new world in which they find themselves. From the time they leave the *Ghost*, they are increasingly "similarly affected," each more and more closely attuned to the "subjective" consciousness of the other, in contrast to Larsen's focus on "the immediate, objective present." As they launch into the open sea, they plight their troth in an exchange reminiscent of that between Jack and Charmian (quoted previously): Maud says, "You are a brave man"; Hump answers, "It is you who are a brave woman" (257). Instead of separating their roles, this exchange unites them in their bravery as they face life and death on the open ocean, their fates sexually indistinguishable. Maud learns to steer the small boat and protects Hump by allowing him to sleep, even as he has sought to protect her; and Hump sees her as "woman, my kind, on my plane, and the delightful intimacy of kind, of man and woman, was possible, as well as the reverence and awe in which I knew I should always hold her" (261). This description of androgynous gender relations anticipates the conclusion of Sherwood Anderson's "Sophistication" a decade or so later: "Man or boy, woman or girl, they had for a moment taken hold of the thing that makes the mature life of man and woman, in the modern world possible"—that indeed Hemingway would try "to take hold of" fictionally in *A Farewell to Arms* and *The Garden of Eden* in the decades ahead. When Maud says that they will "stand watches just as they do on ships," Hump replies, "I don't see how I am to teach you. . . . I am just learning for myself." Maud answers, "Then we'll learn together" (262). As Hump's undeclared love is increasing they also become "good comrades, and we grew better comrades as the days went by." Although even a "robust woman" would have been frightened by "the terrible sea, the frail boat, the storms, the suffering, the strangeness and the isolation of the situation," all this "seemed to make no impression upon her who has known life only in its most sheltered and consummately artificial aspects" (271). Fully aware of their predicament, she remained "sure of permanence in the changing order of the universe." The contrast with the earlier "squealing" women is striking.

Ashore, Maud helps Hump to build the *two* huts, the separation necessitated, it should be remembered, by editor Gilder's fears regarding the book-buying public, but it does emphasize their complementary androgyny. Hump, "alone in my little hut," thinks that "a tie, or a tacit something, existed between us which had not existed before" (297). Maud even gives advice, learned from reading David Starr Jordan and from conversation with Larsen, on how to deal with the seals, and she leads the assault for the skins with which to make a roof; from this knowledge, they seek the "young bulls, living out the loneliness of their bachelorhood and gathering strength against the day when they would fight their way into the ranks of the benedicts," much as Hump himself has been doing (291). Hump's adoring celebration, "my woman, my mate [which] kept ringing in my head," is saccharine, but less so in the context of his full awareness of her role in their survival and his recognition that she was "living the life of a savage and living it quite successfully." As such a woman, she has contributed to his "manhood, rooting it deeper and sending through it the sap of a new strength" (398). Thus her non-feminine contributions to their endeavors on the island are verbally reinforced by sexual innuendo. This passage would apparently be as far as London could go, under Gilder's editorial eye.

But not so. Maud's greatest physical assistance is in stepping the mast on the wrecked *Ghost*. She is absolutely essential in the operation, and London must have enjoyed getting the description past Gilder. Maud recognizes that the mast suspended in the air by the "shears-tackle," which had originally failed because of its "shortness," is "not over the hole. . . . Will you have to begin all over?" But with Hump's "instructions for lowering away," the "butt of the mast" after several carefully defined adjustments is perfectly fitted:

> [In the] lantern light, we peered at what we had accomplished. We looked at each other, and our hands felt their way and clasped. The eyes of both of us . . . were moist with the joy of success.
>
> "It was done so easily after all," I remarked. "All the work was in the preparation."
>
> "And all the wonder in the completion," Maud added. "I can scarcely bring myself to realize that that great mast is really up and in; that you have lifted it . . . swung it through the air, and deposited it here where it belongs." (348–50)

Whether or not the author of "A Kiss Endured" was conscious of what she was saying, unquestionably the Charmian of the letters must have relished what her lover had written. It remains for the two lovers in their androgynous completion, to which the entire novel has been pointing, to deal with Larsen and return from Endeavor Island to society. Larsen in his blindness yet attempts to kill Hump and burn the ship, but he soon dies, an undaunted materialist, his final word, "Bosh!" As they bury him at sea, symbolically disposing of the extremity of his brutish masculinity, Maud, still the idealist but from the breadth of understanding she has achieved, whispers, "Goodby, Lucifer, proud spirit"[8]—no longer the sweetly good woman but the passionately good woman.

In Boone's analysis of *The Sea-Wolf*, he sees the imminent return of Hump and Maud to civilization as "transforming the text's originally infinity-bound quest into a circular return and a recuperation of the familiar." In contrast to other quest romances, Boone asserts, this return thematically supports "an already existing ethos" of conventional gender roles and textually is evidence of London's failure "in maintaining the open-ended imperatives of the [quest] mode" as the novel has the happy ending of the sentimental romance (209). In comparing *The Sea-Wolf* to these other works, Boone underscores dimensions for which London has not always been given credit, although Watson has observed that at a time when *Moby-Dick* was nearly forgotten, *The Sea-Wolf* is evidence that London "read it more creatively than any novelist had yet done, building on its major motifs and absorbing the literary tradition that lies behind it" (61). But Boone's conclusion that the novel falls short in these comparisons needs further examination. One does not have to claim that London's achievement is on a level with that of Melville and Twain—or even overlook what Watson calls the "saccharine conventionality" that too often characterizes the narrator's language and attitude in telling the love story—to see that *The Sea-Wolf* maintains both a thematic and a textual integrity. Clearly Hump and Maud during their sea voyage have experienced a change toward androgyny. They are different in themselves and in relation to each other. And surely Boone overstates when he says that in contrast to the "independent identities" of Ishmael, Huck, and Billy, Hump and Maud are dependent on each other. As London's letters reiterate, and as the development of the characters supports, he is interested in showing a man and a woman who complement each other in an ideal androgynous union because each has a sense of individual identity that transcends conventional concepts of gender roles. Moreover, the writer of the letters, one who for many years signed himself "Yours for the Revolution," desired a transformed society based on individuals freed from fallacious and debilitating conventionality.

Such a motif is explicitly evident throughout the novel. At the end, Hump and Maud are fitted to live with each other, both personally and professionally (as literary critic and poet), no longer intellectually and emotionally encapsulated, as each had been earlier, in what Ann Douglas has termed a feminized American culture.[9] In effect, then, the quest motif, with its metaphysical implications, is joined to the theme of androgyny, with its social implications. The quest is not so much abandoned as given a potential social dimension, a dimension not sufficiently recognized—in part, it must be admitted, because London offers only scattered hints about the involvement of Hump and Maud on their return to the society that has warped not only them but Wolf Larsen as well. The hints are there, however. In *The Sea-Wolf*, London in a textual innovation merges the quest romance with the social novel as Fitzgerald was to do a generation later in *The Great Gatsby*. London had promised Brett something "utterly different" in his novel. Whatever its flaws, London delivered on his promise, achieving a highly original thematic and textual contribution to the American literary canon.

Making a Heterosexual Man

Gender, Sexuality, and Narrative in the Fiction of Jack London

SCOTT DERRICK

Gender and sexuality are both difficult subjects in Jack London's fiction. On the one hand, as I shall argue, the reader of his tales and novels confronts a boundary-violating play of desire between masculinity and femininity and between the homoerotic and heteroerotic, which can make London seem to be a writer of surprising liberatory impulses. The reader also confronts a narrative rigidity, which insists on the fundamental importance of maternity to women, which privileges competitive violence as the intrinsic center of masculinity, and which engineers a containment of its own homoerotic impulses. I intend to explain such contradictions by looking at certain repeated patterns, or tropes, in a variety of London's fiction. The reader of London repeatedly encounters versions of certain scenes relating to gender and sexuality, and I base my reading on the assumption that the meaning of such scenes becomes clear intertextually, not in the relative isolation of the usual practice of constructing a reading of individual tales and novels.[1]

I will proceed by elaborating in three sections a series of interrelated subthemes connected to gender and sexuality. In the first, I examine the general opposition in London's fiction between moments that seem to violate conventions of gender difference and moments that work to keep those conventions intact. I suggest that this contradiction might be understood in terms of the "New Woman" of turn-of-the-century culture and her relation to the traditional, maternal woman of the nineteenth century, both of whom attract and threaten the male figures in London's fiction. The consequence is a politically ambiguous, fetishistic structure in which signs of power are both granted to women and taken away.

In the second section, I suggest that much of London's overdetermined treatment of gender difference must be understood in terms of sexual difference as well, and in terms of London's attempt to contain the complex homoeroticism of his writing. London's fiction works to distinguish between his homosocial love of men and an eroticism phobically rejected as lower-class filth and feminization. This splitting of desire paradoxically allows an "innocent" gaze at clean, white male bodies, though the erotic may be punished through apocalyptic violence. These metaphors, in turn, also suggest the interrelations of sexuality and class.

In the final section, focusing on *Martin Eden* and *The Sea-Wolf*, I suggest that London employs a narrative teleology aimed at the construction of heterosexual masculinity to repress and marginalize a finally unacceptable and disruptive homoeroticism. As a consequence, the homoerotic in London's fiction suggests the difficulty of articulating the otherness of the body and its desires, and hence the problem of the unconscious.

Cross-Dressing, Cross-Behaving, and Gender Difference

Jack London regularly depicts gender in contradictory and conflicting ways. On the one hand, London values heroines who possess masculine characteristics and often seem to violate gender boundaries.[2] In *The Sea-Wolf*, for example, Maud Brewster appears in masculine apparel, seems regarded by Van Weyden as one of American literature's premier writers, and at crucial moments offers to wield a club in Van Weyden's defense. Frona Welse in *A Daughter of the Snows*; Saxon Brown Roberts in *The Valley of the Moon*; Lizzie Connolly in *Martin Eden*; and Grace Bentham in "The Priestly Prerogative," a story in London's early collection *The Son of the Wolf*, all in a variety of ways owe their attractiveness to their divergence from feminine norms.[3] London also values men whose masculinity contains feminine traces, men like Billy in *The Valley of the Moon*, who speaks of his body in terms of its exhaustible supply of "silk"; or the Malemute Kid, who "despite his tremendous virility . . . was possessed of a softer, womanly element"; or Martin Eden, who "under that muscled body . . . was a mass of quivering sensibilities" (34) and who, like both Joe Fleming in *The Game* and Wolf Larsen in *The Sea-Wolf*, possesses fair, soft, feminine skin.[4]

On the other hand, London's fiction also contains conservative and re-

actionary elements and works to preserve signs of sexual difference, often
quantitative but sometimes qualitative as well. For example, Van Weyden reminds us in *The Sea-Wolf* that Maud, regardless of her ability, was still "so
much the woman, clinging and appealing, sunshine and dew to my manhood" (233). Even her compassionate solicitude for the dying Wolf Larsen
was "compelled" by "the woman of her" (233), and he refers to her in his
"pet, secret phrase" as "one small woman" (266). This insistence on her essential femininity even *as* she crosses gender boundaries has a mantralike
quality for Van Weyden and seems designed to protect his fledgling manhood. For example, even after she seems ready to brain Larsen with the seal
club, he concludes as she begins "weeping convulsively" that "after all, she
was only a woman" (256). This "woman" gets her peculiar kind of strength
from her propinquity to nature. Van Weyden comments that "often and often, her last reserve force gone, I have seen her stretched flat on her back
on the sand in the way she had of resting and recuperating" (224). Lest we
miss the implications of this, Hump later tells us that he "remembered
Michelet's 'To man, woman is as the earth was to her legendary son; he has
but to fall down and kiss her breast and he is strong again'" (238). Though
in one sense weaker than her male counterpart, she has access to the formidable powers of nature and acts as a kind of circuit breaker, capable (if
switched on) of transferring that power to him.[5]

The size and nature of the gap between genders vary from text to text
in London, but he seems to believe that the barrier of difference is constituted by an inbred "nature" of man and woman. For example, in *White Fang*
(1906), some kind of inherited predisposition makes London's dog-hero refrain from committing acts of violence against a female, which "would require nothing less than a violation of his instinct."[6] In *Martin Eden*, a similar biological imperative motivates Ruth Morse. As London writes, "Her desire that Martin take a position was the instinctive and preparative impulse
of motherhood. She would have blushed had she been told as much" (274).
In *The Game*, Genevieve finds her boxer attractive because she was "moulded
by all her heredity to seek out the strong man for mate, and to lean against
the wall of his strength" (23).

Throughout his fiction, London insists on a containing grid of "natural"
biological roles, even as he authorizes transgressions of gender boundaries.
Perhaps the best example of how conflicted and contradictory London's position on gender could seem is a letter written in 1903 to Charmian Kittredge,
his eventual wife and a likely model for Maud Brewster.[7] In it London simultaneously posits an enormous similarity and an unbridgeable difference:

"We are so alike in so much, that, as you have remarked, perhaps we are too alike. . . . But there is a great difference between us, . . . and that difference is your essential femininity and my equally essential masculinity. . . . You are, when all is said & done of women the most womanly; and I, I hope, am somewhat of a man."[8]

The conflicts in London's work—his desire to embrace an adventurous femininity, to license at least some deviation from conventional male roles, and still to preserve the integrity of basic gender categories—might be understood in terms of what Carroll Smith-Rosenberg has called the problem of the androgynous "New Woman" in the late nineteenth and early twentieth centuries. In this period, women gained significant access, for the first time, to American colleges and universities and, as a consequence, demanded even wider social reforms.[9] Anna Strunsky, a socialist headed for Stanford[10] with whom London had a passionate infatuation prior to his attachment to Charmian Kittredge, articulates a kind of credo for the New Woman in *The Kempton-Wace Letters*, the collaborative epistolary look at love she and London published in 1903. Strunsky's character, Dane Kempton, writes that "today there is a change in attitude. Woman is new-born in strength and dignity, and the highest chivalry the world has ever known is in blossom. She is an equal, a comrade, a right regal person. She is no longer a means but an end in herself, not alone fit to mother men but fit to live in equality with men."[11] Strunsky's passage has a "both-and" structure that quietly preserves maternity as a crucial component of womanhood. The persistence of this concept of maternity has traditionally been the most successful disciplinary weapon used against women and, Smith-Rosenberg argues, devastatingly effective in controlling the "New Woman" in the early twentieth century.[12] Given London's fascination with biological categories and evolutionary thinking, it seems not surprising that his fiction should contain conservative figurations of maternity as a kind of feminine essence. In most naturalist fiction, after all, sexuality is synonymous with reproduction, and reproduction constitutes a hidden essence of life in general, arranged for the preservation and evolution of the species.

London works both the conservative and liberationist sides of the "woman question" and finally seems comfortable with neither. Frona Welse may best articulate this ambivalence, close to incoherence, in *A Daughter of the Snows* (1902): "I am no woman's rights' creature; and I stand, not for the new woman, but for the new womanhood. . . . I do try to be consistent; . . . but you can see neither rhyme nor reason in my consistency. Perhaps it is because you are unused to consistent, natural women; because, more likely, you are only familiar with the hot-house breeds. . . . They are not natural or strong; nor can they mother the natural and strong" (118).

If London often employs maternal instinct as an anchor of sexual difference, he also seems uncomfortable with women who conform most closely to cult-of-true-womanhood maternal values. Maud Brewster, in *The Sea-Wolf*, is one of London's least maternal creations, but even she has a dangerous moral purity, which both challenges Van Weyden's own genteel values and threatens to restrict his ability to survive the brutality of the *Ghost*. When Larsen engages in dangerous "man-play" (160), which leads to the loss of Mugridge's foot, she urges Hump to intervene. He responds by insisting that she does not understand the "laws" of this brave new world. "You bring with you certain fine conceptions of humanity, manhood, conduct and such things," he tells her, "but here you will find them misconceptions" (162).

Repeatedly, in Jack London's fiction, the "hot-house" woman threatens masculinity with her noncomprehension of its necessities and realities, and hence she threatens the masculine ethos of naturalist writing as well. The Maud who does not understand "rough man-play" might also not understand London's man-play prose, even as Ruth Morse, in *Martin Eden*, fails to appreciate the masculine strength of Martin Eden's prose. Ruth reads his work, and Martin values her precisely for her feminine insulation from his realities. When she responds to one of his tales by editorializing, "*We know there are nasty things in the world*," Eden "cuddled to him the notion of her knowing, and chuckled over it as a love joke. . . . He thanked God that she had been born and sheltered to such innocence" (168). Eventually, Martin seems to agree with Brissenden, who sees such women as Ruth as "prattling out little moralities that have been prattled into them, and afraid to live life."[13] The subjugation of Martin to Ruth suggests the felt subjugation, which also persistently troubled other nineteenth- and twentieth-century male writers, of a male writer to a female reader. Although the turn of the century everywhere contains a broad crisis of the relation of masculinity to the maternal,[14] a specifically literary maternity helps produce the reformulating of masculinity evident in so much naturalist prose.

The unsolvable alteration between conventional and outlaw femininity suggests a fetish structure that underlies much of the treatment of gender in London's fiction. Freud argues that the fetish, a defense against male castration anxiety, grants to women a substitute for the penis, a disguise of which lack threatens the male with his own potential loss.[15] To Freud, the fetish "remains a token of triumph over the threat of castration and a safeguard against it; it also saves the fetishist from being a homosexual by endowing women with the attribute which makes them acceptable as sexual objects" ("Fetishism," 216). Freud's claim requires careful unpacking in reference to London's novels and tales. When London's women seem most androgynous in terms of their participation in male culture, we often see scenes of appropriation of some piece of the male technology of violence. As mentioned previously, for example, in *The Sea-Wolf* Maud Brewster repeatedly appears in male dress, which elicits a highly interested response from Humphrey Van Weyden, and she also brandishes and uses clubs. At still another moment, she insists on relieving Van Weyden at the helm of the small craft they use to escape from the *Ghost*. As Van Weyden tells us: "I turned the oar over to her and obeyed. I experienced a positive sensuous delight as I crawled into the bed she had made with her hands. The calm and control which were so much a part of her seemed to have been communicated to the blankets" (202). In this case, Hump seems to take a masochistic delight in relinquishing his newfound masculinity, so that Maud's assertiveness translates into his passivity.[16]

In Jack London's other tales and novels we find similar moments, in which a woman's attractiveness seems cemented by her appropriation of signs of masculine privilege. In *A Daughter of the Snows*, Frona Welse figuratively and literally threatens Vance Corliss with a whip. After she apologizes for having "raised her coiled whip to strike" (108), Corliss jests, "I notice the dogs your whip falls among come nevertheless to lick your hand and to be petted" (111). In "The Son of the Wolf," a short story from which London's first collection takes its title, Scruff MacKenzie enjoys a fetishistic "pleasure/danger" moment with the native woman he has selected for his wife: "She brought herself to her knees . . . and shyly unbuckled his heavy belt. . . . But her next move disarmed his doubt, and he smiled with pleasure. She took from her sewing-bag a moosehide sheath. . . . She drew his great hunting-knife, gazed reverently along the keen edge, half tempted to try it with her thumb, and shot it into place in its new home."[17]

Quite often, in London's Klondike stories, the fetishism that London uses to regulate masculine ambivalence toward the feminine functions to negotiate class and racial differences between women as well. In "The White Silence," for example, the first tale of *The Son of the Wolf*, London relates the ability of native women to undertake male hardships and execute male tasks with a certain matter-of-factness.[18] For native women to become erotic objects, they must possess suggestively white features, in which case his stories assume an obsession with dress, with veiling and unveiling, with putting on and taking off. For example, the native woman mentioned above in "The

Son of the Wolf" is "in features, form, and poise, answering more nearly to the white man's type of beauty" (25–26). In "The Wife of a King," in the same collection, the native Madeline can handle a dog team for hundreds of miles, but she still has an "exquisitely turned foot and ankle," which allows her access to the imagined sexual power of bourgeois femininity.[19] After the Malemute Kid and his associates train her in feminine graces, they find themselves subject to her new authority: "Yielding to the intoxication of the moment, and of her own power, she had bullied, and mastered, and wheedled, and patronized them . . . and instinctively, involuntarily, they had bowed . . . to that indefinable something in woman . . . while Malemute Kid, utterly abandoned, had seized the broom and was executing mad gyrations on his own account" (176–77). In this passage, Madeline's ascension into white womanhood also seems paired with the Malemute Kid's transgression of his own gender, signified here by his passionate whirl with the fetishistic broom, which is a kind of cross-dressed phallus. Madeline-as-fetish takes on a magical power, which augments the pleasure of her viewers masochistically to "forget" the nature of her creation. In reality, however, male power remains intact. Practically speaking, the success of a band of men in creating feminine beauty as a commodity will undercut the claims of women to autonomy and respect.

In the case of white women in the Klondike, the dynamics of attraction work in the opposite direction. The woman unable to acquire an Indian-like facility for the trail, such as the execrable Mercedes in *The Call of the Wild*, is a contemptible figure. When forced to walk in order to lighten the sled, "she let her legs go limp like a spoiled child."[20] Much more desirable is the admirable Grace Bentham in "The Priestly Prerogative," "a slender girlish creature . . . who urged and encouraged her husband, . . . who broke trail for him when no one was looking, and cried in secret over her weakling woman's body" (122).

In still other examples from London's fiction, we find women appropriating what has been labeled "the gaze" in contemporary feminist film theory. To the extent that men traditionally have had the power of actively looking in art at women who have conventionally been the objects of representation, the presentation of women exercising such a prerogative also suggests the possibility of a fetishistic structure. In *Martin Eden*, for example, when Martin briefly returns to the "old days" of street brawling, the woman who *causes* the contest seems to drink in the spectacle: "While he kept a wary eye on his antagonist, he glanced at Lizzie. Usually the girls screamed . . . but . . . she was looking on with bated breath, leaning slightly forward, so keen was her interest" (423–24). In *A Daughter of the Snows*, Frona Welse also enjoys gazing at scenes of danger. We are told that "when . . . violent assault and quick death seemed most imminent, the first officer had stolen a glance at the girl by his side. He had expected to find a shocked and frightened maiden countenance, and was not at all prepared for the flushed and deeply inter-ested face which met his eyes" (4). In another episode, in *The Game*, Gene-vieve, already disguised as a boy, watches the boxing match through a se-questered "peep-hole" (107). This peep-hole signifies her appropriation of the male power of gazing and her continued sequestration from the "eyes" that "blazed" (142) in the ring, from the gazes of Ponta, which "sweep the audience with his hatred" (171), and from Joe's own eyes "flashing the light and glitter of steel" (165). Joe, in turn, seems feminized by her scrutiny as she watches him disrobe, displaying skin "fair as a woman's" (113) and a body that seems to be "Dresden china, to be handled gently and with care" (117). These violations of gender convention, however circumscribed, prove fatal to them both. Joe dies in the ring, and Genevieve plunges into a new per-ception of feminine marginality. The "Game," she finds, makes "woman piti-ful, not the be-all and end-all of man, but his toy and his pastime" (179).

All of these moments, in various ways, enact an economy of presence and absence between the genders. The signs of feminine strength often seem paired with a pleasurable male masochism, indicating that in London's nar-ratives feminine strength and masculine strength exist in a state of tension, at times explicit and obvious and at other times muted and scarcely per-ceptible. For instance, in the first two examples of the female gaze (given above), the text renders the male's own perception as a "glance" of divided attention. In the third, Genevieve's position is simultaneously powerful and completely disempowered.

An additional and perhaps even more compelling example of an inverse relation between masculine and feminine power occurs in *The Valley of the Moon*. In it, Saxon, emboldened by "the memory of her fighting forefathers," commits the impropriety of watching a labor riot in front of her house (188). Her gaze immediately finds as object the vulnerable body of the "round-bel-lied, cigar-smoking leader" of the antistrike forces: "In some strange way, she knew not how, his head had become wedged at the neck between the tops of the pickets of her fence. . . . His hat had fallen off, and the sun was making an astounding high light on his bald spot. The cigar, too, was gone. . . . She saw he was looking at her. One hand . . . seemed waving at her, and al-most he seemed to wink at her jocosely, though she knew it to be the con-tortion of deadly pain" (188). In this case, the leader of the strikebreakers seems reduced and humiliated precisely because he is the immobile and "framed" recipient of a female gaze, which reveals to him the full extent of his losses and his weaknesses.

The politics of such depictions are complicated. It is not clear that the fetishistic structures inhabiting London's fiction negate the progressive potential of his nonconventional women characters, any more than the adolescent perception that all altruism contains elements of self-interest means that we should dispense with altruism altogether. In much of London's fiction, however, conventional women arguably are a greater threat to men than women who serve as male adventure companions, and we recognize this precisely by the phobic intensity of their depiction.

The White, the Clean, the Homoerotic

London's love of masculinity necessarily raises the common question of homoeroticism in his work. As opposed to the ambiguous biographical evidence on whether London ever engaged in explicitly homosexual relations, the textual evidence seems relatively clear concerning the strength of London's love of masculine culture and athletic male bodies.[21] This love generates in London's fiction identifiable strategies of homophobic displacement and suppression.

London had no difficulty in admiring the male body and in attributing feminine traits to it, which seems to argue for a blurring of object choice. The most famous such passage is Van Weyden's long look at the unclothed Larsen: "I must say that I was fascinated by the perfect lines . . . and . . . the terrible beauty of it. . . . But Wolf Larsen was the man-type, the masculine, and almost a god in his perfectness. As he moved about or raised his arms the great muscles leapt and moved under the satiny skin. . . . His body, thanks to his Scandinavian stock, was fair as the fairest woman's. . . . I could not take my eyes from him" (116).[22] The transfer of a desirable femininity to Larsen renders him a dangerously seductive object even to a heterosexual man. As I have argued, London also transfers male characteristics to women, but the dynamics of such a transfer are necessarily different. Such a transfer suggests the sublimation of a prohibited male homoeroticism by finding desired male characteristics in women, but this need makes heterosexual desire less identifiable and conventional.[23]

Examples of homoeroticism sublimated into heterosexuality are common in London's prose. In a well-known letter London wrote to his future wife, Charmian, close to the time of *The Sea-Wolf*'s publication and at the height of their initial passion, he admits to her the strength of his love of men: "Shall I tell you a dream of my boyhood and manhood? . . . I . . . knew always—that there was a something greater I yearned after . . . that . . . made those woman-loves wan things and pale. . . . For I had dreamed of the great Man-Comrade." Relating this dream seems to have been London's way of testing his female companion's tolerance for a desire he advances cautiously: "I have held a woman in my arms . . . and in that love-moment have told her. . . . And the woman grew passionately angry, and I should have wondered had I not known how pale and weak it made all of her that she could ever give me" (*Letters*, 1: 370). The question of what London "should have wondered" intrigues: Is his sexual identity at stake? In any case Charmian—as opposed to Bessie Maddern London, his first wife—seems to have appealed to Jack partly because of her ability to impersonate this longed-for male companion. As he says at the beginning of this letter, "You are more kin to me than any woman I ever knew."

Even in *The Valley of the Moon*, perhaps London's most successful imaging of heterosexual love and companionship, the frame-tale of adventure invoked by Billy and Saxon is the homosocial/homoerotic one of *Robinson Crusoe*. When Billy offers to serve as Saxon's Friday, he invokes an adventure originally involving only men. Indeed, Billy early confides to Saxon that his deepest desires have always been for things masculine: "I've never cared for girls—that is, not enough to want to marry 'em. I always liked men better" (91). Billy's relation to the unconventional Saxon leaves room for, and even absorbs and satisfies, Billy's homoerotic passions.[24]

If London often seems to work homosexual desires through heterosexuality, he has other narrative strategies that simultaneously seem to express and contain them. First, one finds a persistent association between the homoerotic and filth. The London short story "In a Far Country" provides a clear example of the connection.[25] This tale involves two effete men, Carter Weatherbee and Percy Cuthfert, who fail to measure up to the manly standard of the Klondike and thus earn the contempt of both their traveling companions and the narrator: "A bucket of water to be brought . . . and these two effete scions of civilization discovered sprains or blisters requiring instant attention" (73). Left to fend for themselves for a winter, they do not bother to undertake a difficult overland trek: "In the absence of fresh vegetables and exercise, their blood became impoverished, and a loathsome, purplish rash crept over their bodies. . . . Next, their muscles and joints began to swell, the flesh turning black, while their mouths, gums, and lips took on the color of rich cream. . . . They lost all regard for . . . common decency.

The cabin became a pigpen, and never once were the beds made" (85–86). Eventually, in a state of mental and physical deterioration, they kill each other. After shooting Weatherbee, Cuthfert, struck by an ax and prone on his unmade bed in a sexually vulnerable position, feels that the "lower portion of the body was useless. The inert weight of Weatherbee crushed him . . . like a bear under a trap" (98).[26]

The violence of the effete pair belies or perhaps suppresses what might be imagined as the potential erotic freedom of the Northland, far from the disciplinary pressures and scrutiny of conventional middle-class culture. After all, London tells us early in the story, the successful sojourner "may estimate success at an inverse ratio to the quantity and quality of his fixed habits. . . . The exchange of such things as a dainty menu for rough fare . . . is after all a very easy matter" (70). Although London speaks about a need to change when one is in the wilderness, in fact our heroes *do* change, rejecting or losing much of the discipline of the body inculcated by civilization. What London seems to require, then, is a degree of change that prevents the more important, seductive, and threatening changes the story depicts.

In *The Sea-Wolf*, Mugridge, the *Ghost*'s cook, again suggests the connection between homoeroticism and filth. Joan Hedrick in *Solitary Comrade* notices the possibility of erotic dynamics between Mugridge and Larsen, the unfathomable "fancy" Larsen takes to him in the early part of the novel (122–23). Van Weyden's own repulsion to Mugridge has a kind of phobic intensity: "I had taken a dislike to him at first, and as he helped to dress me this dislike increased. There was something repulsive about his touch. I shrank from his hand; my flesh revolted. And between this and the smells arising from various pots boiling and bubbling on the galley fire, I was in haste to get out into the fresh air" (27). Like Van Weyden himself, Mugridge has feminine characteristics—the former notes his "effeminate features running into a greasy smile" (27). Like the effeteness of Cuthfert and Weatherbee, Mugridge's feminization suggests a possible audition as an erotic object and a defense against such desire, compounded by the text's immediate and phobic rendering of his body. The positive desire that London's characterization suppresses, however, may be available in London's depiction of a predecessor of Mugridge's, in *The Cruise of the Dazzler* (1902), his tale of California boyhood piracy.[27] Here, young Joe gravitates to the Oakland docks and sees a fishing boat called the *Ghost*. In its cabin, he watches a "young fellow of nineteen or twenty who was engaged just then in cooking. . . . The sleeves, rolled back to the elbows, disclosed sturdy, sun-bronzed arms, and . . . his

face proved to be equally bronzed and tanned. . . . While he worked he talked
with a companion on deck" (243). Eventually, the cook and his companion
retire for an intimate dinner at a tiny table. We are told that "all the romance
of Joe's nature stirred at the sight" (244). *The Sea-Wolf* completely reverses
the valence of this scene of all-male domesticity, while preserving its focus
on a figure invested in the sensual task of cooking for other men. It repudi-
ates, but it does not avoid, the category of the erotic, and its emphasis on
disgust for Mugridge's body works to unveil the erotic content of the earlier
idyllic scene.

London extends the uncleanliness of Mugridge, in *The Sea-Wolf*, to the
world of the forecastle, where men live together in homosocial intimacy: "It
smelled sour and musty, and . . . I saw every bit of available wall-space hung
deep with sea-boots, oilskins, and garments, clean and dirty. . . . The air was
thick with the warmth and odor of their breathing, and the ear was filled
with the noise of their snoring and of their sighs and half-groans" (109–10).
Immediately after Larsen survives an attack in this realm of the body, Van
Weyden admires his "perfect lines" and "satiny skin." The juxtaposition suggests a difference between Larsen's body and the disreputable bodies of the
crew and consequently a difference in Van Weyden's scrutiny of them. London also uses race to draw a pointed distinction between attraction to a "feminine" male body and the body of the masculine Larsen. First, we are told
that one of the hunters, "Oofty-Oofty," was "a beautiful creature, almost
feminine in the pleasing lines of his figure," with a "softness and dreaminess
in his large eyes which seemed to contradict his well-earned reputation for
strife and action" (113–14). Then we are told that Oofty-Oofty had lines that
"in so far as they pleased" were "feminine," but Larsen was "the man-type,
the masculine, and almost a god in his perfectness" (116).[28]

London's narrative separates Larsen from the contagion of the erotic by
demonizing the lower-class racial body as the real place of fluid, odor, and
warmth, consequently effecting a sublimation of homoerotic energy into an
apparently innocent, homosocial gaze. London usually insists upon the cleanliness and whiteness (two allied but different tropes) of the bodies free for
his scrutiny. For example, in *The Game*, the fair-skinned Joe harangues
Genevieve on the cleanliness of the fighter's body: "Hard all over. . . . Now
that's what I call clean. Every bit of flesh an' blood an' muscle is clean right
down to the bones. . . . No soap and water only on the skin. . . . I tell you it
feels clean" (27–28).

A similar obsessiveness in *Martin Eden* seems tied to London's complicated class politics as well. After seeing Ruth, Martin feels "a crying need to

be clean . . . if he were ever to be worthy of breathing the same air with her"
(81). He fears that his place will always be "with all that is low . . . in dirty
surroundings among smells and stenches" (146). Once again, sanitation has
sexual implications—this time, however, in Ruth's conversation with her
mother. According to Mrs. Morse, her children must have a "heritage" that
is "clean," and Martin "is, I am afraid, not clean. Your father has told me of
sailor's lives, and—and you understand" (214). Martin himself seems to agree
with this assessment. Early in the novel he remembers "jails and boozing-
kens, fever-hospitals and slum streets" and other women, whom he characterizes as "a grotesque and terrible nightmare brood—frowsy, shuffling
creatures . . . gin-bloated hags of the stews and all the vast hell's following
of harpies, vile-mouthed and filthy, that under the guise of monstrous female form prey upon sailors" (35–36). Although this passage from *Martin
Eden* graphically demonstrates that London's intertwined anxieties are not
confined to homoeroticism, it also reinforces the perception that the juxtaposition of filth and relations between men has erotic implications, since
filth here seems explicitly sexual in a heterosexual context.

To the barriers of class, race, and cleanliness London builds against eroticism between men might be added the threat of apocalyptic violence, such
as erupts at the end of "In a Far Country" or in *The Sea-Wolf*, where Mugridge suffers a dismemberment by a shark, as a consequence of orders given
by Larsen, with whom he had an inexplicably favorable relationship. While
being towed through the sea by a rope as punishment for insufficient cleanliness, he is attacked by a shark and emerges with "the right foot . . . missing, amputated neatly at the ankle," with "a fountain of blood gushing forth"
(160). Mugridge's loss uncannily resembles the fate of Otoo, in "The Heathen," one of London's most homoerotically suggestive stories.[29] In this tale,
a beloved native companion, who becomes "brother and father and mother,"
saves the narrator from a shark attack by offering himself as a substitute meal.
When he at last surfaces, "both hands were off at the wrist, the stumps spout-
ing blood. . . . 'Otoo!' he called softly. And I could see in his gaze the love
that thrilled in his voice" (389).

Horrific violence also erupts at the end of *The Call of the Wild*, as the
Yeehats put an end to Buck's sojourn with Thornton. After finding body after body with arrows protruding, the enraged Buck attacks so ferociously
that Indians "shot one another with the arrows; and one young hunter, hurl-
ing a spear, . . . drove it through the chest of another hunter with such force
that the point broke through the skin of the back and stood out beyond"
(82). The various components of the scene work as a terrible expression and
suppression of Buck's love for Thornton.[30]

Martin Eden's homoerotic love for Brissenden, a relation based on London's passionate friendship with George Sterling, also contains traces of violence against the body and engineers the beloved body's disappearance. Brissenden suffers from consumption and has periodic hemorrhages; indeed, London describes his face as "cadaverous" (363). His writing itself figures as violence to Martin Eden: "It was terrific, impossible; and yet there it was, scrawled in black ink across the sheets of paper. . . . It was a mad orgy of imagination, wassailing in the skull of a dying man who half sobbed under his breath and was quick with the wild flutter of fading heart-beats" (364). Brissenden understands his poem as a transmutation of corruption, a survival of the "sweet illusions and clean ideals" of his "simple" youth. He figures his refusal to publish it as an aversion to the body, as his unwillingness to "have it pawed over and soiled by a lot of swine" (366).

When Brissenden takes Martin to see other male intellectuals, the odyssey is attended by imagery of filth and of dismemberment. Brissenden promises to show him "the real dirt," so he "won't be lonely anymore," and warns, "Watch out, they'll talk an arm off of you" (369). The most formidable of the intellectuals seems to be the "handsome, brunette" Kreis (372). When Brissenden decides to stir controversy, he points up Martin's attractiveness, introduces the erotic, and invokes violence and dismemberment: "Here's fresh meat for your axe, Kreis, . . . a rose-white youth with the ardor of a lover for Herbert Spencer" (374). Martin has a defender in Norton, who looks sympathetically at him "with a sweet, girlish smile." After Brissenden's death, Martin thinks briefly of reencountering the "real dirt," but experiences a never-explained phobic aversion: "But at the last moment . . . he recoiled and turned and fled through the swarming ghetto. He was frightened at the thought of hearing philosophy discussed, and he fled furtively, for fear that some one of the 'real dirt' might chance along and recognize him" (413). The often noted undermotivation of Eden's eventual suicide may result in part from the novel's inability to articulate the problem of his homoeroticism. Unable to enter the world of the "real dirt," he nonetheless loses his interest in women, which, as Lizzie Connolly tells him, is "all right enough for sissy-boys," but not for someone who "ain't made that way" (456).

Making a Heterosexual Man: Teleology and Narrative

In the full flush of her infatuation, the passionate Lizzie Connolly blurts out to Martin Eden, "You could do anything with me. You could throw me in the dirt an' walk on me" (427). Little does she seem to realize that her association with dirt may be precisely the problem for Eden. In London's work, almost all questions of gender and sexuality are class questions as well, linked to desires for upward mobility and respectability. Lizzie represents his past, and his eventually disillusioned desires focus entirely on class ascent. As he says of his former lower-class companions, "Their mode of life, which had once been his, was now distasteful to him. . . . He had exiled himself" (429). Thus "dirt," often in London's work a metaphor of sexual distaste, serves as a sign of class distaste as well, often unlinked to sexuality, or, by extension, as a sign of distaste for the kind of sexual experience lower-class life makes available.[31]

In London, then, two of the novel's most conventional, intertwined, and restrictive plots, the plot of class mobility and the marriage plot, work to place desire in a straitjacket. In order to "rise" in the world, one has to be or become the right kind of man with the right kind of woman and live the right kind of life.[32]

In *Martin Eden,* for example, Martin's desires for Ruth and for self-improvement are born instantaneously, and the most immediate sign of their entwining is his purging of associations and memories that threatened to "flood him" (35). Although the opening pages of *Martin Eden* overtly represent Martin's discovery of desire—the desire that motivates class-bound ambition—they read like the instantiation of primal repression. A jumbled, inchoate richness of desire, memory, and experience yields to the obsessive teleological focus of the novel. The advent of "Ruth" converts Eden's past into "filth," a metaphor that "blots" from his consciousness initial and diverse memories: "weak and sickly faces of the girls of the factories"; the "simpering, boisterous girls from the south of Market"; the "women of the cattle camps, and swarthy cigarette-smoking women of Old Mexico"; the "Japanese women, doll-like, stepping mincingly on wooden clogs"; the "Eurasians, delicate featured, stamped with degeneracy"; and "South-Sea Women, flower-crowned and brown-skinned" (36). Equally striking are his never-to-be-repeated memories of relations with other men, of "that hot, starry night, . . . the flaming passion in the Mexican's face, . . . the sting of steel in his neck, and the rush of blood, the crowd and the cries, the two bodies . . . locked together and . . . tearing up the sand" (38). As Martin molds his tumultuous life to conform to her comfortable standards of behavior, it is no wonder he refers to her "sublimated beauty" (35).

What Eden's desire for Ruth registers, then, is precisely the constraint of hegemonic cultural values upon desire, and their dependence on what Billy at the end of *The Valley of the Moon* reiterates as "renunciation" in the service of upwardly mobile heterosexuality (498). Eden will never again allow himself the adventures he remembers here, though he will stubbornly insist on their value to his writing. It might be observed that the presence of such memories in Eden's prose, like the presence of such material in London's prose, points to literature's paradoxical liberation and containment of desire. On the one hand, literature allows the representation and experience of material unacceptable in polite society, even if a narrative suggests such material, or the experience that generates it, is unacceptable. "Renunciation" always marks the presence of the renounced. In this sense a renunciation of the homoerotic may also be an exploration of the homoerotic, the content of which as a cultural category owes much to pathologizing rhetoric. In constricting terms, the literary registers a pressure against culture that must submit to the terms culture supplies for its articulation. These are not only standards of literary value, but finally also the narrative forms, the convincing and compelling plots, to which a writer has access at any historical moment.[33] The intolerable inertia of such forms, their capacity for intransigent resistance to desire, may well generate violence.[34]

In his psychoanalytic narrative of the development of adult sexuality, Freud works to confine homosexuality to renounced desires of the infantile, the primitive, and even the animal past of the species, and to make heterosexuality the proper goal of personal and cultural development. In his discussion of "inversion" in a famous footnote to *Three Essays on Sexuality*, Freud argues that

> psycho-analysis considers that a choice of an object independently of its sex— freedom to range equally over male and female objects—as it is found in childhood, in primitive states of society and early periods of history, is the original basis from which . . . both the normal and the inverted types develop. Thus . . . the exclusive sexual interest felt by men for women is also a problem that needs elucidating. . . . In inverted types, a predominance of archaic constitutions and primitive psychical mechanisms is regularly to be found.[35]

This development, in which individual progress recapitulates the history of the species, involves a transition from an animal, all-fours anality to an upright, genital-centered heterosexuality, as Freud makes clear in another footnote in *Civilization and Its Discontents*. Such a development makes "normal" heterosexuality itself a sublimation: "With the assumption of an erect posture by man and with the depreciation of his sense of smell, it was not only his anal erotism which threatened to fall a victim to organic repression, but the whole of his sexuality so that since this, the sexual function has been accompanied by a repugnance . . . which . . . forces it away from the sexual aim into sublimations and libidinal displacements."[36] The same metaphors Freud uses to express and contain the homoerotic as primitive, infantile, bestial, and repugnant are constantly at play in Jack London's fiction. In London's work, however, the homoerotic possesses a disruptive, inchoate energy that it surrenders in Freud, even as it assumes a clear but confining narrative shape.

Freud's linking of homoeroticism to bestial primitivism involves a profound cultural paradox, since characterizations of the gay man as he emerges in late-nineteenth- and early-twentieth-century culture stress his dandification and effeteness. This paradox inhabits London's most distinctive account of heterosexual development and homosexual suppression, *The Sea-Wolf.* Humphrey Van Weyden must forgo his intense civilization and the literary, aesthetic life he shares with another man, Charley Furuseth. He must abandon the consequences of a course of development apparently gone wrong so he can overcome his lack of interest in women.[37] Although Hump has been "surrounded by women" all his life, his relation to them has been "aesthetic and nothing more" (168). In fact, when his future mate, Maud Brewster, boards the *Ghost,* Van Weyden feels "strangely afraid of this woman" (141).

What allows this development, as I have argued, is Maud's essential androgyny, which allows Hump to transfer a desire for men to a female object. Further, Hump's intense identification with Larsen, despite erotic moments, is "saved" from homosexuality by what I have described as the text's attempt to differentiate the "clean" and "white" from the "filthy" or anal body and by Larsen's unremitting ferocity. As in the Oedipus myth, the son's desire for the father hides behind a facade of mutually maintained competition, hatred, and even violence. This identification with a violent and ostensibly heterosexual man, who attempts eventually to rape Maud, seems to be a necessity if Hump is to master heterosexuality. As Joseph Boone argues, Larsen facilitates the transformation of desires for other men into desires to dominate men and nature, and he facilitates a transcendence of fears of women through domination as well. Although Van Weyden retains a genteel and delicate side, the example of Larsen's dominance makes this gentility possible for Hump in a sexual relation with Maud. He holds his partial identification with Larsen in reserve as a guarantee of at least quantitative gender difference.

As a triumph of the novel's project of sublimation, the terms of this identification are altered by the novel's sadistic torture of Larsen, who undergoes a slow paralysis before finally expiring. As his anesthetized body loses its ability to feel or act, he becomes a kind of disembodied phallic trope, literally described in linguistic terms: "The man of him was not changed. It was the old, indomitable, terrible Wolf Larsen, imprisoned somewhere within that flesh. . . . No more would he conjugate the verb 'to do' in every mood and tense. 'To be' was all that remained to him— . . . to will . . . and in the spirit of him to be as alive as ever, but in the flesh to be dead, quite dead" (259). This torture suggests that Hump's passage to heterosexual masculinity requires a dangerous bodily identification with other men, yet the final consolidation of a heterosexual identity involves a suppression of the body and its wayward, decentering desires. The will to heterosexuality in London's writing produces a remaindered homoeroticism visible only as a text repressed, as a series of free-floating moments that nevertheless contribute a disruptive energy to his narratives. The homoerotic thus stands as the central sign in London's fiction of a body and sexuality that exert force on human existence, but lie beyond any easy understanding or articulation.[38] This body and this sexuality compete with more conventional renderings of physical life and desire.[39]

London wrote incessantly about nature and physical life, but his uses of the biological often work to construct a stable, knowable world from which he can extract principles of behavior. Not only does Darwinian natural selection explain and support a masculine struggle for dominance, but it explains sexuality as well in terms of the reproductive search for one's "mate." The dynamism of London's fiction, however, results precisely from the pressure of the excluded, the barely repressed, against his own formulations. The narrative accommodations London makes with existence, like Hump's nascent manhood, are always threatened by remaindered physical desires, which London would like to torture or discipline into submission.

The whole of this interplay in London's writing occurs against his background assertions that we can know nothing of enduring value about human life. This consciousness surfaces as the trope of "whiteness," present in the first tale of his first collection of short stories, "The White Silence," and in the meditation on alcoholism, *John Barleycorn* (1913), as "white logic."[40]

The "passive phase of the white silence" has a "stupefying" effect: "All movement ceases, the sky clears, . . . the slightest whisper seems sacrilege, and man becomes timid. . . . Sole speck of life journeying across the ghostly wastes of a dead world, he trembles at his audacity, realizes that his is a maggot's life, nothing more" (7). In *John Barleycorn*, written toward the end of London's career, an alcohol-induced "white logic" produces unlivable wisdom: "I am truth. . . . Appearances are ghosts. Life is ghost land, where appearances change, transfuse, permeate each the other and all the others. . . . You are such an appearance. . . . All an appearance can know is mirage. You know mirages of desire. These very mirages are the unthinkable and incalculable congeries of appearances" (192). London's repetition of "mirage" implies both a knowledge of the inadequacy of the culturally given and an inability to articulate or imagine anything beyond its borders. In these passages London's whiteness seems to yield only negative formulations and can only insist on the unsubstantial and inadequate nature of all representations. Its cynicism is unrelentingly oppositional, and it can find no positive articulation of desire.[41] Consequently, whiteness suggests the authentic difficulty of the writer's task: the imperviousness of experience to the writer's obstinate questionings, and the related resistance of narrative to the marginalized sensations, blank misgivings, and unarticulable desires that flood the interstices of human existence like white noise.

At the same time, the invocation of whiteness as an epistemological boundary may suggest the facility with which such boundaries—however philosophically authentic—also serve the needs of repression. Eve Kosofsky Sedgwick has recently argued that it is simplistic to speak of ignorance as a unitary sum of what lies beyond the realm of knowledge. Instead, ignorance always occupies a particular position in some realm of knowledge and works to legitimate some claims to truth and to delegitimate others. Even if certain kinds of questions have no easy answers, for example, does a focus on such questions mask the implications of what we do know? Is ignorance always strategic? [42]

"Whiteness," which in white logic suggests intolerable truth, is often a sign of homoerotic desire in London's fiction. Indeed, even the story "The White Silence" thematizes the problem of love between men. In it, the Malemute Kid explicitly confesses that his attachment to Mason produced jealousy toward the latter's wife "from the first time she had come between" the two of them. This theme accompanies other tropes that signify the disruption of the homoerotic in London's fiction. In the description of the passive phase of white silence, for example, we find images of bodily corruption—the "ghostly wastes of a dead world" and the traveler's status as a suggestively phallic "maggot." Even the disaster that befalls Mason is suggestive. To some extent like Larsen, whose paralysis is total, and even more like Percy Cuthfert of "In a Far Country," he ends up "paralyzed from his hips" and thus sexually anesthetized.

As a signifier of repression, then, whiteness may reflect in London, as it does in other American writers, a periodic desire to bury particular anguishes of subjectivity beneath an obliterating image of that anguish. Whiteness seems to negate the difficult, twisted interrelations of race, class, sexuality, and gender in American culture. Such a trope, however, may also advertise the pressure of what it represses or displaces. London was honest enough—and troubled enough—to render his anguish in such a way that its nature might be suggested.

Social Darwinism, Gender, and Humor in 'Adventure'

CLARICE STASZ

Jack London reached adulthood during the tumult of American imperialism. In 1893, historian Frederick Turner stunned the public with his thesis that the American frontier was closed; quite naturally some responded by urging American incursions abroad. Within the next few years the country would gain Hawaii (through a bloodless coup led by conservative businessmen) and become a major influence in the Philippines and Panama. Although both economic and Christian missionary interests spurred these advances, the ideology of Social Darwinism provided the rationale.

As popularized at the time, Social Darwinism was reduced to a crude argument claiming the survival of the fittest among individuals within society and among societies as well. The doctrine appealed to the privileged Anglo-Saxon elite because it reinforced ethnocentric and evolutionist attitudes toward so-called primitive peoples. Thus businesspeople could exploit natives because it was their superior right to do so, and missionaries could claim to be bringing the advantages of Christian morality to the heathens.

Jack London was well read in the varieties of Social Darwinism, more complex than the popular view, and he understood the theory to be more than a simple "top dog wins." He knew from Darwin, for example, that the key to species survival was cooperation, hence his leanings toward workers organizing and socialism. Yet having been raised by a race-proud mother and exposed to the anti-Asian hostilities rampant in the Bay area, he could not help absorbing some of the ideology's crude racist slant.

But London was to have the unusual opportunity to visit lands with "primitives," first in the Yukon, then Hawaii, finally the South Seas, and thus test the theory firsthand. As a consequence, a significant portion of his fiction concerns interracial contact between the White Man and the Primitive. Given his personal development and questioning, along with the complexity of Social Darwinism itself, it is possible to interpret his views as racist in some cases and not in others.

Along with the conscious ideology of Social Darwinism, society in London's day was on the threshold of a pivotal, subliminal shift in gender expectations with regard to both femininity and masculinity.[1] With no frontier to conquer, men had to develop new arenas to express dominance and aggressiveness, new rules for the masculine pecking order; with more personal mobility, women were searching for expression beyond the walls of the home. London's writings, both fiction and private correspondence, express his awareness of this transformation.[2] Privately, he developed a psychology of integrating so-called masculine and feminine qualities within one's self. Socially, he reflected on men's and women's roles through his fiction, where he explored the values and the disadvantages of patriarchy. This examination is best seen in the misunderstood *The Little Lady of the Big House,* a devastating critique of masculine dominance.

I will examine London's reflections on these themes as voiced in a minor novel, *Adventure.* Here London weaves his experiences in the Solomon Islands with stories told to him by colonials living there at the turn of the century. This tale may be likened to a sketch, a rough model rejected in later variations on the theme. Its failure as literature has less to do with its outmoded ideology than with its inadequacies of technique, notably the control of humor, but these aspects of *Adventure* are intertwined.

On July 9, 1908, Jack London and the *Snark* crew landed at Pennduffryn Plantation in the Solomon Islands, which would be their base. Their hosts were Englishmen Tom Harding and George Darbishire, whose business was trading and copra. Other whites in the plantation compound were Harding's wife, Baroness Eugenie, and Claude Bernays, the plantation manager. Melanesians under contract, treated not much better than slaves, provided the labor. The hosts soon regaled the crew with stories of murders of white schooner captains and head-hunting attacks upon plantation whites. Charmian observed the first night that in her boudoir was "a rack of rifles, always loaded and ready, and I am to keep my revolver with me day and night" as protection against uprising.[3]

Tropical disease mocked the lush beauty of the blue lagoons, the coral reefs underneath crisscrossed by the purple shadows of the feathery palm trees lining the beaches. The entire crew of the *Snark* had malaria, yaws, and infected ulcerations. London suffered an additional curious ailment—his hands swelled up, the skin thickened, then peeled off in many layers. Partly because of their poor health, the Londons spent the next three and a half months at Pennduffryn, with brief explorations of nearby islands. During this stay London completed "The Heathen" and began *Adventure*, using the plantation and several of its inhabitants (even a vicious "nigger-hating" mongrel named Satan) as the model for the fictional Berande Plantation. That Social Darwinism was key can be seen in the notes he wrote at the time: "She reads her Kipling & catches a consciousness of themselves as farmers on the fringe of empire builders. Make the love affair very tantalizing. She—a wild thing that did not want to be caught. Motif. The imperial race, farming the world. . . . Her final conversion to fact that blacks are vermin."[4]

On October 25, 1908, London wrote George Brett that he had completed 20,000 words of "a short Solomon Island novel—love story and adventure," which he expected to complete in two months.[5] In fact, he was so weakened by his various ailments that five months later he informed Brett that he had accomplished only 40,000 words.[6] It was May 3, 1909, before he could send the completed 75,000-word manuscript off to John Cosgrove, editor of *Collier's Weekly*, to be considered for serialization.[7] Cosgrove declined, as did *Hampton's Magazine*. Eventually *The Popular Magazine*, an action and adventure journal, bought the serialization rights, and Macmillan, which had been sitting on the manuscript for almost two years, brought it out in 1911.[8]

The editorial resistance to the work was reasonable, for the final version cries for extensive cutting and editing. When Benjamin Hampton advised that he could publish only 40,000 words, Jack defended the length: "There is one unfortunate thing about my writing, namely, that I *weave*. This makes it impossible to cut radically to the extent that you suggest. Possibly, all-told, a thousand or so words might be cut from this story, and still leave a clear, sensible narrative; but the man doesn't live who could cut 30,000 words out of *Adventure*, and leave anything but insane gibberish."[9] In fact, as with other of London's lesser works, trimming would have strengthened the narrative.

Written under stressful conditions, *Adventure* easily competes for the nadir of London's longer tales. The characters are cartoons, the suspense episodes flat, and the racism raw. The triad love story, a favorite plot device of London's, is feeble. In his critical overview of London, Earle Labor relegates the novel to a single footnote in which he calls it "a warmed-over version of *A Daughter of the Snows*."[10] In his cogent study of London's novels, Charles

Watson excludes *Adventure* from consideration, noting that it is "perhaps the most readable" of his lesser novels and praising its narrative power.[11]

Yet London himself, while acknowledging that the work was not a major one, defended its value. The ever-present threat of violence and disease, the whites' abuse of the natives, the basic crude aggression for survival, all captured his imagination; but it would be other works, such as "The Red One" and certain stories in his *South Sea Tales,* wherein he would more successfully present this land of darkness. A major component of the story's deficiency concerns its use of humor to serve the characterizations and the plot, along with its failure to use comic rhetoric effectively.

Adventure's plot is slight. Joan Lackland, a Hawaiian-born white tomboy, suddenly appears in the Berande Plantation house of fever-ridden David Sheldon. His partner has died, as has her father, with whom she was adventuring, so Dave and Joan are the only whites on the island. She ministers to him, shows intellect and daring in this dangerous environment, and pressures him into accepting her as a partner. He continually objects to her demand because a white man and woman alone together give a poor impression, but she eventually wins out. Although various action episodes intervene, the main storyline concerns Sheldon's falling in love with Joan, and her stubborn resistance to him, as told from his point of view. Two potential rivals appear at different points—Christian Young, the Tahitian-English descendant of a *Bounty* crew member, and John Tudor, a gold-hunter. Eventually Tudor under Joan's care recuperates from malaria, and one day he makes a pass at her that she rebuffs. When Sheldon confronts Tudor, the two end up agreeing to a "modern duel," hunting each other in the jungle. After wounding Tudor, Sheldon is delighted to hear Joan say she is ready to marry him, the last line of the book being "I am ready, Dave."

The subplot concerns the whites' encounters with South Sea Island natives, including Joan's Polynesian workers, the Melanesian plantation indentured servants, and various bushpeople, including headhunters. Upon arrival, Joan disapproves of Dave's hostility toward the darker races, but with exposure to native menace and the sight of white heads hanging in a smokehouse, she adopts his less tolerant, racially superior attitude. As Sheldon explains, "[In the tropics] the black, the brown, and the yellow will have to do the work, managed by white men. The black labor is too wasteful, however, and in time Chinese or Indian coolies will be imported." When Joan asks if the black will then die off, he agrees, for "the unfit must perish" (113–14). Her accepting such views is assisted by the repeated episodes of threat, including uprisings by plantation workers, an attack by headhunters on Tudor's gold-prospecting unit, and a nearby tribe's invasion of the plantation. Joan's conversion to race dominance is sealed when she uses her whip to beat a recalcitrant worker.

Joan Lackland fits a familiar mold of female characters from London's fiction, known at the time as the New Woman. Her most developed first appearance is Frona Welse in *A Daughter of the Snows*.[12] The only child of an Alaskan capitalist, Frona violates the Victorian strictures of ladyhood by wearing skirts that show her ankles, being adept at various athletics (including boxing), speaking her mind, and befriending a prostitute. Jack's second wife, Charmian, would in life exemplify the ways of the New Woman and become the model for Dede Mason in *Burning Daylight* and Paula Forrest in *The Little Lady of the Big House*.[13] Jack claimed that the model for Joan Lackland was Armine von Tempsky, a young friend who had been raised on the Haleakala Ranch in Hawaii and who shared many qualities with Charmian.[14] Preferring cattle drives to dances, Armine had the forthright independence of a cowboy, and although Joan Lackland may seem unbelievable to some, her actions reflect a form of gender rebellion common at the time. This was, after all, the decade when women's clubs mobilized for numerous social campaigns, and the suffrage movement was revitalized. And particular to the younger rebellious women was a hardy resistance to marriage.[15]

With regard to Joan's erotic appeal, however, it is clear London had Charmian in mind: "Her attitude is romance of adventure & damn sex—when he makes love to her, at first, she is so vexed that she gets in angry rages—once, cries. That is what makes the love affair so tantalizing. He is swept off his feet by sight of her great masses of hair drying after a swim."[16] (In the final version, no such encounter takes place.)

Dave Sheldon, on the other hand, is trapped in a more traditional view of femininity. From the beginning he has difficulty with Joan's temperament: "Her quick mind and changing moods bewildered him, while her outlook on life was so different from what he conceived a woman's outlook should be. . . . Her temper was quick and stormy, and she relied too much on herself and too little on him, which did not approximate at all to his ideal of a woman's conduct when a man was around. . . . At any rate, she did not look the part. And that was what he could not forgive" (75–76). Of English birth and education, he cannot conceive of a woman as a business partner and complains that her moral reputation is in danger. One solution is to force her to leave, which worries him because he would be sending her off alone, unprotected; the other is to marry her. Since to marry her is to accept a woman with "unfeminine" ways, either option threatens his expression of masculinity.

London's major device for elaborating Joan's independence is providing her a sarcastic voice. When the weakened Dave disputes her forcing him to rest, objecting that he has his plantation to attend to, she replies with humor in her eyes, "Don't you want to know about *me*? Here am I, just through my first shipwreck, and here are you, not the least bit curious, talking about your miserable plantation?" (48). Later on she mocks his asking her if she is an American by parrying, "You're English, aren't you?" (58). And several days later, she further teases him for being impolite by impugning his Englishness. Just in case the reader does not catch her humor, London often includes references to the laugh lines around her eyes.

These conversational ridicules continue through half of the story. Referring to Satan, she remarks that the dog is smarter than Dave Sheldon, for it is able to identify her workers as (racially superior) Tahitians rather than Melanesians. Another time she says she will find her own island plantation and concludes her mocking remarks with, "Find some spot where I shall escape the indignity of being patronized and bossed by the superior sex" (121). Following one argument, she jeers amusedly, "I suppose you've been accustomed to Jane Eyres all your life. That's why you don't understand me." As she walks away from that encounter, she laughs and calls out, "You're hoping a 'gator catches me, aren't you" (126–27).

London makes similar use of sarcasm, mockery, and teasing to establish the independence of female characters in some of his other works. Frona Welse similarly puts down Vance Corliss for his conventional views of femininity in *A Daughter of the Snows*.[17] Even the richly drawn and long-suffering Paula Forrest in *The Little Lady of the Big House* uses sarcasm, though more subtly, to cue her husband that she is distressed over his preoccupations with his work—"You think in statistics and percentages, averages and exceptions. I wonder, when we first met, what particular formula you measured me up by."[18] Because ultimately the subjugation of women is built upon their being silenced by men, to have a character speak in an assertive, critical manner efficiently establishes her rejection of patriarchy. Significantly, by portraying Dave as something of a boor, seldom quick with repartee, London further confirms Joan's dominance. Furthermore, in conversations with male characters who respect her prowess, Joan speaks directly and does not use deprecatory humor.

More than speech sets Joan's character. She exhibits great physical courage and wiliness, goes off alone and cleverly acquires a trading schooner, confronts with poise violent Melanesian workers, swims in the lagoon despite the alligators, and handles her gun accurately when necessary. She is so finely drawn and presented so much more admirably than any other character that the men, even Dave himself, seem little more than cartoons. Consequently, her capitulation is even more incredible because she seems more competent and capable than the lucky hero. While writing the story, London teased Charmian that he was falling in love with his heroine, and this emotional overidentification may be at the root of the imbalance, for throughout most of the story her character is exteriorized, as viewed by Dave Sheldon.[19]

Since Dave's perceptions dominate, the tracking of the love story consists primarily of Dave's reflections about Joan, interspersed between the action episodes. In his first lengthy meditation, Dave "stumble[s] upon the clew to her tantalizing personality," that she is a *boy* in her viewpoint (134–36). Consequently, he identifies with her by allowing that she has masculine qualities, and he retains superiority in his own mind by regarding her as immature. Yet when she asks to be his partner, he objects that to do so he would have to marry her because she is a woman. Her problem, he thinks, is that she has a boy's mind and a woman's body, which he believes she denies. Despite his confusion and anger over her being "a masquerader. Under all her seeming of woman, she was a boy, playing a boy's pranks," he falls in love with her (220). This is similar to London's own confused attitude toward Charmian, whom he often referred to as a "boy" or a "twin brother," appellations she thought complimentary.

In fact, Joan, like the real-life Charmian, is well aware she is a woman, sexually mature, for she wears lacy underwear and finds Christian Young and John Tudor attractive. She surprises Dave when she returns from a trip dressed uncharacteristically in brown slippers, brown openwork stockings, and a skirt that gives glimpses of her ankles. Again he proposes to her, unsuccessfully, and expresses his love. Soon afterward, Joan remarks that he is changing, that he could be a good husband, one who considers his wife a free agent. But by this point in the story she no longer uses humorous forms, and she metamorphoses into a "traditional female." Unfortunately, little in Dave's behavior corroborates her sudden shift in perception, and the archaic duel situation that follows only reinforces the patriarchal ideology. Joan's submission, with her sudden identification of Dave with her father, is utterly unbelievable. Proof of patriarchy's victory, Dave refers to her as his "little girl" (400).

The original notes to the story do not suggest such a facile capitulation on Joan's part nor excessive patronizing by Dave. He succeeds in teaching her that Melanesians are more fearsome than Polynesians, but she exhibits none of the submissiveness that marks her in the final version.

If certain forms of humor too often determine the character of Joan Lackland, the absence of other forms significantly detracts from the story. Most notable here is irony, a technique London would use to great effect at times in his later writing. An ironic tone concerning the major characters, for example, might have left the reader of *Adventure* aware that the couple would hardly live happily ever after. Such irony well defines the complexity of relationships in *The Little Lady of the Big House* or "The Kanaka Surf."[20]

More important, irony would have removed the most disagreeable part of the plot, its unadulterated racism. It is surprising that critics have not addressed this feature of *Adventure*, because it stands in strong contrast to London's other South Sea tales in this regard.[21] In some of these stories irony is the plot motive. For example, in "The Chinago" the ironic misspelling of a name sends the innocent protagonist, a Chinese worker, to the guillotine. The message is clear, that the superior attitude of the colonizers brings injustice upon the colonized. The title character of "Mauki" is able to take advantage of another irony, his brutal master's succumbing to disease, to behead him. This plot implicitly mocks the idea of the white race being the fittest to survive. In other stories, ironic commentary by the narrator or characters illumines London's questioning of pure Social Darwinism. The drinking buddies in "The Inevitable White Man" discuss how "in direct proportion to the white man's stupidity is his success in farming the world. . . . Tip it off to him that there's diamonds on the red-hot ramparts of hell, and Mr. White Man will storm the ramparts and set old Satan himself to pick-and-shovel work."[22]

Adventure, on the contrary, though written at the same time as these works, which are more ambivalent or critical, presents white racism without apology and indeed resolves in support of it. In accord with the imperialistic fervor of the day, the whites never question their right to exploit native lands and people, and they use violence because, they explain, the natives are violent toward one another. London also borrows from common stereotypes in describing the Melanesians as monkeys, the frequent analogy matching the cartoons prevalent in the newspapers then. Although he made similar references in other South Sea stories, the natives were not so crudely drawn; in fact, they were often invested with admirable qualities. Consequently, the Spencerian system of social dominance is fully reinforced: male over female, white over black, with race the deciding factor. Joan sacrifices her struggle for equality with white men and receives in return the guarantee of superiority over men (and women) of other races. Her attitude is shown toward the end when she chides Dave for dueling, because "white men shouldn't go around killing each other."[23] Whites should not act like other races, in other words.

One must wonder, then, how London could simultaneously produce such varying interpretations of race and sex. When he was writing the novel, he was depressed and in pain, consequences of his puzzling illness. Charmian noted that his nerves were growing unsteady. He was practiced in writing daily no matter his feelings or physical comfort, but perhaps his illnesses were cramping his creativity by changing the very biochemistry of his brain. Although London's intermittent disabilities are well documented, their influence on his uneven inventiveness has yet to be detailed.

More demonstrable is London's and Charmian's own ambivalence concerning Social Darwinism by this point in their lives. With regard to sexism, their views were less complicated. Throughout the South Seas the Londons encountered various taboos concerning "Mary" (*bêche-de-mer* for female) and joked about them. He quipped about seeing "Charmian's proud spirit humbled and her emperious queendom of femininity dragged in the dust."[24] She enjoyed sneaking into tribal male sanctuaries and teasing Jack in return about how uninteresting they were. London supported woman's suffrage, and he was unusual for the time in his view of marriage as a comradeship.

With regard to racism, however, their attitudes were confused. Both Jack's and Charmian's accounts of the Solomons mix expressions of white superiority with those of empathy and compassion for the native people. One senses a struggle going on, with the scientific ethos of the age pressing on one side, and their own private, contrary interpretations on the other. Charmian, for example, could be insulted that an Asian man did not make more room for her on the sidewalk in Honolulu, yet acknowledge that some Solomon bushmen were more intelligent than some of the white colonizers. Adding to these mixed impressions was the alien Solomon Island culture, with its body tattooing and piercing, its head-hunting practices. Several years later, the Londons learned that both Bernays and a trading captain they had met were beheaded during native uprisings. Such practices could only reinforce the imperialist credo of the day that white Christian civilization could improve life for these peoples. Yet the Londons were not close-minded, nor had they a personal investment in imperialism, so they remained ambivalent.

Jack London did not require consistency of himself, which is why disagreement is intense concerning the sincerity of his socialism, the depth of his racism, and the exact shape of his spirituality. In addition, a most pragmatic writer, he self-consciously molded his novels, meant to be published first as serials, for the audience. He wanted *Adventure* to be a diversion, an exciting entertainment, and a source of income. Just as he kept sex out of some novels to appease Mrs. Grundy and inserted spiritualism in *The Star Rover* to satisfy the faddish occultists, so he may have maintained the prevailing social views of the day for this plot. It is the South Sea short stories that express morally complex and socially critical views of imperialism and Social Darwinism.

London's vacillation and ambiguity reflected that of the age. During the Progressive Era, Americans were trying to resolve similar inconsistencies between idea and reality. Woman's sphere was no longer limited to the household, Christian Progressives and socialists were successfully challenging a tiny white capitalist elite, African Americans were organizing for more civil rights, and immigrant workers were changing the social order through unions and by retaining certain Old World ways. Consequently, London found outlets for both traditional and radical interpretations of imperialism. *Hampton's Magazine*, which refused to serialize *Adventure*, published "Strength of the Strong," "Mauki," and "The Terrible Solomons."

London's selling to the conservative market is also evident in his suppression of the erotic. It is sex that compels Dave Sheldon to excuse Joan's rebellion against Victorian views of femininity, for whatever her opinions and actions, she retains her female biology. Joan seems consciously to flaunt this quality to pressure Dave, and she thus hints at men's weakness as defined in the Victorian era, their submission to carnal desire. Were this subtext more explicit, the story would offer the critique of masculinity London developed more fully in *The Little Lady of the Big House*. Such suppression occurs in many of London's love stories and explains why he deserves criticism for excessive romanticization of women. Yet what appears sugary to modern readers would have been thought realistic by the bourgeois of London's day, who honored women for that very stifling of their sexuality. Indeed, what captured London's heart in real life was Charmian's bridging certain Victorian qualities in talk and manner with a New Woman's frankness concerning lust. But London's readers were more willing to hear challenges to racism than to gender expectations.

In capitulating to convention in *Adventure*, however, London shut off the most productive part of his creativity, his ability to identify with the character so completely that the reader participates in the character's journey. As long as Joan Lackland is sarcastic, the reader identifies with her attitude, but once she drops this speech, she loses verisimilitude, for she has now been twisted to meet the demands of Dave Sheldon, the representative of patriarchy and racism who forces her to become his ideal. Were London to have written in the ironic tone of *The Little Lady of the Big House*, the reader would close *Adventure* chuckling because Joan Lackland won the hand, for Sheldon must accept her modern view of womanhood. Instead, by silencing Joan Lackland's voice and sexuality, Jack London silences his own.

"The Way Our People Came"

Citizenship, Capitalism, and Racial Difference
in 'The Valley of the Moon'

CHRISTOPHER HUGH GAIR

The conclusion of Jack London's novel *Burning Daylight* (1910) manifests a generic shift from naturalism to Howellsian realism that establishes the family as a unit occupying a privileged space beyond the reach of the capitalist marketplace. By moving to a nearly self-sufficient, Jeffersonian rural idyll, the protagonists Elam and Dede Harnish gain a degree of moral agency impossible in the determined worlds of the city—where much of the novel is set—and of naturalist fiction. This transformation is problematic for various reasons, the most important of which are: first, that the Harnishes' escape from the market requires money earned in that market and salvaged from Elam's self-generated financial ruin by having the smallholding legally transferred to Dede's name; and, second, the move depends upon a retreat into history and into the economic structure of the nation at least fifty years earlier. Thus the concluding chapters of *Burning Daylight* display a tension between the Harnishes' moral agency and financial independence and the lives of the rural poor, the latter determined by factors such as war and the railroad's extortionate freight rates.

In *The Valley of the Moon*,[1] which in many ways retraces the themes of *Burning Daylight*, the shift from urban to rural is rewritten in a manner that tackles both these problems. Unlike Elam and Dede, the working-class protagonists Saxon and Billy Roberts have no assets in the city and leave Oakland on foot with their few possessions strapped to their backs. Their success in establishing a new life, in the same countryside around Glen Ellen as presented in *Burning Daylight*, therefore depends on their ability to survive in the competitive world, without the head start of an unmortgaged property. In addition, the couple's picaresque journey through multiracial California recognizes and describes the economic transformations that revolutionized farming after the Civil War. During their travels, Saxon and Billy learn that there is no more viable government land available to settlers, and they become experts in the literature of the "new" farming. Despite the affinity they feel for their pioneering ancestors, they are forced to acknowledge the differences in their own situation as they symbolically retrace the steps of their parents and of their Anglo-Saxon progenitors. The novel thus contains an anxiety about race "purity" and the decline of the "original" settlers in California, which the discovery of the Valley of the Moon—ironically, the name given to the land by the displaced Native Americans, the true original settlers—seeks to alleviate. In *The Valley of the Moon*, then, the protagonists' journey can be viewed as a way of coming to terms with a history largely denied in the conclusion to *Burning Daylight*.

In this essay, I will pursue three related issues. I explain briefly London's repeated use of the motif of urban to rural movement, in order to investigate the degree to which his new solutions in *The Valley of the Moon* answer the problematic relationship of genre and history. I adopt and challenge Walter Benn Michaels's essay "Race into Culture: A Critical Genealogy of Cultural Identity" (1992), to examine London's treatment of race anxiety in the face of the Progressive "Melting Pot." My account concerns the tensions between two kinds of storytelling, in this case the conflicting generic structures of naturalism and sentimental fiction. To develop this approach, I adapt Winfried Fluck's recent reappraisal of *Uncle Tom's Cabin*, in which he analyzes the cultural functions of the sentimental narrative and questions how anxieties about the distance between social and moral reference points (such as *The Valley of the Moon*'s challenge to the protagonists' faith in Anglo-Saxon supremacy) are fictionally resolved. Finally, I argue that the apparent triumph of the sentimental, domestic (female) voice in the novel represents an abandonment of the socialist tendencies in London's earlier fictions and an embrace of the middle-class culture rejected in *Martin Eden* (1909). Although the sentimental narrative advocating family is as much a political ideology as any other, I suggest that this is disguised by its constant pairing with the "natural," whether in biological or environmental terms. The resulting investigation of the "natural," especially with regard to Saxon Brown Roberts as homemaker and potential mother, identifies the degree to which she embodies rather than opposes what Mark Seltzer calls the "circulating medium of capital itself."[2]

I

During the crisis confronting Saxon Roberts when her husband, Billy, is jailed for assaulting their lodger, she has mental blackouts as well as "a strange feeling of loss of self, of being a stranger to herself." The narrator attributes these symptoms to "the beginning of an illness that she did not know as illness. All she knew was that she felt queer. It was not fever. It was not cold. Her bodily health was as it should be, and, when she thought about it, she put her condition down to nerves—nerves, according to her ideas and the ideas of her class, being unconnected with disease" (246). This "nervous" condition prompts a questioning of religious belief, in which Saxon concludes that there is no God, no immortality, and that "the universe was unmoral and without concern for men." Blaming the "man-made world" of class conflict and poverty—that is, the conditions created by a capitalist system of production—for the madness and horror that have crushed her domestic economy and induced her miscarriage, Saxon abandons the notion that existence is "ordained" by God. The effect is that looking "thus at life, shorn of its superrational sanctions, Saxon floundered into the morass of pessimism" (254–55). The benevolent determinism of God is replaced by the pessimistic determinism of the market economy, which removes any link between action and reward. In order to escape this despair, she does not return to a faith in a discredited God, but instead decides to "work for . . . happiness" in life, in exchange for acceptance of an eternal "black grave" (256).

Saxon's "illness" and her proposed "cure" embody familiar early-twentieth-century ideology. Jackson Lears charts the "shift from a Protestant ethic of salvation through self-denial toward a therapeutic ethos stressing self-realization in this world" and sees the transformation as a "modern historical development, shaped by the turmoil of the turn of the century."[3] Within the interdependencies of urban market life, it was increasingly hard to sustain the illusion of autonomous selfhood, and in *The Valley of the Moon*, Saxon's loss of faith, baby, money, and (temporarily) memory and husband— that is, the constituents of her "identity"—all depend on decisions made by labor and financial leaders a long way from the individual's control. As a result of her rejecting religious belief, Saxon is unable to anchor herself to a particular view of reality, and she drifts into a condition she calls "nerves," which Lears classifies as "normlessness, or anomie."[4] Her position is thus similar to that of the eponymous protagonist of *Martin Eden*, the more so since Saxon also loses her class affinities, regarding her working-class neighbors as "stupid," but distancing herself from the epithet.

Unlike Eden (who commits suicide before he can begin his planned new life in the South Seas), Saxon does find "self-realization in this world," and, as Lears suggests, this therapeutic rejuvenation involves a flight to "nature," a "nostalgia for the vigorous health allegedly enjoyed by farmers," and, most important, the belief that in a secular universe the process of self-realization is, in itself, "the largest aim of human existence."[5] Thus, not only do Saxon and Billy find a "natural" valley, which they instantly recognize as "our place" (485), but they also recover their health, so threatened by violence and disease in the city. They understand that the discovery of the Valley of the Moon allows them to complete the self-realization commenced when they quit the city. Here, they can "work like hell" (487) to fulfill the potential of both self and land. It is no surprise, then, that the novel closes in the same manner as *Burning Daylight*, with the pregnancy of the female protagonist and with the couple surveying a fertile natural world, in this case, "a doe and spotted fawn [looking] down upon them from a tiny open space between the trees" (530).

Self-realization depends, however, on finding a master narrative to replace the discredited faith in God and class allegiances. Thus, Saxon and Billy turn to their pioneering ancestors to discover "themselves," in a movement in which, paradoxically, the self remains decentered. Their initial attraction to each other is based on their both being "old American stock" (23), and the book seeks a solution to the problematic question of "Americanness" in an increasingly multiracial society. The dilemma at the heart of the novel involves the separation of self from race, which implicitly results in the separation of self from self. As Anglo-Saxons, the Robertses believe that they must shape their own destinies—what Saxon calls "self-sufficingness" (178)—yet as urban poor, they are at the mercy of forces beyond their control. As long as this is so, Saxon and Billy are not true Anglo-Saxons (what they consider "real" Americans) and are therefore not themselves. The move to the country is an attempt to close this gap.

Before taking a more detailed look at just what constitutes an "American" according to the logic of London's narrator and protagonists, we should briefly glance at what, for them, is *not* American. London starts with a seemingly hegemonic sketch of the healthy improvements in constitution when first- or second-generation Irish Americans are compared with their parents. At the Bricklayers' picnic, where Saxon and Billy are introduced, the narrator points out:

> It was too early for the crowd, but bricklayers and their families, laden with huge lunch-baskets and armfuls of babies, were already going in—a healthy, husky race of workmen, well-paid and robustly fed. And with them, here and

there, undisguised by their decent American clothing, smaller in bulk and
stature, weazened not alone by age but by the pinch of lean years and early
hardship, were grandfathers and mothers who had patently first seen the light
of day on old Irish soil. Their faces showed content and pride as they limped
along with this lusty progeny of theirs that had fed on better food. (10)

This description, which shares the parental pride of the old folk it represents,
portrays an America of abundance into which immigrants are easily assim-
ilated. The process appears straightforward, and American identity seems
to come with being born inside the national boundaries. The older generations cannot hope to become American, since they remain "undisguised" by
their adopted clothes and their proximity (biological and geographical) to
their children. All that they are permitted is a kind of associate citizenship,
made possible because the nation provides wealth enough for workers to
support extended families.

It soon becomes clear, however, that for Saxon and Billy, as well as for
the narrator, the gap between legal citizenship and "true" Americanness cannot be bridged. After telling Billy about the Saxons, she explains, "We're Saxons . . . all the Americans that are real Americans, you know, and not Da-
goes and Japs and such" (21–22). As they move through California on their
quest for the Valley of the Moon, observing the vast farms and fortunes of
Portuguese, Dalmatians, and Asiatics, each race is excluded from "true" integration not because of what they do but because of what they are not—
Anglo-Saxon.[6] Indeed, it is repeatedly stressed that the ethnic groups have
succeeded because they share the Puritan settlers' work ethic, whereas the
descendants of the pioneers have lost it. But even here, assimilation is rejected by the Robertses, who become increasingly interested in leisure time
and aesthetic pleasures as pursued by the affluent white communities they
encounter. For them, the Ben Franklinism that will reappear with Jay Gatsby
(another immigrant son denied access to the American aristocracy) is either
an anachronism or a device manipulated to increase production without the
accompanying gains for the individual worker.

As quickly as other groups succeed in corresponding to historical defi-
nitions of "American," the issue of nationality and culture is reinvented in
terms of the search for self-realization. Clearly, it is impossible for "new" settlers to become "real Americans," as Saxon understands this phrase, since
they lack the genetic birthright. Nevertheless, the process of self-realization
implies that to be born a Saxon—even to be named "Saxon"—does not automatically confer membership in the Anglo-Saxon race. Instead, it is only
the first half of a doubling process in which birth and action must be united.

Before looking more closely at the underlying reasons for this symbolic fusion, we need to examine the ways the process is enacted in *The Valley of the Moon*.

II

In his comparison of Thomas Nelson Page's *Red Rock* (1898) with Willa Cather's *A Lost Lady* (1923) and F. Scott Fitzgerald's *The Great Gatsby* (1925), Walter Benn Michaels identifies in Cather a repudiation of the Progressives' political nationalism: "Americanism would now be understood as something more than and different from the American citizenship that so many aliens had so easily achieved." It should be clear from my brief description of "Americanness" that London was repudiating this political nationalism a decade earlier. Curiously, however, Michaels claims that

> it is true that the major writers of the Progressive period—Dreiser, Wharton, London—were comparatively indifferent to the question of American national identity. . . . It was as if, during the period when industrial America was devoted to assimilating and "Americanizing" its immigrants as quickly and thoroughly as possible, only those confronted with what seemed to them the unassimilable "Negro" were compelled to produce an account of the constitutive boundaries of the American.[7]

Michaels is overgeneralizing, circumnavigating (by the nonspecificity of "comparatively indifferent") the extent to which Progressive Era novelists *were* concerned with national identity. By positing a homologous culture, he refuses to sanction the possibility of London (or Dreiser or Wharton) producing an account of the "constitutive boundaries of the American," which would oppose the Progressive ethos.

Michaels's claims are most easily (and productively) refuted via an application of his own ideas to *The Valley of the Moon*. In his essay, Michaels charts the shift by which

> if identification with the Indian could function at the turn of the century as a *refusal* of American identity [in *Red Rock*], it would come to function by the early 1920s as an *assertion* of American identity. . . . The Indian-identified "aristocratic" family [the Forresters in *A Lost Lady*] . . . provides the technology enabling an Americanism that will go beyond the merely national American citizenship offered by the state. But to provide this technology the family . . . must in particular cease to be the site of a certain indifference to racial difference (the family "black and white") and must be made instead into the unequivocal source of racial difference.[8]

Thus, in *A Lost Lady*, Cather describes Captain Forrester's "lonely defiant note that is so often heard in the voices of old Indians." Michaels points out that this association is "exceptionally misleading," since the pioneers and the railroad men were the cause of the Indians' destruction. However, he claims that being an Indian never preempted killing other Indians, and he argues that "the fact that the pioneers are now themselves a vanishing race only confirms the identification." Blinded by the headlights of modernity, the pioneers look back to the *prenational*, precorporate—that is, pre–Civil War—America of a now valorized Indian. In this way, they are able to recover their own difference from and superiority to mere American citizens.[9]

The ease with which Michaels's reading of Cather can be mapped onto *The Valley of the Moon* demonstrates the historical inaccuracy of his argument. First, Billy's and Saxon's ancestors have lived in America "hundreds of years," and their parents all crossed the Plains by wagon train (21–22). Both their fathers returned to the East to fight in the Civil War, proving their credentials as prenational occupants of the land and as founding fathers of an "undivided" country and of the State of California (granted statehood in 1850). In addition, their type is repeatedly seen as a vanishing race and, almost obsessively, as Indians. Saxon's father is described as being "wild as a Comanche . . . his long hair flyin', straight as an Indian . . . ; just as he cut a swath through the Johnny Rebs in Civil War days, chargin' with his men all the way through and back again, an' yellin' like a wild Indian for more" (295). This association with perfect health and aggressive vitality is equated with his failure to prosper: if "a weak heart, or . . . kidney disease, or . . . rheumatism" had forced him to settle down and keep his Market Street lots, his kind would have had more chance of survival in the emerging urban marketplace of post–Civil War America (294–95). Settling down, however, would mean renouncing the right to call oneself a "pioneer" and would entail becoming a "citizen." The pioneer spirit is doomed to perish because of its supposed similarity to that of the Native Americans. In addition, it is doomed because of the corporate, anti-individualistic nature of urban postwar America: the perceived self-determination of the pioneer is replaced by the deterministic laws of the market.

As a result of this inability to shape their own lives and of mass immigration, also a product of the nation's economic transformation, Billy, Saxon, and their friends Bert and Mary adopt Bert's moniker the "last of the Mohegans," directly linking their own fate to that of the vanished Indians. At Billy and Saxon's wedding supper, Bert tells Billy that he is "a Mohegan with a scalplock. An' you got a squaw that is some squaw, take it from me. Minnehaha, here's to you—to the two of you—an' to the papooses, too, gosh-dang them!" (118). This wedding toast turns increasingly sour: Bert dies in a fight with scabs and police (his final words repeat his "last of the Mohegans" refrain), Saxon's premature baby dies, and Mary becomes a prostitute (191–272). The nostalgia for a dying race becomes most pronounced when Saxon and Billy travel through the "foreign land" of the river country of northern California:

> The workers of the soil teemed by thousands, yet Saxon and Billy knew what it was to go a whole day without finding any one who spoke English. They encountered—sometimes in whole villages—Chinese, Japanese, Italians, Portuguese, Swiss, Hindus, Koreans, Norwegians, Danes, French, Armenians, Slavs, almost every nationality save American. . . . And Saxon, looking at [Billy's] moody face, was suddenly reminded of a lithograph she had seen in her childhood. It was of a Plains Indian, in paint and feather, astride his horse and gazing with wondering eye at a railroad train rushing along a fresh-made track. The Indian had passed, she remembered, before the tide of new life that brought the railroad. And were Billy and his kind doomed to pass, she pondered, before this new tide of life, amazingly industrious, that was flooding in from Asia and Europe? (437–38)

The equation of a "foreign land" with foreign peoples, all of whom have arrived well after the Civil War, makes the Indian analogy particularly apposite for Billy and Saxon. Like the Indian in the lithograph, they feel overrun by the sheer volume of new life, and like the first Native Americans, they are unable to recognize "their own" land, in which all the familiar landmarks have been replaced. Unlike the Indian, however, the Roberts family does eventually find a place to settle, apparently unthreatened by newcomers. Michaels's contention that the family has become a "source of racial difference" is confirmed by the novel's title: only in the Valley of the Moon, the translation of the Indian name "Sonoma," and a place as yet uncolonized by "foreigners," can the "true" Americanness of the family unit be established.

It may well be argued here that the original British settlers of California were never under real threat of being swamped by immigrants in the early twentieth century; urban development and most factors of production were firmly in the hands of white Anglo-Saxon Protestants. However, as I indicated earlier, being Anglo-Saxon—and hence American—in *The Valley of the Moon* requires more than the accident of birth. If immigrants are precluded from full assimilation, this does not guarantee that the pioneers' descendants are automatically "Americans." According to the logic of the novel, to be an Anglo-Saxon requires action as well. Therefore, when Mary becomes a prostitute, she rejects her cultural identity and turns herself into the embodiment of capital in an economy that denies self-realization. Instead of the possibility of finding herself—the project undertaken by Saxon—Mary exchanges herself as a commercial object that parodies the self-referential quest for physical and psychic vitality: "Saxon looked at her old friend curiously, with a swift glance that sketched all the tragedy. Mary was thinner, though there was more color in her cheeks—color of which Saxon had her doubts. Mary's bright eyes were handsomer, larger—too large, too feverish bright, too restless. She was well dressed—too well dressed; and she was suffering from nerves. She turned her head apprehensively to glance into the darkness behind her" (272). Mary represents the excesses of the culture of consumption and is, indeed, consumed by that culture. Unlike Saxon, she is unable to unite birth and behavior and consequently forgoes the right to a "self."

Later in his essay, Michaels discovers the same doubling process as that undertaken by Saxon at work in Oliver La Farge's *Laughing Boy* (1929). Reiterating the notion that cultural identity—here, being a Navajo—involves birth and behavior and therefore an element of choice, Michaels stresses that

> Slim Girl's learning to weave, to ride, and to sleep out under the stars are represented by the text as her attempt to exercise a "right" granted her by birth but requiring at the same time that she lay claim to it. *Laughing Boy* enacts, in other words, the project of becoming Navajo, a project made possible only by the fact that there's a sense in which Slim Girl isn't a Navajo and made fulfillable only by the fact that there's a sense in which she is.[10]

Clearly, this passage also illustrates the analogous attempts by Saxon to live up to her name and birthright, in a novel published sixteen years before La Farge's. In order to truly "be herself," Saxon must lay claim to her heritage. She begins by "reconstructing in her vision that folk-migration of her people across the plains" (178), and she uses this vision to allegorize the capital/labor troubles in Oakland as the "Plains" that she and Billy must cross to find their "pleasant valley land" (297). Simple allegory is not enough, however, and the couple must actually recreate their ancestors' journey in order to find themselves. This necessitates camping, learning the sounds of the nonhuman world, plowing and hunting (Billy) and milking (Saxon), purchasing a wagon and horses, and finally locating their Valley of the Moon. The pair even move inland, but are oppressed by the heat and head "west across the wild mountains," exclaiming, "West is best," in echo of their forebears. To find their cultural identity and become themselves, Saxon and Billy must do "authentic" American things. The discrepancy between their actual past and their race's past is "the enabling condition for the appearance of cultural identity as a project, the project of lining up [their] practices with [their] genealogy."[11] The belief that Billy and Saxon have succeeded in the doubling process is reaffirmed when he tells her that "he had a harem, and that she was his second wife—twice as beautiful as the first one he had married" (416). Through the doubling of birth and behavior, Saxon *becomes* not only "herself" but also her name—a fusion of signified and signifier that corresponds with and reaffirms the superimposition of projected and actual selves.

III

But finding a self depends also upon re-creating the actions of others. Thus, as should by now be clear, a self can only be realized in the novel by being mapped onto its ethnic origin. The very term "realization" should warn us, however, that the process is not as simple as London would have us believe. In order to realize a self, the individual must speculate on the eventual union of birth and behavior, which the fates of Bert and Mary demonstrate is by no means guaranteed. Since the notion of autonomous self-hood is an illusion, it remains necessary to consider Saxon and Billy's embroilment in networks wider than the ethnic oneness they seek. In particular, their place in the "entanglement of relations,"[12] which defines the capitalist economy they try to escape, demands closer scrutiny. Unsurprisingly, as in *Burning Daylight*, this wider project of cultural mapping must address the tension between opposing narrative impulses in the text. On the one hand, the naturalism that denies the agency of the individual defines life in the amoral universe of urban capitalism; on the other, the increasingly dominant voice of the sentimental romance promotes the possibility of a private life outside these forces and in contrast to the instabilities of self inherent in urban existence. A brief outline of these respective narrative strands, situating them within the wider cultural field, will enable us to conclude with some observations on the nature of this generic discontinuity.

As we have already seen, in the early chapters of *The Valley of the Moon*, neither Saxon, as principal focalizer, nor the narrator, as commentator on characters and events, holds much hope for individual or collective agency in the city. Saxon's half-brother, Tom, the only active socialist in the novel, is an idealistic and ineffectual dreamer, who would abandon Oakland himself if he were not totally subservient to his wife. His faith in "reasonableness and justice" is juxtaposed to the demonstrable bias the courts show toward corrupt businessmen. While J. Alliston Forbes serves less than two years for massive corporate fraud, the sixteen-year-old Archie Danaker is sentenced to fifty years for stealing a few dollars from a drunk (172–73). Saxon shares the narrator's skepticism, believing that urban conditions reduce men to animals (189) and seeing Tom's "weary, patient look . . . the bent shoulders, the labor-gnarled hands" as symbols of "the futility of his social creed" (185).

It is important to note that there is more than a renunciation of socialism occurring here. The flaws in the logic of much naturalist fiction become apparent in what eventually leads to the generic "triumph" of the sentimental romance in the later stages of the novel. *The Valley of the Moon*, like the majority of London's earlier work, and like Norris's *The Octopus*, Dreiser's *Sister Carrie*, Sinclair's *The Jungle*, and Crane's *Maggie*, represents both the iniquities of turn-of-the-century corporate capitalism and the philosophical belief that nothing can be done to alter the situation. Naturalism's claim to be a catalyst for change is perpetually undermined by its own combination of pessimistic determinism and Social Darwinism, which denies the worth of individual agency. The naturalist self exists in and is created by a world of constant relatedness, without which it would cease to exist, and in which it is constantly driven by a combination of impersonal internal and external forces. Thus, as we have seen, the "characters" of Saxon, Billy, Bert, and Mary are decentered by forces they do not understand or control, which have the power to rob them of themselves. Although individuals are able to express discontent (for example, by comparing their own situation with that of their ancestors), they cannot reconcile their moral indignation to a reconstruction of the preferred social order.

In addition, as a result of its problematic relationship with hegemonic culture—that is, the extent to which its attempt to register dissatisfaction with the market economy is voiced in the language of that economy—naturalism sees no contradiction in embracing both a damning critique of workers' conditions and an appreciation of the goods a consumer culture can provide. The first and second chapters of *The Valley of the Moon* show the ease with which the two attitudes are paired. The novel opens with a Dickensian description of the horrors confronting the "piece-work ironers of fancy starch" (3). Saxon and Mary are distracted when

> the elderly woman brought another interruption. She dropped her iron on the shirtwaist, clutched at the board, fumbled it, caved in at the knees and hips, and like a half-empty sack collapsed on the floor, her long shriek rising

in the pent room to the acrid smell of scorching cloth. The women at the boards near to her scrambled, first, to the hot iron to save the cloth, and then to her, while the forewoman hurried belligerently down the aisle. The women further away continued unsteadily at their work, losing movements to the extent of a minute's set-back to the totality of the efficiency of the fancy-starch room. (4)

Clearly, the passage is designed to illustrate the inequalities of capitalism—the piece-workers are ironing "fancy starch"—and the dehumanizing effects of the work on the worker. Thus, the old woman is successively described as "an entrapped animal" (3), a "half-empty sack," and as "shrieking like a mechanical siren" (4). The other ironers are conditioned to save first the cloth, and they are constantly supervised by a senior employee. Those only emotionally upset by the commotion are obliged to place the Taylorized "efficiency" of their operation, and the financial loss they may cause, above any sympathy they feel for their colleague.

In contrast, the opening of the second chapter, like Dreiser's well-known descriptions of Carrie Meeber in her lace collars and soft new shoes, represents the fulfillment of desires themselves made available by consumer capitalism.[13] At the Bricklayers' picnic

Saxon smiled with appreciation, pointed out her foot, velvet-slippered with high Cuban heels, slightly lifted the tight black skirt, exposing a trim ankle and delicate swell of calf, the white flesh gleaming through the thinnest and flimsiest of fifty-cent black silk stockings. . . . On her white shirtwaist was a pleated jabot of cheap lace, caught with a large novelty pin of imitation coral. Over the shirtwaist was a natty jacket, elbow-sleeved, and to the elbows she wore gloves of imitation suede. The one essentially natural touch about her appearance was the few curls, strangers to curling irons, that escaped from under the little naughty hat of black velvet pulled low over the eyes. (10–11)

Saxon wears these clothes, the products of the culture of consumption, because they allow her to represent—or embody—the desires created in her by the women's magazine advertisements she pins on her wall (7). As Michaels points out in *The Gold Standard*, "capitalism not only provides the objects of fear and desire . . . it provides the subjects as well." Thus, in the same way that Saxon's nervous illness resulted from the forced removal of parts of her identity, her self-satisfaction here is pleasure with the self as a product of market forces. In both cases, selfhood is shaped by the artistic practice of naturalism, which participates in consumer culture's "insatiable appetite for representation."[14]

This insistence on market conditions determining selfhood is at odds with and explains the emergence of the other generic force in the text. Whereas naturalism insists on the constant interrelatedness of subjects and objects— they are all created by the logic of the market—the romance is a space allowing for the "radical autonomy of persons" or what Henry James called "experience disengaged, disembroiled, disencumbered."[15] Thus, where naturalism denies the possibility of mending the rupture between the social and the moral, this act of reparation is at the heart of sentimental fiction. If, in *The Valley of the Moon*, the notions of "radical autonomy" and "experience disengaged" need to be modified in order to include the shift from a self defined by the market to one defined ethnically, then this task must be performed alongside a linking of the family's revised situation with London's reappropriation of sentimental fiction.

Uncle Tom's Cabin (1850) is a text that epitomizes the desire for a certain "indifference to racial difference (the family 'black and white')," which Michaels locates in mid- to late-nineteenth-century literature. Like *The Valley of the Moon*, though with different conclusions, it is concerned with national and familial self-definition, and both books argue for what Winfried Fluck has described (discussing *Uncle Tom's Cabin*) as the ability of "the power of the heart, of natural emotion and moral sentiment, to penetrate to the perception of a moral order—a sentimental epistemology which also has the effect of putting women in the position of superior moral authority."[16] In London's novel, the *combination* of a narrative initially highlighting the futility of the male social (dis)order—the "man-made world" (255) of strikes and riots—but later shifting to a sentimental voice places women in the "position of superior moral authority." It is Saxon who persuades Billy to leave Oakland, and she instigates the reconstruction of the couple's lives. It is also Saxon who initiates the fear about the future of the Anglo-Saxons, echoing Fluck's contention that sentimental fiction is generated by a "profound anxiety about its own moral referent." Saxon and London's race anxiety generates a form able, at least symbolically, to alleviate that anxiety by creating a world in which the social and the moral orders "finally coalesce."[17] In this, the novel confirms formally what we have already seen thematically: the shift transforming the family into the source of racial difference occurs in the genre most fully defined by its faith in the family as the center of all moral values.

In order to illustrate this alignment of the social and the moral, the narrative veers between melodramatic representations of city life—Bert's death, Saxon's miscarriage, Billy's boxing and union injuries—and the possibilities offered by family life. Again, Fluck's reading of *Uncle Tom's Cabin* provides useful insights into the narrative effects of these contrasts. Pointing out that it is the threat of a family breakup—Eliza's fear of separation from her child—that opens Stowe's novel, he asserts that

> the skillful narrative evocation of a fear of a painful separation must be placed within the larger context of a moral order if it is to be effective. If the reader is to be shocked into an awareness of the vulnerability of the moral order, he or she must also be confronted with an image of that which is threatened; in other words, with versions of an intact order that can serve as a norm and countermodel for the staging of its possible breakup.[18]

In *The Valley of the Moon*, the fear and the actuality of separation are juxtaposed to the threatened idyll of family life. Before the industrial turmoil that results in Billy's imprisonment and the loss of the baby, Saxon and Billy's cottage is represented (albeit deceptively) as the site of an "intact order." Although the home is marked by the invasion of market strategies of production and consumption—for example, Saxon secretly exercises in a "systematic way" and reads women's magazines for ideas on preserving her looks (146), thus presenting herself to Billy as a finished product—it is also the site of the happy family. They are vulnerable because of their dependence on wider cultural determinants, but Saxon's repeated visions of her ancestors' lives and her homemaking abilities do create at least a simulacrum of the order that prevailing social conditions forestall. The prime task of the sentimental narrative is to create a place in which the moral and the social can safely correspond. Hence the need to leave the city and search for the Valley of the Moon, and the eventual reconstruction and extension of the "American" family.

The principal difference between *Uncle Tom's Cabin* and *The Valley of the Moon* resides in the opening chapters of London's novel. Whereas Stowe's sentimental design includes the melodramas that threaten the domestic idyll, London incorporates them within the naturalist aesthetic. Fluck points out that Stowe's melodramatic discourse is "designed to act out a terrible suspicion . . . the impression must grow that the incessant violations of the moral order are committed without due punishment and proper moral retribution." Within the melodrama, the existence of the moral order is called into question, and the "fear that it evokes is that the characters with which the reader sympathizes might have been left alone . . . in a hostile universe." Only at the last minute, once these effects have been maximized, does religious reassurance arrive.[19] In the secular world of naturalism, this fear cannot be removed through divine intervention, since the universe is indeed proved to be either hostile or indifferent. Life in the city offers no opportunity for Saxon to rediscover her belief in God. Instead, at the moment of her greatest despair, knee-deep in water and surrounded by rats (261), she is rescued by a young boy advocating the "freedom and motion" of his boat. Unable to visualize a God capable of permitting such urban degradation, London updates the sentimental narrative and reconstructs it around the process of self-realization. Instead of God and Little Eva, he introduces a "small, bright-painted and half-decked skiff" (261) and a boy called "Jack," who, like a secular Eva (or maybe Huck Finn), offers an example of an idealized alternative to everyday experience.

IV

In *The Valley of the Moon*, London thus attempts a fusion of form and content via a move away from both naturalism and socialism. The first is replaced by the sentimental narrative of self-realization; the second is replaced as an ideal condition by the happy family. I have already demonstrated one way in which the project of self-realization is undermined. To conclude, I will show how even this perceived escape from the determining tendencies of the culture of consumption is threatened.

At the most superficial level, London never answers the question of why Saxon and Billy should be free of market conditions simply because they leave the city. They go into business as market gardeners, and Billy lands a contract hauling for the local brickyard, but as Charles N. Watson, Jr., has pointed out, "one cannot but wonder how soon his enterprise will succumb to the economic chaos he has struggled to escape."[20] Paradoxically, will is expected to triumph over economic reality in the Valley of the Moon, though it was unable to do so in Oakland.

One potential solution to this dilemma again depends on London's abandonment of socialism as a viable counter to inequality. Whereas in *The Iron Heel* and *Martin Eden*, London emphasizes the interconnectedness of leisure and toil—for instance, during Martin Eden's spell in the hotel laundry—in *The Valley of the Moon*, they are increasingly depicted as alternatives. Earlier I suggested that London's portrayal of the woman collapsing in front of Saxon and Mary was "Dickensian." His rhapsodic treatment of the middle-class world of private life is equally so, depending as it does on the contrast between it and the proletarian world it surrounds. In an analysis of *Oliver Twist*, D. A. Miller argues, "Much as delinquency is circumscribed by middle-class private life, the indignation to which delinquency gives rise is bounded by gratitude for the class habits and securities that make indignation possible."[21] The same process operates in *The Valley of the Moon*. Not only do Saxon and Billy look back on the horrors of the city, they do so in a manner that valorizes the "beauty and charm" of the "middle-class home" (339) and suggests that this is a place of safety, beyond the economic cycle. This seems to be a kind of anti-naturalist proletarianization in reverse, in which, rather than slipping Hurstwood-style into the realms of determinism, the working class escapes into the world of free will. Thus, Billy and Saxon are able to feel secure in their new home because they own property and Billy has "become a man of affairs" (512).

To express the transformation this way reminds us that, rather than escaping the market, the Robertses have started to "use their heads" (499) and become employers instead of laborers. They adopt the middle-class values of their new neighbors and disguise an ideological stance as a "natural" way of life. The plan to live on "Easy Street" (528) means that they must become the very capitalists they opposed in Oakland, marketing the clay they discover on their land, mortgaging, and borrowing (527–28). From this point of view, Saxon and Billy gain freedom from determinism not because they "become" themselves or Anglo-Saxons; rather, they assume the privileges of the middle classes.

From the perspective of early-twentieth-century consumer society, this discrepancy assumes its own logic as a conflict. The tension in the closing stages of the novel between the desire to attain self-realization and the necessity of matching oneself to a standard to achieve this—whether the standard is Anglo-Saxon or middle-class behavior—is actually a *product* of the double bind of the culture of consumption. On the one hand, Saxon needs to recover "herself" from an economy that defines her in terms of, for example, the clothes she wears, a process requiring a reflex produced by her culture; on the other, the only way she can do this is by reducing ethnicity to its constituent parts, which are subsequently mastered by Saxon and Billy in a kind of ethno-Taylorization process. In an examination of Henry James's *The American*, Mark Seltzer finds a similar conflict between "standardization and self-aggrandizement," and he suggests that "in *The American* at least this conflict takes the form of a double discourse, a sort of double-entry bookkeeping, in which one hand writes standards and statistics even as the other continues to write a romance of self-possession and self-identity." As we have seen, *The Valley of the Moon* employs a "double discourse" for the same reasons. To become what she desires, Saxon absorbs and reproduces the "standards and statistics" of race and, when she has acquired land, of the new farming methods. Like James's Christopher Newman, her identity depends on representation, and "identity is guaranteed by the imperative of resembling oneself, as a copy repeats an original."[22] However, like James, London also writes self-identification in terms of a "romance of self-possession." This doubling process makes *The Valley of the Moon* one of London's least effective attempts to posit an alternative to hegemonic capitalism. Both in its overt embrace of bourgeois values, and in its attempt to escape these values via a construction of self and "Americanness" in terms of ethnicity, the novel depends upon a discourse of auto-Taylorization. Either way, self-realization is redesigned as a project of standardization in which "individuality" is systematically managed, by means of the procedures of the production line, into a reproduction of an original.

"Zone-Conquerors" and "White Devils"

The Contradictions of Race in the Works of Jack London

ANDREW J. FURER

"A symposium on Anglo-Saxon supremacy!" exclaims Frona Welse, in Jack London's first novel, expecting to find her views affirmed by her fellow "zone-conquerors," London's term for what he saw as the Anglo-Saxon's tendency to conquer the peoples of the various climatic "zones"—the Arctic, the tropics:

> We are a race of doers and fighters, of globe-encirclers and zone-conquerors. We toil and struggle . . . no matter how hopeless it may be. . . . Will the In-dian, the Negro, or the Mongol ever conquer the Teuton? Surely not! The In-dian has persistence without variability; if he does not modify he dies, if he does try to modify he dies anyway. The Negro has adaptability, but he is servile and must be led. As for the Chinese, they are permanent. All that the other races are not, the Anglo-Saxon, or Teuton if you please, is. All that the other races have not, the Teuton has. What race is to rise up and overwhelm us?[1]

Although Frona seems an unwavering champion of white supremacy, her creator's views of this question are far from constant. In several of Lon-don's Pacific tales, for example, he valorizes Chinese and Hawaiian ances-try: Ah Chun "perceived little details that not one man in a thousand ever noticed. . . . He did not . . . figure in politics, nor play at revolutions, but he forecast events more clearly than the men who engineered them. . . . Ah Chun was a power. . . . [He] was a moral paragon and an honest business man."[2] Stephen Knight, "athlete, . . . [was] a bronzed god of the sea . . . [with] a quarter-strain of tropic sunshine in his veins. . . . [Dorothy Sambrooke] . . .

pleasur[ed] in the memory of the grace of his magnificent body, of his splendid shoulders, of the power in him."[3]

Much of London's writing deals with conflicts between the individual and the collective, and his views of race constitute a substantial part of the drama of such struggles. London is unquestionably attracted to ideals of white superiority; he created a series of Anglo-Saxon supermen, such as Wolf Larsen of *The Sea-Wolf. Martin Eden*—one of the few of London's 50 books that his publisher, Macmillan, kept in print for most of the twentieth century—contains several passages of blatantly anti-Semitic material.[4] From one perspective, such racist views could be construed as a response to social and biographical pressures. London was six years old when the first Chinese Exclusion Act was passed, in response to Californians' fears of having to compete in a depressed job market with thousands of Chinese laborers; he was in his mid-twenties when the Exclusion Act was indefinitely extended. Biographer Andrew Sinclair notes that London's mother told her son that he was from a distinguished American family, that he was "better than the Irish and Italians and other people who had recently come to the United States," and that he had "a birthright which he must defend from them."[5]

London, however, frequently subverts those views in works such as "Chun Ah Chun," "Koolau the Leper" (1909/1912), and "The Mexican" (1911/1913). These works and other similarly antiracist pieces, a significant part of his later work, have been overshadowed by his widely anthologized Alaskan fiction and such well-known novels as *The Call of the Wild, The Sea-Wolf,* and *Martin Eden.* As a result, the richness and complexity of this powerful and prolific author have yet to be fully recognized, especially in regard to his racial views.[6] London overcomes his pro-Anglo-Saxon bias only where the environment is less harsh and, more important, wherever he finds or creates non-white protagonists of superb courage and power. Their exceptional qualities—whether of body, mind, or spirit—allow the author, without anxiety, to elevate the so-called inferior races (what he elsewhere calls "mongrels" or "scrubs") to a cultural position equal to or even superior to that of whites. London introduces a "man [or woman] on horseback" who is not a "blond beast."

Critics, both favorably and unfavorably inclined toward London, have found his views on ethnicity to be essentially racist. Among writers with a negative view of London, William E. Cain is especially harsh. In a review of London's collected letters, Cain notes London's "contempt for black, brown and Jewish people" and "his reiterated racist . . . ballyhoo" and asserts that "it would be misleading . . . to imply that in his fictional and nonfictional

work London overcomes the disfiguring ideas that he espouses in his letters."[7] In his recent book, *Bodies and Machines* (1992), the New Historicist
Mark Seltzer remarks upon "the terroristic . . . racial violence" in London's
stories of "the great white . . . North."[8]

Even such sympathetic London scholars as Earle Labor, Charles N. Watson, Jr., and Susan Nuernberg acknowledge the powerful appeal that racism
had for him, noting that he reflected racial views then highly popular, such
as those of Benjamin Kidd.[9] Labor emphasizes "the sad historical fact . . .
that many of the leading 'scientific' thinkers of [London's] age embraced various doctrines of white supremacy and that millions of decent Americans
bought books which blatantly preached 'racial egotism' and taught their
readers to 'despise the lesser breeds.'"[10] Watson states that "notions of Anglo-Saxon supremacy were in their heyday, and London's fiction often reflected—and perhaps contributed to—their advance."[11] Nuernberg concurs
in this view, adding that at the time, America needed to justify its imperialist policies.[12] Most London scholars interested in this issue also are careful
to point out instances of antiracism in his work, noting that his views in this
area, as in so many others, are "a bundle of contradictions" (Labor, "London's Pacific World," 214). However, there have as yet been few attempts to
link his paradoxical views of Anglo-Saxon superiority, miscegenation, and
the non-white races.

Before discussing the ways London's antiracist works powerfully val-
orize the non-white races and ridicule ideas of white supremacy and racial
"purity," I must first comment briefly on several works in which he seems
most deeply invested in his Anglo-Saxon supremacist views, so we can understand the strong appeal that white supremacy held for him. In *A Daughter of the Snows*, he has Frona and other characters sing frequently the praise
of the Anglo-Saxon. Frona gives the lengthy lecture, "We are a race of doers
and fighters . . . "; Captain Alexander proclaims that "the white man is the
greatest and best breed in the world" (85). Frona's suitor, Vance Corliss, exclaims, "These battlers of frost and fighters of hunger! I can understand how
the dominant races have come down out of the north to empire. Strong to
venture, strong to endure, with infinite faith and infinite patience, is it to be
wondered at?" (146).

He and Frona then take turns reciting verses from Norse sagas: London
calls her a "furred Valkyrie" (ironically, Frona is of Celtic origin). Corliss,
London writes, feels "strangely at one with the white-skinned, yellow-haired
giants of the younger world" (148) and sees the "sea-flung Northmen, great-
muscled, deep-chested, sprung from the elements, men of sword and sweep,

marauders and scourgers of the warm southlands! The din of twenty centuries of battle was roaring in his ear, and the clamor for return to type strong
upon him" (148). Here we see one of the main appeals for London of Anglo-
Saxon supremacist ideology: a positive form of atavism, a clean and pure reversion to type. A return to the life of such "sea-flung Northmen" is very different from the brutish, degrading, criminal, or diseased kinds of atavism
he portrays in *Before Adam* (1906) or "When the World Was Young"
(1910/1913)—the protagonist of the later story, though the author describes
him as an "early Teuton," behaves more like a caveman.[13] The degraded type
of atavism is a common obsession among naturalists; Frank Norris, for example, wrote two novels, *Vandover and the Brute* (1914) and *McTeague* (1899),
about such degeneration.[14] In *A Daughter of the Snows*, London champions
an Anglo-Saxon supremacy based on a strife-filled heritage. He nonetheless
represents the race not only as the "smiter and destroyer" of the ancient world
but also as its "builder and law-giver" (147), morally superior to other races,
untainted by deception and deviousness, doing its sins "openly, in the clear
sight of God" (201). Its origins are also free of the taint of urban civilization,
since the race comes from the sparsely populated North: "This is the world,
and we know of fact that there are very few people in it, else there could
not be so much ice and sea and sky" (261).[15] Celebrating the Anglo-Saxon
gives London a way to bless the lower forces—the "brute"—in the human
being, rather than condemn them.

In this view, he departs from the evolutionary theory of one of his men-
tors, Herbert Spencer: "out of the lower stages of civilisation higher ones can
emerge, only as there diminishes [the] pursuit of . . . revenge and re-revenge
which the code we inherit from the savage insists on."[16] Spencerian social
evolution "incorporates the concept of definite stages; progress is from the
'militant' to the 'industrial' type of society."[17] The same year that London
published *A Daughter of the Snows*, Spencer stigmatized contemporary mil-
itaristic sentiments as signs of degeneration and "re-barbarisation"; he sees
an unfortunate atavistic return of "barbaric . . . ideas and sentiments, and
an unceasing culture of blood-thirst."[18] London, however, at least in his first
novel, finds that under certain harsh conditions (such as those obtaining
in the Arctic), the recrudescence of Anglo-Saxon "barbaric" traits is a desirable phenomenon.

Even in this work, one of the most racist of London's novels, there are
signs of antiracism. Gregory St. Vincent, who initially "correspond[s] well
to [Frona's] idealized natural man and favorite racial type" (133), turns out
to be a liar and a moral and physical coward. Furthermore, one Indian char-

acter wonders to herself "that the accident of white skin or swart made master or servant as the case may be" (191). There are at least the beginnings here
of a dialogue about simplistic assumptions of racial superiority.

London's late novel *The Mutiny of the Elsinore* includes another such instance of antiracist material in an otherwise virulently racist work, a hint at
thin spots in the armor of Anglo-Saxonism. *Elsinore*'s narrator repeatedly
trumpets the glories of the blond races: "Yes, I am a perishing blond . . . ,
and I sit in the high place and bend the stupid ones to my will; and I am a
lover, loving a royal woman of my own . . . breed, and together we occupy,
and shall occupy, the high place of government and command until our kind
perishes from the earth."[19]

Alongside such passages, however, the novel features episodes depicting
an extremely courageous and capable non-white character. Initially a servant, he is later shown to be a master of men, at least in combat. The narrator, in the midst of a fierce battle with the mutineers, suddenly sees his
Japanese valet, Wada, "charg[e] like a buffalo, jab [a mutineer] . . . in the
chest with the spear he had made and thrust [the mutineer] . . . back and
down" (*Elsinore*, 339). Despite the narrator's representation of him as merely
a servant, Wada emerges as a figure of power, as effective in battle as any
white man aboard the *Elsinore*.

Just as there are hints of egalitarian views in some of London's more
racist works, there are also several places, especially in his journalism, where
he praises a non-white race yet reveals an anxious xenophobia. In much of
his war and personal correspondence on the Russo-Japanese War, and in articles such as "The Yellow Peril" (September 25, 1904), written later on similar topics, London praises the Japanese highly: "as to the quietness, strict-
ness and orderliness of Japanese soldiers it is very hard to find any equals
in the world."[20] Furthermore, he states, they are "a race of warriors and their
infantry is all that infantry could possibly be."[21] Comments such as these,
however, eventually lead to fear and disquietude: "The Japanese are so made
that nothing short of annihilation can stop them," he writes while watching
their successful attack on the Russians at Antung, their men "streaming
darkly" to the attack. Later that day, London sees some Russian prisoners:

> I caught myself gasping. A choking sensation was in my throat. . . . I found
> myself suddenly and sharply aware that I was an alien amongst these brown
> men who peered through the window with me. And I felt myself strangely at
> one with those other men behind the window—felt that my place was there
> inside with them in their captivity, rather than outside in freedom amongst
> aliens.[22]

He also praises the Chinese for being as adept economically as the Japanese are militarily. The threat of efficiency and overwhelming numbers represented by the cooperation of the two races makes him anxious:

> Four hundred million indefatigable workers (deft, intelligent, and unafraid to die), aroused and rejuvenescent, managed and guided by forty-five million additional human beings who are splendid fighting animals, scientific and modern, constitute that menace to the Western world which has been well named the "Yellow Peril."[23]

Although he admires these two races, en masse they frighten him. Their valorization of the collectivity and devaluation of the individual seems both inhuman and immoral to him. He declares, "The Japanese is not an individualist. He has developed national consciousness instead of moral consciousness. . . . The honor of the individual, per se, does not exist. . . . Spiritual agonizing is unknown to him" ("Yellow Peril," 349). Joan London, in her biography of her father, notes that upon his return to San Francisco from the war, his socialist comrades had to listen to him curse "the entire yellow race in the most outrageous terms" and declare that "I am first of all a white man and only then a Socialist."[24]

The fear of the horde (vigorously painted in chapter 23 of *The Iron Heel* in general terms and in "The Unparalleled Invasion" [1910/1914] in specifically anti-Asian terms) is a powerful one. In his short story collection *The House of Pride*, however, fear of the Yellow Peril almost entirely disappears. When London gives Asian and other non-white characters individuality accompanied by exceptional ability, his anxiety dissolves into admiration, and he begins to see numerous ways in which people of color are superior to Anglo-Saxons. Indeed, in contrast to the racial views in his journalism and in such fictions as *A Daughter of the Snows*, the title, *The House of Pride*, alone is provocative: the title story illustrates the pernicious pride and racism of a white character, but the only justified and morally correct pride expressed in all these stories is that of Polynesians, mixed breeds, and Asians.

Chun Ah Chun is one of those who has much to be proud of—he is a philosopher merchant-king, who arrived in Hawaii as a mere peasant: "He was essentially a philosopher, and whether as coolie, or multi-millionaire and master of many men, his poise of soul was the same" ("Chun Ah Chun," 152). In his daily life, he solves "problems such as are given to few men to consider" (153). Ah Chun is a Chinese Cowperwood or Rockefeller, but with none of the character flaws of these fictional and nonfictional titans of finance. After only three years working on a sugar plantation, Ah Chun starts his own business, having discovered, as had London early in life, "that men did not become rich from the labor of their own hands" (154). Ah Chun then goes into the labor-importing business and many others, amassing a fortune. He is a man of great vision, imagining Honolulu as a modern city with electricity while it was still a primitive sand-blasted settlement set on a coral reef.

His career totally refutes Frona's contention that the Chinese are unable to adapt to new conditions. Further, Ah Chun eventually comes to preside over "an atmosphere of culture and refinement second to none in all the islands" (169). No one in Hawaii is too proud to visit him. Later, when he leaves Hawaii to retire to his native land, first landing at Macao, Ah Chun encounters racism at the finest hotel there—the clerk tells him that Chinese are not permitted, and the manager scornfully insults him. He leaves and then returns after two hours, having bought the hotel. During the months following, he increases the hotel's earnings from 3 percent to 30 percent, meriting a description that London elsewhere (see, for example, "The Inevitable White Man" [1910/1911]) reserves for the white race: he is "inevitable," a man of power and mastery, not unlike many of London's dominant Anglo-Saxon protagonists, such as Wolf Larsen or Martin Eden: "Chun Ah Chun had long exercised the power of a king" (186).

This story includes not only a non-white master of men but also a description of the benefits of miscegenation, a practice London criticized harshly in his Mexican War correspondence, among other places.[25] Ah Chun marries a woman who is part Anglo-Saxon and part Polynesian, with the former predominating. They produce fifteen sons and daughters, among whom, the author writes, "the blend of races was excellent" (161). These offspring are very beautiful, precisely because of their mixed blood. Their father "had furnished the groundwork upon which had been traced the blended pattern of the races. He had furnished the slim-boned Chinese frame, upon which had been builded the delicacies and subtleties of Saxon, Latin, and Polynesian flesh" (162). They are also intelligent and well educated: one son goes to Harvard and Oxford, two others go to Yale, and the girls go to Mills, Vassar, Wellesley, and Bryn Mawr. It is true that his high-spirited family causes him many problems, but they are still exceptional progeny. Further, London uses them to show that white society's adherence to ideals of racial purity is itself impure and up for sale. When Ah Chun has trouble marrying his daughters to highly placed whites, he begins to give his daughters large dowries: "That will fetch that Captain Higginson and his high family along with him" (179), he says. Suddenly, his daughters are regarded as eligible.

This is not the only story in which London praises the fruits of miscegenation. In "The Seed of McCoy" (1909/1911) a descendant of the *Bounty* mutineers and Pitcairn Islanders saves a ship with a cargo of burning wheat and pacifies its frantic and mutinous crew through his Christlike calm and mastery of seamanship. McCoy, great-grandson of the McCoy of the *Bounty*, replies to an aggressive inquiry into his identity by stating, " 'I am the chief magistrate,' . . . in a voice that was still the softest and gentlest imaginable."[26] The captain and the mate of the burning ship, the *Pyrenees*, initially judge McCoy by his shabby clothes: "that this barefooted beachcomber could possess any such high-sounding dignity was inconceivable" ("The Seed of McCoy," 265). They soon find, however, that this mixed-breed is able to ease the fears of the crew and revive their weary souls. "[McCoy's] smile was a caress, an embrace that surrounded the tired mate and sought to draw him into the quietude and rest of McCoy's tranquil soul" (264). Later, when the crew seems ready to mutiny because of the ship's delayed landfall, "their faces convulsed and animal-like with rage" (270), McCoy's presence, "the surety and calm that seemed to radiate from him, . . . had its effect" (274): "His personality spoke more eloquently than any word he could utter. It was an alchemy of soul . . . profoundly deep—a mysterious emanation of the spirit, seductive, sweetly humble, and terribly imperious. It was illumination in the dark crypts of their souls, a compulsion of purity and gentleness vastly greater than that which resided in the shining, death-spitting revolvers of the officers" (307). Ironically, McCoy is the product of a clash between white men and Tahitians. The whites, McCoy says, were "terrible men . . . they were very wicked. God had hidden His face from them" (310). The Tahitians' response to these men was little better: "The mutineers . . . killed all of the native men. The [native] women helped. And the natives killed each other. Everybody killed everybody" (310). Yet the mixing of the blood of these two races produces the Christlike McCoy. In this story, London allows that while racial strife brings out the worst in humanity, miscegenation can bring out the best.

It is likely that London's views of the benefits of hybridization, as expressed in many of the *House of Pride* stories, were influenced by his friendship with horticulturalist and philosopher Luther Burbank. In June 1906, Burbank wrote to London:

> The splendid book "White Fang" received and I thank you *most* heartily for this esteemed token of your friendship. We shall all enjoy reading it very much and if it is as good or better than the "Call of the Wild" and some others that you have given us it will have great educational value to say nothing of its value

as a most absorbing story. We will tap it this evening and if I don't get up for breakfast tomorrow morning it will be your fault I am sure. Here goes my best wishes for you and Charmian for a prosperous and happy voyage.[27]

According to Ken Kraft and Pat Kraft, London, a "repeat visitor" to Burbank's ranch, "loyally planted Burbank cactus on his ranch for stock feed, in the teeth of warnings from University of California agricultural experts."[28] London's biographer Clarice Stasz, in addition to remarking upon London and Burbank's friendship, notes the resemblance of Darrell Standing, the "agriculturist" protagonist of London's science fiction novel, *The Star Rover*, to Burbank. In *The Training of the Human Plant* (1907), written during the year that he first met London, Burbank emphasizes "the opportunity now presented in the United States for observing and, if we are wise, aiding in what I think it is fair to say is the grandest opportunity ever presented of developing the finest race the world has ever known out of the mingling of races brought here by immigration."[29] He also claims that "by the crossings of types, strength . . . intellectuality . . . [and] moral force" have "been secured" (12). Another passage from Burbank suggests an additional source of hybridization's attraction for London:

> Just as the plant breeder . . . notices sudden changes and breaks . . . when he joins two or more plants of diverse type from widely separated quarters of the globe,—sometimes merging [a] . . . wild strain with one that, long *over-civilized, has largely lost virility,*—and just as he finds among the descendants a plant which is likely to be stronger and better than either ancestor, so may we notice constant breaks and changes and modifications going on about us in this vast combination of races, and so may we hope for a far stronger and better race . . . a magnificent race, far superior to any preceding it. (9, emphasis added)

In Burbank's account, hybridization can be the basis for biological social reform, a kind of racial therapy to rid *fin de siècle* Americans of "over-civilization." In "Chun Ah Chun," London champions a Chinese titan of finance, but he also, as noted above, praises the great beauty and ability of Ah Chun's children, who are "one thirty-second Polynesian, one-sixteenth Italian, one-sixteenth Portuguese, one-half Chinese, and eleven thirty-seconds English" (160).

London was writing about the benefits of interbreeding, however, even before he met Burbank. In "The Story of Jees Uck" (1902/1904), the protagonist of which is an Alaskan "mixed-breed," London states, "What with the vagrant blood in her and the heritage compounded of many races, Jees Uck developed a wonderful young beauty."[30] In addition, she displays a capacity for decisive and powerful action; seeing Amos, the man who has tried to poison her husband, Neil Bonner, she "spring[s] like a tigress upon Amos and with splendid suppleness and strength bend[s] his body back across her knee" ("Jees Uck," 257). London represents her as a counterirritant to the jaded Anglo-Saxon race: she constitutes "an immeasurable sum of pleasurable surprise to the overcivilized man that had . . . [caught] her up. . . . In Jees Uck he found the youth of the world—the youth and the strength and the joy" (262–63).

London also found people of superb strength and endurance among the natives of Hawaii. "Koolau the Leper," in the same collection as "Chun Ah Chun," provides a capable non-white character who achieves personal triumph in the face of overwhelming odds and a significant disability, while poignantly illustrating the evils that whites had brought into the South Seas. The story begins with Koolau detailing the whites' injustice to the Polynesian lepers. He says to his followers, "Because we are sick they take away our liberty. We have obeyed the law. We have done no wrong. And yet they would put us in prison. Molokai is a prison. . . . It is the will of the white men who rule the land. . . . They came like lambs, speaking softly. . . . To-day all the islands are theirs."[31] Here London casts a negative light on Roosevelt's ideal of "speaking softly and carrying a big stick." Koolau and his people are thrice-wronged, as Kapalei, a former jurist, who is now "a hunted rat" (56), indicates:

> The sickness is not ours. We have not sinned. The [white] men who preached the word of God and the word of Rum brought the sickness with the coolie slaves who work the stolen land. I have been a judge. I know the law and the justice, and I say to you it is unjust to steal a man's land, to make that man sick with the Chinese sickness, and then to put that man in prison for life. (57)

London emphasizes the moral superiority of the Polynesians by giving this speech to a man of high rank and great insight who has been brought low by the greed, hypocrisy, and arrogant callousness of Anglo-Saxon invaders.

Earle Labor, in his essay "Jack London's Pacific World," sees this story as "representative of London's attitude toward the underdog" (211), but although Koolau and his people are undoubtedly persecuted, Koolau, despite his deformity, is a figure of mastery and power. He had been a "lusty, whole-bodied youth" (90), and now, an expert marksman, he feels "a . . . prod of pride" because more than 100 men, London writes, "with war guns and rifles, police and soldiers . . . came for him, and he was only one man, a crippled wreck of a man at that. They offered a thousand dollars for him, dead or alive" (78). As Labor states, "He is indomitable spiritually—a . . . magnificent rebel" (211). Koolau holds a mountain passage against the soldiers for two days, then during a parley, he announces with pride and dignity: "I am a free man. . . . I have done no wrong. All I ask is to be left alone. I have lived free, and I shall die free. I will never give myself up" ("Koolau," 86). The soldiers pursue him for six weeks, but his "sure rifle" and his wilderness abilities frustrate their efforts, so they abandon the attempt and leave the Kalalau Valley to him. Ironically, he thus regains some of the stolen lands, and lives for two more years.

James I. McClintock states that Koolau "salvages his individual dignity but dies according to 'the law' enforced by whites."[32] The ending of the story, however, seems to undermine this interpretation. As Koolau lies dying of his disease, having escaped the white "law" in the Kalalau Valley, he recalls his youth and his mastery over nature, and, London writes, "his last thought is of his Mauser, and he pressed it against his chest with his folded, fingerless hands" ("Koolau," 91). His last act is that of a warrior. It is true that his people have deserted him, but this shows that—in London's view—in spite of a dark skin, and a disease seemingly emblematic of degeneration, Koolau overcomes the Nietzschean "man on horseback," whose virtues are beyond race.

In 1908, while recuperating in Australia from bowel surgery and malaria, which had caused him to give up his *Snark* voyage, London accepted an assignment from the *New York Herald* to cover the world championship heavyweight bout between Tommy Burns and Jack Johnson. Early in his article on the fight, London argues for race solidarity, seeming to align himself with the dominant racial politics of the day, which assumed that white would and should cleave to white, black to black, and so on: "Personally I was with Burns all the way. He was a white man, and so am I. Naturally I wanted to see the white man win. Put the case to Johnson and ask him if he were the spectator at a fight between a white man and a black man which he would like to see win. Johnson's black skin will dictate a desire parallel to the one dictated by my white skin."[33] London goes on, however, to give Johnson his due: "Because a white man wishes a white man to win, this should not prevent him from giving absolute credit to the best man, even when that best man was black. All hail to Johnson" (146). Despite feelings of racial solidarity, London does not stint his praise for Johnson: "What . . . [won] on Saturday was bigness, coolness, quickness, cleverness, and vast physical superiority" (146). Racial stereotypes are absent from London's presentation of a "superior mind in a superior body" figure that he so admires, one who in this case happens to be black.[34] Indeed, given his portrait of the "inevitable white man" in other texts, the language London uses to compare Burns and Johnson is striking.

The fight, he says, "had all the seeming of a playful Ethiopian at loggerheads with a small and futile white man, of a grown man cuffing a naughty child, of a monologue by one Johnson, who made noise with his fist like a lullaby, tucking one Burns into his little crib in Sleepy Hollow" (147).[35] In London's account, the only thing Johnson does wrong is that he does not knock Burns out when he has the chance.[36] The author, for all his early protestations about identifying with the white man here, seems in his egotism to identify with Johnson, who is clearly an exceptional individual and a master of men. Johnson was "superb. He was impregnable . . . as inaccessible as Mont Blanc" (148), a rather ironic simile. An August 18, 1911, interview in the *Medford Sun* bears the headline, "Prefers Jack Johnson's belt to the Crown of King George; Jack London Admires Fighters." The piece quotes London as declaring, "I would rather be heavyweight champion of the world . . . than King of England, or President of the United States, or Kaiser of Germany."[37]

London also covered Johnson's fight against James Jeffries, "the Great White Hope." The racial issues at this Reno fight were even more explicit than in the Burns contest. As Richard Bankes says, the promoter Tex Rickard advertised the fight as "the ultimate test of racial superiority" (*Stories of Boxing*, 151). As a result, several hundred men roamed the streets of Reno, threatening to kill Johnson if he won. Interestingly, in London's early articles on the fight (he was to write one each day for the ten days preceding the fight, as well as an article about the fight itself), he inverts the era's stereotypical opposition of civilized white man and savage black man—he declared that Johnson's abilities were those of a scientific boxer while Jeffries' were those of a primitive fighter: "Jeff is a fighter, Johnson is a boxer. Jeff has the temperament of a fighter. Old mother nature in him is still red of fang and claw. He is more a Germanic tribesman and warrior of two thousand years ago than a civilized man of the twentieth century" ("No. 2" [June 24, 1910], 157).[38] Johnson also appears to be more sophisticated intellectually than Jeffries. The latter is a silent fighter; on the other hand, Johnson displays "genuine wit, keen-cutting and laughter provoking" ("No. 5" [June 27, 1910], 165). He reveals "positive genius" in placing his blows during a fight. Like London's other supermen—Ernest Everhard and Martin Eden, for example—Johnson combines a powerful, creative mind and a superb body.[39] If Martin is laborer as artist and intellectual, Johnson is boxer as artist and intellectual: "[Johnson] is a marvel of sensitiveness, sensibility and perceptibility. He has a perfect mechanism of mind and body. His mind works like chain lightning and his body obeys with equal swiftness" ("Jeffries-Johnson Fight" [July 4, 1910], 182).

It is not only among Asians, Polynesians, and blacks that London discovers masters, but among the "breeds" (as he calls them) of Mexico as well. In "The Mexican," Felipe Rivera has the spiritual indomitability and the physiological power of London's Anglo-Saxon heroes: he has a "deep chest," tough-fibered flesh, an "instantaneousness of the cell explosions of the muscles, [and] . . . fineness of the nerves that wired every part of him into a splendid fighting mechanism."[40] Furthermore, London is careful to note that "Indian blood, as well as Spanish, was in his veins" (261). Rivera, like Koolau, is a tragic figure—a sympathetic fellow revolutionist says, "He hates all people. . . . He is alone . . . lonely" (251). Nonetheless, he is admirable both in his strength and his ideals: he is a boxer who fights for money to help fund a socialist revolution in Mexico. Those in his revolutionary cell, the Junta, are unaware of how Rivera gets money to bring them, but they are well aware of his force and dedication: "To me he is power—he is the wild wolf,—the striking rattlesnake," says one. To another, "He is the Revolution incarnate. . . . He is the flame and spirit of it, the insatiable cry for vengeance" (251).

McClintock states that Rivera is "that mysterious, inevitable, telic power that goes beyond intellectual commitment, even beyond patriotic emotion" (*White Logic*, 129). Unlike the whites in the fight game, he boxes not just for money, but for a glorious ideal and for the welfare of others. London states, "Danny Ward fought for money, and for the easy ways of life that money would bring. But the things Rivera fought for burned in his brain" (269). This, along with his exceptional muscular powers, makes him triumphant. Although he has an often unprepossessing exterior, he displays the melding of superior spirit and superior body, which London so worships in his Anglo-Saxon heroes—Elam Harnish, for example.[41]

In Rivera's ultimate fight—upon which depend $5,000 and the guns necessary to start the revolution—he finds that "all Gringos were against him, even the referee" (278), who counts long seconds when his opponent is down and short seconds when Rivera is. Through his strength and quick intelligence and his keen senses ("Rivera's ears were a cat's, desert-trained"), however, he triumphs over the whites' conspiracy of unfairness. (London refers to Rivera's handlers, who are white strangers, as "scrubs," a phrase he uses elsewhere as a derogatory term for mixed breeds.) Although his opponent is "the coming champion" and is helped by "the many ways of cheating in this game of the Gringos" (289), such as muttering vile racist insults to Rivera during the fight, Rivera is something much more, an "Übermensch": although only a boy of eighteen, "he had gone through such vastly greater heats that this collective passion of ten thousand throats, rising surge on surge, was to his brain no more than the velvet cool of a summer twilight" (288). Furthermore, like Ernest Everhard in *The Iron Heel*, he is a superman who is nonetheless devoted to the cause of the masses: "resplendent and glorious, [Rivera] saw the great, red Revolution sweeping across his land. . . . He was the guns. He was the Revolution. He fought for all Mexico" (282). After he has won the bout, "the Revolution could go on" (290). The skinny, dark mixed-breed is a far cry from the "blond beasts" of much of London's power-worshiping fiction, but this superior individual fighting for the people combines the two attributes London valued most: individual mastery and dedication to the socialist cause.

London's attraction to supermen and women of his own race is widely known. As I have tried to show here, however, he recognizes that exceptional individuals exist among other races, and he champions such figures as well. Indeed, his final, unfinished novel, *Cherry*, displays one of the most accomplished of his female characters, a young Japanese woman who combines the best of her Asian heritage with an excellent Western upbringing. She is "a finished creation of many a million years, a jewel of the quick, a selected culmination, a last biological and aesthetic word of womanhood" (1).[42] Cherry is also a born linguist and a scholar: "only a scholar could trip her while at the same time running the equal risk of being tripped by her" (14). Although London seems to use her to argue against miscegenation, and to make a case for racial purity as the way for each culture to produce its best citizens, the fact that intellectually and culturally she is a product of Hawaii's polyglot society subverts this view.

London's sympathy for the underdog is well known. Nonetheless, it is precisely his admiration for the spiritual and physical power to be found among those whom popular opinion of his day held to be inferior that persists through all the contradictions of his racial views. Many of these supermen and superwomen tend to emphasize, in their distinction, the benefits of self-culture and argue for a model of success that emphasizes differentiation rather than subordination to the greater social good. Characteristically, London often ignored such implications of his own views and valorized the collective over the individual. In 1916, London wrote to resign from the Socialist Party, claiming that it had lost its revolutionary fire. In this letter, in perhaps his final words on the race issue, questions of power and courage are inextricably linked to those of race and class: "If races and classes cannot rise up and by their own strength of brain and brawn, wrest from the world liberty, freedom and independence, they never in time can come to these royal possessions."[43]

Political Leprosy

Jack London the 'Kama'āina' and Koolau the Hawaiian

JAMES SLAGEL

When we teach English as a subject, we teach literature and language, often politics, and occasionally the politics of language and literature. Sometimes politics forces its way into apparently innocuous discussions. Such a passage of playful banter turned powerful political statement is a brief exchange between Charmian and Jack London as they lounged side by side during their second day in Hawaii, a conversation she initiated and then recorded in *Jack London and Hawaii*:

> "You are a *malihini*—did you know that?"
> "No, and I don't know it now. What is it?"
> "It's a newcomer, a tenderfoot, a wayfarer on the shores of chance, a—."
> "I like it—it's a beautiful word," Jack curbed my literary output. "And I can't help it, anyway. But what shall I be if I stay here long enough?"
> Recourse to a scratch-pad in my pocket divulged the fascinating sobriquet that even an outlander, be he the right kind of outlander, might come in time— a long time—to deserve. It is kamaai-na, and its significance is that of old-timer, and more, much more. It means one who belongs, who has come to belong in the heart and life and soil of Hawaii. "I'd rather be (*'kamaaina'*) than any name in the world, I think. . . . I love the land and I love the people."[1]

Although it is fair to group London with Melville, Twain, Stoddard, Stevenson, and Michener as a visitor to the Islands, we must acknowledge London's desire to become a *kama'āina*, as evidenced in his writing by lush descriptions of the land and generally sensitive portrayals of the people, and in his life by his remaining in Hawaii until failing health necessitated his return to the Valley of the Moon. Unlike those other *haole* (white) writers, the man called sailor, farmer, adventurer, pirate, genius, and philosopher (as well as racist) desired above all to be a *kama'āina*, literally, a child of a land.

Some in the Hawaiian community would argue that any such attempt would be futile; only one born in Hawaii or of Hawaiian blood can be a *kama'āina*. Others believe it to be a function of time; one becomes a *kama'āina* after a certain period of time in the Islands, regardless of sympathies or values. Still others, including the Londons, believe that by coming to appreciate all that is Hawaiian, a *malihini*, or newcomer, can achieve the distinction of "adopted son," if you will, as opposed to *nā kanaka maoli*, the indigenous Hawaiians or true children of the land. To fall within this broader definition of *kama'āina*, London the "outlander" first had to develop a respect for the relationship between the people and the land, which, in turn, led to an acceptance by this union of flesh and soil that was Hawaii.

Acceptance came hard: the conflict between London's philosophical beliefs and his seemingly more emotional infatuation with Hawaii was evident in the incongruities between his personal dealings with the Islanders and his writing. Initially, London's view of Hawaii was blurred by Social Darwinist leanings and the resultant ethnocentric, white supremacist corollaries, which subordinate the Hawaiians to the more capable Anglo-Saxons. In the end, his path to acceptance was, as it should be, his fiction. One piece in particular, "Koolau the Leper," shows genuine empathy with *nā kanaka maoli*.[2] When London finally lays lonely yet defiant Koolau to rest in a ginger blossom thicket in the Kalalau Valley, he closes one of the most controversial stories and opens one of the most bitter debates in Hawaiian *haole* literary history, a debate that kept his work off local bookstore shelves and the writer all but shunned by the white population in Hawaii.

London's stated desire to be more than a passing observer and recorder of a foreign culture, then, cannot be dismissed as a whimsical comment uttered on a pleasant day. Still, however sincere London's attempt to become part of the Hawaiian culture, he was the product of a Western heritage, education, and life experience, and he thus possessed a Western perspective. In a discussion of this perspective, an application of the paradigm established in Edward Said's *Orientalism* proves useful.[3] Hawaii, of course, is not part of the Orient as discussed by Said, that is, the Middle or Near East; nor is it part of the Japan/China-centered Far East, which America obsesses over; nor is it any more Eastern than Western in its philosophical, institutional, or cultural heritage. Rich in its own history and cultural identity, Hawaii is nonetheless Oriental as opposed to Occidental in terms of providing an Other for the Western reader.

Although the composition of this Other is less the issue than London's existence apart from it, an understanding of its construction allows useful comparisons to the characters in London's Hawaiian fiction. Stephen Sumida, in his discussion of Hawaiian literary traditions, outlines Western writers' fascination with and search for the "exotic," an erotic, languid extension of the European pastoral but set in the South Seas.[4] When we are dealing with the Pacific Island cultures, equating this Exotic with Orientalism as a means of coming to grips with our perceptions as Westerners, rather than developing a real understanding of the culture, requires some qualification. Said points out that the Occident's view of the Orient is imbued with a rich tradition of competition (actually, dominance and subservience); the relationship of the Occident to the Exotic is comparatively fresh, less than four centuries old, and, at least initially, based on a purely fanciful understanding. Where Europe sees the Orient through the nostalgic "what was" or "what was perceived to be," America has viewed the Exotic through "what could be." Both distortions show the Occident's desire to dominate; each creates a discourse based on "Western projections unto and will to govern" the culture (Said's phrase) and a virtual reality created by extrapolating from ill-informed texts.

In the case of the Exotic in general, and Hawaii in particular, those texts were grounded in the imaginative fiction created by the likes of Defoe and Swift, Rousseau's concept of the Noble Savage, the journals of the eighteenth-century South Pacific explorers—most notably, James Cook and Samuel Wallis—and later the provocative fiction of Stevenson, Melville, and others.[5] Melville's *Typee* (1846), set in the Marquesas Islands, initially perpetuated, then challenged the stereotype of an unblemished and dignified people living a carefree and quietly fulfilling existence in idyllic surroundings. Indeed, as the Western population in Hawaii steadily grew throughout the nineteenth century, and with it the recognition that sets of values differed between diverse peoples, especially between the missionaries and *nā kanaka maoli*, so did the number of pejorative tracts being shaped by and shaping Western perspectives. Given two opposing yet presumably accurate truths within the Exotic discourse, the Occident had to decide, as Sumida puts it, which view was "more true—that the natives were peaceful, domestic sorts, noble inhabitants of a paradise; or that the natives, although useful for replenishing the ships' stores, were depraved and were to be shot at the first threat of harm to the visitors."[6]

Shortly before London's first arrival in Hawaii, one writer in particular, Mark Twain, seemed to address this duality. In typical fashion, Twain's keen observations and wry comments satirize both visions.[7] Through his fictitious traveling partner, Mr. Brown, a parody of the boorish American abroad, Twain outlines many of the annoyances that, though superficial, tend to undermine the image of paradise. Brown's tirades against the scorpions, cockroaches, and "santipedes," as well as his diatribes mocking the language and customs, provide Twain the luxury of judging a culture under the guise of judging the judge.

However, Twain's historical narratives and comments on his own encounters with the native people reveal his ambivalence. He alternates jabs at such "barbaric" customs as human sacrifice with attacks on the selfish and intolerant *haole* intruders. One only has to read Twain's account of Captain Cook's death at Kealakekua Bay and his description of Britain's brief annexation of the kingdom in 1843 to be convinced of his sympathy for *nā kanaka maoli*. Yet he chides the missionaries for delivering the concept of Hell to a carefree, unburdened people, and at the same time he acknowledges, in a rare moment of sincerity, that "the wonderful benefit conferred upon the people by the missionaries is so prominent, so palpable, and so unquestionable, that the frankest compliment I can pay them, and the best, is simply to point to the conditions of the Sandwich Islanders of Captain Cook's time and their condition today. Their work speaks for itself."[8] The Occidental's placing himself in a position to make such a choice, and thus control the Exotic, is more germane to the discussion of perspective than which choice is made.

Such was the Exotic that London encountered; given a blank sheet of paper, what Hawaiian would he describe? The writer takes chances when he incorporates leprosy, a heinous serpent introduced into the garden by the West through the East. At one point in Hawaiian history, to utter the word in public was to commit a misdemeanor, and some 40 years before London's arrival, Twain had been admonished not to discuss the disease in his letters to the *Sacramento Union* for fear of losing readers in the business community.[9]

By transforming a bit of recent Hawaiian lore regarding a native leper's refusal to submit to the *haole* government, and thus raising the protagonist to near legendary status, London appears in "Koolau the Leper" to exploit the diseased few for the elevation of the healthy yet oppressed many. More important, he asks and answers political questions about the distribution of power, which *haole* society considered inappropriate. Was the writer the sensationalist, the betrayer of friends, and the "untruthful and ungrateful bounder," in the words of Lorrin Thurston, London's close associate who also spoke for the indignant white community?[10] Or was London simply writing as a *kamaʻāina*, the true child of the land Charmian claimed he longed to be? Or, given the relationship between the two perspectives, could he not be one without being the other?

A misplaced emphasis on the *fear* of leprosy that appears to be so pivotal invites the first conclusion. A closer look at the protagonist, especially in relation to the protagonists of London's two other "leper stories," Jack Kersdale in "Good-bye, Jack" and Lyte Gregory in "The Sheriff of Kona," reveals that the physical components of the disease, in particular the contagiousness, are minimized and that "Koolau the Leper" is the powerful and enduring political statement of a man struggling with and finally, in Hawaii's case, rejecting the imperialism spawned by Social Darwinism, ethnocentric doctrine, and Western perspectives on the Exotic.

In order to understand more clearly the political implications of both the disease and the story, the reader must have a passing familiarity with the political climate of turn-of-the-century Hawaii. Only fourteen years prior to London's 1907 visit, Hawaii was ruled by a native monarch. Queen Liliuʻokalani was the last in a line of *aliʻi* (rulers) that began when Kamehameha the Great united the islands and commanded his people to lay down their weapons in 1810. In an attempt to maintain sovereignty in a changing world, the *aliʻi* had for nearly a century played the more powerful French, British, and Americans against each other, a strategy that could only postpone the inevitable. Throughout the last half of the nineteenth century, overzealous missionaries arrived, condemned, and saved, and various nations' warships were an intimidating presence in Honolulu harbor.

By the 1890's, though Liliuʻokalani was popular with the native population, her hold on the throne was tenuous; the powerful white minority, mostly American plantation owners and businessmen, had difficulty with the financial and social impediments she created. This dissatisfaction led to the illegal overthrow of the monarchy and the movement toward annexation in 1893. Originally condemned by the United States, though installed with the consent and support of its representative to the kingdom, the Provisional Government quickly achieved stability and diplomatic recognition. By the time of London's arrival, the Hawaiian Republic was a territorial possession, and the Hawaiian people were powerless and landless wards of a self-serving collection of *haole* businessmen.

Many of the principals of the 1893 insurrection were still prominent in Hawaiian society in 1907, and the Londons met three of the most important. Lorrin Thurston and Sanford Dole, two of the architects of the overthrow and framers of the constitution, were now the editor of the *Honolulu Advertiser* and a prominent judge, respectively. Thurston, though something of a blackguard and a political opportunist, became a close friend of London's. Along with their wives, the two traveled extensively together, taking short trips on horseback to the windward side of Oahu and a longer trip to the neighboring island of Maui. They adopted Hawaiian names, the Londons becoming Lakana and Lakana Wahine (woman) and the Thurstons, Kakina and Kakina Wahine. The friendship and the correspondence, though strained at times, remained intact for the rest of London's life.

In August 1907, the Thurstons arranged a breakfast meeting between the Londons and the Doles. Though little is known of what they discussed, the Londons were undoubtedly impressed with the judge. Charmian said of Dole, "Jack always warms to the instance of the gallant resistance made by him and another stripling, holding the Palace doors against an infuriated mob during an uprising incident to a change in monarchs. 'Can't you see them? Can't you see the two of them—the glorious youth of them risking its hot blood to do what it saw had to be done!' he cries with growing appreciation of the sons of men."[11] That the Londons were attracted by the imperialist cause as much as the exuberance of youth is evident in Charmian's assertion later that day that Hawaii "is an example of a truly benevolent patriarchy."[12]

Such cavalier comments present the Londons as naive, blithely unaware of the plight of *nā kanaka maoli* they claimed to love. Yet Charmian displays sensitivity when she writes of the members of the "vanishing race" whose "eyes look only an innocent equality of sweet frankness, and their feet step without fear the soil they can but still feel is their own." These conflicting sentiments are perhaps best resolved in Charmian's account of their brief encounter with Liliu'okalani in May 1907, during one of the deposed queen's infrequent public appearances. After describing at length the queen's dignity and understandable "cold hatred of everything American," Charmian concludes with a romantic, somewhat wistful defense of social Darwinism tempered by compassion: "My sympathy for one, is very warm, toward her. There is no gainsaying that truism, 'survival of the fittest,' in the far drift of the human, and the white indubitably has proved the fittest; but our hearts are all for this poor old Queen-woman; although I could not help wondering if she would have liked us any better had she known."[13] If the missionaries destroyed the Hawaiians culturally and the businessmen ravaged them politically, the most salient manifestation of the assault was the physical toll the introduced diseases took on the native population. Liliuʻokalani had seen four-fifths of her people "swept out of existence by the vices introduced by foreigners";[14] the most devastating of these plagues in the later years of the monarchy and early years of the republic was leprosy. The source of the disease was unknown, but the Hawaiians called it *maʻi aliʻi* (the royal sickness) or *maʻi Pākē* (the Chinese sickness), believing it to be introduced by the Chinese "coolies" who were imported to work the plantations when the vanishing native population could not or would not. Although the disease was not race-specific, the overwhelming majority of victims were *nā kanaka maoli*, and the government, in an attempt to save the race and placate the frightened healthy population, passed an act in 1865 to isolate victims on an almost inaccessible peninsula on the island of Molokai.

Initially, conditions for the victims were brutal. Ripped from family and home, ceremoniously pronounced "walking dead," and shipped to a strange island, they were often forced to swim to shore through crushing surf, only to find themselves, shelterless and foodless, also in the state of anarchy that is expected among people with no tomorrow. Robert Louis Stevenson, a source familiar to the Londons and quoted by them both in their writings about the Islands, said of the early days of the settlement on Molokai: " ʻAole kanawai ma keia wahi!'—'There is no law in this place'—was their word of salutation to newcomers; cards, dancing, and debauch were the diversions; the women served as prostitutes, the children as drudges; the dying were callously uncared for; heathenism revived; okolehao (alcohol distilled from taro roots) was brewed, and in their orgies the disfigured sick ran naked by the sea."[15] Physical conditions improved greatly during the next 40 years as the lepers moved from victims to patients, thanks largely to the selfless work of a Belgian priest, Father Damien, and medical advances in treating, if not curing, the disease. *Kōkua*, or volunteer helpers, were often allowed to accompany patients, and morale seemed greatly improved. Yet Stevenson captured the anguish of that initial band of victims, which lingered on for many patients during London's time, and perhaps remains with the few residents living in Kalaupapa today: "Many must have conceived their ostracism to be grounded in malevolent caprice; all came with sorrow at heart, many with despair and rage."[16] In perception as well as truth, leprosy was a political issue.

London's own fascination with the disease predated his arrival in the Islands. He had visited several leper settlements and lazar houses, and Charmian writes that within five weeks of landfall, Jack had been "deftly pulling wires to bring about a visit for us both to the famous Leper Settlement on Molokai." Dinner guest Lucius E. Pinkham, president of the Board of Health, was anxious to arrange the trip, feeling that London would give a sympathetic and fair account. The Londons spent the first week of July at Kalaupapa.

The Londons, immediately impressed with the order, cheerfulness, and vitality of the settlement, spent the next four days participating in sporting events, researching the subject in the doctors' libraries, visiting the grave and the church of Father Damien, admiring the humanitarian efforts of Superintendent Jack McVeigh and Dr. William Goodhue, and listening to the songs and stories of the patients. Jack's thorough satisfaction with the quality of life at Kalaupapa is revealed in Charmian's account of his jest, shared with his wife and McVeigh: " 'Why, look here, Mate Woman,' he panned, 'we could, if ever we contracted leprosy, live here according to our means. I could go on writing and earning money, and we could have a mountain place, a townhouse down in the village, a bungalow anywhere on the seashore that suited us, set up our own dairy with imported Jerseys, and ride our own horses, as well as sail our own yacht.' "[17] This flippant statement, intended no doubt for the company present, should be viewed more as a reflection of London's positive impressions of the settlement than of his insensitivity to the patients, although later writings indicate his strong belief that the patients' perceived plight was exaggerated.

Midway through the stay, a patient engaged London in a conversation regarding pride and a concern for the outside world's perceptions of the settlement. He implored the writer to "give the public a breeze" about the patients, and Charmian thought she saw "in Jack's active eye a hint of the fair breeze to a gale that he would set ablowing on the subject of 'the fellows on Molokai.' "[18] London's response, "The Lepers of Molokai," was completed within three days of the visit. An unabashedly positive view of the work going on in the settlement, the article was well received by Pinkham, McVeigh, Goodhue, and, no doubt, the patients themselves. London expressed his self-satisfaction in a letter to Hayden Carruth, literary editor of *Woman's Home Companion*: "While leprosy may be a distasteful subject, I think I have handled it fairly decently for your readers; and that I have given a side of it that has not hitherto been given to it—namely, the happier, brighter side."[19] Indeed, the article reads variously as a travel brochure for a tropical paradise ("The Settlement of Molokai enjoys a far more delightful climate than even

Honolulu"), a call for the doctor's canonization ("too much praise cannot
be given [Dr. Goodhue] for the noble work he has done"), a testimonial aimed
at the needlessly concerned (" 'They are so contented down there,' Mr.
Pinkham told me, 'that you can't drive them away with a shot gun'"), and a
forceful, unqualified defense of the policy ("That a leper is unclean, however,
should be insisted upon; and the segregation of lepers . . . should be rigidly
maintained"). If the article could be distilled to a single point, it would not
be unfair to quote London's assertion that "one thing is certain. The Leper
in the Settlement is far better off than the leper who lies in hiding outside."[20]

There is no reason to believe that "The Lepers of Molokai" is anything
but a sincere reflection of Jack London's views on a fascinating topic. The
essay might have been his last public writing *about* leprosy, but these words
were not his last *involving* the disease, a distinction London felt compelled
to explain in a letter to the *Honolulu Advertiser*. As one of Hawaii's "most
salient characteristics," leprosy was a fair target to be exploited in fiction.
Such was the nature of writing, London charged,[21] and thus the topic in three
of London's first six Hawaiian stories.

It is interesting to speculate on the sources of London's leper trilogy. Perhaps he gleaned ideas from his friend Alexander Hume Ford, who poured
out "whacking good material—for stories" during dinner at the end of the
Londons' first week in Hawaii. Certainly he heard one version of the Koʻolau
legend from *Snark* shipmate Bert Stolz, whose father was the sheriff Koʻolau
had killed fourteen years earlier. No doubt during his stay at Kalaupapa, Jack
was inundated with the stories of those afflicted, and that experience cannot be minimized: Charmian's account of departing Honolulu on the *Noeau*
appears almost verbatim as the climactic scene in "Good-bye, Jack," and the
description of the Kona coast in "The Sheriff of Kona" mirrors Jack's speaking of that region as he rested at a friend's house at Holualoa in late August.[22]
In a letter to Thurston in the midst of the storm that followed the stories'
publication, London would only say that they were local in origin: "I have
written three leper stories, everyone of which was told me by you Hawaiians."[23]

Yet London's choice of material reveals a mind struggling to reconcile
conflicting obligations to philosophical convictions, friends, and conscience.
Although his apparent confusion over the *haole* community's indignation
following the publication was genuine, his defense that the stories were
"purely fictional" sounds hollow. In fact, London's version of Koʻolau's exploits is so similar to an account published the preceding year by Kahikina
Kelekona (John G. M. Shelton), there can be little doubt of the intended par-

allel.[24] Kelekona's *Kaluaikoolau!*, written in the Hawaiian language and dedicated to *nā kanaka maoli*, focused on the journals of Pi'ilani, Ko'olau's wife, who returned to society shortly after her husband's death and gave a firsthand account of the family's sojourn.

Briefly, Kelekona's retelling of Pi'ilani's story is one of shared tragedy and all-conquering love. Having monitored his early symptoms of leprosy for four years, and after receiving the government's orders to prepare for the voyage to Molokai in 1893, Ko'olau declared his intent to obey so long as his wife and young son, Kaleimanu, would be allowed to remain with him. Pi'ilani recalled their pact: "And we agreed together to live patiently together in the hardships of this life, and that death only would separate us. We made a sacred oath before All Powerful God to fulfill this with determination and without retreat."[25]

At a meeting of area lepers, Sheriff Louis Stolz denied Ko'olau's request, and Ko'olau stated that he would remain on Kauai. Stolz's subsequent attempt to ambush Ko'olau forced the leper to kill the sheriff. Convincing the other lepers to surrender for deportation and avoid the appearance of complicity in Stolz's death, Ko'olau, along with Pi'ilani and Kaleimanu, who by now was showing symptoms of leprosy himself, sought refuge in the wilderness of the Kalalau Valley. Soldiers of the Provisional Government followed. Ko'olau shot and killed two, and the search was quickly abandoned. For the next few months, except for a chance encounter with some sympathetic acquaintances, the family remained in seclusion, moving constantly in the valley and living off the land.

Kaleimanu's condition worsened, and upon his death the couple prayed for strength to continue. For the next year, as they wandered the Kalalau Valley, Pi'ilani became frightened by the increasing severity of Ko'olau's symptoms: strong stomach pains, weakness, and periods of confusion. Her husband, too, saw the end approaching, and they discussed Pi'ilani's inevitable return to society:

> Tell the truth if you are questioned, saying that mine was the trouble, which you and the child followed with me to the end, and that you fulfilled the oath you swore. And my only command to you is, when the time comes, that you bury my gun with me, we will sleep together in the belly of the earth, because you had nothing to do with the gun. I alone used it and when I go, we go together; when my work is done, its work in this world is done.

Soon after, Ko'olau became comatose and then died, and Pi'ilani immediately became aware of her loneliness. An interesting contrast to London's final scene, her powerful description of Ko'olau's burial captures the proud and loyal love that defines her story:

> I spread out the fragrant leaves of the forest over the earth on the bottom and the sides until all was ready for the last task, fetching my beloved husband's body. I knelt by his side and sent my prayers to the feet of the God in the high heavens. Then I lifted him onto some branches and dragged him to his final resting place in the beloved soil of his native land. There I laid him to sleep with his favorite gun on his breast, fulfilling his last command to me. Giving praise to the Heavenly Father, I covered him over with leaf tips, and the earth swallowed him up and hid him, returning dust to dust, ashes to ashes, in the name of Almighty God. . . . I planted all around with slips from the forest, kissed the earth and left him there sleeping the sleep of seasons.[26]

Although the story takes place in the year of the overthrow of the monarchy, aside from an attack on the Provisional Government's brutal attempt to coerce help from the family's friends through terrorism, Kelekona does not mention the *haole*/Hawaiian conflict. The question of the Provisional Government's right to break the bonds of marriage and separate husband from wife is not a political one; Ko'olau and Pi'ilani would not recognize the right of any government, *haole* or Hawaiian, to supersede God's law of holy marriage. Perhaps I oversimplify when I say that Pi'ilani's is a love story, tragic and true.

Hawaiian literature scholar A. Grove Day, in his foreword to a collection of London's Hawaiian stories, asserts that the differences between the historical account of Ko'olau and London's fiction are unimportant, citing the two protagonists' defiant spirits as the thematic link.[27] However, London's relationship with the Hawaiian people is revealed, not in the sympathetic retelling of the story, but in the conscious changes the writer makes. The setting and the situation no doubt appealed to what readers and critics would label London's naturalist slant. Of more interest here, though, is London's attempt to alter the Exotic to create a *new* tradition, one in which he can perhaps find a niche. Comparing the points of departure of Pi'ilani's narrative and those of "Koolau the Leper" illustrates London's appreciation of the underdog, the weaker combatant pitted against the more fit in the struggle for survival, as well as a disappearance of the racism that his long-held belief in Social Darwinism helped create. Three revisions in particular support this contention: the replacement of family with a renegade band of fellow lepers, the elimination of Christian references, and the exaggeration of Ko'olau's symptoms.

London's decision to exclude Pi'ilani and Kaleimanu changes the nature of the conflict. Although the political ramifications of the Provisional Government's reaction to the family's act of defiance and the political implications of the sheltering land are apparent to a reader familiar with the circumstances surrounding the overthrow, such nuances could easily be lost on London's predominantly Mainland readers. Pi'ilani's love story is therefore transformed into a quest for freedom. Ko'olau's refusal to be separated from his family is replaced with a more general defiance rooted in hatred for the *haole* conquerors and in a bond with the land: "We were born here. Here we have lived. And here shall we die."[28] To London's reader, there is no place for man-woman love in this politically charged portrait of the Hawaiian, only the compelling, sexless love for the *'āina*, the stolen land.

A powerful image that highlights this distinction is the rifle in the hands of the dead man. To Pi'ilani, the rifle is a symbol of Ko'olau's final act of protection, his acceptance of blame for the trouble caused. The rifle is subordinated to the relationship it preserves. There is no need to pass it on; the bond between the lovers has been broken temporarily by the death of one, and further fighting would be senseless.

For London, Koolau's last thought is of the Mauser he clutched. The gun represents the struggle for an empty freedom that consisted of little more than scurrying like an animal just beyond the reach of the persistent pursuer. Yet Koolau is a hero, solely because of the struggle. As the rifle becomes bigger than life, we cheer Koolau's attacks and mourn his defeat. This is more than compassionate Social Darwinism made fiction: The *haole* will win the battle for survival, but only because of their "strange persistence," their "terrible will." Persistence defeats dignity, and genuine empathy for the Hawaiian people replaces mere compassion.

If love is the foundation of Pi'ilani's tale, the couple's Christian beliefs are the basis of this love. Ko'olau and Pi'ilani draw much strength from their Christianity; indeed, it is their pledge to God that gives authority to their binding love and justifies the murder of the three lawmen. The flight itself is ordained by God, and the wilderness is a manifestation of God's protecting grace. According to Pi'ilani, "The Three Heavenly spirits regard us with love and sprinkle their Holy Spirit over us and spread their wings as refuge for us. Therefore, on our arrival at our refuge, our first action was to bend our knees and give praise to the Heavenly One and thanks for our care and guidance."[29] On the other hand, a positive experience with the *haole* religion becomes a diversion for London's reader. Although the juxtaposition of the introduced religion and the introduced disease creates powerful irony, the effect of Christianity on *nā kanaka maoli* is an issue London wisely chooses to avoid: his story is not one to evaluate a trade-off between the certainty of stolen land and the possibility of eternal life. Christianity is prominent in Pi'ilani's story of two people "united under the shelter of the Holy Trinity," a faith built on Hawaiian spirituality, but London must establish stronger cultural divisions in his political tale.

Consequently, religion is ignored, and emphasis is placed on the missionaries as manipulators. Stripped of their spiritual armor, they are cynically equated with the unscrupulous businessmen:

> They were of two kinds. The one kind asked our permission, our gracious permission, to preach to us the word of God. The other kind asked our permission, our gracious permission, to trade with us. That was the beginning. Today all the islands are theirs, all the land, all the cattle—everything is theirs. They that preached the word of God and they that preached the word of Rum have foregathered and become great chiefs.[30]

These explicit attacks on the missionaries were likely the true source of Thurston's agitation and public outcry. He no doubt felt some threat, as he claimed, in London's once again bringing leprosy to the reading world's attention. But Thurston, the grandson of a missionary, and Dole, the son of a missionary, had to feel betrayed by London's scathing comments on the messengers of God in "Good-bye, Jack": "The fruit of the seed of the missionaries (the sons and grandsons) was the possession of the islands themselves—of the land, the ports, the town sites, and the sugar plantations. The missionary who came to give the bread of life remained to gobble up the whole heathen feast."[31] In London's stories, Christianity becomes less a religion than a tool of imperialism, the heirs of the missionaries and the leaders of the insurrection are exposed as hypocrites, and deception joins persistence as the conquering *haole*'s most noteworthy attributes.

The elimination of Koʻolau's Christianity leads to blatantly political statements, but the boldest and most controversial deviation from the original tale is the exaggeration of Koʻolau's symptoms. In Pi'ilani's account, he exhibited none of the physical distortions associated with the extreme cases of leprosy London observed at Kalaupapa. His symptoms were more internal: severe cramps and weakness afflicted his body, and he became prone to periods of incoherence. In truth, London's accounts of flapping ears and fingers burned to the stumps were the exception. Yet, charged with sensationalism and the exploitation of the patients London befriended at Kalaupapa, he chooses to discuss in graphic detail the most grotesque and frightening ravages imaginable: "Their hands, when they possessed them, were like harpy-claws. Their faces were the misfits and slips, crushed and bruised by some mad god at play in the machinery of life. Here and there were features which the mad god had smeared half away, and one woman wept scalding tears from twin pits of horror, where her eyes once had been."[32]

Beyond the terror, such a description evokes a sense of loss. As is common with London's writings and those of other literary naturalists, the characters regress to their animal roots. They become "huge apes marred in the making," climbing and crawling with the goats and rats as the *haole* bombard them into submission. "They were creatures," London writes, "who had once been men and women," but that was before the *haole* came. Those who took the land took their humanity.

It is especially ironic that this disfigurement should happen to *nā kanaka maoli*, a race London regarded as unparalleled in physical attractiveness. The healthy "sun-ripe Junos" and "bronzed Apollos" who sing and dance and are all "flower bejewelled and flower crowned" in "Good-bye, Jack" now sing and dance, in a diseased world of the *haole*'s making, "a barbaric love-call such as might have come from the dark forest depths of the primeval world."[33] In a sense, all the *haole* left the Hawaiian was beauty, the skin on his back; to emphasize the completeness of the cultural genocide, London robs him of that, and even proud, defiant Koolau, like a wild animal, crawls into a hole to die.

Leprosy, then, becomes an appropriate and powerful backdrop for the struggle against imperialism London apparently was beginning to appreciate in the later years of a short life. It is possible that the story, with details altered, simply reflects Koʻolau's actual feelings, that London is relating the truth as he understood it, though the pen that replaced Piʻilani with a band of decaying peers easily could have resolved a conflict between truth and story. This playing loose with the facts makes London's decision to glorify a character's refusal to relocate to Kalaupapa, a fate London personally thought far preferable to the inevitable slow death from the disease unchecked, that much more interesting. To make a political point, the writer dismissed his own feelings about an appropriate response to the disease, risked the alienation of his friends at Kalaupapa by implying the worst about the settlement, and invited the wrath of the powerful *haole* establishment that hosted his stay. But what is the political statement London makes?

An initial temptation is to read "Koolau the Leper" as an allegory. Certainly, allegorical elements are present in the setting, the characters, and the plot, and a reasonable extension of these elements might be to view the group's abandoning Koolau as symbolic of the Hawaiian sovereignty movement's inability to organize, or perhaps they embody the Social Darwinist's contention that inferior people lack the ability to cooperate and consequently deserve to perish.

Yet if the story is an allegorical call to arms to a nation essentially bereft of warriors for five generations, it becomes a call to cultural suicide. Koolau's pointing out that the *haole's* perseverance is what his own race lacked is a reflection of the widespread resignation to fate that characterized his peaceful and practical people; 25 years earlier, King Kalakaua, when told that his race was dying out, responded, "I've read lots of times that great races died out, and new ones took their place; my people are like the rest."[34] If we follow the allegory, we are left with ambiguous feelings: we revel in Koolau's temporary victory over the *haole*, ubiquitous but little else, and we are frustrated and saddened by the inevitable death of Koolau and, simultaneously, the Hawaiian nation.

If not a call to action, "Koolau the Leper" runs the risk of being viewed as a sentimental eulogy for the dying race. Yet *haole* readers are inspired by Koolau's defiance beyond the universal appeal of the rebel fighting injustice. In the Hawaiian setting, there is something poignant about Koolau's bond with the *'āina* and his absolute refusal to leave his native island. For London to write about this bond from a Hawaiian's perspective would have been, if not impossible, presumptuous; for him to write about it from the perspective of a *malihini* on the way to becoming a *kama'āina* is an expected outgrowth of the changes occurring in the writer's life. The *haole* protagonists in the other two leper stories, Jack Kersdale and Lyte Gregory, represent the two extremes in this transformation.

Structurally, "Good-bye, Jack" and "The Sheriff of Kona" appear more alike than different. Each focuses on an Island-born *haole* with a noteworthy attribute that a likable and somewhat intrusive narrator describes through an anecdote. Each is then exposed to leprosy, and the reader is left to judge the man based on his reaction to the situation. These similar structures invite comparison, which, in the context of the political sentiment established by "Koolau the Leper," yields a wealth of insight into London's view of the place of the *haole* in Hawaii.

The character of Jack Kersdale is tainted from the beginning. After London's opening paragraph explains sarcastically how the missionaries civilized *nā kanaka maoli* almost to extinction, we discover that Kersdale comes from missionary stock. A society man, a club man, a yachtsman, and a Yale graduate, Kersdale has a formal, detached relationship with the Islands. "His head was crammed fuller with vital statistics and scholarly information concerning Hawaii Nei"[35] than any other Islander the narrator had encountered. Yet with this knowledge comes little to suggest an intimacy with the people or the land: His enjoyment of the climate and the sun, his propensity for dancing and singing and wearing flowers behind his ears, shows only the most superficial appreciation of Hawaii Nei.

His is a world apart from *nā kanaka maoli*. At the age of sixteen, he played a credible role in the overthrow of the monarchy, an incident casually mentioned as testimony to his courage, but one that reveals as much about his loyalties. His wealthy and privileged world, like that of the visiting Londons, is one of breaking horses at Von Tempsky's Haleakala Ranch or attending parties at Dr. Goodhue's Kona bungalow, the site of the centipede incident used to define Kersdale's courage.[36]

There is something tainted in Kersdale's soul as well. A staunch defender of the settlement at Kalaupapa, he takes a perverse pleasure in watching the patients deported from Honolulu harbor. The sincerity of his lengthy defense of the settlement, an account lifted almost verbatim from London's "Lepers of Molokai" article, at this point in the story is irrelevant; the suffering of the families being separated is real, and converting family tragedy into a spectator sport reveals the monster in Kersdale.[37]

With the stunning revelation at the end of "Good-bye, Jack," the issue is less the reality of the environment at Kalaupapa, more Kersdale's true perception of that environment, and even more Kersdale's hypocrisy. We do not mock the failure of his courage, for even the most courageous man would blanch at the possibility of leprosy. Yet this is a man who minutes earlier extolled the virtues of the paradise these wailing victims were to enjoy. Those words are too recent for us to miss the irony. London's message is echoed in another scolding letter to Thurston: "To your saying, As a man thinks, he is, let me add a rider, As a man is, so is the world. Thus in the eyes of the man who has just dined, all the world is well-fed. Make your own application."[38] Although few readers are callous enough to relish Kersdale's fate, it is difficult to muster sympathy for the man who mocked the mourning Hawaiians. Kersdale, a lifelong resident of the Islands, remained a *malihini*; he never appreciated the people or the *'āina*, and, not surprisingly, his reaction at the end reflects his personal fear, not the anxiety of being separated from a land he loved.

Even before the character of Lyte Gregory is introduced, London sets a more refreshingly reverent tone in "The Sheriff of Kona." In lieu of the political commentary that introduces "Good-bye, Jack," London begins his story with a lengthy panegyric on the beauty of the Kona coast: a lotus land

it is, with "a mountain wind, faintly balmy, fragrant and spicy, and cool, de-
liciously cool, a silken coolness, a wine-like coolness—cool as only the mountain wind of Kona can be cool."[39]

The ode to the land segues so seamlessly into a description of Lyte
Gregory that the two become synonymous, and the narrator Cudworth builds
on the natural imagery and robust interaction with the ʻāina in painting his
picture of the protagonist: "We fished sharks on Niihau together. We hunted
the wild cattle on Mauna Kea and Mauna Loa. We broke horses and branded
steers on the Carter Ranch. We hunted goats through Haleakala. He taught
me diving and surfing until I was nearly as clever as he, and he was cleverer
than the average Kanaka." Built "like the chieftains of old Hawaii," Gregory
is indeed a kamaʻāina—his love for the land is balanced with his love for the
native people. We learn that Gregory fought fiercely in the revolution on the
side of the monarchy, and therefore on the side of nā kanaka maoli, a detail
that initiates the comparison to Kersdale, and he carries out his unpleasant
task of rounding up the lepers with as much compassion and understanding as possible, as his initial restrained response to Stephen Kaluna's accusations proves.

Perhaps the most intriguing aspect of Gregory's personality is revealed
in the anecdote. While Kersdale's impressive courage is consistent with both
haole and kanaka virtues, Gregory's attribute is Island-born. His ability to
draw the needed card and his confidence to bet without looking at that card
reflect a certain connection with a higher entity. The Hawaiians speak of
mana, of having a divine association with this force. Often manifested in
specific talents or skills, mana also takes the form of a more nebulous mys-
tical power, bestowed by a divine authority.[40] Through his magical albeit superficial poker incident, Gregory demonstrates this spiritual relationship
with the good as clearly as Kersdale demonstrates his bond with the bad.

Many readers consider "The Sheriff of Kona" less than a great work
largely because of the disjointed and unsatisfying resolution of the conflict:
Gregory is left leprous but living in Japan; he is guilty of betraying his conscience by abandoning Kalaupapa, yet he is removed from his land. As a
leper, he seems to have escaped, but as a kamaʻāina, Gregory confronts a fate
far worse than Kersdale's. Gregory is forced to live the rest of his life separated from the land he loved, and London emphasizes this pain by mini-
mizing the symptoms and, consequently, the reader's awareness of the leprosy.

As a common thread in three stories, leprosy becomes something of a
badge of honor as well as a curse. The malihini Kersdale is never portrayed

as leprous or sensitive; we withhold our sympathy. Gregory, the *kama'āina*, evokes sympathy with his early symptoms of the disease and his longing to return home. Koolau the Hawaiian, the image of his ravaged body firmly instilled in the reader's mind, earns the most respect in his struggle for dignity and communion with the *'āina*. In a twisted sense, Kersdale never earns the right to be viewed as a leper, and Gregory comes perhaps as close as a *haole* can to the pain of the Hawaiian people. Similarly, London the writer and the non-Hawaiian reading public can never hope to become Koolau: we cannot know his pain, nor can we enjoy his dignity. At best, the *haole* reader vicariously becomes Lyte Gregory, less than Hawaiian but more than a casual visitor to Islands. We strive, like London and through London, to become *kama'āina*.

The degree to which Jack London achieved the status of *kama'āina* is uncertain. There is no litmus test for an outsider's acceptance into a foreign culture, and we are forced to use subjective standards. Obviously, London was not born in the Islands; nor did he reside in Hawaii long enough to qualify as a *kama'āina* merely as a function of time, although the creation of the Island-born protagonist John Lakana (London) in his last short story, "The Water Baby," might indicate the author's self-perception or desire. London's love of the land never wavers. The agrarian novels he penned and his work at his own Beauty Ranch in California attest to his reverence for the *'āina*; however, the Hawaiians cannot claim sole possession of this reverence, and London seems from early on to appreciate the land around him.

Ideally, the question of London's relationship with the Hawaiian people should be answered by the people themselves, and we must rely on anecdotal evidence. In an oft-quoted piece, Charmian relates the incident of a ukulele player in a Hawaiian orchestra in San Francisco, a young Hawaiian man who spoke through much emotion upon hearing of London's death, "Better than any one, he *knew* us Hawaiians—Jack London, the Story Maker. . . . The news came to Honolulu—and people, they could not understand. . . . They could not believe. I tell you this: Better than any one, he knew us Hawaiians."[41]

Equally touching is Charmian's story of the *mele*, the song Hawaiians composed for Jack and presented at his farewell *lū'au* in 1916, a series of long stanzas punctuated by a sweet refrain:

> Haianaia mai ana ka puana,
> No Keaka Lakana neia inoa.
>
> This song is then echoed,
> 'Tis in honour of Jack London.[42]

On a more personal level, I can speak to the enduring nature of London's relationship with the Islands. I teach at the Kamehameha Schools, a unique college-preparatory institution established more than a century ago by a descendant of the Hawaiian monarchy for the education of native Hawaiian children. Like many indigenous peoples compromised, betrayed, and eventually consumed by the Western world, Hawaiian students exhibit a certain skeptical resentment toward Western writers, especially when so much beautiful and important Hawaiian literature has been ignored in favor of these visitors. Yet Jack London, more than many other visiting *haole* writers, touches the lives of the students. In a story like "Koolau the Leper," my students see a sympathetic, somewhat indignant white writer speaking *to* a proud culture and *for* an otherwise unheard (to the ears of these students) segment of the population.

In the final analysis, London the writer will be judged on his writing, mostly the more popular fiction. As readers with late-twentieth-century sensibilities, we are tempted to view as clumsy and patronizing his early-twentieth-century attempts to redefine the traditional Exotic of Defoe, Rousseau, and Melville. London certainly misses much of the poetry that implicitly defines Hawaiian values in the writing of Pi'ilani and Ko'olau, and the overstated and vulgar presentation in some of his Hawaiian material might be as much a reflection of his lack of understanding as it is a necessary component of his literary style.

His loving respect for the Hawaiian people and his sympathy for their struggle against the ever-growing *haole* are evident in these early stories, though some readers regard these same stories as exploitive, and later stories, especially "The Bones of Kahekili," appear to present the Hawaiian groveling before the omnipotent white rancher, "a source of life, a source of food, a fount of wisdom, a giver of law, a smiling beneficence, a blackness of thunder and punishment."[43] If "The Water Baby" can be viewed as London's last word on the matter, the Hawaiian is in the end elevated to a transcendental level: the wisdom and wholeness of the old Hawaiian compared to the more "civilized" whites are brought to surface in the relationship between Kohokumu and the *haole* Lakana. At best, London's portrayal of the Hawaiian people is a heavily qualified success; the writer seemed on more solid ground when he attempted to distinguish between *malihini* like Jack Kersdale and *kama'āina* like Lyte Gregory and, perhaps, John Lakana.

Of course, such judgment with no historical context is blatantly unfair and perhaps off the point. Even an effective writer like London must be judged as much on intent as product when we try to ascertain his feelings about a subject dear to him, and we must be allowed to consider London's attempt as much as his success in coming to appreciate Hawaii Nei. In truth, no writer, regardless of talent, could portray the fierce pride and simple dignity of Koolau the Leper without feeling some of that pride himself. Having recently commemorated the 100th anniversary of the overthrow of Queen Liliu'okalani, I believe using Jack London to help Hawaiian children gain an appreciation for the best the *haole* have to offer in terms of compassion and respect is a gratifying extension of his time spent in the Islands. It is an appropriate legacy for a man known for much, but wishing to be remembered as Keaka Lakana, *kama'āina*.

Historical Discourses in Jack London's "Shin Bones"

TANYA WALSH

I think that there are only three places that are of value enough
to be taken. One is Hawaii. The others are Cuba and Puerto
Rico.

—James Blaine, U.S. Secretary of State, 1889

Incidentally, I may state that never in the history of Hawaii
has Hawaii bulked so large in American interest as she is bulk-
ing right now.

—Jack London, 1915

Jack London made his first trip to the Hawaiian Islands in 1904, and his extended visits continued until shortly before his death. In 1915 he wrote to
Ralph Kasper, "We came to Honolulu to stay three weeks. It looks as if we
shall stay three months."[1] Hawaii would provide London a rich source for
his writing, and when encouraging a young Japanese writer from Hawaii,
one who insisted on using the conventional settings and plots of most American fiction, London said to him, "I can only repeat to you to go ahead and
study the profession of writing, and to remind you that you have, here in
Hawaii, an exceptional field hitherto unexploited in literature."[2] It was advice that London himself heeded.

London's attitude of respect for the Islands and its inhabitants was not
shared by all who visited. His personal library contained numerous travel-
ogues and histories of Hawaii, and these works displayed contempt for and
superiority to the Hawaiian people.[3] In *The Making of Hawaii*, a volume from
London's library containing his copious marginal notes, William Freeman
Blackman writes about white superiority, the Hawaiians' drunkenness, and
the claim that superior races could not survive long in the tropics.[4] In
other works, such as C. S. Stewart's *Journal of a Residence in the Sandwich Islands*, the author repeatedly refers to the people of Hawaii as heathens in
need of salvation.[5] London's respect for the Hawaiians appears anomalous,
for even his contemporaries continued to compose narratives like these.

Katherine Fullerton Gerould, in her travelogue, *Hawaii: Scenes and Impressions* (1916), perpetuates racist attitudes similar to C. S. Stewart's nearly a century earlier: "[Hawaiians] have never learned to improve on Caucasian ideas. . . . But you must not expect them to go further: you must not expect them to like work, or to care how foolish their clothes look."[6] London's respect for the Islands and its people was apparently an independent stance.

In 1916, the year of his death, London, whose health was failing, went to Hawaii. During this period he discovered the writings of Carl Gustav Jung, which would change the nature of his final works—his narrative style moved in a distinctly modern direction, anticipating the modernist movement in the 1920's. London's last fictions address such modern concerns as time, history, psychology, feminism, and the autonomy of the narrative voice itself. His development paralleled the early work of Joyce and Woolf, who overtly addressed history and the nature of texts. During this final stay in Hawaii in the spring of 1916, London composed one of his most complex narratives, the short story "Shin Bones." Originally titled "In the Cave of the Dead" when published posthumously in *Cosmopolitan* in 1918, it was later anthologized in a collection of Hawaiian stories entitled *On the Makaloa Mat* (1919).[7]

This story is one of London's more obscure yet finely crafted narratives. Through the framing device of a first-person narrator/auditor, "Shin Bones" is the tale of a Hawaiian prince's ancestry and his own Anglocentrism and modernization. It is in 1916 that Prince Akuli tells his history to a white auditor. Descended from the *ali'i*, or Hawaiian royalty, Prince Akuli is the last in his family's line. He is Oxford-educated, and he is merely a royal figurehead (he often travels around his island in a limousine). His narrative is primarily about his ancestry and his mother's predilection for maintaining ancient customs long gone from the now Americanized Islands. The principal custom he discusses is that of gathering and saving the bones of ancestors. Prince Akuli tells how he and his mother's aging retainer retrieved ancestral bones from a secret burial cave that had been in use for 800 years. While in the cave, Akuli covets the shin bone of an ancestor three centuries dead; he collects it, and the shin bone of her slain lover, and he keeps them as personal talismans. But as he ends his narrative, he realizes that the ancient customs are gone and that his gesture has been an empty one. Akuli concludes with a cynical exclamation, "This is the twentieth century and we stink of gasoline."[8]

"Shin Bones" reveals London's concern with history, how we know it, how we interpret it, and how we preserve it. Wanting to represent events accurately, London read many books about Hawaii and made extensive mar-

ginal notes in sections on the colonization by whites.[9] As Hayden White has
observed,

> Historical discourse should not be considered primarily as a special case of
> the "workings of our minds" in its efforts to know reality or to describe it, but
> rather as a special kind of language use which, like metaphoric speech, sym-
> bolic language, and allegorical representation, always means more than it
> literally says, says something other than what it seems to mean, and reveals
> something about the world only at the cost of concealing something else.[10]

History can never be wholly objective; it is always shaped figuratively by the
creator of the discourse. In other words, historical discourse uses the same
tropes as any other writing, and the composer determines the nature of the
figurative writing, thus revealing something about himself or herself. Stephen
Greenblatt says that literary discourse is itself a "matrix [in which history]
is created and recreated."[11] Furthermore, in Bakhtinian terms, there exists
in London's fiction "a plurality of equal and unmerged voices and con-
sciousnesses, a genuine polyphony of fully valid voices . . . a plurality of con-
sciousnesses, with equal rights and each with its own world."[12] London's narrative about Hawaiian history continually calls into question a matrix,
polyphony, or dialogue of historical voices.

    In the text of "Shin Bones," there are two primary historians, Prince
Akuli and the nameless, Caucasian narrator. The prince's version of history
is distinctly Anglocentric, influenced by the British and the American presence in Hawaii and also by his Oxford education. As he tells the story of his
mother, it becomes evident that her interpretation of history is equally ethnocentric. But these two interpretations create an interesting juxtaposition:
Akuli's historical discourse accomplishes quite the opposite of his Anglocentrism; it creates a void from which his "Hawaiianness" emerges. The ethnocentrism of his mother, Hiwilani, however, only accentuates how much
influence British and American customs have had on her. And then the first-
person narrator colors the discourse with his version of the prince's story,
condemning the British colonization and the American annexation of Hawaii.
Thus each character is unable to escape history or to attain objectivity in the
telling of it. Each narrative is another discourse in a polyphony of historical discourses and is able to exist independently.

    The inability to fully absorb and understand one's personal history is
the result of Hawaii's colonization and annexation.[13] The ancient Hawaiians
willingly exchanged their culture for another culture. Stephen Greenblatt remarks on incorporating such historical "fact" into fiction: "History loses its

epistemological innocence, while literature loses an isolation that had come to seem more a prison than a privilege."[14] Hawaiians saw in the British and the Americans a way to progress beyond their "primitivism." And London, through historically grounded fiction, brings about dialogues between various interpretations of these events. Thus in Hawaiian history, the exchange of Hawaiian culture for British and American values parallels the economics of sandalwood, whaling, and sugar plantations.[15] The Hawaiians became fewer in number and more modernized while losing their heritage; the Caucasians became exceedingly wealthy.[16] In "Shin Bones," London addresses from the viewpoint of two distinct narrators the larger cultural context produced by this Anglo-American influence, as well as how selfish economic interests alter history and culture.

As Linda Hutcheon comments, "Artist, audience, critic—none is allowed to stand outside history, or even wish to do so." She quotes Hayden White: "A specifically *historical* inquiry is born less of the necessity to establish that certain events occurred than of the desire to determine what certain events might *mean* for a given group, society, or culture's conception of its present tasks and future prospects."[17] This quotation summarizes my central concerns about "Shin Bones." White's assertion that all historical writing is discursive rather than empirical leads us to examine the historical discourse of the prince, the narrator, and London himself. What do the events in the story have to do with the teller? How do their personal biases affect the tellings? How do these three function, not as historians, but as historiographers? How do they reconstruct the past? How does each make meaning with what has been reconstructed? And what, ultimately, is the reader's role? The narrative complexity of "Shin Bones" invites all of these inquiries.

"Shin Bones" is a short story written by a white American male, and narrated by a white American male steeped in Hawaiian culture, in which a Hawaiian of royal descent recounts his heritage under the shadow of wealth, an English education, the twentieth century, and the annexation of Hawaii by the United States. The story is interrupted by an old Hawaiian woman, obviously of the peasant class, weaving a lei for Prince Akuli while he recounts his history to a white man sympathetic to native Islanders. "Shin Bones" seems ripe for a culturally based reading. This story can be interpreted as a narrative questioning the nature of historical discourse, since there are three discourses that are simultaneous: the prince's, the narrator's, and Jack London's.

The setting of "Shin Bones" is the fictional Hawaiian island of Lakanaii. It is odd that London would fabricate an island, especially since most of his audience knew about Hawaii. In a discussion of London's "The Water Baby," Earle Labor notes that *Lakana* is Hawaiian for "London," which makes intriguing the Anglo implications of the fictional setting in "Shin Bones."[18] The story opens with Prince Akuli discussing his mother and old Hawaiian customs:

> It was a sad thing to see the old lady revert. . . . In her last years Hiwilani went back to the old ways and to the old beliefs—in secret, of course. . . . [She] had gone quite native at the last, sleeping on mats on the hard floor—she'd fired out of the room the great, royal, canopied four-poster that had been presented to her grandmother by Lord Byron, who was the cousin of the Don Juan Byron and came here in the frigate *Blonde* in 1825. (178)

From the outset, a concern with history, custom, heritage, and culture is made clear. The British influence on Hawaii and the prince is manifested in the allusion to Byron's *Don Juan*. It is true that Lord Byron, the poet's cousin, commandeered a ship to Hawaii in 1825, but calling the poet "Don Juan Byron" creates a literary parallel between the ironic hero of the epic poem and the failed, cynical protagonist of London's story: a Prince Squid (the English translation of Akuli) who is not really a prince. But the prince's narrative becomes doubly ironic as his mother, descended from the purest *ali'i*, "goes native." Not only does he align himself and his family with the British, he shows that ultimately the Hawaiian culture wins as his mother "reverts." In this same passage, Prince Akuli describes his mother's passion for collecting the bones of her ancestors. Far from being simply a morbid fictional construct of London's, the collection of bones is an ancient Hawaiian tradition. It is, in a sense, a collector's physical manifestation of his or her own historical discourse.

The burial of the dead is a complex ritual in Hawaiian culture, of which London was keenly aware. Commoners' grave sites, often the caves formed by lava tubes, were public knowledge, but those of the *ali'i* were known only to the person responsible for the burying.[19] The burial ritual was based on the concept of *mana*, an individual's uniqueness and power; the *ali'i*, being of the noblest of royalty, possessed the most *mana*. This remained in the bones of the deceased and could be tapped by the one who had them.[20] According to Toni Han, "The bones of the dead were guarded, respected, treasured, venerated, loved or even deified by relatives; coveted and despoiled by enemies. Flesh decays, but bones survive as everlasting reminders; in essence, bones represent the immortality of an individual, as well as a link between the living and their progenitors."[21] This is the reason why Hiwilani desires these sacred remnants. In the nineteenth century, King Kalakaua started the bone-hunting craze. Relatives would take the bones as keepsakes, as Hiwilani does, to discover their own history. Rather than writing a traditional historical discourse, Hiwilani returns to and reconstructs her past. Her son, Prince Akuli, works in a more "literary" fashion, but this reflects his historical biases.

Prince Akuli's education at Oxford came about because his mother wants the bones of her grandfather and her mother, and through sorcery she convinces her old retainer, Ahuna, accompanied by the prince, to retrieve them from the secret burial cave. Ahuna is the only person who knows the location of the cave; after his death, the bones will be interred forever. Akuli refuses to go, but his mother promises to convince his father to send him to Oxford, knowing that he is completely taken with British culture and authors. Akuli, accompanied by Ahuna, makes the journey to retrieve the bones. And the prince is eventually sent to England. Ahuna and Akuli fall prey to different yet equally powerful authoritative discourses.[22] Ironically, Ahuna's belief in tradition and superstition is the very thing that sends the unbelieving Akuli to England, where he will discard all vestiges of that past.

Most of the prince's narrative is about this sojourn to his ancestors' tomb, but his discourse is as biased with Anglocentrism as his mother's is with her ethnocentrism:

> Old drunken Howard had lent me his Tennyson, and I had mooned long and often over the "Idyls of the King." Here were the three, I thought—Arthur and Lancelot and Guinevere. This, then, I pondered, was the end of it all, of life and strife and striving and love, the weary spirits of these long-gone ones to be invoked by fat old women and mangy sorcerers, the bones of them to be esteemed of collectors and betted on horse races and ace-fulls or to be sold for cash and invested in sugar stocks. (200)

The prince's cynical historical discourse is clearly the result of his English education and the colonization and annexation of Hawaii. Yet while he is in the crypt, he steals two shin bones. As much as he tries to deny the remnants of the ancient Hawaiian in the modern man, Prince Akuli is painfully aware they lurk beneath the surface.

In opposition to Prince Akuli is Kanau, his father, who is fully cognizant of the historical and cultural importance of the bones, but disregards this knowledge for the sake of profit. Like his wife, he collects bones and other relics buried with the dead. But he does not use them to reconstruct history; he sells them to collectors so he can invest in sugar and bet on horses. Ahuna says of Kanau: "There is no sacredness in Kanau. His mind is filled with sugar and the breeding of horses. I do know that he sold a feather cloak his grandfather had worn to that English collector for eight thousand dollars, and the money he lost the next day betting on the polo game between Maui and Oahu" (196). Kanau has absorbed the worst qualities of English and American entrepreneurs. He literally sells his heritage and ostentatiously squanders his profits, behavior associated with the decadent wealthy. Kanau looks at life only in terms of monetary profit and loss. Akuli's parents provide a cacophony of discourses between which the prince is divided. This is reflected in the narrative structure of "Shin Bones."

The overarching voice of the first-person narrator is another historiographic discourse in the stratum of voices. This layering of tellers shows the complexity of narrating historical discourses, for as Mikhail Bakhtin notes, " 'I' can only realize itself on the basis of 'we.'"[23] The first-person narrator can immediately bring both the prince's tale and his own to the dialogic level of the "we." This narrator is an acquaintance of the prince's; they met in South Africa during the Boer War. He is a *malihini*, or white outsider, but he is the prince's traveling companion on this day when Akuli chooses to tell his history. In a narrative structure resembling Conrad's *Heart of Darkness*, this nameless narrator recounts the prince's tale, providing a frame for the narrative and someone for the prince to talk to, as well as reminding the reader that this is indeed text, for the narrator introduces numerous breaks in Akuli's story.

London's admiration for Joseph Conrad is well documented, and the similarity between the narrative structure of *Heart of Darkness* and "Shin Bones" is undeniable. The first-person narrator of London's text recounts Prince Akuli's tale of a clandestine journey, much as the narrator of Conrad's novella tells of Marlow's tale of his journey up the Congo. The narrator's frequent interruptions alert the reader of *Heart of Darkness* that this is the reconstruction of a narrative set in London, not the Congo. Similarly, "Shin Bones" is set in modern Hawaii, not during Akuli's teenage years, and the narrator's breaking into the story so reminds the reader. Additionally, through this framing in both texts, we see not only the narrative made more complex but also the evils of imperialism in Africa and the indictment of colonialism in Hawaii. At the conclusion of Conrad's work, however, Marlow is a changed man, decidedly more resigned and nihilistic about human nature. In "Shin Bones" the narrator does not give in to the prince's cynicism; he retells the story in a manner showing his deep respect for the Hawaiian people, regardless of how the prince feels about them. This continuous exchange of points of view about culture and history between Prince Akuli and the narrator lends depth to London's narrative.

The narrator's reconstruction of history is certainly on the side of the ancient Hawaiians, who allowed their lands to be taken from them by greedy capitalists. After watching the old woman present her completed lei to the prince, the narrator states:

> Oh, truly, to be an *alii* in Hawaii, even in this second decade of the twentieth century, is no light thing. The *alii*, utterly of the new, must be kindly and kingly to those old ones absolutely of the old. Nor did the prince without a kingdom, his loved island long since annexed by the United States and incorporated into a territory along with the rest of the Hawaiian Islands—nor did the prince betray his repugnance for the odor of the hala. He bowed his head graciously; and his royal condescending words of pure Hawaiian I know would make the old woman's heart, until she died, warm with remembrance of the wonderful occasion. The very grimace he stole to me would not have been made had he felt any uncertainty of its escaping her. (190)

Prince Akuli's divided attention is treated sympathetically in light of his nation's history. This second version of history in "Shin Bones" causes the text's underlying concerns to surface within its polyphony. The long-running dichotomy in the native population, created by British colonization and American annexation, is encapsulated in the narrative voices of London's story.

All of the history of Hawaii figures prominently in the weave of London's "Shin Bones." Behind the behavior of Prince Akuli, Hiwilani, and Kanau is the British and American influence and its varying effects on each individual: Hiwilani longs for her lost heritage; Kanau is completely absorbed by the white hegemony. Prince Akuli faces the nightmare of history and the nightmare of the future as well, for he is a modern man.

Having more in common with Stephen Dedalus than with Humphrey Van Weyden, Prince Akuli feels the burden of the past more acutely than anyone else in the narrative. He has his Hawaiian past, but his Anglocentric past affects his historical discourse in modern Hawaii. When in the tomb of his ancestors, he can recall the past only in language that bears Hawaiian and English influences. He must live with the burden of the glorious past, but he must also face what seems a bleak, capitalist-inspired future. In Europe, World War I is under way; the prince remarks as he gazes upon his new lei: "It stinks of the ancient, . . . I stink of the modern. My father was right. The sweetest of all is sugar up a hundred points, or four aces in a poker game. If the Big War lasts another year, I shall clean up three quarters of a million over a million" (192). In this passage and in his exclamation, "This is the twentieth century and we stink of gasoline," he indirectly shows his concern for having lost a pre-white past, and he indicates his wariness about the future's lack of promise—unless he cares only about making money. There is a certain cynicism in his voice, revealing his alienation from both worlds. The prince is caught between "going native" and going Anglo-American modern, the same bind that ostensibly landed him at Oxford. This is why he possesses the bones of his ancestors and a limousine. Ironically, because the prince lives in the present and remembers the past, he can never hope to "go native"; he is already too "white." Like his father, the prince has given up his heritage for the sake of profit. Unlike his father, he is all too aware of this, and it tortures him into a cynicism about the past, present, and future.

Through Hiwilani and Akuli, all these issues are made manifest, but obversely. Hiwilani's "going native" has only stressed her Anglocentrism, and Akuli's Anglocentrism has only emphasized his Hawaiian heritage, exemplified by his inability to live satisfactorily in the present because he is haunted by the past. Thus London implies that in a cultural exchange, economic implications and factors always prevent the culture from being what it once was. Changing one hegemony for another forever influences the culture that was absorbed. This may seem novel and exciting, but one eventually yearns for what was lost. Unfortunately, history cannot be altered; some may try to recapture it, some may be trapped in it, and some may attempt to interpret it. In "The Politics of Knowledge," Edward Said observes, "Victimization, alas, does not guarantee or necessarily enable an enhanced sense of humanity. To testify to a history of oppression is necessary, but it is not sufficient unless that history is redirected into intellectual process and universalized to include all sufferers."[24] For Hiwilani and Prince Akuli, this is the horror of their situation: Hiwilani makes no attempt to intellectualize the past, and the prince has overintellectualized it to the point of cynicism and solipsism. Both mother and son lack a sense of humanity. And this lack is further emphasized by the first-person narrator.

Throughout, Prince Akuli's discourse is rendered discontinuous. Interestingly, whenever the narrator interrupts, he refers to the same image, the old Hawaiian woman stringing the lei for the prince, whom she recognizes. The prince is disgusted at the action but accepts the lei graciously out of his sense of royal duty, again showing the conflict between old and new values. He later flings the lei into the bushes when she is gone, which suggests that the modern wins out. The parts of the narrative that involve this woman serve two purposes: to show that the prince cannot escape his heritage and to draw attention to the historical discourses at work in London's text.

The narrator's choice—his sympathetic portrayal of an old woman string-ing a lei for a member of royalty who is a mere figurehead and who scorns the Hawaiian ways—shows his bias toward and respect for the common peo-ple, those who were forgotten by their rulers and exploited by the sugar barons. Second, he makes continual reference to the rape of the land and the annexation of the Islands, revealing his dislike for this now well established power structure: "It is true that the hala smelled most freshly strong, yet was the act beautiful to me, and the old woman herself beautiful to me. My mind leaped into the prince's narrative so that to Ahuna I could not help liken-ing her" (190). Clearly, the narrator's discourse is anything but objective. Hence we have another historical discourse distinctly reflecting the biases of its creator. The narrator does more than simply recount the prince's narra-tive. The old woman was not a part of the prince's tale; the narrator chose to interrupt the story and include her. But the issues of the nature of his-torical discourse do not end with the nameless narrator; they resonate on yet another discursive level.

The amount of research Jack London undertook about Hawaii before beginning to write fiction about the Islands additionally makes this story a historical discourse by London. As Bakhtin notes, "Through the agency of artistic form the creator takes up *an active position with respect to content*."[25] Since London is the ultimate crafter of this fiction, he obviously controls all of the discourses here and is himself a participant in the polyphony. The his-toriography of "Shin Bones" can thus be carried to yet a third level. London, in his fictional account of a prince alienated from his heritage who tells a white man, sympathetic toward the way the Islanders have been treated, a story about that heritage, is telling his own history of Hawaii's colonization and annexation. In 1916, London wrote,

> The *haoles*, or whites, overthrew the Hawaiian Monarchy, formed the Dole Republic, and shortly thereafter brought their loot in under the sheltering folds of the Stars and Stripes. There is little use to balk at the word "loot." The white man is the born Looter. And just as the American Indian was looted of his continent by the white man, so was the Hawaiian looted by the white men of his islands. Such things be. They are morally indefensible. As facts they are irrefragable—as irrefragable as the facts that water drowns, that frost bites, and that fire incinerates.[26]

The nature of London's historical discourse is undeniable here. His figura-tive language clearly condemns American interests in Hawaii. London goes on to say that Hawaii is a paradise for the well-to-do, those privileged few who can afford it.[27] This bias is present in the telling of "Shin Bones," in which London conflates fiction and history, creating fictional characters in order to present his interpretation of Hawaiian events. Bakhtin has said that "the author's discourse about a character is discourse about discourse."[28] Thus even under the umbrella of fictional discourse, the protean nature of the recording of history is evident. Cultural assumptions, as Bakhtin notes, influence the historical discourses of character, author, and reader: "The simple selection of an epithet or a metaphor is already an active evaluative act with orientation in both directions—toward the listener and toward the hero. *Listener and hero are constant participants in the creative event*, which does not for a single instant cease to be an event of living communication involving all three."[29] The characters in "Shin Bones" are influenced by their cultures when they create their discourses. London, wealthy, white, and a former socialist, interprets the texts as a point of view on the side of the exploited, but knowledgeable about the exploiters. And according to Bakhtin, this extends to the reader, who, depending on his or her culture, participates variously in the polyphonic dialogue created by the prince, the narrator, and London.

London's narrative strategies in "Shin Bones" clearly place him among modern, rather than naturalist or Victorian, writers. Gone from this narrative are the nineteenth-century conventions prevalent in London's earlier work. London, in 1915, was creating a new style of fiction, one that raised more questions than it answered. Prince Akuli is akin to Eliot's J. Alfred Prufrock in his cynicism, nihilism, and solipsism. Like Stephen Dedalus and Prufrock, Akuli resorts to "silence, exile, and cunning" and is far too cynical to ever "eat a peach." No longer at the mercy of nature, London's later characters battle with themselves and the often painful self-knowledge they possess. Like Dedalus, Akuli is trying to awaken from the nightmare that is history.

This break from Victorian conventions extends to the content of the work as well. London clearly condemns imperialist attitudes toward native populations, and particularly toward women. In September 1904, British author Charles Warren Stoddard presented London with a copy of his collection of Hawaiian stories, *The Island of Tranquil Delights*.[30] Stoddard's anthology concludes with a photograph of a nude Hawaiian woman seductively lying among carefully arranged tropical foliage.[31] This final image is a patent objectification of the woman, an attitude absent from "Shin Bones" and London's other Hawaiian works.

London gives his characters their own voices; they are autonomous individuals, not objects to be exploited for the sake of the curious and the greedy. And these many voices suggest a dialogue between past and present to reconcile the ambivalence experienced by modern Hawaiians like Prince Akuli, as well as the sense of regret displayed by his companion, the narrator. In "Shin Bones," indeed, there is a call for the elimination of a single authoritative voice. All absolutes are subject to question; there is no one interpretation of history, but several interpretations existing simultaneously. This dialogue extends beyond the text to include the reader, for, as Bakhtin says, "the artistic interaction of author, listener, and hero may exert its influence on other domains of social interaction."[32] Thus in the dialogic matrix of "Shin Bones," Prince Akuli's failure need not be the reader's. The reader, or listener, can become yet another voice in the polyphony.

The Myth of Hope in Jack London's "The Red One"

LAWRENCE I. BERKOVE

"The Red One" is an artistic, powerful, but perplexing story. Written at the peak of London's intellectual and literary development, the story is thickset with psychologically suggestive situations, with ambiguities and ironies, with odd parallels and paradoxes, and with mythological and literary allusions. These allusions at first may seem ornaments to the fabric of the tale, but on closer inspection they turn out to be functional. They pattern the way the story unfolds and progressively reveal the grounds for London's skepticism that humanity can fulfill its aspirations to civilization.

There are several reasons why this intriguing story is not better known. The most obvious is that, until recently, it has been hard to locate. Completed in May 1916,[1] it was originally published, posthumously, in October 1918 both in *Cosmopolitan*, where its title was changed from "The Message," and in the anthology, *The Red One*.[2] It was not reprinted until 1972, when Thomas Clareson included it in his *A Spectrum of Worlds*; only with the publication of the Library of America's 1982 edition of *Jack London: Novels and Stories*, the 1990 edition of *Short Stories of Jack London*, and Stanford's 1993 edition of the *Complete Short Stories of Jack London* did the story at last receive wide circulation.

Another reason is the mistaken but widespread assumption that London is only a "popular" author, that he is not suitably "literary" for serious scholarship. On the contrary, the poetic complexity of the story is why even scholars who are familiar with "The Red One" have only reconnoitered it with a handful of brief studies of it. Most of these studies have merely categorized the tale, variously, as a work of science fiction, of naturalism, of fantasy, of proto-Jungian psychology, or as an echo of Conrad's *Heart of Darkness*.[3] Each of these categories has some merit, but as partial treatments of the story they underestimate its uniqueness and sophistication.

A technical problem that also might have slowed the interpretation of this story has been whether it could be justly approached from a Jungian perspective. Although the story is strikingly suggestive of that influence, until now there has been no support for assuming that London was familiar with Jung. In what is now one of his most frequently quoted statements, Jack London in 1916 described to his wife, Charmian, his feelings upon reading Carl Jung's newly published *Psychology of the Unconscious*: "Mate Woman, I tell you I am standing on the edge of a world so new, so terrible, so wonderful, that I am almost afraid to look over into it."[4] Thanks to the pioneering work of such scholars as Earle Labor, James McClintock, and Jeanne Campbell Reesman, the stories written after London read that book are now recognized as being profoundly influenced—inspired, actually—by Jungian psychology. More than that, they are also being acknowledged as among his best. This emphasis has placed great weight upon the probable date of London's encounter with Jungian thought. The English translation of *Psychology of the Unconscious* became available in the summer of 1916, and London appears to have read it in June. If this marks London's introduction to Jung, then "The Red One," completed in May, is even more remarkable because if it preceded London's contact with Jungian psychology then London would have had to arrive independently at some of the same insights as Jung.

I have discovered information, however, that makes possible a date earlier than the summer of 1916 for London's first contact with Jungian thought. Although the English translation of *Psychology of the Unconscious* was published in 1916, it was by no means the first translation of Jung's work. Between 1907 and January 1916, fifteen other works had been translated, including two monographs—one in 1909 and the other in 1915.[5] An extensive criticism of Jung also appeared in English as early as 1910.[6] Although the facts of these early translations and discussion do not constitute proof that London read them, they do indicate that Jungian ideas had currency in the United States before 1916 and that London's lively interest in psychology may have led him to them, even secondhand. London, according to David Hamilton, had begun to read Freud as early as 1912 and to integrate Freudian ideas into his work by 1914.[7] It is not farfetched to think that London had read the works of other psychologists as well, and that he read *Psychology of the Unconscious* when it first came out because he had encountered Jung's thought elsewhere.[8]

Although there might well be Jungian elements in "The Red One," I believe that the story is still too early to be considered as Jungian as, for example, his later stories "The Water Baby" or "Like Argus of the Ancient Times." In any case, there was too much going on in London's mind in May 1916 for "The Red One" to be restricted to any single influence. The tale instead reflects London at that dramatic and exciting moment in his life, when his mind was churning with such powerful stimuli as Freudian as well as Jungian theory, mythology, Darwin, reflection on the implications for civilization of World War I, skepticism, and mysticism. As London weighed and balanced these tremendous considerations and attempted to integrate them with his previous experience, his art was at its peak, and in "The Red One" he recorded fictionally an extraordinary, unified impression of his world at a pivotal moment in time.

The story opens with the English naturalist Bassett recollecting his captivation by a strange but heavenly sound while he was searching for a rare butterfly on Guadalcanal, one of the Solomon Islands in the South Pacific. London associated Melanesia, which includes the Solomons, with sickness, evil, and humanity at its most degraded. As Labor puts it, "If Polynesia was London's version of Paradise Lost, then Melanesia was his version of the Inferno."[9] Entering the jungle to locate the sound, Bassett is ambushed by bushmen who kill his bearer and injure him. In the process of escaping the natives, Bassett kills some of them and inadvertently flees toward the interior. Then follows a waking nightmare in which Bassett, fevered and semi-delirious from insect bites, penetrates ever deeper into the heart of the jungle stinking "with evil," guided only occasionally by repetitions of that magnificent sound. He encounters monstrous, parasitic, and decadent "life-forms that rooted in death and lived on death" (582) and tiny villages of cannibals who tortured their human victims. Bassett's ordeal of survival of the fittest reduces him within a matter of days from a civilized scientist to a savage whose gun alone makes him superior.

Bassett, at the point of death, is saved by Balatta, a bushwoman so ugly to him as to seem "apish," who brings him back to her tribe of headhunters. As he is nursed back to partial health and learns the tribal language, he meets Ngurn, the "devil-devil" priest or medicine man. They eventually become cronies, for Ngurn in his way shares Bassett's aspiration to wisdom. Ngurn's way is to cure heads in the smoke of the devil-devil hut and exchange secrets with them.

When Bassett learns from Ngurn that the majestic sounds Bassett finds irresistible come from the god of the tribe, "the Red One," also called the

"Star-Born," he pressures Balatta, who loves him, to take him to the place of the Red One. She does so, but secretly and in terror, for the place is taboo to females and the penalty is a week of slow torture before death. The Red One is a ball, 200 feet in diameter, of an unearthly, iridescent cherry-red metal, resting in a pit dug out of a mesa and surrounded by human sacrifices, some still dying from torture. Bassett is convinced that it came—or was sent—from somewhere in space. Even when lightly touched, its surface quickens into sounds. The glorious peals that enthrall Bassett come, however, from its being struck by a "king post"—an elaborately carved battering ram. But each wonderful sound represents, ironically, another sacrifice inhumanly made to the Red One.

When Bassett returns to the village, he realizes that his illness will not leave him long to live. He therefore strikes a bargain with Ngurn, offering to yield his head, which Ngurn covets, for the privilege of seeing and hearing the Red One once more, up close. The story ends with Bassett, in his final auditory ecstasy, fancying, just as Ngurn's steel bites into his neck, "the vision of his head turning slowly, always turning, in the devil-devil house beside the breadfruit tree" (598).

It is necessary to pause and expand upon the symbolism and suggestive situations. They add power to the tale and might even seem the main attractions in themselves did not London discourage this by complicating them with ambiguity and irony, thus subordinating them to his skeptical conclusion. For example, despite its association with human sacrifice, the central image of the Red One is beautiful as well as terrible, and it contains the promise of good as well as bad. It may therefore be seen not only as a symbol of death but, paradoxically, also as a symbol of hope or life. As a symbol of hope, the Red One might be "a child of intelligences" (592) from superior civilizations in outer space. As an ovular symbol of life, red as blood and round, the Red One represents potential and is essentially passive. It has no sound, no voice of its own until struck or stimulated. The most effective of these objects is the "king post" ram, a phallic symbol. But this, too, is represented ambiguously and ironically as a symbol of destructive potency. Amid the dead and the dying in the Red One's pit are many totem poles from defeated tribes, some of them adorned with the helmet motif—another phallic symbol. The king post, itself decorated with helmet motifs, therefore represents the superior violent masculinity of Ngurn's victorious tribe.

Bassett's "penetration" of Guadalcanal is another example of ambiguous and ironic masculinity. Adding to the sexual implication of "penetration" is that Guadalcanal itself is a female symbol: an island, surrounded by fluid. Its potent center, the Red One, is surrounded by additional female symbols: the protective rings of beach, jungle, grasslands, hills, and village. Bassett penetrates each of these rings on his way to the core. But Bassett's masculinity is limited—he makes it on his own only through the grasslands and then has to be aided by Balatta the rest of the way. Bassett may be masculine in his consciousness and rationality, expressed in his profession as a scientist, yet even in England, we are told, for him woman's sexual charm "had never been robust" (588). In a further irony, his name suggests the hound bred to catch small burrowing animals, like rabbits. But the Red One is not small game, and neither is it "captured." On the contrary, Bassett, having penetrated Guadalcanal up to the Red One, does not go all the way, nor can he get out again. This implies a masculinity as well as a personal deficiency.

If the story is approached from a Jungian perspective, and Bassett is regarded as a sort of ego, Ngurn functions ambiguously as his "shadow."[10] Bassett regards Ngurn as "a fore-runner of ethics and contracts, of consideration, and gentleness in man" (598)—a sort of precursor of civilization—but Ngurn's civilization is, in the final analysis, as limited to externals as Bassett's. The devil-devil priest and medicine man sits in the "ashes of death" (585) and broods darkly upon the mysteries. Ngurn talks to heads and seems to expect replies. However much he may delude himself, Ngurn does not get into the heads he collects, nor would he find much of the wisdom he professes to seek in the head of Bassett, who is educated but not wise.

Balatta serves the purpose of Bassett's "anima," the female side of a male personality. She is unadorned female: primitive, elemental, and instinctual. Although she acts largely on unconscious impulses, she is generous, ready to serve, and represents love.[11] But Bassett considers her "unthinkably disgusting" (588) and suitable only to be used, and to achieve his purpose he is quite willing that she be sacrificed: "Yet did Bassett insist on having his man's will satisfied, at the woman's risk, that he might solve the mystery of the Red One's singing, though she should die long and horribly and screaming" (590). Bassett regarded all women as subservient, inferior, and "animated by the cosmic verity of sex" (589). In imparting this overbearing attitude to Bassett, London both loads the case against Bassett and personally distances himself. London in his own life had long since come to value women as equals of men.[12] Bassett's ingratitude for Balatta's devotion and his inability to appreciate her inner qualities are major deficiencies.

The three main characters together would constitute an integrated self, but separately they all fail. Balatta sets herself up to die for love of Bassett when she accompanies him on his final visit to the Red One, for the place is taboo to women and Ngurn must uphold the law. Bassett dies for one last ecstatic experience, but without penetrating the mystery of the Red One. Ngurn lives on, but he is at best the progenitor of an evolving culture that appears doomed to fall short of achieving wisdom, just as Bassett's has.

This is suggested by the implicit comparison of the two cultures' attitudes toward sacrifice. Ngurn's tribe is bloody, typifying "the pitiless rule of natural selection" (594), and barbaric, sacrificing humans liberally to the Red One. It is so skilled in torture that Bassett "realized that he was yet a tyro in knowledge of the frightfulness the human was capable of wreaking on the human" (590). Nevertheless, Bassett, having reverted to barbarism in wandering through the jungle, also assents to both torture and sacrifice when he does not prevent Balatta from going with him on his last visit to the Red One. Bassett and his gun, moreover, not only arrived at Guadalcanal from "civilization" on a "black-birding" ketch—a slave ship—but as "a scientist first, a humanist afterward" (589), he was so determined to "extract from the heart of the Red One the message of the world from other worlds" that he was willing to destroy "the entire population of Guadalcanal" (595). Similarly, Ngurn, in order to extract wisdom from the heads of people of other tribes, has them killed and decapitated. In brief, just as Bassett and Ngurn may be seen to be ironic doubles, so may their respective cultures. Given that London wrote the story during World War I, which was then in mid-course, he might have been implying that both Ngurn and his culture were less barbaric than Bassett and his, and that the story of civilization is one of regression rather than advancement.

What takes this story beyond a series of thought-provoking but undirected parallels and paradoxes is London's subtle use of a series of literary and mythological allusions that increasingly shape a pessimistic conclusion. The three allusions present in the first paragraph of "The Red One" all have settings that suggest the end of an old order and the coming of a new, but demonstrate in themselves a graduation from optimism to pessimism. The first compares the "liberation of sound" emanating from the Red One to "the trump of an archangel." This probable reference to Gabriel, together with the quoted phrase, prepares the reader for good tidings. The second allusion, to walls of cities falling down "before so vast and compelling a summons," is to Joshua. Like the first, this reference also has a culturally favorable connotation, but may in context also allude ironically to the extermination of the Guadalcanal villages by the Red One's aggressive tribes. But the third, likening the sound to "the mighty cry of some Titan of the Elder World vexed with misery or wrath" (578), recalls the Titans supplanted by the Greek gods and reflects pain, frustration, failure, and defeat. Thus the first paragraph subtly outlines and forecasts the outcome of the story.

A note of ambiguity is established several paragraphs later with an allusion to Childe Roland and his dark tower (579). Again, we are reminded of an imminent encounter of great import, but as in Browning's poem, neither the issue involved nor the likely consequence of the confrontation is made manifest.

After Bassett penetrates the outer jungle of Guadalcanal, "abruptly, as if cloven by the sword of God in the hand of God, the jungle terminated" (582). The referent of this powerful simile is delayed several paragraphs until Balatta appears, "innocent of garb as Eve before the fig-leaf adventure" but "as unbeautiful a prototype of woman as [Bassett], with a scientist's eye, had ever gazed upon" (583). In this subtle and complex allusion, which is the central image of the story, London has evoked Eden and Darwin's *Descent of Man*. It may seem strange to think of a ferocious and cannibalistic culture as Edenic, but London is being anthropological and relativistic rather than biblically faithful. If Eden ever existed, he implies, it probably was like this.

This understated but potent allusion has major ramifications for the story. If Balatta is an Eve, then Bassett is an Adam. But he is an Adam who despises his Eve. To him, "the sight of her was provocative of nausea and the contact of her provocative of despair" (589). Nevertheless, this Adam's decision, like that of the first Adam, will affect the genetic future of the race. Furthermore, London treats the Eden story as myth, which enables him to put other myths on a par with it. This is parallel to Jung if not actually Jungian: although no myth is absolutely true, all myths contain some valuable human truth.

The Eden allusion is ironically continued in the description of Ngurn's dwelling, "the devil-devil house in the shadow of the breadfruit tree" (584). In Eden was the tree of life as well as the tree of knowledge of good and evil. The punishment for eating the fruit of the latter was death, and Adam and Eve were exiled lest they eat the fruit of the tree of life and live forever. The breadfruit tree recalls both the Edenic trees, one with fruit and the other with bread, the staff of life. In the shadow of a tree of life, therefore, is a house of death, and it guards the forbidden knowledge of the secrets of life and death and also the mysteries of the Red One, temptingly cherry-red. This allusion, in other words, is foreboding in its association of knowledge with death.

What Bassett's scientific training enables him to deduce about the Red One is signified by the next allusion, to the statue of Memnon (589). Memnon, a fabled king of the Ethiopians, was the son of Aurora and Tithonus and was killed in combat with Achilles. A statue of him on the Nile supposedly gives off mysterious sounds when struck by the sun's rays. Bassett abandons his hypothesis that the Red One became "vocal" when the sun struck it when he realizes that its sounds are associated with sacrifices and occur at night as well as in the daytime. Later, this realization plus his personal discovery that the Red One is hollow means that it is no messenger but might contain a message. He concludes that "no thing of chance was it," but that it came from the stars, "a creation of artifice and mind" (592), possibly from advanced beings. The rest of the story reflects Bassett's failure to appreciate the distinction between messenger and message and act on it.[13]

The possible deadliness of the message is hinted at when Bassett's first visual impression of the Red One is that it seems to be a pearl (590). Brown connects this allusion to Matthew 13:45–46: "Again, the kingdom of heaven is like unto a merchantman, seeking goodly pearls: Who, when he had found one pearl of great price, went and sold all that he had, and bought it" ("A Perfect Sphere," 83, 85). The reference to eternal life is the apparent meaning, but the allusion makes more sense if read ironically, because what Bassett actually "buys" is death.

The ironic inversion of biblical allusions intensifies when Ngurn is described as functioning "religiously for himself and the twelve tribes under him." Clearly, the twelve tribes of Israel are being summoned to mind in this shocking comparison. Bassett, who views Ngurn's tribe as evil, apish, and irrational, spells out the blasphemy: "It was as if God's Word had fallen into the muck mire of the abyss underlying the bottom of hell; as if Jehovah's Commandments had been presented on carved stone to the monkeys of the monkey cage at the Zoo; as if the Sermon on the Mount had been preached in a roaring bedlam of lunatics" (593). London did not find it necessary to suggest what some superior observer from space might think of European nations revering the Bible and slaughtering one another in a world war.

Another foreshadowing of Bassett's end occurs when Ngurn informs him that "no white man . . . had gazed upon the Red One and lived" (595). This statement recalls God's warning to Moses in Exodus 33:20: "Thou canst not see my face: for there shall no man see me, and live." Bassett briefly hopes to recover his health, escape back to "civilization," and return with an armed expedition that would kill everyone who keeps him from learning the Red

One's message. But when his health deteriorates and he realizes that his death is imminent, no alternative remains but to make the best of Ngurn's law, gaze upon the Red One—and die.

Two more allusions, one overt and one indirect, appear in the last paragraph of the story, both seemingly linked to heads, but actually to minds. Bassett's final vision of "his head turning slowly, always turning" in Ngurn's devil-devil house is prepared for by his knowledge that Ngurn respected him as a wise man and that Ngurn desired to devote himself to "the long learning and hatching of the final wisdom that will be mine before I die." If Bassett consents to yield his head, Ngurn tells him, "I promise you, in the long days to come when I turn your head in the smoke, no man of the tribe shall come in to disturb us. And I will tell you many secrets, for I am an old man and very wise, and I shall be adding wisdom to wisdom as I turn your head in the smoke" (596). The idea of learning from a severed head occurs in a number of myths around the world, particularly the story of Mimir, which London might have known,[14] but the allusion here is ironic.

Norse myth describes Mimir as an exceedingly wise man. He was one of the Aesir, the gods of Asgard, and a favorite of Odin's. While on a mission to the Vanir, the opponents of the Aesir, Mimir was decapitated by them. The Vanir then sent Mimir's head back to Odin. "Odin took Mimir's head and cradled it. He smeared it with herbs to preserve it, so that it would never decay. And then the High One sang charms over it and gave back to Mimir's head the power of speech. So its wisdom became Odin's wisdom—many truths unknown to any other being."[15] For all Ngurn's confidence, however, and his appearance as an intellectually curious man, the story does not reveal him to be particularly wise. The romantic rationale of learning wisdom from Bassett's head is appealing, but the omniscient narrator has told us what is in Bassett's head, and it is not wisdom. Furthermore, Ngurn's practice of "curing" heads may be a grimly ironic pun. Indeed, when a head is cut off and smoked, it is "cured" of seeking wisdom or thinking about truth. This allusion, therefore, leads to a false conclusion unless taken ironically.[16]

The overt allusion to Medusa also is deceptive—self-deceptive, actually—on Bassett's part. Just as he feels Ngurn's hatchet bite into the back of his neck, "it seemed that he gazed upon the serene face of the Medusa, Truth" (598), and Bassett has a final vision of his turning head in Ngurn's devil-devil house. The equation of the Medusa's face with truth, however, is Bassett's and not the narrator's. Bassett's point of view is not always reliable, and his error is signaled by his peculiar identification of Medusa with truth. Medusa, according to the account of Apollodorus, was a Gorgon whose face, topped by writhing snakes in place of hair, was so horrible that whoever looked on her was turned to stone. When Perseus killed her with Athena's help, he gave her head to Athena, who placed it upon the aegis, Zeus's shield, which she always carried.

London depicts in Bassett, therefore, a man who confuses wisdom for truth, who looks upon Medusa instead of Athena, and who in so doing sets himself up for death without knowing either wisdom or truth. His ecstasy when the Red One is struck may mark a sensory high point, but not an intellectual one. All the convictions he derived from that final sound, that "archangels spoke in it," that "it was invested with the intelligence of supermen of planets of other suns,"[17] that "it was the voice of God," and that "the interstices of matter were his, and the interfusings and intermating transfusings of matter and force," all these soaring "insights" are fantasies of a mind that wanted certainty so badly that it deluded itself.[18]

Two last allusions provide us with a means of tying together London's fable. Implicit in this story is the legend of Pandora—in Greek myth the first woman, a kind of Eve—who unwisely opened a box from which all of mankind's troubles escaped, but in which yet remained life's greatest good—hope. The Red One, though fearsome, may contain hope for man. But it is never opened, and its secret remains sealed.

As we have seen, the Red One in its similarity to an ovum may serve as a symbol of life. Life holds the potential for both bad and good, respectively represented by the Red One's angry and threatening sounds and its archangelic sonorities. Despite the gruesome acts done in its name, however, the Red One itself is innocent and passive; it is like an egg as yet unpenetrated. Were that to happen, it might turn into something else, possibly something good. A risk is involved, of course, in finding out.

For all his "wisdom," Ngurn never attempts to find out what is inside the Red One. He causes the phallic king post to bump up against it in an ironic sort of foreplay, but he never contemplates penetration. But Bassett almost penetrates it. On his first and furtive visit to the Red One, "forgetful of safety, of his own life itself, entranced by the wonder of the unthinkable and unguessable thing, he raised his knife to strike heavily from a long stroke, but was prevented by Balatta." This is the turning point of the story.[19] The terrified Balatta begs him not to strike, and ironically, "he yielded automatically to his gentler instincts and withheld the knife-hack" (592).

London here completes the Eden-Darwin parallel by inverting the Eden myth. An Adam and Eve once again face a momentous decision, and again they make the wrong choice. Unlike Eve, Balatta wishes to obey the taboo of her god; unlike Adam, Bassett would have broken it. In the Eden story and this one, Adam and Bassett err by being wrongly gentle—indulgent—with their mates. And in both stories the pair are punished with death.[20] In the Eden myth death comes eventually, after exile and a cursed life; in Guadalcanal, it comes instantly for Bassett and, presumably, in a week's time after torture for Balatta.

The difference between the two stories is that between the Bible and Darwin. In the Bible, Adam and Eve defied a divine injunction limiting their intellectual inquisitiveness and paid the price for their folly. In "The Red One," there is no such divine injunction, just human taboos (Bassett, in fact, creates his own), and to obey them is folly. What makes good theological sense in the Bible makes no sense at all in London's parable of evolution. If human progress is to be made, he intimates, nothing is sacred but human life.

Although Balatta represents love and potential life, she lacks the intellectual curiosity necessary to advance the quality of life. Ngurn represents the shadow side of Bassett, ethics and an appreciation of mystery, but he lacks the knowledge and daring—the manliness—necessary to penetrate the Red One. And though Bassett is intellectual, he is inhumane; he would wipe out the population of Guadalcanal to find his answers. He also lives too much in his mind: "To him, human life had dwarfed to microscopic proportions before this colossal portent of higher life from within the distances of the sidereal universe" (592). The outstanding qualities of each of the three might have been combined in a way beneficial to the race, but these are unintegrated, and the hope they represent is lost.[21]

The last allusion in the story derives from the island chain in which Guadalcanal is located: the Solomons. "The Red One" is about the search for truth, but before truth can be apprehended, there must be wisdom. The reference to the wisdom of Solomon remains an ironic backdrop to this story of human folly, of intellectual timorousness, superstition, and arrogance. London's studies of psychology seem to have revealed to him human potentialities, which were too seldom integrated to bring about the progress he yearned for. In the myths of the race, London found warnings of the same shortcoming. And in Darwin, London could read that "superior" life forms could be extinguished while primitive ones survived. No matter which set of myths London consulted, therefore, biblical, cultural, psychological, or scientific, they offered the same negative conclusion in every case: wisdom eludes man or is of no avail, and truth is beyond his reach.

McClintock observes of London that "joy and terror had always struggled with one another in his work either to complement one another or for final control."[22] Describing London's state of mind in 1916, Charmian reports that London's investigation of many minds "brought to him . . . yet more disillusion with the human element that had already suffered much in his regard." She sees this disillusion at work in London's creation of Bassett: "His ultimate discouragement with the endless strife of humanity even unto the modern horrors of the Great War, are in the mouth of his puppet [Bassett]."[23] Charmian's statements need not be taken as the last word on London to nevertheless grant that "The Red One" does not reflect much optimism for the human race.

The Red One could be a symbol of hopeful life or a symbol of sanguinary violence, but this story grimly posits that hope is doomed to be drowned in blood. London believed that an integration of intelligence and imagination with sensibility (in Jungian terms, masculine and feminine traits, respectively) was needed to move the race forward along an evolutionary path. Because in May 1916 he did not see this occurring, "The Red One" therefore represents his fear that the growth of human intelligence divorced from other humane qualities would lead to the bleak alternative that strife is life, and to a pitiless process of random natural selection that is equivalent to human regression.

Afterword

The Representative Man as Writer/Hero

EARLE LABOR

> It makes a great difference to the force of any sentence whether there be a man behind it or no. . . . Through every clause and part of speech of a right book I meet the eyes of the most determined of men; his force and terror inundate every word; the commas and dashes are alive; so that the writing is athletic and nimble,—can go far and live long.
>
> —Emerson, "Goethe; Or, The Writer"

Several years ago I noted the connection between Goethe's *Wilhelm Meister's Apprenticeship* and London's *Martin Eden*, but I had overlooked Emerson's startlingly relevant essay on Goethe until Jeanne Campbell Reesman discovered it for me.[1] Emerson's description of Goethe seems to have been tailor-made for London: "hundred-handed, Argus-eyed, able and happy to cope with this rolling miscellany of facts and sciences, and by his own versatility to dispose of them with ease; a manly mind, unembarrassed by the variety of coats of convention with which life had got encrusted, easily able by his subtlety to pierce these and draw his strength from nature, with which he lived in full communion." With further aptness, Emerson describes Goethe as a realist and materialist who "would have no word that does not cover a thing"; the user of a simple style that strips away worn-out convention; an autodidact interested in science, especially in the science of human nature.[2]

The parallels between London and Emerson's American scholar, as Cassuto and Reesman have suggested in their Introduction, are equally close. The true scholar, says Emerson, is "Man Thinking"—by which he means the human being "in the right state" or "the whole man." The three major influences that mold the character of this figure are Nature, the Past (best represented in books), and Action. All three are readily apparent in the shaping of London's character as well as in his works. And the last, Action, though not primary, is crucial. "Life lies behind us as the quarry from whence we get tiles and copestones for the masonry of to-day," Emerson explains. "I

217

learn immediately from any speaker how much he has already lived, through
the poverty or the splendor of his speech."[3]

The splendor of London's speech is due in considerable measure to the
richness of experience that informed it. Only lately, however, have his critics come to realize that he gained at least as much of this experience through
the "felt life" of books as through the "raw life" of direct encounter. Furthermore, as Cassuto and Reesman instructively remark, the "emphasis on
the events of Jack London's life has drawn attention away from the writing,
which was always the central activity within that life." The distinctive contribution of the thirteen essays collected in this volume is that they focus essentially if not exclusively upon this "central activity" within London's life.
Perhaps what is most noteworthy is that this kind of critical scrutiny is so
recent—that it has, in fact, come to maturity only during the past generation. Let me underscore this fact with some personal reminiscence and brief
recounting of the recent history of London scholarship.

At the 1963 conference of the Michigan College English Association, held
on the campus at Adrian College (where I was a newcomer serving an ad-
ministrative/teaching stint), MCEA President Sam Baskett introduced me
to the assembly as "the other Jack London scholar." That label reflected not
only our special scholarly camaraderie but also Jack London's peculiar academic status in the early 1960's. Sam and I were not the only self-confessed
Jack London scholars in the United States, of course; but there were barely
a handful of others—King Hendricks at Utah State, Gordon Mills at the University of Texas, Clell Peterson at Murray State, Alfred Shivers at Stephen F.
Austin, and Franklin Walker at Mills College. Except for these, virtually nobody in the academic establishment seemed to think London worth serious
scholarly attention. That had been London's literary predicament for a quarter century following his death, as is witnessed by the representative opinions of some of the country's leading critics, culled from Joan Sherman's *Reference Guide*:

> "He had only to tell his life over again—to make a story of it in the newspa-
> per sense—to feed the romanticism of the big urban populations. London be-
> came a sort of traveling salesman of literature, writing to his market, offering
> 'red blood' and adventure." (Lewis Mumford, *The Golden Day*, 1926)

> "We find the primitive man, who is also the superman of Nietzsche's dreams,
> in the guise" of Larsen, Eden, Daylight, Roberts, and Standing. Ernest Ever-
> hard, "merely the superman in red," and the others are Jack London "as he
> felt himself to be. . . . It was on the egotistic level that his books were con-
> ceived"; and the one character he could depict "is so much a product of his

dreams, so nearly a personal myth, that we cannot find it convincing." (Granville Hicks, *The Great Tradition*, 1933)

"It is almost certain that his vogue is passing, for there is something imper-manent in the very nature of the literature of violence." (Arthur H. Quinn, *American Fiction: An Historical and Critical Survey*, 1936)

From London's tales, O'Neill "brought wholesale butchery and violence to contemporary primitivism." O'Neill's atavism in *The Emperor Jones* suggests London; Anna Christie resembles the "Amazon" in "The Night-Born"; and the "rather witless radical talk of the type that London used to indulge in so handsomely" appears in *The Hairy Ape*. (Oscar Cargill, *Intellectual America*, 1941)[4]

These examples fairly represent the stereotypes of London that prevailed for the generation after his death. But such attitudes began to be seriously challenged during the 1950's by a few maverick critics. After completing his dissertation, "Jack London's Fiction: Its Social Milieu," at Berkeley, Sam Bas-kett published essays on London in *American Literature* and *American Quar-terly*; and his Introduction to the 1956 Rinehart edition of *Martin Eden* was the first definitive treatment of this seminal novel.[5] Gordon Mills also pub-lished pioneering essays in such prestigious journals as *American Quarterly* and *Nineteenth-Century Fiction*.[6] Maxwell Geismar, Kenneth Lynn, Walter Rideout, C. C. Walcutt, and Conway Zirkle included substantial commen-taries on London in their books.[7] And at the end of the decade, Clell Peter-son published three perceptive London articles in the *American Book Col-lector*.[8] These were harbingers of good things in the next generation.

The 1960's may be rightly seen as the watershed of Jack London schol-arship. A number of significant London books were published during this decade: *The Bodley Head Jack London*, edited by Arthur Calder-Marshall; the Pathfinder edition of *The Call of the Wild* and *White Fang*, with an intro-duction by Abraham Rothberg; Richard O'Connor's *Jack London: A Biogra-phy*; Matthew Bruccoli's scholarly Riverside edition of *The Sea-Wolf*; the Signet Classic editions of *The Sea-Wolf* and *The Call of the Wild*, with sub-stantial essays by Franklin Walker; King Hendricks and Irving Shepard's *Let-ter from Jack London*; my Perennial Classics edition of *Great Short Works of Jack London*; Franklin Walker's *Jack London and the Klondike*; and Hensley Woodbridge, John London, and George Tweney's comprehensive *Jack Lon-don: A Bibliography*.[9] Also published during the 1960's were King Hendricks's monographs *Creator and Critic* and *Jack London: Master Craftsman of the Short Story*, C. C. Walcutt's *Jack London* (in the University of Minnesota Pam-phlets on American Writers series), and a new edition of Joan London's *Jack*

London and His Times.[10] Whereas the first issue of *American Literary Scholarship* in 1963 gave Jack London less than a sentence, subsequent issues in the series granted him multiple pages—due in considerable measure to the new forum provided by the *Jack London Newsletter*, inaugurated by Hensley Woodbridge in 1967.

London studies burgeoned during the next decade, beginning with the 1970 publication of *Jack London Reports*, edited by King Hendricks and Irving Shepard.[11] Richard Weiderman founded Wolf House Books for the purpose of publishing Londoniana, including not only out-of-print London materials but also such important new books as James McClintock's pioneering study of London's short stories.[12] Weiderman also published several issues of *The London Collector*, "a non-profit amateur literary magazine dedicated to a study of the life and works of Jack London." At the same time, David Schlottmann began publishing his occasional newsletter *What's New About London, Jack?* as well as *The Wolf*, his annual monograph for presentation at the Jack London Birthday Banquet, inaugurated in 1970 by Russ Kingman. Kingman and his wife, Winnie, had recently moved from Oakland to Glen Ellen, where their Jack London Bookstore and Research Center was destined to become a mecca for collectors and scholars alike. Three important reference works appeared during the 1970's: Dale Walker and James Sisson's *The Fiction of Jack London: A Chronological Bibliography*, Woodbridge's revised and enlarged bibliography, and Joan Sherman's *Reference Guide*.[13] Dale Walker also published two important studies of London's fantasy fiction, *The Alien Worlds of Jack London*, followed two years later by *Curious Fragments*.[14] In 1973, Peregrine Smith issued a new and enlarged edition of Franklin Walker's *The Seacoast of Bohemia*, which included vital information about London's association with George Sterling and such fellow Carmel artists as Mary Austin and Jimmy Hopper.[15] Lois and Cliff Rather published their beautiful limited edition of *Jack London, 1905* in 1974.[16] My *Jack London* (in the Twayne U.S. Authors series), the first book-length critical introduction to London's literary achievement, also appeared in 1974; McClintock's *White Logic*, the first book-length treatment of London's short fiction, appeared in 1975. In 1976, four major journals—three in the United States and one in France—celebrated the centennial of London's birth with special issues.[17] In addition to Sherman's *Reference Guide*, Andrew Sinclair's problematical *Jack* appeared in 1977.[18] The next year Ray Wilson Ownbey's *Jack London: Essays in Criticism* confirmed the conviction that London scholarship had produced a substantial body of first-rate works.[19] The decade ended with the publication of Richard Etulain's *Jack London on the Road*, Dale Walker's *No Mentor But Myself*, and—finally—a reliable biography: Russ Kingman's *Pictorial Life of Jack London*.[20]

London's bandwagon continued to gain momentum in the 1980's, given impetus by several useful new editions of his works: Earl Wilcox's comprehensive casebook on *The Call of the Wild*, Joseph Simon's handsome edition of *The People of the Abyss*, Howard Lachtman's *Sporting Blood* and *Young Wolf*, Donald Pizer's densely packed two-volume Library of America edition (containing five novels, three books of nonfiction, twenty-five short stories, and four socialist essays), Stanley Wertheim and Sal Noto's *Dearest Greek*, my *Klondike Trilogy* (three newly rediscovered stories), Sal Noto's *Jack London's California* and *With a Heart Full of Love*, Dale Walker's *In a Far Country*, and the heavily reviewed three-volume Stanford edition of London's letters.[21] Two noteworthy biographical studies appeared during the 1980's: Joan Hedrick's frustrating *Solitary Comrade* and Clarice Stasz's illuminating *American Dreamers*.[22] Also casting important new light on London's works were Charles Watson's pioneering study, *The Novels of Jack London*, and Carolyn Johnston's thoughtful exposition of London's socialism, *Jack London—An American Radical?*[23] David Mike Hamilton's *"The Tools of My Trade"*: *Annotated Books in Jack London's Library* provided conclusive evidence that London amply fulfilled Emerson's second major requirement for the American Scholar: the influence of the Past, principally through books.[24] Other notable publications were Homer Haughey and Connie Kale Johnson's illustrated *Ranch* and *Homes* albums, Gorman Beauchamp's succinct Starmont Reader's Guide to London's science fiction, and James Lundquist's *Jack London: Adventures, Ideas, and Fiction*.[25] The short-lived but invaluable journal published by D. Michael Bates, *Jack London Echoes*, provided articles by London buffs and scholars and, perhaps even more important, reminiscences by London's only surviving daughter, Becky, as well as "Profiles" of outstanding figures in Jack London studies. To fill the vacuum left when *Echoes* was discontinued, Russ Kingman launched the *Jack London Foundation Newsletter* in 1989. One of the most encouraging academic phenomena of the decade was the inclusion of London sessions in the annual programs of the College English Association, the American Literature Association, the Modern Language Association, and the Popular Culture Association.[26] That London had been rediscovered not only by the academic Establishment but also by the U.S. Postal Service was dramatically evidenced in 1986, on Saturday, January 11 (the day before what would have been London's 110th birthday, had he lived another 70 years), at a special First Day of Issue ceremony in Glen Ellen, California, celebrating the new 25-cent Jack London stamp in the Great American Series.[27]

Public as well as scholarly interest in London has scarcely diminished during the 1990's—in fact, it appears now to be growing exponentially. The 1990 Macmillan edition of London's 50 best short stories has been adopted by the Book-of-the-Month Club; London's *John Barleycorn* has been published as a Signet Classic; William C. Brown published Jim Bankes's edition of London's boxing stories; Oxford University Press has included Jack London in its World's Classics series; Stanford University Press has published London's *Complete Short Stories*; Reader's Digest has published a volume of London's stories in The World's Best Reading series; and London has been added to Viking/Penguin's distinguished Portable Library.[28] The horizons of London scholarship have been significantly widened by the recent publications of Mark Zamen's study of London's public-speaking career; Eugene Lasartemay and Mary Rudge's investigation of the vital nurturing relationship between Jack and his loving African-American "mother," Jennie Prentiss; Tony Williams's painstakingly researched survey of London's contributions to the film industry; Jacqueline Tavernier-Courbin's intensive critical study of *The Call of the Wild*; Twayne's new edition of the TUSAS *Jack London*, substantially revised by Jeanne Reesman and myself; Susan Nuernberg's extensive collection of critical essays on Jack London; and Daniel Dyer's definitive annotated edition of *The Call of the Wild*.[29] A most important tool for London scholars is the *Definitive Chronology*, which Russ Kingman completed the year before his death in 1993.[30] The editing of the *Jack London Foundation Newsletter* has been undertaken by Russ's widow, Winnie Kingman, who also serves now as executive director of the Foundation. Although Woodbridge's *Jack London Newsletter* ended publication in 1989, it has been succeeded by the *Foundation Newsletter*; the *Jack London Journal*, inaugurated by James Williams at the University of Chicago; and *The Call*, the newsletter of the Jack London Society, organized in 1990 under the leadership of Professor Reesman at the University of Texas in San Antonio.

The new Jack London Society may be viewed as a symbol of the London renascence—or, more accurately, *nascence*—since it is only during the past generation that London studies have really come of age. The essays in *Rereading Jack London* validate the impressive course that such studies have taken. The range of critical approaches—representing current trends in literary theory as well as the scope of London's own literary achievements— is, frankly, astonishing. Moreover, several of the essays were originally delivered at the first Jack London International Symposium, held in Sonoma, California, in 1992. That one of the world's predominant centers for scholarly research—the Henry E. Huntington Library—volunteered to serve as host for the second symposium in 1994 is significant. We have come a long way, indeed, from those lonely days when Sam Baskett and I felt as if we were the only two Jack London scholars willing to admit it. I guess our main concern now is the happy worry that we may even be lost and forgotten in the crowd.

But there is no worry that Jack London will be lost and forgotten again. He is established now as a major figure in American literary history—our first and perhaps our greatest Writer as Folk Hero. No other writer, not even our beloved Mark Twain, has so thoroughly captured the essential themes of the American Dream in his meteoric career—and none has so completely captivated American readers of all ages. A legend in his own time, and a mythic figure for all time, London has indeed proven to be, in fact, the archetypal kosmos that Walt Whitman so desperately longed to be: the poet/seer embraced as lovingly by his people as he embraced them. Whitman's inspiration, Ralph Waldo Emerson, who described the writer—the poet—as the greatest of his representative men: "He is the true and only doctor [or teacher]; he is the only teller of news, for he was present and privy to the appearance of what he describes."[31] Elsewhere, in his essay "Greatness," Emerson remarks, "Whilst degrees of intellect interest only classes of men who pursue the same studies, as chemists or astronomers, mathematicians or linguists, and have no attraction for the crowd, there are always men who have a more catholic genius, are really great as men, and inspire universal enthusiasm. A great style of hero draws equally all classes, all the extremes of society, till we say the very dogs believe in him." This comment, better than any I know, explains Jack London's extraordinary universal appeal.[32]

Since Leonard Cassuto and Jeanne Reesman have so appropriately introduced the selections in this volume with reference to Emerson, it is only fitting that I conclude with like reference. "The man is only half himself," Emerson informs us, "the other half is his expression."[33] The great value of this edition emanates from the new insights its contributors give us into Jack London's "other half."

Reference Matter

NOTES

Cassuto and Reesman: Introduction

1. Jack London, *Martin Eden* (New York: Macmillan, 1909), 109.

2. Ralph Waldo Emerson, *Representative Men*, in *Complete Works*, vol. 4 (Boston: Houghton Mifflin, 1876), 19.

3. Jerome Loving, *Emerson, Whitman, and the American Muse* (Chapel Hill: University of North Carolina Press, 1982), 175, 180.

4. Maurice Gonnaud, *An Easy Solitude: Individual and Society in the Works of Ralph Waldo Emerson*, trans. Lawrence Rosenwald (Princeton: Princeton University Press, 1987), 371–72; Emerson, *Representative Men*, 61.

5. Gonnaud, *Easy Solitude*, 372; Emerson, *Representative Men*, 11, 190.

6. Friedrich Nietzsche, *Twilight of the Idols / The Anti-Christ*, trans. Michael Tanner (New York: Penguin, 1990), 85.

7. Friedrich Nietzsche, *The Will to Power*, ed. Walter Kaufmann, trans. Walter Kaufmann and R. J. Hollingdale (New York: Vintage, 1968), 505.

8. Emerson, *Representative Men*, 12, 9, 16–17, 31–32.

9. Charles Child Walcutt, *American Literary Naturalism: A Divided Stream* (Minneapolis: University of Minnesota Press, 1956).

10. Emerson, *Representative Men*, 7; Emerson, "The American Scholar," in *Nature, Addresses and Lectures* (Boston: Houghton Mifflin, 1903), 95; Emerson, "Literary Ethics," in *Nature, Addresses and Lectures*, 159; Emerson, "The American Scholar," 98–99.

11. Donald Pizer reevaluates naturalism as humanistic in his *Realism and Naturalism in Nineteenth-Century American Literature*, in which he notes tension in these works between "the subject matter of the naturalistic novel and the concept of man

which emerges from this subject matter," a concept that offers a "compensating hu-manistic value . . . which affirms the significance of the individual and of his life." Though the naturalist appears to suggest that the individual may be only a cipher in his amoral world, "the imagination refuses to accept this formula as the total mean-ing of life and so seeks a new basis for man's sense of his own dignity and impor-tance." Such a view enriches London studies, for his works, perhaps more than any of the other naturalists', seek the spiritual solace that Emerson described as imma-nent in Nature and that Pizer describes as a possibility in naturalist narratives. In tale after tale the subject may appear to be physical survival, but the real aim seems to be spiritual union with the human community, past and present. Sometimes this yearning takes the form of humanism, and sometimes socialism, feminism, or en-vironmentalism. But the urge is to find and adopt a creed that will allay the fears oc-casioned by the White Silence of a naturalist universe. See Donald Pizer, *Realism and Naturalism in Nineteenth-Century American Literature*, rev. ed. (Carbondale: South-ern Illinois University Press, 1984), 10–11. Elsewhere, Pizer hints at this context for reading London when he says of London: "His fiction, it is now realized, touches upon some of the central myths of the Western experience. And his life epitomizes a distinctive moment in American cultural history (reflected as well in the career of Theodore Roosevelt) when the idea that it was necessary to engage all ranges of experiences vigorously and with passion again became, as in the age of Emerson, a moral imperative" (Pizer, "Jack London," in *The Reader's Companion to American History* (New York: Houghton Mifflin, 1991).

12. Joel Porte, "Emerson: Experiments in Creation," in Boris Ford, ed., *The New Pelican Guide to English Literature*, vol. 9: *American Literature* (New York: Penguin Books, 1988), 85–96.

13. Daniel Borus, *Writing Realism: Howells, James, and Norris in the Mass Market* (Chapel Hill: University of North Carolina Press, 1989). For a study of the more spe-cific relationship between writing and consumerism at this time, see Rachel Bowlby, *Just Looking: Consumer Culture in Dreiser, Gissing, and Zola* (New York: Methuen, 1985).

14. Jonathan Bishop, *Emerson on the Soul* (Cambridge: Harvard University Press, 1964), 214; Emerson, *Representative Men*, 191.

Williams: Commitment and Practice

1. Charles N. Watson, Jr., *The Novels of Jack London: A Reappraisal* (Madison: University of Wisconsin Press, 1983), 3.

2. Christopher P. Wilson made a significant step in this direction. In his chapter on London in *The Labor of Words*, he puts London's professional status in relation to the marketplace, principally the magazine boom of the late nineteenth and early twentieth century. I do not agree, however, that London's work can be understood only as commodity, his audience only as consumer, and the author only as an arti-san "haunted by Keatsian realms of Beauty and Truth" (Christopher P. Wilson, *The*

Labor of Words: Literary Professionalism in the Progressive Era [Athens: University of Georgia Press, 1985], 112). I agree that London borrowed from the model of the artisan, but, more significantly, he borrowed from the model defined by nineteenth-century romantic poets and continued by late-nineteenth-century British aesthetes. In recounting London's training as a writer in 1896–97, Wilson does not mention London's immersion in British aestheticism, let alone any evidence that he knew British literature. Wilson's assertion that London was "haunted" comes after his reading of *Martin Eden* as unmediated autobiography. Wilson cannot admit to London's knowledge of British literature and British literary practice—even though it could help to "prove" his "hauntedness"—or any early influences other than marketplace advisors (such as *The Writer*) because he is constrained by his presupposition that London was only an artisan, "our first proletariat writer" (ibid., 96).

3. For such attempts, see, for example, Earle Labor and Jeanne Campbell Reesman, *Jack London: Revised Edition* (New York: Twayne, 1994), xiv, 82; and Mark Pittenger, *American Socialists and Evolutionary Thought, 1870–1920* (Madison: University of Wisconsin Press, 1993), 209.

4. Barthes, "The Death of the Author," in *Image, Music, Text*, trans. Stephen Heath (New York: Noonday Press, 1977), 147. Barthes's familiar formulation is that the word *author* does not have a concrete existence, that authorship becomes part of the experience of the text. In another well-known statement, Michel Foucault says that the author's name helps define the relation between the historical figure and the text, as an integral part of the text's discursive field (Foucault, "What Is an Author?" in *Language, Counter-Memory, Practice*, trans. Donald F. Bouchard and Sherry Simon, ed. Bouchard [Ithaca, N.Y.: Cornell University Press, 1977], rpt. in *Critical Theory Since 1965*, ed. Hazard Adams and Leroy Searle [Tallahassee: Florida State University Press, 1986]). However, some traditional critics and scholars see themselves as having weathered a post-structuralist storm, and for them the figure of the author and the methodology for its discovery remain intact. "But in spite of all the theoretical controversy over the relevance and place of the author, a great deal of literary study as it is routinely carried on from day to day continues to be fundamentally biographical in approach" (Jack Stillinger, *Multiple Authorship and the Myth of Solitary Genius* [New York: Oxford University Press, 1991], 8). Because London studies is especially susceptible to biographical criticism (biographies of London far outnumber studies of the author and his work), it is imperative that new views of authorship receive practical testing.

5. See Donald Pizer, ed., *Jack London: Novels and Stories, Novels and Social Writings* (New York: The Library of America, 1982); and Harry R. Warfel, Ralph H. Gabriel, and Stanley T. Williams, eds., *The American Mind: Selections from the Literature of the United States* (New York: American Book Company, 1937), 1004–7.

6. Foucault, "What Is an Author?" 148. In the broader context of "reconstructing individualism," Thomas C. Heller and David Wellbery write that "reconstruction" "does not imply a return to a lost state but rather an alternative conceptualization

of the experience of subjectivity" (Introduction, in Heller, Morton Sosna, and Wellbery, eds., *Reconstructing Individualism: Autonomy, Individuality, and the Self in Western Thought* [Stanford, Calif.: Stanford University Press, 1986], 2). A number of theoretical models offer themselves as guides to the consideration of authorial identity:
Jungian archetypes, psychoanalytic postulations of narrative constructions of the
self, and ethical and moral theories of identity and selfhood. The last seems best
suited to the exploration of that specific identity known as author, especially within
the context of professionalization, because ethical theory can and often does center
on practice. Practice, as a manifestation of authorship, cannot occur in isolation.

7. Any attempt to historicize the authorial figure of Jack London, or, in other
words, to place him as an object of attention in his cultural, social, and political milieu, will first have to confront the traditional summary of events of his time and
their general characterization. The panic of 1893, the formation and disintegration
of Coxey's army, the discovery of gold in the Klondike, the evolution of photography, and the war with Spain occurred while the United States was the scene of
three key trends: industrial and financial development through consolidation/in-
corporation; world power enforced by military strength; and general protest and dispute voiced against the incorporating and military powers. Jack London was personally involved in four of these five specific events and a major figure of one of the
trends.

8. See Akeel Bilgrami, "What Is a Muslim? Fundamental Commitment and Cultural Identity," *Critical Inquiry* 18 (Summer 1992): 821–42.

9. Ibid., 828.

10. Ibid.

11. Ibid., 827.

12. Heller and Wellbery put it this way: "Thus [given the disintegration of classical individualism], strategies emerged to relocate the experience of individuality in
the indeterminacies left around the edges of competing structures. Of course, the
sense of selfhood that appeared in these gaps could not assume the coherence and
consistency of the classical representation. . . . One theme that organizes many of
these endeavors is the modern notion of authenticity. . . . [Yet] it would be difficult
to claim that the strategies for differentiating authentic from inauthentic individualism provide a happy solution to the modern problem of reconceptualizing the individual. . . . However well motivated, the revival of a discourse emphasizing inten-
tion, autonomy, and responsibility echoes the 'jargon of authenticity' that Adorno
perceived in the rhetoric of the existentialists" (9–10, 12).

13. Bilgrami, "What Is a Muslim?" 830, 831. Thus he refutes G. A. Cohen's insistence on "the self's irreducible interest in a definition of itself." Cohen mistakenly
attempts to escape material conditions. Authenticity is not synonymous with autonomy, or stasis, but this is where Cohen and even Williams could lead us.

14. Bilgrami, "What Is a Muslim?" 828.

15. Earle Labor, Robert C. Leitz, III, and I. Milo Shepard, eds., *The Letters of Jack
London*, 3 vols. (Stanford, Calif.: Stanford University Press, 1988), 2: 675.

16. In his discussion of sincerity, Christopher Wilson typically limits himself to exploring London's identity as an artisan. Wilson turns "sincerity" into a synonym for "passion," as in London's phrase "impassioned realism." He then wants to prove that passion is subverted by commercialism and professionalism by converting it into "forceful prose" (525). My contention is that Wilson seriously misconstrues "sincerity" by ignoring its widest application. Critics, some wildly different from Wilson, have construed this letter as London's telling Brett that his public persona constitutes his most marketable commodity. This reading, however, ignores all that he says about sincerity and about not caring how his books—specifically, *The Road*—do in the marketplace, an issue I discuss below.

17. By *model*, I mean a key word that works in dialectical relation to those key words that describe subject-formation. *Model* points to the system by which one can organize and marshal one's individual practices of authorship. A model grants one a protocol to deal with publishers, agents, and editors. It gives one a method to submit one's work. It may even actively determine the content of the work, how one composes, how one revises, or whether one should do so. Martha Woodmansee, in her study of the relation between the formation of the author-subject and copyright law, delineates three general models: the craftsman, the divinely inspired poet, and the genius, inspired from within. See Martha Woodmansee, "The Genius and the Copyright: Economic and Legal Conditions of the Emergence of the 'Author,'" *Eighteenth-Century Studies* 17 (Summer 1984): 425–48, rpt. in Woodmansee, *The Author, Art, and the Market: Rereading the History of Aesthetics* (New York: Columbia University Press, 1994), 35–55.

18. Arthur Fosdick, "Don'ts for Writers," *The Writer* 12 (Sept. 1899): 129.

19. Woodmansee, "The Genius and the Copyright," 427.

20. Franklin Walker, *Frank Norris: A Biography* (Garden City, N.Y.: Doubleday, Doran, 1932), 165.

21. George Brett to London, September 18, 1907, folder 5, Macmillan Company Collection, New York Public Library.

22. See Alan Trachtenberg, *Reading American Photographs: Images as History, Mathew Brady to Walker Evans* (New York: Hill and Wang, 1989), 176.

23. London, *Martin Eden* (New York: Macmillan, 1909), 109; *Letters*, 1: 329.

24. Joan D. Hedrick points out that in *The Call of the Wild* London "attempted the same plot" as in *A Daughter of the Snows*: "the decivilization of the hero in the Northland" (Joan D. Hedrick, *Solitary Comrade: Jack London and His Work* [Chapel Hill: University of North Carolina Press, 1982], 100).

25. See Labor and Reesman, *Jack London*, chap. 1.

26. In the same letter, Brett reiterated his admiration for the book and said, "I note your determination to adhere to the ordinary form for the publication of this book [that is, not in a cheap 75-cent cloth edition] and we shall, of course, govern ourselves accordingly. I admire your courage in deciding, notwithstanding what must be the hostile attitude of the ordinary press, in appealing in the first instance, wholly to the audience naturally friendly to the publication of such a book." Don't

compare *The Iron Heel*, he said to London in pointed reply to London's January 16, 1907, letter (*Letters*, 2: 663), to "such a sordid piece of work as the 'Jungle.' . . . To compare your book with this one is like, I think, comparing a piece of creative imagination with the reporter's story of what he saw in the case of any given incident or accident" (Brett to London, January 23, 1907, folder 5, Macmillan Company Collection). Clearly, Brett accepted London on his own terms because the publisher understood the author to be exactly who the author wanted to be, an understanding that surpasses commercial interests but takes commercial form, as Brett insists.

27. Hedrick quotes this letter at length and in her brief analysis comes to generally the same conclusion: "Remaining true to his deepest inner needs was essential for the artist" (Hedrick, *Solitary Comrade*, 157). But her next statement shows what she is really after: "Yet this alone would not sell his work." Like many critics and biographers, Hedrick sees London's artistic choices determined not by any sense of identity or practice of fundamental commitments but by the paradox of how to be a money-making artist.

28. See McClure to London, June 22, 1900, London Collection. Charles Watson, whose chapter on *A Daughter of the Snows* is the shortest of his nine case studies, says that "on the strength of the moderately favorable reception of *The Son of the Wolf*, [London] persuaded S. S. McClure to send him $125 a month while the novel was in progress" (Watson, *The Novels of Jack London*, 18). This necessarily brief account—Watson is after all offering readings of the novels, not analyzing London's entire authorial career—is wrong in three ways. First, *The Son of the Wolf* was not published until April 7, 1900 (see James E. Sisson III and Robert W. Martens, *Jack London First Editions: A Chronological Reference Guide* [Oakland, Calif.: Star Rover House, 1979], xxiii), and McClure wrote in February 1900 that he wanted to publish a book by London (see McClure to London, Feb. 1, 1900, London Collection). Actually, McClure had read "An Odyssey of the North" in the *Atlantic Monthly* and was thus moved to begin his relation with London. Second, it was McClure, not London, who did the persuading. See the McClure correspondence for 1900 in the London Collection. Third, the contract was not for the length of time it took to write a novel; it was for five months.

Perhaps Watson relied on Andrew Sinclair's similar recounting of the contract: "The stories in *The Son of the Wolf* were well received. . . . S. S. McClure, always seeking new talent for his magazine and publishing house, put Jack on a retainer of $125 a month to keep him for a year while he wrote his first novel" (Andrew Sinclair, *Jack: A Biography of Jack London* [New York: Pocket Books, 1977], 67). Wilson's account, like Watson's, is brief and inaccurate: "Coveted by McClure and then dropped, he was taken up by Macmillan" (Wilson, *Labor of Words*, 106). When it comes to financial dealings, Wilson is completely silent about authorial agency. The source of confusion as usual begins with London himself. He told Elwyn Hoffman and Cloudesley Johns that McClure had given him a contract: "Expect to devote the next five months to the writing of a novel for McClure Phillips Co. They have agreed to give me an income of One twenty-five per month till the thing is done" (*Letters*, 1: 197). A cursory reading would miss London's estimation that five months should be enough time to write the novel; unfortunately, the editors of *Letters* footnote this passage with the following remark: "S. S. McClure agreed to pay JL an advance against royalties of $125 per month while he wrote the novel *A Daughter of the Snows*" (ibid.). Here is the way London explains it to Cloudesley Johns: "Did I tell you McClure has bought me (as you would call it), but as I would say, has agreed to advance me one hundred and twenty-five per month for five months in order that I may try my hand at a novel?" (ibid.).

29. See Phillips to London, Dec. 26, 1900, London Collection.

30. This figure includes an estimated $600 in advances for *God of His Fathers*. See Phillips to London, Oct. 21, 1901, and Dec. 20, 1901, London Collection.

31. *Letters*, 2: 675.

32. Phillips to London, May 3, 1901, London Collection. This letter actually was begun on April 17.

33. James Williams, "The Composition of Jack London's Writings," *American Literary Realism* 23 (Winter 1991): 78.

34. Phillips to London, May 29, 1901, London Collection.

35. See Ray Stannard Baker, *American Chronicle: The Autobiography of Ray Stannard Baker* (New York: Charles Scribner's Sons, 1945), 139–40.

36. *Letters*, 1: 250.

37. See Williams, "Composition of London's Writings," 78.

38. London, "Nam-bok the Unveracious," *Children of the Frost* (New York: Century, 1902), 59.

39. Phillips to London, August 29, 1901, London Collection.

40. *Letters*, 1: 261.

41. Phillips to London, August 29, 1901, London Collection.

42. *Letters*, 2: 675.

43. The rejection of the stories was both politically and aesthetically motivated. *McClure's* was of course a conservative magazine, with a certain amount of openness toward new trends in American political thought. In 1900, Viola Roseboro, McClure's chief manuscript reader, had fought for "The Question of the Maximum," when London submitted it; she may have been the only one to do so. Ray Stannard Baker had questioned how much London had kept to himself certain revolutionary principles. But at this point, in 1900, Baker would not have been familiar with London's work; he had not made his trip to California. So there were not strong enough objections to refuse "The Question of the Maximum," and Roseboro persuaded the more cautious editors. Later, when Phillips had sent Baker to California to visit London, he and London had engaged in political discussion at great length and high heat (see Baker, *American Chronicle*). This was not so much an ideological difference as an instinct against radical or revolutionary change; yet London had clarified their real political differences. Hence, when London submitted "Wanted,"

Baker could more accurately convey London's political intentions and how much they ran counter to his employer's. Hearing Baker's assessment, even Roseboro capitulated. She was certain now that she and London were in different political camps.

Jane Kirkland Graham, Roseboro's biographer, asserts that *McClure's Magazine*, represented principally in correspondence with London by Roseboro, "asked him to conform to the policy of the magazine, which he refused to do; in asking London not to advocate Socialism in the magazine, V. R. was only acting in conformity with the policy of *McClure's*, which was always suggesting need of reform, but avoiding utopias. London was angry" (Jane Kirkland Graham, *Viola, the Duchess of New Dorp* [Danville, Ill.: N.p., 1955], 70–71). Graham's narrative certainly rings true, but I have been unable to track down any of the correspondence, other than what I cite, which she seems to rely upon. That is, I have not found documentary evidence that someone at the magazine asked London to downplay or eliminate his socialism and that London was angry.

44. *Letters*, 1: 245.

45. See Harry Golden's untitled reminiscence—dated April 30, 1971—of a meeting he had with London in the fall (most likely September) of 1913 (Oakland History Room, Oakland Public Library). This reminiscence will be published under the title, "At the Saddle Rock with Jack London and Ed. Morrell" in the second number of the *Jack London Journal* (1995).

Auerbach: *"Congested Mails"*

1. Edward B. Clark, "Roosevelt on the Nature-Fakirs," *Everybody's Magazine* 16 (June 1907): 770–74, supplemented by Theodore Roosevelt, "Nature Fakers," *Everybody's Magazine* 17 (Sept. 1907): 427–30. Calling Roosevelt a member of the Ananias Club (a liar), London replies in "The Other Animals," *Collier's* (Sept. 5, 1908), 10–11, 25–26. See also Roosevelt's letter to his friend and fellow target of attack John Burroughs (Mar. 12, 1907), as well as his subsequent angry response to *Collier's* editor Mark Sullivan (Sept. 9, 1908), in Eltinge E. Morison, ed., *The Letters of Theodore Roosevelt* (Cambridge: Harvard University Press, 1952), 5: 617, 6: 1220–23. Roosevelt ends his letter to Sullivan by saying that he would no more enter into a serious controversy with London about his fiction than he would seriously engage the writer's views on social or political reform.

2. For three recent popular accounts of this still-raging controversy, see Marian Stamp Dawkins, *Through Our Eyes Only: The Search for Animal Consciousness* (Oxford: Freeman, 1993); Elizabeth Marshall Thomas, *The Hidden Life of Dogs* (Boston: Houghton Mifflin, 1993); and Vicki Hearne, *Animal Happiness* (New York: Harper-Collins, 1994). For a more unusual, highly original view interrogating modern science's historical construction of the relation between humans and animals, see Donna Haraway, *Primate Visions* (New York: Routledge, 1989).

3. Cited in Charles Child Walcutt, *American Literary Naturalism: A Divided Stream* (Minneapolis: University of Minnesota Press, 1956), 96–97.

4. Christopher Wilson, *The Labor of Words: Literary Professionalism in the Progressive Era* (Athens: University of Georgia Press, 1985).

5. Walter Benn Michaels, *The Gold Standard and the Logic of Naturalism: American Literature at the Turn of the Century* (Berkeley and Los Angeles: University of California Press, 1987), particularly the introduction ("The Writer's Mark"); Michael Fried, *Realism, Writing, Disfiguration: On Thomas Eakins and Stephen Crane* (Chicago: University of Chicago Press, 1987); Mark Seltzer, *Bodies and Machines* (New York: Routledge, 1992). A fourth important recent study of American naturalism is worth noting here: Lee Mitchell, *Determined Fictions* (New York: Columbia University Press, 1989). Mitchell's discussion is at once conceptually broad and methodologically narrow. The strong claims he makes for naturalism's radical undermining of conventional philosophical assumptions about personal agency and identity are based on a series of rather traditional stylistic analyses (examining syntactical repetition, for example) that focus in isolation on individual naturalist texts (a single short story, in the case of Jack London).

6. Jack London, *The Call of the Wild*, in Donald Pizer, ed., *Jack London: Novels and Stories* (New York: The Library of America, 1982).

7. The comparison to Kipling and Seton is frequently made, but often in rather general terms. See, for instance, James Lundquist, *Jack London: Adventures, Ideas, Fiction* (New York: Ungar, 1987), 100.

8. Seltzer, *Bodies and Machines*, 166.

9. London claimed, with perhaps some justification, that he was "unconscious" while writing the novel. See Joan London, *Jack London and His Times: An Unconventional Biography* (New York: Doubleday, 1939; Seattle: University of Washington Press, 1968), 252.

10. Christopher Wilson briefly notes the same paradox, but perhaps too optimistically claims that the two plots work in "counterpoint" (*Labor of Words*, 104).

11. For an interesting and important discussion of naturalist plotting, see June Howard, *Form and History in American Literary Naturalism* (Chapel Hill: University of North Carolina Press, 1985). Emphasizing the binary opposition between nature and culture, Howard admits that such antinomies are "unstable" (53) in London's *White Fang*. Yet she relies on such a structuralist model (Greimas's semiotic rectangle) in a way that too readily accepts as givens London's constructed oppositions.

12. In a footnote, Walcutt briefly ponders the same sorts of questions, which he leaves unanswered. See Walcutt, *American Literary Naturalism*, 311 n. 22. It might be argued that Social Darwinism would work precisely to naturalize the notion of human mastery, but Buck's atavistic reversion to savagery would more logically remove him from the human realm entirely.

13. Ibid., 106.

14. This striking phrase is used in a series of essays on the relation between human and animal psychology written in the 1880's by George John Romanes, a pro-

fessor and popular explicator of Darwin, whom London cites in his *Collier's* reply to Roosevelt. See George Romanes, *Essays* (London: Longmans, Green, 1897), 71, 75.

15. Howard, *Form and History*, chaps. 3–4.

16. This summary of Hegel's master/slave dialectic is based on Alexandre Kojève, *Introduction to the Reading of Hegel* (Ithaca, N.Y.: Cornell University Press, 1980), 3–70, quotation on 42. By seeing Hegel (as read by Kojève) as the source for London's Nietzsche and Marx, I am not making claims for direct influence; while to my knowledge Hegel is not mentioned by London in his letters or essays, Hegel powerfully informs American literature's conceptual foundations, as a recent collection of essays has suggested. See Bainard Coward and Joseph G. Kronick, eds., *Theorizing American Literature: Hegel, the Sign, and History* (Baton Rouge: Louisiana State University Press, 1991). For a fleeting allusion to Hegel pertaining to London, see Joan D. Hedrick, *Solitary Comrade: Jack London and His Work* (Chapel Hill: University of North Carolina Press, 1982), 138.

17. Kojève, *Introduction*, 52, 64.

18. London's joke is even more pointed in the serialized version of the story, which was first published in *The Saturday Evening Post*, a mass-circulation magazine with a large format closely resembling a daily newspaper. We thus begin the story by reading the news of Buck reading the news.

19. Seltzer, *Bodies and Machines*, 224–25.

20. Jack London, "How I Became a Socialist," in Pizer, ed., *Novels and Social Writings*, 1117–20.

21. London started writing *The Call of the Wild* some time during December 1902 and was finished by the middle of January 1903; the novel was serialized the following summer (beginning June 1903) in *The Saturday Evening Post*. In addition to writing the novel, and the essay on socialism, and preparing *The People of the Abyss* for publication the following fall, London during this intense six-month period also produced *The Kempton-Wace Letters* (published anonymously; co-authored by Anna Strunsky), bought the sloop *Spray* to sail around San Francisco Bay, began writing *The Sea-Wolf* (virtually completed by the end of the year), separated from his wife and children, and fell in love with his future wife, Charmian Kittredge.

22. What is important here is that London conceived of the writer's work in terms of rationalized production. Kojève, *Introduction*, 65. Basing class distinctions on the difference between mental and manual labor, London uncharacteristically falls prey to a vulgar Marxism, an argument all the more surprising, since his essay was published by the prominent socialist editor John Spargo, who in other contexts criticized such confused and unscientific thinking. See Daniel T. Rodgers, *The Work Ethic in Industrial America, 1850–1920* (Chicago: University of Chicago Press, 1978), 219–20, 229. Presumably securing London's famous name for the socialist cause would be more important than the depth of his analysis itself.

23. See Charles N. Watson, Jr., *The Novels of Jack London: A Reappraisal* (Madison: University of Wisconsin Press, 1983), 36, for a brief comparison between *Black*

Beauty and *The Call of the Wild*. Watson also offers an interesting comparison between *The Call* and *White Fang* (85) that shows the plots' structural similarities, despite the latter's ostensible reversal of direction. For the suggestion that *The Call of the Wild* functions in some ways as a slave narrative, I am indebted to my student Benjamin Diamond.

24. Earlier in the narrative (27–28) Spitz falls through the ice, leaving Buck on the slippery edge, straining in a panic along with Dave and François to pull the dog back up and thereby save themselves, all linked to the sled by the traces. The writing of these two fictional abyss passages is clearly informed by London's terror of falling into the social Pit.

25. Later in the narrative, in describing Buck's newfound "pride in himself" as a killer, London remarks that in Buck's physical swagger this pride "advertised itself . . . as plain as speech" (77). The shift from pride in work to pride in killing is thus matched by the shift from writing to public (advertised) speaking.

26. Like Thornton, London was wounded, maimed during the writing of *The Call of the Wild* in a manner almost too good to be true: "A heavy box of books fell on me, striking me in a vital place" (London to Anna Strunsky, dated Jan. 20, 1903). Here the hazards of a career in letters take on a tangible dimension. See Earle Labor, Robert C. Leitz, III, and I. Milo Shepard, eds., *The Letters of Jack London*, 3 vols. (Stanford, Calif.: Stanford University Press, 1988), 1: 339.

27. There are numerous historical analyses of this crisis. See, for example, Joe L. Dubbert, "Progressivism and the Masculinity Crisis," in Elizabeth H. Peck and Joseph H. Peck, eds., *The American Man* (Englewood Cliffs, N.J.: Prentice-Hall, 1980), 303–20; T. J. Jackson Lears, *No Place of Grace: Antimodernism and the Transformation of American Culture, 1880–1920* (New York: Pantheon, 1981); and E. Anthony Rotundo, *American Manhood* (New York: Basic Books, 1993), chaps. 10–11.

28. Theodore Roosevelt, "A Colonial Survival," in *The Works of Theodore Roosevelt* (New York: Scribner's, 1926), 12: 306.

Crow: Ishi and London's Primitives

1. "Homecoming in the California Visionary Romance," *Western American Literature* 24 (1989): 3–19.

2. See Jeanne C. Reesman, "The Problem of Knowledge in Jack London's 'The Water Baby,'" *Western American Literature* 23 (1988): 201–15, for a discussion of London's discovery of Jung.

3. Watson, *The Novels of Jack London: A Reappraisal* (Madison: University of Wisconsin Press, 1983), 49–50.

4. Jacqueline Travernier-Courbin has made such an analysis of these novellas, and she has seen the application to London's other California novels, though our analyses and conclusions differ in many details. She does not discuss *Before Adam* or *The Scarlet Plague*. See "California and After: Jack London's Quest for the West," *Jack London Newsletter* 13 (1980): 41–54.

5. See Earle Labor, "From 'All Gold Canyon' to *The Acorn-Planter*: Jack London's Agrarian Vision," *Western American Literature* 11 (Summer 1976): 83–101, for a discussion of London's advanced ecological concerns.

6. *Before Adam*, biographical introduction by Willy Ley, epilogue by Loren Eiseley (New York: Macmillan, 1962), 137.

7. Ibid., 154, 154–55.

8. See James Lundquist, *Jack London: Adventures, Ideas, and Fiction* (New York: Ungar, 1987), 170; and Watson, *The Novels of Jack London*, 187.

9. *The Scarlet Plague* (New York: Macmillan, 1929), 181.

10. See Theodora Kroeber, *Ishi in Two Worlds* (Berkeley and Los Angeles: University of California Press, 1976); and Ursula K. Le Guin, *Always Coming Home* (New York: Harper and Row, 1985). Theodora may have idealized the relationship of Alfred Kroeber and Ishi, and the placing of Ishi in a living exhibit on vanished tribes may be read as an act cultural imperialism.

11. Kroeber, *Ishi in Two Worlds*, esp. 99.

12. David Mike Hamilton, *"The Tools of My Trade": The Annotated Books in Jack London's Library* (Seattle: University of Washington Press, 1986), 228. See *Tribes of California* (Berkeley and Los Angeles: University of California Press, 1976 [1877]), 277. Powers was one of the sources used by Theodora Kroeber.

13. My thanks to Professor Susan Gatti of Indiana University of Pennsylvania for pointing out this reference. London may have heard or read of Ishi's archery practice with Dr. Saxton Pope or his arrow-making and bow-making demonstrations at the museum. It is even possible that London witnessed one of the demonstrations.

14. Labor, "London's Agrarian Vision," esp. 95–100.

15. See Edward W. Said, *Culture and Imperialism* (New York: Knopf, 1993), esp. 25–26 on *The Heart of Darkness*.

16. James Clifford, *The Predicament of Culture: Twentieth-Century Ethnography, Literature, and Art* (Cambridge: Harvard University Press, 1988), 11–12, 16.

17. In this connection, see Clifford's hostile reading of a "Primitivism" exhibition at the Museum of Modern Art, ibid., esp. 202.

18. *The Valley of the Moon* (Santa Barbara, Calif.: Peregrine Smith, 1975 [1913]), 2: 297.

Peluso: Gazing at Royalty

I would like to thank Joss Lutz Marsh for her interest in this topic as it developed into a presentation for her session at the 1992 MLA convention. I am also indebted to Leonard Cassuto, Jay Williams, and, especially, Jeanne Campbell Reesman for probing editorial remarks that have improved this discussion in a variety of ways.

1. Earle Labor, Robert C. Leitz, III, and I. Milo Shepard, eds., *The Letters of Jack London*, 3 vols. (Stanford, Calif.: Stanford University Press, 1988), 1: 310.

2. Turn-of-the-century expansionism is covered in David Healy, *U.S. Expansionism: The Imperialist Urge in the 1890s* (Madison: University of Wisconsin Press,

1970); Samuel P. Hays, *The Response to Industrialism: 1885–1914* (Chicago: University of Chicago Press, 1957), 163–87; and Robert Wiebe, *The Search for Order, 1877–1920* (New York: Hill and Wang, 1967), 224–55, 256–62. The Columbian Exposition is discussed in Alan Trachtenberg, *The Incorporation of America: Culture and Society in the Gilded Age* (New York: Hill and Wang, 1982), 208–34, esp. 214–17.

3. Raymond Williams, *The Country and the City* (New York: Oxford University Press, 1973), 165, emphasis added.

4. Ibid., 166. See also Asa Briggs, *Victorian Cities* (New York: Harper and Row, 1963, 1965), 68, 326–27. Focusing on actual experience within a city rather than on textual representations, Kevin Lynch analyzes the interrelations between observer and observed in his discussions of "legibility" and "imageability," in *The Image of the City* (Cambridge: MIT Press, 1960), esp. 2–8, 9–12, 78–83, 85–88, 131. And for related discussions, see William Sharpe and Leonard Wallock, "From 'Great Town' to 'Nonplace Urban Realm': Reading the Modern City," in Sharpe and Wallock, eds., *Visions of the Modern City: Essays in History, Art, and Literature*, Proceedings of the Heyman Center for the Humanities, Feb.–Mar. 1983 (New York: Columbia University Press, [1983]), esp. 24–25; as well as Steven Marcus's treatment of Engels's view of Manchester, in "Reading the Illegible," in H. J. Dyos and Michael Wolff, eds., *The Victorian City: Images and Realities*, 2 vols. (London: Routledge and Kegan Paul, 1973), 1: 257–76.

5. See Peter Keating, introduction to *Into Unknown England, 1866–1913: Selections from the Social Explorers* (Manchester: Manchester University Press, 1976), 11–32, esp. 11–13, 20–21; Deborah Epstein Nord, "The Social Explorer as Anthropologist: Victorian Travellers Among the Urban Poor," in Sharpe and Wallock, *Visions of the Modern City*, 118–30, esp. 120–22; Briggs, *Victorian Cities*, 60, 325–26, 328–29; and see also P. J. Keating, "Fact and Fiction," in Dyos and Wolff, *The Victorian City*, 2: 585–602, esp. 585–86, 593. The term "abyss," which had been in circulation for some time, began in the 1880's and 1890's to take on new connotations as it was increasingly associated with "class fear" of diseases or rebellion, in particular "the growing militancy of the working-class movement" (Keating, *Into Unknown England*, 20; and see 20–21: London is mentioned on 21). Andrew Sinclair's "A View of The Abyss," in Jacqueline Tavernier-Courbin, ed., *Critical Essays on Jack London* (Boston: G. K. Hall, 1983), 230–41, and Keating's introduction to *Into Unknown England*, 10–32, are important for placing London in relation to the British tradition of urban writing; they do not, however, examine how his construction of the East End modified that tradition or the implications of those modifications.

6. This paragraph draws extensively on Edward W. Said, *Orientalism* (New York: Pantheon, 1978), 49–73, esp. 54–55, quotations on 55. See also Colin Mercer, "Baudelaire and the City: 1848 and the Inscription of Hegemony," in Francis Barker et al., eds., *Literature, Politics and Theory: Papers from the Essex Conference, 1976–84* (London and New York: Methuen, 1986), 18, 29.

7. The *locus classicus* of London's fear of returning to the poverty of the "Social

Pit" is his essay "How I Became a Socialist," in Donald Pizer, ed., *Jack London: Novels and Social Writings* (New York: The Library of America, 1982), 1117–20.

8. The fullest account of his ambivalence toward the urban underclass is Joan D. Hedrick, *Solitary Comrade: Jack London and His Work* (Chapel Hill: University of North Carolina Press, 1982), 59–71; and see 68 and 94, regarding his embrace of the middle class. See also Carolyn Johnston, *Jack London—An American Radical?* (Westport, Conn.: Greenwood Press, 1984), 75, 77.

9. Virtually every commentator on London has noted the tensions and conflicts in his politics, though explanations have varied. Joan London, *Jack London and His Times: An Unconventional Biography* (New York: Doubleday, 1939), at times quite hostile, goes so far as to call her father a political "ignoramus" (190) whose understanding of socialism "was at best muddled" (171; and see 179–91, 206–7, 215, 336–37, 368). However, she also recognizes that despite his political naivete and his eventual estrangement from the cause (257, 263, 330, 333–35, 350–53, 368), her father could also be a vehement champion of it (288, 294–95, 297–303, 304–5). Andrew Sinclair, *Jack: A Biography of Jack London* (New York: Harper and Row, 1977), links London's politics to everything from his fear of falling back into the social pit (e.g., 31–32) to personal conflicts (125–26, 165–66) to matters of health (66, 109, 156). Joan Hedrick follows Kenneth Lynn in viewing London's socialism as "an intellectual link" but "a social break" from his experiences as a wage worker (*Solitary Comrade*, 39). And Carolyn Johnston concludes that London's socialism was deeply indebted to "traditional American values and the democratic political tradition, with an ample infusion of [agrarian] utopianism" (*London—American Radical?*, 182; strong summaries of her thesis appear on 92, 97, 181–86, esp. 182, 184). My own view is closest to Johnston's.

10. On London's early phase, see Johnston, *London—American Radical?*, chap. 2, esp. 29, 31–32, 35–36, 38–39, 51; and Joan London, *Jack London and His Times*, chap. 14, esp. 181, 187, 189; see also 206–7. On his later phase, see Johnston, chap. 4, esp. 110, 115–16, 118–19, 133–34; and Joan London, 288–96, 300–305. Both phases reveal a somewhat qualified commitment to socialism. For instance, even after two years as a card-carrying socialist, London still submitted campaign pieces to "the aristocratic Fifth Ward Republican Club" (Joan London, 173). Similarly, although he wrote some of his most compelling socialist fictions during his revolutionary phase (see Hedrick, *Solitary Comrade*, 169–87), he was unable to commit himself to anything more than a dubious introduction to Alexander Berkman's memoirs (Johnston, 153–54; Joan London, 318–19) and, a few years later, was ambivalent about the Mexican Revolution (Johnston, 154–57; Joan London, 338–53; Sinclair, *Jack*, 201–4).

11. Conceived of before he went to the East End (*Letters*, 1: 302) but not written until after he returned from there (*Letters*, 1: 338), "How I Became a Socialist" details a "conversion" to socialism framed, with its references to "a healthy Western city" (1117) and "what sociologists love to call 'the submerged tenth'" (1119), by language and ideas heavily indebted to *People*.

12. Arguably, in light of London's growing estrangement and eventual defection

from the Party—certainly no small part of which was due to his views on imperialism (Johnston, *London—American Radical?*, 154–57)—this strand of his politics might be considered the central one.

13. The account of American socialist responses to imperialism on which I have drawn is Hubert Perrier, "The U.S. Left on War and Empire, 1880–1920," in Serge Ricard, ed., *An American Empire: Expansionist Cultures and Policies, 1881–1917* (Aix-en-Provence: Université de Provence, 1990), esp. 111–18; and see Healy, *U.S. Expansionism*, 100. On the conflicted racialism of socialists, see Perrier, "The U.S. Left," 116, 112; and Johnston, *London—American Radical?*, 94–95. London's view on the Spanish-American conflict is in *Letters*, 1: 12.

14. Perrier, "The U.S. Left," 117–18.

15. Discussions of London's combination of evolution and socialist politics are in Johnston, *London—American Radical?*, 47–49, 50–53, 77, 133–34, 155–56, 157; Sinclair, *Jack*, 33, 74–75; and *Letters*, 1: 88–93, 98–101, 132, 188.

16. The imperialistic strain in London's commitment to racial supremacy was as strong as it was complex, often tainting what might easily be mistaken for simple valorization of non-white races. For example, in "Koolau the Leper" (1909), London critiques America's currently shoddy colonial policy by affirming Hawaii's worthiness for full statehood through a positive representation of the non-white protagonist Koolau. But the point here is about American imperialism, not a valorization of Hawaiian values, customs, and meanings. Defined by his iconographic quality, Koolau is admirable insofar as he embodies traditional American values, which, London implies, require changing a policy of exploitative expansionism to one designed around eventual statehood. Owing little if anything to indigenous Hawaiian values, Koolau emerges as a symbolic figure in a decidedly American allegory of individualism and freedom, even sounding by the story's conclusion like a revolutionary patriot when he declares, "I am a free man . . . I have lived free, and I shall die free" (in Pizer, *Novels and Social Writings*, 896). In short, London urges America to a stronger imperial policy in the Pacific on the grounds that the best Hawaiians resemble Americans and therefore the Islands deserve, as it were, to be annexed. Or, put another way, London clears the path toward annexation by imagining Hawaii as sufficiently worthy of American imperial designs. The point that Hawaii is important primarily, if not exclusively, as an instrument in American imperial activities is reinforced in 1916 with "My Hawaiian Aloha," in King Hendricks and Irving Shepard, eds., *Jack London Reports: War Correspondence, Sports Articles, and Miscellaneous Writings* (New York: Doubleday, 1970), 379–402, where London's recollection of the Islands is again presented in terms of fundamental American values—specifically, "manifest destiny" (380). Complimenting Hawaii for being a "melting pot" (396), London argues throughout for a forward-looking American imperial policy so that when the Islands attain statehood America will not lose out in the "conflicting courses of empires" to the "Mongolian (represented by the Japanese)" (380; and see 399–400). The cultural chauvinism embedded in these attitudes toward Hawaii, which clearly emerge

from expansionist debates at the turn of the century (Healy, *U.S. Expansionism*, 25, 28, 52–53, 55–56, 132–34, 170, 175–76), also help explain curious pieces like his 1916 essay "Our Guiltless Scapegoats: The Stricken of Molokai," in Hendricks and Shepard, *Jack London Reports*, 375–79, where a sympathy for the Hawaiian lepers co-exists with a recommendation that America export its own lepers to the Molokai settlement. Here again, it is not Hawaii that is being privileged, but Anglo-Saxon superiority.

17. Jack London, *The People of the Abyss* (New York: Grosset and Dunlap, 1907), 32.

18. I am referring to Strong's *Our Country* (1885) and *Expansion Under New World Conditions* (1900). See discussions of Strong's important place in what Friedrich W. Horlacher calls the "semantic environment" of imperialism ("The Language of Late Nineteenth-Century American Expansionism," in Ricard, *American Empire*, 35–38); and see Richard Hofstadter, *Social Darwinism in American Thought*, rev. ed. (Boston: Beacon Press, 1955), 178–79; Wiebe, *Search for Order*, 238; and Healy, *U.S. Expansionism*, 38. In his copy of Strong's *Expansion*, London himself marked passages relating to American materialistic and racial superiority (David Mike Hamilton, *"The Tools of My Trade": The Annotated Books in Jack London's Library* [Seattle: University of Washington Press, 1986], 267). London's general affiliation with Strong's ideas is made even clearer by Horlacher's discovery in *Our Country* of "the myth of the chosen people, . . . of predestination, . . . of the promised land, . . . of manifest destiny, . . . of the westward course of empire, . . . of white, Anglo-Saxon supremacy, the pioneer myth, the transplantation myth, the success myth, etc." ("Language of American Expansionism," 37). As I will show, it is precisely these values and ideals that London himself uses in *People*.

19. In a provocative essay, Alfred Hornung uses autobiographical evidence from *The Road* and *John Barleycorn* to argue that London's entire life and work were a form of expansionism, which Hornung defines as a struggle to survive enacted by an outsider who opportunistically subverts conventions (Hornung, "Evolution and Expansion in Jack London's Personal Accounts: *The Road* and *John Barleycorn*," in Ricard, *American Expansion*, 197–213, esp. 199, 201–2, 204–5). Although appealing, Hornung's view that all such acts are performed solely to gain personal freedom misses the important ways in which London was engaged in larger cultural projects.

20. In a letter to Anna Strunsky, London highlights this point. Speaking first of "the supreme beastiality or unhumanness" of the East Enders, he goes on to say, "Nor . . . should I like to be a West Ender" (*Letters*, 1: 309). What London would *like* to be is what he already is, an American.

21. Regarding attitudes of Anglo-Saxon superiority present in his childhood, see Joan London, *Jack London and His Times*, 23; Johnston, *London—American Radical?*, 7; and Hedrick, *Solitary Comrade*, 17. On their persistence into his adult life, see Joan London, 210–15, 283–85, 338–53, esp. 350–53; Johnston, 42–48, 93–94, 106 n. 98, 154–57, 184; and Sinclair, *Jack*, 107–8, 202–3. On London's attachment to the narrative of self-reliance in the form of Horatio Alger stories, see Hedrick, 6–10, 15–16, 24,

25, 33, 60; and Johnston, 8, 29. London obviously had class divisions and imperialism on his mind during his East End project (see *Letters*, 1: 304, 305; Sinclair, "View of The Abyss," 232–33; and Joan London, 239–40).

22. Or, in Colin Mercer's incisive phrasing, "Narrative declares action *and* produces it" ("Baudelaire and the City," 26).

23. Said, *Orientalism*, 7. However, American desires for positional superiority were not free from complication. They were deeply marked by "ambivalence toward Europe" and Great Britain (Wiebe, *Search for Order*, 257, and see 226, 237–38, 256–58; see also Hofstadter, *Social Darwinism*, 181–84; and Healy, *U.S. Expansionism*, 22–33). And as Healy observes, the new imperialism was in many ways motivated precisely by uneasiness about the nation's position amid "a world of empires" (esp. 22, 28). London's use of the colonizer stance, then, might be seen as reinscribing common national sentiments—even as it allows ambivalence toward England's East Enders (sympathy and revulsion) it ultimately affirms American national supremacy, which thereby enables imperialism.

24. Brooks Adams, "The New Industrial Revolution," *Atlantic Monthly* 87 (1901): 165; and see 161, 164. Adams is treated in Hofstadter, *Social Darwinism*, 186–89; and Healy, *U.S. Expansionism*, 101–2, 109, 115–16, 176–77.

25. Although the doss lines, workhouses, missions, and so forth are the characteristic "thematic units" that identify districts within large urban areas (see Lynch, *Image of the City*, 68, 104), places like Trafalgar Square (or the coronation there) form the "landmarks" (ibid., 78–83) around which urban knowledge is organized.

26. In this paragraph I have been following closely Mercer, "Baudelaire and the City," 25–26, 28. Jacqueline Tavernier-Courbin, "Introduction: Jack London: A Professional," in Tavernier-Courbin, *Critical Essays*, 11, also alludes to a parallel between London and Baudelaire.

27. Increasingly shifting toward administrative and commercial importance, especially in relation to the empire, the city of London in the closing years of Victoria's rule became familiar as the "world city" and the center of empire (Briggs, *Victorian Cities*, 323–24, 328, 371). By exploiting "what is there to be known" about this transition in order to produce "what needs to be known," London reinforces his own imaginative history.

28. London's relationship to the market has been hotly debated. Joan London, for instance, insists that her father wrote for money and was indebted to his audience as much for material survival as for the psychological security that came from feeling free of poverty and physical labor (*Jack London and His Times*, 90–91, 136, 168–69, 172, 176, 192–93, 198–201, 227, 230, 232–33, 234–37, 254, 317–18, 322–24). Taking these insights in a different direction, Joan Hedrick ventures that London's attempt to tell the truth in and earn a living from his writings was a dilemma of many serious American writers (*Solitary Comrade*, 151–68, esp. 154–55, 157–58). Similarly, Jacqueline Tavernier-Courbin suggests that Jack London was a serious writer whose claims of writing for profit were actually defense mechanisms for subverting po-

tential criticism of his work ("Introduction," 2–4). Regardless of the particular accent given to London's concerns, virtually everyone agrees that because his livelihood depended on selling books, considerations of the market were rarely far from his mind.

29. Quoted in Joan London, *Jack London and His Times*, 237.

30. Quoted in Mercer, "Baudelaire and the City," 32.

31. The "vender of brains" remark appears in Jack London, "What Life Means to Me," in Philip S. Foner, ed., *Jack London: American Rebel* (New York: Citadel Press, 1947), 395. And see esp. 395–96 where differences between physical and mental labor are repeatedly understood through the language of commodification. It is also worth mentioning that like "How I Became a Socialist" this essay is indebted to London's East End project. When he discusses his conversion from laborer to "brain merchant," for example, he uses language and ideas from *People* to explain the shift. In this sense, London's contact with the East End poor seems to have sharpened for him not only his commitment to socialism and Anglo-Saxon superiority but to authorship as well. *People* thus becomes a key document for understanding his politics and his art.

32. The comment appears in a 1907 edition of *People*. And see Johnston's analysis (*London—American Radical?*, 77–78).

33. London's meticulous construction of himself as an American in England militates against Marie L. Ahearn's attempt to link his book to new journalism in "*The People of the Abyss*: Jack London as New Journalist," *Modern Fiction Studies* 22 (1976): 73–83. Claiming London's "personal involvement" and "participation" (74–75), Ahearn herself also notes that such participation is compromised by his squeamishness (76), his objective commentary (76, 80), or his own awareness of his difference (77). Add to this London's continual allusions to literary texts and to studies by middle-class writers *about* the poor—neither of which would likely have been read *by* the poor— and such "personal involvement" becomes highly questionable, as it does when we learn that he used a camera and guides (see Sinclair, *Jack*, 89–90). And see Mercer, "Baudelaire and the City," 21–22, for a related discussion.

34. Keating, "Fact and Fiction," 587–88.

35. Ibid., 589–91.

36. David M. Potter, *People of Plenty: Economic Abundance and the American Character* (Chicago: University of Chicago Press, 1954).

37. Quoted in Keating, "Fact and Fiction," 592. The ways in which urban writings used tropes of exploring unknown territory is treated in Keating, introduction, *Into Unknown England*, 13–18; and see *People*, 13, 15.

38. London in this sequence seems to be intentionally suppressing his awareness (and later use) of such books as Charles Booth's monumental seventeen-volume study (*People*, 213, 297) because in a letter to an American editor in 1906, he talks proudly of just this use of secondary-source material (*Letters*, 2: 548–49; Hamilton, *Annotated Books in London's Library*, 18). Similarly, he intentionally avoids posing

solutions in *People* (*Letters*, 1: 318) even though he knew of them (*Letters*, 1: 312). In fact, he only consented to include a discussion of possible solutions when prodded by his publisher (*Letters*, 1: 331 n. 2); and even then, as I discuss below, they had a decidedly American slant.

39. See, for instance, George R. Sims, *How the Poor Live and Horrible London* (N.p., 1889), esp. "The Dark Side of Life."

40. Quoted in Keating, *Into Unknown England*, 65. Similarly, it is possible to take the measure of its staged quality by noting that, despite the apostrophe, London used the agency as a mailing address while he was on his European tour (*Letters*, 1: 314–15).

41. *The Concise Oxford Dictionary of Literary Terms*, s.v. "elegy."

42. Patrick Brantlinger, *Rule of Darkness: British Literature and Imperialism, 1830–1914* (Ithaca, N.Y.: Cornell University Press, 1988), 42. And see 37–38, where Cook & Son is explicitly implicated in the transmutation of imperialist conquest into tourism.

43. Ibid., 44.

44. The conserving function of elegy is important: "the emotion, originally expressed as a lament, finds consolation in the contemplation of some permanent principle" (*Princeton Encyclopedia of Poetry and Poetics*, 2d ed., s.v. "elegy"). Here, obviously, the notion of imperialism is that "permanent principle."

45. Michel Foucault, "Truth and Power," in Colin Gordon, ed., *Power/Knowledge: Selected Interviews and Other Writings, 1972–77* (New York: Pantheon, 1980), 133.

46. The pessimistic undercurrent of imperialism is covered in Hofstadter's discussion of Brooks Adams and others (*Social Darwinism*, 185–92) and in Healy, *U.S. Expansionism*, 99–109, esp. 108–9. Anti-imperialism is treated in Healy, 213–31, 232–47; Hofstadter, 192–96, esp. 192, 194; Wiebe, *Search for Order*, 241, 260–62; and Hays, *Response to Industrialism*, 183–85. But imperialists and anti-imperialists actually shared many central assumptions (Healy, 49, 54–56, 173, 239, 243–47); indeed, as Healy points out, even though they opposed imperialism (taking foreign territory), nearly all anti-imperialists endorsed expansionism (acquiring contiguous land or establishing trading centers in distant territory) (Healy, 49, 55, 246). London at least knew Adams's work (see Hamilton, *Annotated Books in London's Library*, 20, 50–51).

47. Wiebe's list reads in part, "Equal opportunity for each man; a test of individual merit; wealth as a reward for virtue; credit for hard work, frugality, and dedication" (Wiebe, *Search for Order*, 136).

48. Mercer, "Baudelaire and the City"; Horlacher, "Language of American Imperialism," 34–35. I do not mean simply that London's endorsement of conservative economics translates into his support of individualism; rather, I am stressing that it also underwrote his radicalism. For example, a year and a half before his East End trip, London accepted the mayoral candidacy of the Oakland Social Democratic Party by asserting, "We demand that which our national platform demands, that which we demand the world over, namely, equality of opportunity" (quoted in Joan London, *Jack London and His Times*, 228). As David Potter has shown, because the

idea of equality of opportunity actually privileges liberty, it lies at the base of American conservative doctrine (*People of Plenty*, 91–92). For Jack London, then, the concept seems to have mediated his belief in both socialism and individualism. Good related discussions are in Johnston, *London—American Radical?*, 28–29, 148–49, 182.

49. Based on invidious comparisons with other nations, the figure is particularly apposite to London's attempt to imagine the United States as the dominant actor in imperialist narratives. As Henry Nash Smith, *Virgin Land: The American West as Symbol and Myth* (Cambridge: Harvard University Press, 1950), says, "Neither American man nor the American continent contained, under this interpretation, any radical defect or principle of evil. But other men and other continents, having no share in the conditions of American virtue and happiness, were by implication unfortunate or wicked" (187; and see Wiebe, *Search for Order*, 226).

50. On the relation between manifest destiny and the new world garden, see H. N. Smith, *Virgin Land*, esp. chaps. 3, 11, 14–17. On Jack London's shift to agrarianism, see Joan London, *Jack London and His Times*, 231–32; Johnston, *London—American Radical?*, 163–64; Earle Labor, "From 'All Gold Canyon' to *The Acorn-Planter*: Jack London's Agrarian Vision," *Western American Literature* 11 (Summer 1976): 94–101; Sinclair, *Jack*, 117–18, 162–63; and Sinclair, "View of The Abyss," 233, 240 n. 13. And on the notion of a distinct American race, see Reginald Horsman, *Race and Manifest Destiny* (Cambridge: Harvard University Press, 1981), esp. 249–55. One might also speculate that London's commitment to the land caused him to turn away from his earlier version of Anglo-Saxon superiority, which had linked the survival of the United States to that of Great Britain (see, e.g., *Letters*, 1: 99–101, 123–24, 128–29, 182, 185). That is, as he committed himself increasingly to the land, he committed himself increasingly to America. As he once proclaimed, "I see my farm in terms of the world, and I see the world in terms of my farm" (quoted in Labor, "London's Agrarian Vision," 99). In this regard, it is also worth mentioning that Thomas Jefferson, to whom Labor likens Jack London (ibid., 98), was not only America's preeminent agrarian but also its foremost expansionist, supporting and endorsing the Lewis and Clark expedition, among other things (and see Healy, *U.S. Expansionism*, 35, 48, 51).

51. See Healy, *U.S. Expansionism*, 39, 87–88, 200; Hofstadter, *Social Darwinism*, 180; and Hays, *Response to Industrialism*, 166–67.

52. See Nord, "Social Explorer as Anthropologist," 125–29. Natural selection was a powerful legitimizing idea for imperialism because it justified and enabled colonial activity as taking place on behalf of a less developed people (see Homi K. Bhabha, "The Other Question: Difference, Discrimination and the Discourse of Colonialism," in Barker et al., *Literature, Politics and Theory*, 155–56; and see Nord, "Social Explorer as Anthropologist," 125). In the United States, theories of Anglo-Saxon superiority made the idea especially appealing to supporters of imperialism (see Hofstadter, *Social Darwinism*, 170–72, 176–77, 179–80, 190; and Healy, *U.S. Expansionism*, 14–16, 122–24). And, as Hofstadter reminds us, Darwin's *Origin of Species* is subtitled *The Preservation of Favored Races in the Struggle for Life* (171).

53. See also Mercer, "Baudelaire and the City," 27. Worth noting, too, are the important parallels in Bhabha's and Raymond Williams's discussions: producing colonial subjects as both knowable and Other is surely a function of "what is desired and what needs to be known."

54. Leonard Cassuto, "Jack London's Class-Based Grotesque," typescript, adopts a similar position when discussing London's use of the grotesque to critique industrial poverty, as does James R. Giles, "Jack London 'Down and Out' in England: The Relevance of the Sociological Study *People of the Abyss* to London's Fiction," *Jack London Newsletter* 2 (1969), who claims that starting with *People* London's urban writing used animal imagery to signal a negative view of atavism (79, 81–83), which, after 1905, is directed toward American urban dwellers (82–83). Regarding this last point, however, it seems that such negative connotations more likely arise from a growing anti-urbanism based on London's agrarianism than on an ideological volte-face that would equate the United States with the East End.

55. Influenced by Brett's shrewd sense of the book market and its desire for happy endings (see Hedrick, *Solitary Comrade*, 163–65), London's final chapter makes a strong case for the argument I advanced in my opening pages regarding the commodification of mind.

56. Wiebe, *Search for Order*, 224, 236–37, 243.

57. For more explicit evidence of London's later interest in Taylor, see Hedrick, *Solitary Comrade*, 25–26 and esp. 239 n. 17. For an assessment of London's views in relation to those of the influential economist Charles A. Conant, whose *The United States in the Orient* (1900) fused efficiency, Anglo-Saxon superiority, and imperialism, see Healy, *U.S. Expansionism*, 194–209, esp. 200, 202–3, 205–6.

58. Sections of the speech are quoted and discussed in Hofstadter, *Social Darwinism*, 180; and Horlacher, "Language of American Expansionism," 38 n. 14. London must have cheered Beveridge's closing, "Pray God the time may never come when mammon and the love of ease will so debase our blood that we will fear to shed it for the flag and its imperial destiny" (Horlacher, 38 n. 14).

59. See H. N. Smith, *Virgin Land*, chaps. 2 and 3, quotation on 37.

Shor: Power, Gender, and Ideological Discourse

1. Quoted in Carolyn Johnston, *Jack London—An American Radical?* (Westport, Conn.: Greenwood Press, 1984), 140 n. 49.

2. Quoted ibid., 126.

3. Quoted ibid., xiii. In fact, according to Johnston, many of the Yale students were so inspired by London's energetic and challenging address that they formed a chapter of the Intercollegiate Socialist Society. See ibid., 116.

4. Jack London, *The Iron Heel* (Westport, Conn.: Lawrence Hill, 1980), 55.

5. See, for example, Nathaniel Teich, "Marxist Dialectics in Content, Form, Point of View: Structures in Jack London's *The Iron Heel*," *Modern Fiction Studies* 22 (Spring 1976): 85–99; and Gorman Beauchamp, "Jack London's Utopian Dystopia and

Dystopian Utopia" in Kenneth M. Roemer, ed., *America as Utopia* (New York: Burt Franklin, 1981), 91–107. For an analysis that stresses the "multiple functions" of the "stratification of voices" and thus goes beyond the double point of view, see Alessandro Portrelli, "Jack London's Missing Revolution: Notes on *The Iron Heel*," *Science Fiction Studies* 27 (July 1982): 181.

6. Joan D. Hedrick, *Solitary Comrade: Jack London and His Work* (Chapel Hill: University of North Carolina Press, 1982), xvi. For other biographical studies of London, see Robert Barltrop, *Jack London: The Man, the Writer, the Rebel* (London: Pluto Press, 1976); Earle Labor, *Jack London* (New York: Twayne, 1974); Joan London, *Jack London and His Times: An Unconventional Biography* (Seattle: University of Washington Press, 1968); Richard O'Connor, *Jack London: A Biography* (Boston: Little, Brown, 1964); and Andrew Sinclair, *Jack: A Biography of Jack London* (London: Harper and Row, 1977). For a concise overview of these works, see my entry, "Jack London," in Paul E. Schellinger, ed., *The St. James Guide to Biography* (Chicago: St. James Press, 1991), 472–73. For a biography of London that situates his radicalism within a divided consciousness and a contradictory era, see Johnston, *London—American Radical?*.

7. Hayden White, *The Content of the Form: Narrative Discourse and Historical Representation* (Baltimore: Johns Hopkins University Press, 1987), 185–213.

8. On the contradictions, see Peter Conn, *The Divided Mind: Ideology and Imagination in America, 1898–1917* (Cambridge: Cambridge University Press, 1983). On the political crises and conflicts that framed the period of Jack London's life (1876–1916), see Nell Irvin Painter, *Standing at Armageddon: The United States, 1877–1919* (New York: Norton, 1987).

9. Jean Pfaelzer, "The Impact of Political Theory on Narrative Structures" in Roemer, *America as Utopia*, 120. For other descriptions of the utopian qualities of *The Iron Heel*, see Tom Moylan, *Demand the Impossible: Science Fiction and the Utopian Imagination* (New York: Methuen, 1986), 6; and Beauchamp, "Utopian Dystopia."

10. For Stuart Hall's concept of "discursive chains" and its connection to the ideological terrain, see Kenneth Thompson, *Beliefs and Ideologies* (London: Tavistock, 1986), 33, 48.

11. Fredric Jameson, *The Political Unconscious: Narrative as a Socially Symbolic Act* (Ithaca, N.Y.: Cornell University Press, 1981), 115. For an insightful interpolation of the ideologeme in utopian fiction, see Moylan, *Demand the Impossible*, 38, 49.

12. Joan London, *Jack London and His Times*, 307.

13. On the theoretical connection between different forms of masculinity and power, see Arthur Brittan, *Masculinity and Power* (New York: Basil Blackwell, 1989). The connection between a discursive force field and power and gender is derived from the work of Michel Foucault. See Foucault, *The History of Sexuality, Volume I—An Introduction*, trans. Robert Harley (New York: Pantheon, 1978); and "The Subject of Power," in Hubert L. Dreyfus and Paul Rabinow, eds., *Michel Foucault: Beyond Structuralism and Hermeneutics* (London: Harvester Press, 1982), 208–26. For

a discussion of Foucault's discursive force field and its link to power and gender in history, see Joan Wallach Scott, *Gender and the Politics of History* (New York: Columbia University Press, 1988), esp. 42. For an excellent overview, see R. W. Connell, *Gender and Power: Society, the Person and Sexual Politics* (Cambridge: Polity Press, 1987).

14. Sinclair, *Jack*, 129.

15. Hedrick, *Solitary Comrade*, 83.

16. For a masterly biography of Debs, which sets out this connection between American manhood and socialism, see Nick Salvatore, *Eugene Debs: Citizen and Socialist* (Urbana: University of Illinois Press, 1982). In a direct reference to Debs and his iconic significance in his short story "The Dream of Debs" (1909), London contrasts the resolve and masculine strength of the organized working class in a future general strike and the weakness and cowardice of the leisured men of the ruling class.

17. Hedrick, *Solitary Comrade*, 15. Although Portrelli notes Everhard's role as working-class hero, albeit one who speaks "for" but not "from" the working class, he neglects, for the most part, London's masculinist portrayal of Everhard. See Portrelli, "London's Missing Revolution," 184–85.

18. Clarice Stasz, "Androgyny in the Novels of Jack London," *Western American Literature* 11 (May 1976): 122, 133.

19. June Howard, *Form and History in American Literary Naturalism* (Chapel Hill: University of North Carolina Press, 1985), 77.

20. Hedrick, *Solitary Comrade*, 28.

21. On the role of Jackson's arm in the education of Avis, see Charles N. Watson, Jr., *The Novels of Jack London: A Reappraisal* (Madison: University of Wisconsin Press, 1983), 113–15. On the metaphors of power in *The Iron Heel*, see Barltrop, *Jack London*, 85.

22. Quoted in John Frow, *Marxism and Literary Form* (Oxford: Basil Blackwell, 1986), 72. On the reconstructive approach, see Dominick LaCapra, *Rethinking Intellectual History: Texts, Contexts, Language* (Ithaca, N.Y.: Cornell University Press, 1983), esp. 23–71. On the deconstructive or semiological decoding method, see H. White, *The Content of the Form*, 185–213.

23. Watson, *The Novels of Jack London*, 104.

24. Painter, *Standing at Armageddon*, 206. For other historical references to the rates of industrial accidents, see James R. Green, *The World of the Worker: Labor in Twentieth Century America* (New York: Hill and Wang, 1980), 13.

25. See, for example, Peter N. Stearns, *Be a Man!: Males in Modern Society* (New York: Holmes and Meier, 1990). In arguing that the absence of Jackson's arm reflects the absence of the authentic working class in *The Iron Heel*, Portrelli also asserts that the "loss of Jackson's arm, torn and chewed by the teeth of the machine, sums up London's strategy of loss, absence, void, fragmentation by which he indicates—by *not* describing them—the essential objects of *The Iron Heel*" ("London's Missing Revolution," 184).

26. Johnston, *London—American Radical?*, 121.

27. For an incisive analysis of the sexual politics of *The Iron Heel*, see Hedrick, *Solitary Comrade*, 188–99. See also Jeff Hearn, *Men in the Public Eye: The Construction and Deconstruction of Public Men and Public Patriarchies* (London: Routledge, 1992); and M. S. Kimmel, "The Contemporary 'Crisis' of Masculinity in Historical Perspective," in H. Brod, ed., *The Making of Masculinities: The New Men's Studies* (Boston: Allen and Unwin, 1987), 121–53.

28. Paul Stein, "Jack London's *The Iron Heel*: Art as Manifesto," *Studies in American Fiction* 6 (Spring 1978): 80.

29. Howard, *Form and History*, 122.

30. On London's evangelical socialism, see Johnston, *London—American Radical?*, 109–45. On the social gospel and Christian Socialism, see Sidney Fine, *Laissez Faire and the General Welfare State* (Ann Arbor: University of Michigan Press, 1964), 169–97; Robert M. Crunden, *Ministers of Reform: The Progressives' Achievement in American Civilization, 1889–1920* (New York: Basic Books, 1982); and R. C. White and C. H. Hopkins, *The Social Gospel: Religion and Reform in Changing America* (Philadelphia: Temple University Press, 1976).

31. Watson, *The Novels of Jack London*, 119.

32. From "The Preacher and the Slave," in *Songs of the Workers*, 34th ed. (Chicago: IWW, 1974), 64. This Joe Hill song was first published in the 1911 edition of the Wobblies' *Little Red Song Book*. See also Philip S. Foner, *The Case of Joe Hill* (New York: International Publishers, 1965).

33. George Speed quoted in Melvyn Dubofsky, *We Shall Be All: A History of the Industrial Workers of the World* (New York: Quadrangle, 1973), 157. On the same page, Dubofsky alludes to this passage from *The Iron Heel* and attests that the novel was "well known to Wobblies." On the IWW, see ibid., 146–70; and Donald E. Winters, Jr., *The Soul of the Wobblies: The IWW, Religion, and American Culture in the Progressive Era, 1905–1917* (Westport, Conn.: Greenwood Press, 1985). See also Peter Carlson, *Roughneck: The Life and Times of Big Bill Haywood* (New York: Norton, 1983). On London and the Wobblies, see Johnston, *London—American Radical?*, 115–16. It is not surprising that the "one big union," which brings the ruling class to its knees in London's "The Dream of Debs," is referred to only as the ILW.

34. Portrelli, "London's Missing Revolution," 186.

35. Quoted in Joan London, *Jack London and His Times*, 333–34.

36. Antonio Gramsci, *Selections from the Prison Notebooks*, trans. and ed. Quentin Hoare and G. N. Smith (New York: International Publishers, 1971), 276.

37. Beauchamp, "Utopian Dystopia," 91.

38. Howard, *Form and History*, 39, 41. See also Conn, *The Divided Mind*, 104–9, where the brief description of London's "ambiguous" socialism also cites the contemporary context.

39. See Painter, *Standing at Armageddon*; Frederic C. Jaher, *Doubters and Dissenters: Cataclysmic Thought in America, 1885–1918* (New York: Free Press of Glen-

coe, 1964); and E. J. Hobsbawm, *The Age of Empire, 1875–1914* (London: Weidenfeld and Nicolson, 1987).

40. On the historical context of masculine concerns, see Stearns, *Be a Man!*. On the masculinist ethos of radical workers, like the Wobblies, see my "Masculine Power and Virile Syndicalism: A Gendered Analysis of the IWW in Australia," *Labour History* 63 (Nov. 1992): 83–99. On the masculine bias in naturalism, see Howard, *Form and History,* 140. Although, as a number of critics point out, the name Everhard came from a Michigan cousin of London's, the gender posturing of the character conveys a strong sense of phallocentric power. See, for example, Watson, *The Novels of Jack London,* 102–3.

41. Quoted in Johnston, *London—American Radical?,* 15. On Nietzsche's influence, see ibid., 79–88.

42. See Geoffrey Harpham, "Jack London and the Tradition of Superman Socialism," *American Studies* 16 (Spring 1975): 23–33.

43. Quoted ibid., 80.

44. See Arthur Lipow, *Authoritarian Socialism in America: Edward Bellamy and the Nationalist Movement* (Berkeley and Los Angeles: University of California Press, 1982); and Glen L. Seretan, *Daniel De Leon: The Odyssey of an American Marxist* (Cambridge: Harvard University Press, 1979).

45. Quoted in Joan London, *Jack London and His Times,* 336.

46. On Coxey's army, see Barltrop, *Jack London,* 41; Johnston, *London—American Radical?,* 11–17; and Painter, *Standing at Armageddon,* 117–21.

47. On the impact of competition and ambition on radical messages and movements during the late nineteenth and early twentieth centuries, see Aileen Kraditor, *The Radical Persuasion, 1890–1917* (Baton Rouge: Louisiana State University Press, 1981). Although Kraditor's comprehension of the role of privatization and segmentation helps to explain the waning of oppositional political formations, her consistent undervaluing of the state's intrusive and repressive role in the public and private sectors and her overvaluation of the democratic constancy of corporate liberalism undermines her interpretation of the general irrelevance and marginality of radical political formations during this period.

48. On the connections between Leninism and the Fighting Groups, see Stein, "Jack London's *The Iron Heel*," 89; and Portrelli, "London's Missing Revolution," 185–86.

49. On Charmian Kittredge, see Johnston, *London—American Radical?,* 79; and Clarice Stasz, *American Dreamers: Charmian and Jack London* (New York: St. Martin's Press, 1988). For a discussion of the New Woman, see Peter G. Filene, *Him/Her/Self: Sex Roles in Modern America,* 2d ed. (Baltimore: Johns Hopkins University Press, 1986), 19–34.

50. Hedrick, *Solitary Comrade,* 15.

51. Portrelli, "London's Missing Revolution," 190.

52. Quoted in Watson, *The Novels of Jack London,* 105.

53. On the influence of Donnelly's *Caesar's Column*, see ibid., 109–12. On the loss of faith in *The Iron Heel*, see Barltrop, *Jack London*, 127.

54. On the vengeful return of the repressed, see Portrelli, "London's Missing Revolution," 189.

55. On naturalist predispositions and proletarianization, see Howard, *Form and History*, 140. London's 1903 journalistic account of the poor of London's ghettos, entitled *The People of the Abyss* (thus the self-referential connection in *The Iron Heel*), contains the familiar tropes of naturalism and features London undertaking a disguise (class transvestism) that Avis and the Fighting Groups take on in different form in *The Iron Heel*.

56. See Beauchamp, "Utopian Dystopia." On how *The Iron Heel* "reveals the radical disjunction between London's political insight and his emotional limitations," see Hedrick, *Solitary Comrade*, 189.

57. On the "transvaluation of values" in other London literary texts, see Johnston, *London—American Radical?*, 88.

58. On the politics of transfiguration, the transvaluation of values, and utopia, see Seyla Benhabib, *Critique, Norm, and Utopia: A Study of the Foundations of Critical Theory* (New York: Columbia University Press, 1986), 13.

59. Walter B. Rideout, *The Radical Novel in the United States, 1900–1954: Some Interrelations of Literature and Society* (New York: Hill and Wang, 1966), 41–42. For the interconnections between London's contradictions and socialism's, see Johnston, *London—American Radical?*, 183–84.

60. See, for example, the essays in John H. M. Laslett and Seymour Martin Lipset, eds., *Failure of a Dream: Essays in the History of American Socialism*, rev. ed. (Berkeley and Los Angeles: University of California Press, 1984); Robert Hyfler, *Prophets of the Left: American Socialist Thought in the Twentieth Century* (Westport, Conn.: Greenwood Press, 1984); and Milton Cantor, *The Divided Left: American Radicalism, 1900–75* (New York: Hill and Wang, 1978). For a concise critical analysis of how those contradictions and divisions led to the eventual failure of American socialism during the first two decades of the twentieth century, see Mike Davis, *Prisoners of the American Dream: Politics and Economy in the History of the US Working Class* (London: Verso, 1990), 40–51.

61. Joan London, *Jack London and His Times*, 379.

Baskett: Sea Change in 'The Sea-Wolf'

1. Bertha Clark Pope, ed., *The Letters of Ambrose Bierce* (San Francisco: Book Club of California, 1922), 105.

2. Earle Labor, Robert C. Leitz, III, and I. Milo Shepard, eds., *The Letters of Jack London*, 3 vols. (Stanford, Calif.: Stanford University Press, 1988), 1: 36, 278.

3. Carolyn Heilbrun, *Toward a Recognition of Androgyny* (New York: Knopf, 1973), x.

4. Anna Strunsky, "Memories of Jack London," *The Bowery News* (June 1962): 8–9.

5. *The Sea-Wolf* (New York: Macmillan, 1904), 199.

6. Joseph Boone, "Male Independence and the American Quest Genre: Hidden Sexual Politics in the All-Male Worlds of Melville, Twain and London," in Judith Spector, ed., *Gender Studies: New Directions in Feminist Criticism* (Bowling Green, Ohio: Bowling Green State University Popular Press, 1986).

7. Charles N. Watson, Jr., *The Novels of Jack London: A Reappraisal* (Madison: University of Wisconsin Press, 1983), 65.

8. In thus regarding Larsen's dimensions, Maud moves, in Heilbrun's terms, beyond what she might have earlier considered "appropriate," a development that is also suggested in the last sentence of the novel: Maud's smile, as she "completed" Hump's expression of love, is "whimsical with love," "whimsical as I had never seen it," recalling an earlier description of Larsen's "whimsical" smiles, the only other appearance of this word in the text (142).

9. Ann Douglas, *The Feminization of American Culture* (New York: Knopf, 1977).

Derrick: Making a Heterosexual Man

1. Such a procedure runs the real risk of flattening individual texts that might each be made to yield a variety of complex readings. I hope this danger will be off-set by the virtues of pointing out the intertextual complexity of certain patterns in London. In any case, any critical procedure has risks and limitations.

2. Several critics have recently argued for the progressive possibilities of London's gender politics. See, for example, Sam S. Baskett, "Sea Change in *The Sea-Wolf*," in this volume (originally *American Literary Realism* 24 [1992]: 5–22). Baskett says that *The Sea-Wolf* argues for a cultivated androgyny, embodied in the often ridiculed relation between Maud and Hump. See also Jeanne Campbell Reesman, "Jack London's New Woman in a New World: Saxon Brown Roberts' Journey into *The Valley of the Moon*," *American Literary Realism* 24 (1992): 40–54. Reesman argues that too little attention has been paid to the late fiction, and she discusses *The Valley of the Moon* as a text with radically experimental gender roles. I believe London's depictions of gender have progressive possibilities at times, but I resist using the metaphor of "androgyny" (see note 9).

3. For passages concerning Maud Brewster, see 155, 141, 220, and 255 in *The Sea-Wolf*, in *The Sea-Wolf and Other Stories*, ed. Andrew Sinclair (New York: Viking Penguin, 1984). See also *A Daughter of the Snows* (London: T. Nelson and Sons, n.d.); *The Valley of the Moon* (New York: Macmillan, 1913); *Martin Eden* (New York: Viking Penguin, 1984); and "The Priestly Prerogative," in *The Son of the Wolf: Tales of the Far North* (Boston: Houghton Mifflin, 1900), 119–44.

4. For two references to Billy's "silk" in *The Valley of the Moon*, see 405 and 410. The passage referring to the Malemute Kid is from London's "The Wife of a King," in *Son of the Wolf*, 167. See also *The Game* (London: William Heinemann, 1905), 113–16.

5. For a discussion of the way an "emphatically male" naturalism manages its anx-

ieties about the reproductive power of women and of a feminine nature, see Mark
Seltzer's *Bodies and Machines* (New York: Routledge, 1992). In a chapter entitled "The
Naturalist Machine," for example, Seltzer argues that Norris's *The Octopus* rewrites
"the colossal mother . . . as a machine of force" and hence produces "a counter to
female generativity" (29). In this rewriting, the man comes to occupy the crucial position of "middleman," asserting an obstetrical control of reproduction (28).

6. Jack London, *White Fang*, in Donald Pizer, ed., *Jack London: Novels and Stories* (New York: The Library of America, 1982), 257.

7. The formidable abilities of Charmian Kittredge emerge most clearly in the
recent biography by Clarice Stasz, *American Dreamers: Charmian and Jack London*
(New York: St. Martin's Press, 1988).

8. Earle Labor, Robert C. Leitz, III, and I. Milo Shepard, eds., *The Letters of Jack
London*, 3 vols. (Stanford, Calif.: Stanford University Press, 1988), 1: 382.

9. To Carroll Smith-Rosenberg, the "New Woman" constituted a revolutionary
demographic and political phenomenon. Eschewing marriage, she fought for professional visibility; espoused innovative, often radical, economic and social reforms;
and wielded real political power. "The New Woman as Androgyne: Social Disorder
and Gender Crisis, 1870–1936," in *Disorderly Conduct: Visions of Gender in Victorian America* (New York: Knopf, 1985), 245. Clarice Stasz argues for the importance
of the New Woman to London's fiction in "Androgyny in the Novels of Jack London," *Western American Literature* 11 (May 1976): 121–33. She makes the strongest
possible case for London's progressive reformulation of gender roles. I believe that
notion of androgyny, which implies a complementary blending of men and women
into a wholeness tragically lost, tends to conceal the complexity of London's relation
to questions of gender.

10. Andrew Sinclair mentions that Strunsky had registered at Stanford, in *Jack:
A Biography of Jack London* (New York: Harper and Row, 1977), 62.

11. Jack London and Anna Strunsky, *The Kempton-Wace Letters* (New York: Macmillan, 1903), 104–5.

12. Smith-Rosenberg argues that in the late nineteenth and early twentieth centuries a deviation from conventional roles often was interpreted as a sign of les-
bianism. And the consequences of the campaign against "deviance" were to increase
marriage rates among women graduates from colleges and to decrease the number
of women undertaking further professional training ("New Woman as Androgyne,"
277–81).

13. Genevieve, in *The Game*, seems to be a marginally more attractive version of
the same kind of conventional woman, one who finds herself attracted to a man she
wants to change. She cannot understand Joe's passion for the violence of boxing and
threatens his masculine status by seeking to remove him from the ring. Nevertheless, she attracts men precisely by her difference. They "stood in awe of Genevieve,
in a dimly religious way, as of something mysteriously beautiful and unapproach-
able" (49).

Kim Moreland, in "The Attack on the Nineteenth-Century Heroine Reconsidered: Women in Jack London's *Martin Eden*," *Markham Review* 13 (1983–84): 16–19, sees the novel as an explicit attack on the conventional heroine of the nineteenth-century woman's novel. For Martin, the most acceptable relation is his homoerotic, misogynist one with Brissenden. Although Ruth cannot transcend her class position, Martin cannot transcend his sufficiently to make a relation with Lizzie Connolly possible.

14. This crisis is reflected in the array of cultural forms aimed at the cultivation of masculinity in the late nineteenth and early twentieth centuries. See Joe L. Dubbert's useful book, *A Man's Place: Masculinity in Transition* (Englewood Cliffs, N.J.: Prentice-Hall, 1979); and Mark Seltzer's "The Love-Master," in *Bodies and Machines*, 147–72.

15. This argument is made in Freud's "The Medusa's Head" (212–13) and "Fetishism" (214–19), in Phillip Rieff, ed., *Sexuality and the Psychology of Love* (New York: Macmillan, 1963).

16. Forrest G. Robinson has an interesting argument concerning *The Sea-Wolf*, in *Having It Both Ways: Self-Subversion in Popular Western Classics* (Albuquerque: University of New Mexico Press, 1993), 55–78: that Maud is actually the dominant figure in the novel, manipulating and controlling the naive Van Weyden with amazing consistency, despite the pattern's status as an "inadvertent" feature of London's text (76). This dominance seems to require that we attribute to Maud conventional feminine "wiles," which leaves unchallenged a masculine ascendancy in the realm of direct action. This ascendancy, in turn, raises the question of how extensive one's claims for Maud's power can finally be. I believe that the relations between Maud and Hump are better accounted for in terms of an ambivalent, fetishistic alteration.

17. Jack London, "The Son of the Wolf," in *The Son of the Wolf*, 21–51, quotation on 28.

18. Jack London, "The White Silence," in *The Son of the Wolf*, 1–20.

19. Jack London, "The Wife of a King," in *The Son of the Wolf*, 160–89, quotation on 173.

20. Jack London, *The Call of the Wild*, in Pizer, *Novels and Stories*, 1–86, quotation on 53.

21. Sinclair reports in his biography that London may have engaged in a homosexual relationship while in prison for vagrancy (*Jack*, 22–24). In addition, one of the great loves of London's life was the bohemian poet George Sterling (see Thomas Benediktsson, *George Sterling* [Boston: Twayne, 1980]). London referred to Sterling as "Greek" and was called "Wolf" in return. It is difficult not to think of the importance of "Greek love" in late-nineteenth-century debates about homosexuality. Louis Crompton argues, in the introduction to *Byron and Greek Love: Homophobia in Nineteenth-Century England* (Berkeley and Los Angeles: University of California Press, 1985), that anyone "intimately familiar with the classics" would recognize the homoerotic implications of the term, but he also says that nineteenth-century schol-

arship suppressed aspects of Greek literature troubling to Victorian morality (11). Both Stasz, in her biography of London and Kittredge (*American Dreamers*, 97), and Benediktsson (*George Sterling*, 30) state that both men would have been shocked at the suggestion of anything erotic in their relationship. Without evidence, however, their certitude seems suspect, and strenuous denials are often a better index of an act's social propriety than of its possible commission. Andrew Sinclair is more cautious but still concludes, "He remained a woman's man and never seems to have slept voluntarily with men" (*Jack*, 24). A letter Sinclair cites from London to Maurice Magnus on the subject of homosexuality, however, seems to me to be less definitive, more coy and self-contradictory than it does to Sinclair (*Letters*, 2: 1042). I know of no detailed account of the sexual life of early-twentieth-century California bohemian culture; such a work would be of great aid in resolving this question. The problem of homoeroticism and the relationship between Sterling and London was framed in Joan London's 1939 biography about as well as it has been in recent texts. She concludes that "both would have furiously resented and denied the inferences that would be readily drawn today," but it was probable that their relationship did contain "some latent homosexuality" (Joan London, *Jack London and His Times: An Unconventional Biography* [New York: Doubleday, 1939], 260). For an account of London's prison adventures, see *The Road*, in Donald Pizer, ed., *Jack London: Novels and Social Writings* (New York: The Library of America, 1982), 235.

22. Several commentators on the novel have noted the homoerotic dynamics of this scene. See Robert Forrey, "Male and Female in London's *The Sea-Wolf*," *Literature and Psychology* 24 (1974): 135–43, who says that repressed homosexuality is key to the novel. Both Joan D. Hedrick, in *Solitary Comrade: Jack London and His Work* (Chapel Hill: University of North Carolina Press, 1982), 122–23, and Charles N. Watson, Jr., in *The Novels of Jack London: A Reappraisal* (Madison: University of Wisconsin Press, 1983), 65–68, cite this passage as evidence of homoeroticism.

23. One persistent argument has been that London believed in androgyny. I believe that the terrain of gender difference is almost always more contested and complicated than "androgyny" implies, though it expresses a useful tolerance for variation from gender norms. As a metaphor, it tends to essentialize gender by taking as givens the feminine and masculine qualities to be blended; it suggests a possible midpoint of perfect and harmonious equality; it implies, as a consequence, that masculinity and femininity represent equal divisions of the social real; it fails to consider how women's transgressions of gender boundaries may still function within a patriarchal economy rather than challenge it; and it does not examine whether "feminine" moments in masculine culture really challenge patriarchy or represent appropriation and/or masochistic pleasure.

24. The love scenes between Billy and Saxon also seem to be authentic enough, even though Saxon has an odd anxiety about her ability to sustain Billy's sexual interest, which she assuages by obsessively laundering her "pretty flimsies." I would not want to argue that desire in *The Valley of the Moon* must be understood as ex-

clusively homosexual or heterosexual. I am arguing, however, that the unacceptability of the former leads London to try to absorb it into the latter, even as he produces homosocial scenes that demonstrate the equivocal success of this effort.

25. Jack London, "In a Far Country," in *The Son of the Wolf*, 69–101.

26. "In a Far Country" has important relations to at least two other texts. Sam S. Baskett notes the possible indebtedness of this tale to Joseph Conrad's "An Outpost of Progress" in his *Tales of Unrest*. The similarities are striking and numerous, but the culmination of the tale on an unmade bed is one of London's additions to whatever material he appropriates. See Baskett, "Jack London's Heart of Darkness," *American Quarterly* 10 (Spring 1958): 66–77. Also of interest is a prose piece London entitled "Housekeeping in the Klondike" (*Harper's Bazaar* 33 [Sept. 1900]: 1227–32), to which Jonathan Auerbach has generously directed my attention. In it, London indicates that the Klondike housekeeper has a "feminine prototype" (1232) in other cultures, and he begins by exclaiming, "Housekeeping in the Klondike—that's bad! And by men—worse. . . . It is bad, unutterably bad, for men to keep house" (1227). The danger in role switching may be specified by his emphasis on the one thing male housekeepers do *not* do for other men: "But there is one thing the cook does not have to do, nor any man in the Klondike—and that is, make another man's bed. In fact, the beds are never made" (1231). This last admission is quite interesting, in terms of the implication that the failure of Cuthfert and Weatherbee to make beds constitutes a special, as opposed to a widely shared, depravity in Klondike culture. The unmade bed in London's essay indicates a repression of the erotic, in the refusal to touch another man's bed, and an openness, an ongoing temptation as well. This temptation, in turn, is arguably denied by the filth of the unmade bed.

27. Jack London, *The Cruise of the Dazzler*, in Arthur Calder-Marshall, ed., *The Bodley Head Jack London*, vol. 2 (London: Bodley Head Press, 1964).

28. My argument is that even disreputable or racially other bodies in London's fiction *are* eroticized. Van Weyden's defenses, a consequence of his scrutinizing the ship's other men, tend to betray the salience of why they were constructed.

29. Jack London, "The Heathen," in Earle Labor, Robert C. Leitz, III, and I. Milo Shepard, eds., *Jack London Short Stories* (New York: Collier Books, 1991), 374–90.

30. What differentiates *The Call of the Wild* from *White Fang* (1906) is that White Fang learns to live in the confines of bourgeois heterosexuality, living beneath the paternal sway of "the love-master" and siring offspring of his own. We might be struck by the lengths to which the novel must go to safely contain its canine hero's love for Weedon Scott.

31. We by definition know too little about what kind of experience this might be, since what we take to be nineteenth-century "sexuality" typically represents the repressive grid of bourgeois morality. Though we should avoid the naturalist error of linking lower-class life with inchoate and somehow undisciplined desire, London's men gesture beyond the boundaries of working-class culture and even the aggressive "realism" of naturalism to experiences too rough, too "unclean," for representation.

32. For a general consideration of the torturous consequences of London's class ascension as it relates to gender, see Hedrick's *Solitary Comrade*, particularly the chapter entitled "The Middle Class" (32–47). To Hedrick, London gives himself a choice between "the man's world of raw power and the woman's world of poetry and 'culture.' . . . Over and over again London was to choose the sentimentalities of middle class culture over the 'old sad savagery' that he had known" (43).

33. Joseph Boone argues that the wilderness in American literature often serves as a "wild zone," which allows an exploration of desires difficult to articulate within the setting of conventional culture. See "Male Independence and the American Quest Romance as Counter-Traditional Genre: Hidden Sexual Politics in the Male World of *Moby Dick, Huckleberry Finn, Billy Budd*, and *The Sea Wolf*," in his *Tradition Counter Tradition: Love and the Form of Fiction* (Chicago: University of Chicago Press, 1987), 226–77.

34. Leo Bersani, to whom my analysis is indebted, argues for an opposition between sexuality and narrative, in *The Freudian Body: Psychoanalysis and Art* (New York: Columbia University Press, 1986), 39–40. For example, in Freud's *Three Essays on Sexuality*, Bersani says, sexuality is theorized in two conflicting ways. It is an incalculable force unknowable in terms of its objects, to which it is merely "soldered"; and it is a confining narrative of stages leading from the polymorphous flux of childhood to adult sexuality. The channel of this teleological narrative confines and pathologizes divergent desires even as it also creates space for their discussion within the discourse of sexuality and calls them into theoretical existence (39).

35. Sigmund Freud, *Three Essays on Sexuality*, trans. and rev. by James Strachey (New York: Basic Books, 1962), 11–12.

36. Sigmund Freud, *Civilization and Its Discontents*, trans. and ed. James Strachey (New York: Norton, 1961), 53.

37. Watson, in *The Novels of Jack London*, notes that *The Sea-Wolf* contains a narrative of male sexual development in which homosexuality plays a role: "Indeed, the central action involves a crisis of sexual as well as intellectual identity. In this crisis, 'masculinity' implies both homosexuality and nihilism (the creed of brute strength), while 'femininity' implies heterosexuality and ethical idealism. Emerging from an abnormally prolonged mother-dependency, Humphrey must pass through an intermediate stage of masculine exclusivity before arriving at a final stage of sexual and philosophical adulthood" (65).

38. Leo Bersani argues, in *The Freudian Body*, that sexuality should perhaps be understood as precisely such a permanently "outside" force: "We desire what nearly shatters us, and the shattering experience is, it would seem, *without any specific content*—which may be our only way of saying that the experience cannot be said, that it belongs to the nonlinguistic biology of human life. . . . Sexuality would not be originally an exchange of intensities between individuals, but rather a condition of broken negotiations with the world" (39–41).

39. The nature of these conventional narratives has been best interrogated by

Michel Foucault. They form the locus of domination, including the "repressive hypothesis" itself. As he argues in *The History of Sexuality*, volume 1: *An Introduction*, trans. Robert Hurley (New York: Vintage Books, 1980), "never have there existed more centers of power; never more attention manifested and verbalized; never more circular contacts and linkages; never more sites where the intensity of pleasures and the persistency of power catch hold, only to spread elsewhere" (49). Positing a body beyond discourse may suggest a return to the repressive hypothesis, although Foucault's contention that all positions within discourse involve an extension of power is still important and valuable. Clearly, a speaking of the body's difference from discourse in discourse must be a difficult process.

40. Jack London, "The White Silence," in *Son of the Wolf*, 1–20; and *John Barleycorn*, ed. John Sutherland (New York: Oxford University Press, 1989). Both passages have figured prominently in London criticism. For a good account, see James I. McClintock, *White Logic: Jack London's Short Stories* (Grand Rapids, Mich.: Wolf House Books, 1975), 47–57.

41. The argument that "whiteness" represents a general epistemological limit in his fiction has been made before. See, for example, McClintock's *White Logic*, 82.

42. According to Eve Kosofsky Sedgwick in *Epistemology of the Closet* (Berkeley and Los Angeles: University of California Press, 1990): "If ignorance is not—as it evidently is not—a single Manichaean, aboriginal maw of darkness from which the heroics of human cognition can occasionally wrestle facts, . . . perhaps there exists instead a plethora of *ignorances*. . . . Insofar as ignorance is ignorance *of* a knowledge . . . these ignorances . . . are produced by and correspond to particular knowledges and circulate as part of particular regimes of truth" (8).

Stasz: Social Darwinism, Gender, and Humor

1. For a view of these changes with regard to masculinity, see Mark C. Carnes and Clyde Griffen, eds., *Meanings for Manhood: Constructions of Masculinity in Victorian Manhood* (Chicago: University of Chicago Press, 1990).

2. See my "Androgyny in the Novels of Jack London," *Western American Literature* 11 (May 1976): 121–33; as well as Stoddard Martin, *California Writers* (New York: St. Martin's Press, 1983).

3. Charmian London, *The Log of the Snark* (New York: Macmillan, 1915), 369.

4. Manuscript notes to *Adventure*, Henry E. Huntington Library, San Marino, Calif. These are unnumbered loose sheets.

5. Earle Labor, Robert C. Leitz, III, and I. Milo Shepard, eds., *The Letters of Jack London*, 3 vols. (Stanford, Calif.: Stanford University Press, 1988), 2: 755.

6. London to Brett, March 3, 1909, ibid., 793.

7. London to Cosgrove, May 3, 1909, ibid., 804.

8. See Jack London to George P. Brett, April 1, 1910, ibid., 882; Jack London, *Adventure* (New York: Macmillan, 1911).

9. *Letters*, 2: 831.

10. Earle Labor, *Jack London* (New York: Twayne, 1974), 162.

11. Charles N. Watson, Jr., *The Novels of Jack London: A Reappraisal* (Madison: University of Wisconsin Press, 1983), xii.

12. Jack London, *A Daughter of the Snows* (Philadelphia: J. B. Lippincott, 1902).

13. Jack London, *Burning Daylight* (New York: Macmillan, 1910); *The Little Lady of the Big House* (New York: Macmillan, 1916). For discussion of Charmian London's influence on his female characters in these and other novels, see my *American Dreamers: Charmian and Jack London* (New York: St. Martin's Press, 1988).

14. Jack London to Joan and Becky London, August 22, 1916, *Letters*, 3: 1566. "One of the Von Tempsky girls, who was a model for Joan Lackland, is just now up from Hawaii and visiting us on the ranch. I wish you knew her and her sister and their strong old father."

15. For a cogent introduction to these changes, see Glenda Riley, *Inventing the American Woman* (Arlington Heights, Ill.: Harlan Davidson, 1987), particularly chap. 6, "'Reordering Women's Sphere': The Progressive Era, 1890–1917."

16. Manuscript notes to *Adventure*.

17. See, for example, *A Daughter of the Snows*, 108–9.

18. *Little Lady of the Big House*, 292.

19. Charmian London, *Log of the Snark*, 389.

20. "The Kanaka Surf" appears in *On the Makaloa Mat* (New York: Macmillan, 1919).

21. Jack London, *South Sea Tales* (New York: Macmillan, 1911).

22. "The Inevitable White Man," in *South Sea Tales*, 238–39.

23. Ibid., 402.

24. Jack London, *The Cruise of the Snark* (New York: Macmillan, 1911), 273.

Gair: "The Way Our People Came"

1. Jack London, *The Valley of the Moon* (New York: Macmillan, 1913; London: Mills and Boon, 1914). For a useful outline of the combination of fictional and autobiographical sources that provided the framework for London's novel, see Charles N. Watson, Jr., *The Novels of Jack London: A Reappraisal* (Madison: University of Wisconsin Press, 1983), 187–210. See also Jack London, *Burning Daylight* (New York: Macmillan, 1910).

2. Mark Seltzer, *Bodies and Machines* (New York: Routledge, 1992), 71.

3. T. J. Jackson Lears, "From Salvation to Self-Realization: Advertising and the Therapeutic Roots of the Consumer Culture, 1880–1930," in Richard Wightman Fox and T. J. Jackson Lears, eds., *The Culture of Consumption: Critical Essays in American History, 1880–1980* (New York: Pantheon, 1983), 1–38, quotation on 4. See also Lears, *No Place of Grace: Antimodernism and the Transformation of American Culture, 1880–1920* (New York: Pantheon, 1981), 3–58.

4. Lears, "From Salvation to Self-Realization," 9.

5. Ibid., 11.

6. For a similar sociological argument concerning the "ethnocentrism [that] leads a people to exaggerate and intensify everything in their own folkways which is peculiar and which differentiates them from others," see William Graham Sumner, *Folkways: A Study of the Sociological Importance of Usages, Manners, Customs, Mores, and Morals* (New York: Dover, 1959 [1906]), esp. 13–15. Sumner identifies a general "rule . . . that nature peoples call themselves 'men'" and regard others as "something else—perhaps not defined—but not real men" (14). In *The Valley of the Moon*, as I will demonstrate, the Anglo-Saxon protagonists repeatedly do the same.

7. Walter Benn Michaels, "Race into Culture: A Critical Genealogy of Cultural Identity," *Critical Inquiry* 18 (Summer 1992): 655–85, quotations on 667, 670.

8. Ibid., 664.

9. Ibid., 665–67.

10. Ibid., 673.

11. Ibid., 679.

12. Seltzer, *Bodies and Machines*, 68.

13. Theodore Dreiser, *Sister Carrie* (Harmondsworth: Penguin, 1981), 98–99; Walter Benn Michaels, *The Gold Standard and the Logic of Naturalism: American Literature at the Turn of the Century* (Berkeley and Los Angeles: University of California Press, 1987), 19.

14. Michaels, *The Gold Standard*, 20, 19.

15. Seltzer, *Bodies and Machines*, 68.

16. Winfried Fluck, "The Power and Failure of Representation in Harriet Beecher Stowe's *Uncle Tom's Cabin*," *New Literary History* 23 (Spring 1992): 319–38, quotation on 322.

17. Ibid., 334, 322.

18. Ibid., 327.

19. Ibid., 329–30.

20. Watson, *The Novels of Jack London*, 210. See Jeanne Campbell Reesman, "Jack London's New Woman in a New World: Saxon Brown Roberts' Journey into the Valley of the Moon," *American Literary Realism* 24 (Winter 1992): 40–54. Reesman claims that the "novel's conclusion surprises with its lack of closure" in an "idyllic yet disturbing open ending" (52).

21. D. A. Miller, "The Novel and the Police," *Glyph* 8 (1981): 127–47, quotation on 131.

22. Seltzer, *Bodies and Machines*, 75.

Furer: "Zone-Conquerors" and "White Devils"

1. Jack London, *A Daughter of the Snows* (New York: Grosset and Dunlap, 1902), 83. These racial views are echoed in some of London's early letters: "The negro races, the mongrel races, the slavish races, the unprogressive races, are of bad blood—that is, of blood which is not qualified to permit them to successfully survive the selection by which the fittest survive" (London to Cloudesley Johns, June 1899, in Earle

Labor, Robert C. Leitz, III, and I. Milo Shepard, eds., *The Letters of Jack London*, 3 vols. [Stanford, Calif.: Stanford University Press, 1988], 1: 87).

2. London, "Chun Ah Chun," in *The House of Pride and Other Tales of Hawaii* (New York: Macmillan, 1912), 154, 156, 169. This story was initially published in *Woman's Magazine* 21 (1910). Dates accompanying short story titles in the text are of initial magazine publication. I use these earlier dates, rather than dates of initial book publication, to emphasize that London's antiracist views are not contained within one narrow segment of his career.

3. London, "Aloha Oe," in *The House of Pride*, 131–32, 142–43, 144.

4. See, for example, the description of the Oakland socialist, "a clever Jew," with "stooped and narrow shoulders," who "stood forth representative of the whole miserable mass of weaklings and inefficients," in chapter 38 of the novel (London, *Martin Eden*, in Donald Pizer, ed., *Jack London: Novels and Social Writings* [New York: The Library of America, 1982], 854).

5. Sinclair, *Jack: A Biography of Jack London* (New York: Harper and Row, 1977), 4.

6. Nineteen of London's works were novels. He worked in nearly every genre, including drama, socialist manifesto, sports journalism, and travel narrative. His subjects include: agriculture, alcoholism, astral projection, big business, ecology, economics, gold-hunting, penal reform, political corruption, prizefighting, seafaring, socialism, war, and wildlife. There are some recent signs that more of his works are being given attention. Jeanne Campbell Reesman has noted that "in his later period in particular (though even here, not without exception), his tendency is toward portraying native peoples of non-Anglo-Saxon background not only sympathetically but as morally superior to Anglo-Saxons" (Introduction to "A Symposium on Jack London," *American Literary Realism* 24 [1992]: 4).

7. Cain, "Socialism, Power, and the Fate of Style: Jack London in His Letters," *American Literary History* 3 (1991): 604–5.

8. Seltzer, *Bodies and Machines* (New York: Routledge, 1992), 223 n. 35.

9. Benjamin Kidd (1858–1916), English civil servant, popular philosopher, and ardent Spencerian, was the author of *Social Evolution* (1894). The book brought him instant fame—within six years of its publication it had been translated into eight languages. Kidd's social philosophy, a simplistic application of the Darwinian concept of natural selection to social evolution, glorified the Anglo-Saxon contribution to history and divided humanity into stronger and weaker races.

10. Labor, "Jack London's Pacific World," in Jacqueline Tavernier-Courbin, ed., *Critical Essays on Jack London* (Boston: G. K. Hall, 1983), 214.

11. Watson, *The Novels of Jack London: A Reappraisal* (Madison: University of Wisconsin Press, 1983), 200.

12. See Nuernberg, "The Call of Kind: Race in Jack London's Fiction" (Ph.D. diss., University of Massachusetts, 1990).

13. London, "When the World was Young," in *The Night-Born* (New York: Cen-

tury, 1913), 84. It is especially, if not exclusively, in the Arctic that this reversion can remain pure, as is evident by the contrast between the fate of atavistic whites there and those in Melanesia. See "Mauki" (1909/1912).

14. Although *Vandover* was not published until twelve years after Norris's death, it seems to have been written during his year (1894–95) as a special student at Harvard. See James D. Hart, ed., *A Novelist in the Making: Frank Norris* (Cambridge: Harvard University Press, 1970), 43–57.

15. Corliss says to Colonel Trethaway, "But it is the living strenuously that holds you," and then implies that "living strenuously" is not only "Frona's philosophy" (220) but that of any right-thinking Anglo-Saxon Alaskan.

16. Spencer, *The Study of Sociology* (London: Kegan, Paul, Trench, 1873), 199. London owned or borrowed dozens of Spencer's works; as David Mike Hamilton notes, "Herbert Spencer's work was part of the bedrock of London's philosophy" (*"The Tools of My Trade": The Annotated Books in Jack London's Library* [Seattle: University of Washington Press, 1986], 256). There are references to Spencer in almost all of London's novels.

17. David Wiltshire, *The Social and Political Thought of Herbert Spencer* (Oxford: Oxford University Press, 1978), 247.

18. Spencer, *Facts and Comments* (New York: D. Appleton, 1902), 133. (London's annotated copy of this work is at the Huntington Library.) These comments reflect Spencer's negative view of the Naval and Military Exhibition of 1901, which was in part a commemoration of the Great Exhibition of 1851. Spencer, in line with his view that the same laws govern the evolution of bodies and societies, and following his theory of "equilibriation," states that societies are either evolving or degenerating; they never stand still.

19. London, *The Mutiny of the Elsinore* (Honolulu: Mutual Publishing, 1987), 337. This novel was serialized as *The Sea Gangsters* in *Hearst's Magazine* from November 1913 to August 1914.

20. London to Charmian Kittredge, Mar. 4, 1904, *Letters*, 1: 415.

21. London, [Description of army in Korea], in King Hendricks and Irving Shepard, eds., *Jack London Reports: War Correspondence, Sports Articles, and Miscellaneous Writings* (New York: Doubleday, 1970), 13, 42.

22. London, "Give Battle to Retard Enemy," in Hendricks and Shepard, *Jack London Reports*, 103, 106.

23. London, "The Yellow Peril," in Hendricks and Shepard, *Jack London Reports*, 347.

24. Joan London, *Jack London and His Times: An Unconventional Biography* (New York: Doubleday, 1939), 284.

25. See, for example, "The Trouble Makers of Mexico" (June 13, 1914), in Hendricks and Shepard, *Jack London Reports*. Writing of the *mestizos*, London declares, "They are what the mixed breed always is. . . . They are neither white men nor Indians. . . . They possess all the vices of their various commingled bloods and none

of the virtues" (177). In the course of this article, London manages a backhanded compliment to Mexico's Indian population (or at least its male half), even as he condemns the country's "mixed-breeds": "[The half-breeds] are child-minded and ignoble-purposed. The stern stuff of manhood, as we understand manhood, is not in them. This stern stuff is in the pure-blooded Indians, however" (180).

26. London, "The Seed of McCoy," in *South Sea Tales*, intro. A. Grove Day (Honolulu: Mutual Publishing Paperback Series, 1985), 262.

27. Burbank to London, June 2, 1906, Jack London Collection, Henry E. Huntington Library. (The first communication between the two appears to have occurred the previous fall, when London wrote to Burbank requesting "a tip as to any kinds of exceptionally good fruits and grapes for me to plant" [London to Burbank, Oct. 7, 1905, Sonoma County Library].) I am not the first to propose the connection between London and Burbank's views of hybridization. Clarice Stasz makes a similar point in chapter 8 of her *American Dreamers: Charmian and Jack London* (New York: St. Martin's Press, 1988). In his autobiography, Burbank describes London as a "big healthy boy with a taste for serious things, but never cynical, never bitter, always good-humored and humorous, as I saw him, and with fingers and heart equally sensitive when he was in my gardens" (Burbank [with Wilbur Hall], *The Harvest of Years* [Boston: Houghton Mifflin, 1927], 225). A photograph of London and Burbank examining spineless cacti is included in Russ Kingman, *A Pictorial Life of Jack London* (New York: Crown, 1979), 171. I wish to thank Earle Labor, Wilson Professor of American Literature, Centenary College, and Sara S. Hodson, Curator of Literary Manuscripts, Huntington Library, for drawing my attention to some of the London/Burbank material mentioned here. I also thank the Huntington for permission to quote from Burbank's letter to London.

28. Ken Kraft and Pat Kraft, *Luther Burbank: The Wizard and the Man* (New York: Meredith Press, 1967) 116, 145.

29. Burbank, *The Training of the Human Plant* (New York: Century, 1907), 5. He also describes this new American hybridization process as "this marvelous mingling of races in the United States" (33).

30. London, *Bâtard and Other Stories* (Oakland: Star Rover House, 1987), 241. "Jees Uck," originally published in the magazine *The Smart Set* in September 1902, was included in London's third short story collection, *The Faith of Men and Other Stories* (1904). The character of Jees Uck represents an exception, of course, to London's tendency to create superior non-white protagonists only in stories set in warm climates.

31. "Koolau the Leper," in *The House of Pride*, 48. This story was initially published in the *Pacific Monthly* in December 1909.

32. McClintock, *White Logic: Jack London's Short Stories* (Grand Rapids, Mich.: Wolf House Books, 1975), 138.

33. Jack London, "Burns-Johnson Fight," in James Bankes, ed., *Jack London: Stories of Boxing* (Dubuque: William C. Brown, 1992), 145. All citations of London's boxing articles refer to this collection, unless otherwise noted.

34. This is not to say that London never lapses into stereotypes in this article: "[Johnson's] face beamed with all the happy, care-free innocence of a little child" (149). Given that London's career coincided with the height of the Jim Crow era, it is remarkable that his prose often escapes from racist language.

35. Phrases like "made noise with his fist like a lullaby" may seem clichéd, but remember that London was among those who invented such idioms.

36. "One criticism, and only one, can be passed upon Johnson. In the thirteenth round . . . [he] should have put Burns out. He could have put him out; it would have been child's play. Instead of which he let Burns live until the gong sounded, and in the opening of the fourteenth round the police stopped the fight and Johnson lost the credit of the knock-out" (150).

37. *Medford Sun* quoted in Bankes, *Stories of Boxing*, xii.

38. In his article on the fight itself (July 4), London heightens this contrast, noting that "the ferocity of the hairy-chested caveman and grizzly giant combined did not intimidate the cool-headed negro" (181).

39. Everhard, the self-educated protagonist of London's socialist novel, *The Iron Heel*, is a blacksmith and a brilliant strategist and theorist of revolution.

40. London, "The Mexican," in *The Night-Born*, 274. This story was first published in *The Saturday Evening Post*, August 19, 1911.

41. Harnish is the hero of London's *Burning Daylight* (1910). Stephen Knight, a mixed breed from the story "Aloha Oe," has a powerful physique of the more outwardly resplendent kind, and thus he is perhaps even more like London's Anglo-Saxon heroes.

42. I wish to thank the late Russ Kingman, of the Jack London Research Center, and I. Milo Shepard, London's literary executor, for allowing me to use the unpublished typescript of *Cherry*, from which all page numbers are taken. As of October 12, 1916, London had announced to Edgar G. Sisson, managing editor of *Collier's*, that he had completed 5,000 words of a new Hawaiian novel, for which he had "only begun to collect possible titles . . . *Cherry*; *The Screen-Lady*; *The Screen-Gazer*; and *Fire Dew*" (*Letters*, 3: 1588). A little more than a month before his death on November 22, 1916, he announced to Sisson that he had completed 15,000 words and was "swinging along on *Cherry*" (London to Sisson, October 23, 1916, *Letters*, 3: 1594).

43. London to the Members of the Local Glen Ellen Socialist Labor party, Mar. 17, 1916, *Letters*, 3: 1538.

Slagel: Political Leprosy

1. Charmian London, *Jack London and Hawaii* (London: Mills and Boon, 1918), 22–23.

2. The name of the historical figure that inspired London's story was Ko'olau, with the Hawaiian *'okina* (glottal stop) between the *o*'s. For the sake of clarity, I will use Koolau to refer to London's protagonist and Ko'olau to refer to the historical figure. In keeping with the Hawaiian language, no *s*'s are placed on plurals. Also, to

avoid confusion, and in keeping with the language of London's time, I will use the term leprosy instead of the preferred designation, Hansen's Disease.

3. Edward Said, *Orientalism* (New York: Vintage Books, 1979).

4. Stephen Sumida, *And the View from the Shore: Literary Traditions of Hawai'i* (Seattle: University of Washington Press, 1991).

5. A. Grove Day, *Pacific Island Literature: One Hundred Basic Books* (Honolulu: University of Hawaii Press, 1971). Day's bibliography and synopses of seminal books, mostly by *haole* authors, provides a solid foundation for the Exotic as perceived by the Occident.

6. Sumida, *And the View from the Shore*, 15–16.

7. A. Grove Day, ed., *Mark Twain's Letters from Hawaii* (Honolulu: University of Hawaii Press, 1975).

8. Ibid., 54–55.

9. Day, "Introduction," ibid., vii. See also Sumida, *And the View from the Shore*, 47.

10. Earle Labor, Robert C. Leitz, III, and I. Milo Shepard, eds., *The Letters of Jack London*, 3 vols. (Stanford, Calif.: Stanford University Press, 1988), 2: 861. Under the pseudonym "Bystander," Thurston wrote his editorial/letter in the *Honolulu Advertiser* following the publication of London's leper stories, initiating a series of public and private letters between the two friends.

11. Charmian London, *Jack London and Hawaii*, 176. Most likely, they spoke about Dole and C. C. Harris at the time of Kalakaua's election in 1874. Lorrin Thurston, in his *Memoirs of the Hawaiian Revolution* (Honolulu: Advertiser Publishing, 1936), wrote: "In the doorway, facing the mob, stood Sanford B. Dole and C. C. Harris, each with a hand on the shoulder of the other, warning the crowd back" (7). In her book *American Dreamers: Charmian and Jack London* (New York: St. Martin's Press, 1988), Clarice Stasz suggests the Londons were manipulated by Thurston and other white leaders in an attempt to persuade the writer to glorify the Islands. Jack's giddy naivete here seems to support that contention.

12. Charmian London, *Jack London and Hawaii*, 177.

13. Ibid., 63, 51.

14. Liliu'okalani, *Hawaii's Story by Hawaii's Queen* (Rutland, Vt.: Charles E. Tuttle, 1964), 367. Liliu'okalani's book is an honest and passionate account of the events surrounding the overthrow, and it is an intelligent antithesis to Thurston's *Memoirs* and other Western writings about this shameful segment of U.S. history.

15. Robert Louis Stevenson, *Travels in Hawaii* (Honolulu: University of Hawaii Press, 1973), 55. London alluded to the Damien letters, which extolled the virtues and defended the practices of Belgian priest Father Damien of Molokai, when he wrote to Thurston (Feb. 1, 1910), stating that Stevenson's writing on leprosy in Hawaii had a greater effect on the world's perception than anything London could write. See *Letters*, 2: 870–71.

16. Stevenson, *Travels in Hawaii*, 53. The current residents of Kalaupapa, treated

Hansen's Disease patients, were initially forced into isolation at the settlement and now reside there by choice.

17. Charmian London, *Jack London and Hawaii*, 119–20.

18. Ibid., 115.

19. London to Carruth, July 11, 1907, *Letters*, 2: 870.

20. Jack London, *The Cruise of the Snark* (London: Seafarer Books, 1971), 106.

21. London to *Honolulu Advertiser*, June 11, 1910, *Letters*, 2: 870.

22. Compare Charmian London, *Jack London and Hawaii*, 105–7, with the *Noeau* departure scene in "Good-bye, Jack" (in *Stories of Hawaii*).

23. London to Thurston, June 11, 1910, *Letters*, 2: 901. London had completed the Hawaiian stories by October 25, 1907, within three weeks of his departure from the Islands. In a letter to publisher George Brett (Oct. 25, 1908), London debates whether to publish them separately or combine them with stories from around the world (*Letters*, 2: 755).

24. Frances Frazier, trans., "The True Story of Kaluaikoʻolau the Leper," *Hawaiian Journal of History* 21 (1987): 1–41. Frazier's is the first English translation of Shelton's 1906 book.

25. Ibid., 8.

26. Ibid., 32, 33.

27. See "Introduction," in Jack London, *Stories of Hawaii*, ed. A. Grove Day (Honolulu: Mutual Publishing, 1968), 11.

28. London, "Koolau the Leper," *Stories of Hawaii*, 42.

29. Frazier, "True Story of Kaluaikoʻolau," 9.

30. London, "Koolau the Leper," 39.

31. Compare London's description with an account from Thurston: "Statements have been made that the 'mission boys,' the sons and grandsons of American missionaries to Hawaii, were ultra-active in the overthrow of the Monarchy. That is true. I come within that distinction. I have been a lifelong acquaintance with the 'mission boys,' and a splendid body of men they were. . . . Instead of using their vantage ground for their personal aggrandizement, they devoted their efforts and influence to winning for Hawaii the fullest possible participation in control of its own affairs as an integral part of the United States. . . . I make special reference to the 'mission boys' here because of the prominence given them by the royalists" (*Memoirs*, 277–78). One wonders if Thurston numbers London among these "royalists."

As much as a rebuttal to London and others, Thurston's book is by and large a futile attempt to carve a respectable niche in Hawaiian history. It should be noted that in 1993 the City Council of Honolulu voted to change the name of Thurston Avenue in recognition of his infamous role in the illegal overthrow and his subsequent manipulation of the Hawaiian people. History, it seems, will not be kind to Lorrin Thurston.

32. London, "Koolau the Leper," 40.

33. Ibid., 43.

34. Gavan Daws, *The Shoals of Time* (Honolulu: University of Hawaii Press, 1968), 292.

35. London, "The Sheriff of Kona," *Stories of Hawaii*, 57.

36. See Charmian London, *Jack London and Hawaii*, 181–82, for the view from Dr. Goodhue's Kona bungalow. The description suggests the opening scene in "The Sheriff of Kona."

37. The similarity between London's opinions on Kalaupapa (*The Cruise of the Snark*, 97–104) and the repugnant Kersdale's views is a bit disconcerting, though Charmian (*Jack London and Hawaii*, 105–7) speaks of the tremendous sympathy she and Jack felt when observing the departure of the *Noeau*, as well as their discomfort at being present for such an intimate scene. We are led to believe that London, unlike Kersdale, would not go there for entertainment.

38. *Letters*, 2: 902.

39. London, "The Sheriff of Kona," 92. The spiritual quality of the land cannot be minimized. In 1843, King Kamehameha III declared Hawaiian sovereignty from Great Britain: "Ua mau ke ea o ka 'āina i ka pono" (The life [some say, sovereignty] of the land is perpetuated in righteousness). Somewhat ironically for *nā kanaka maoli*, this has since become the state motto.

40. Mary Kawena Pukui, E. W. Haertig, and Catherine A. Lee, *Nānā I Ke Kumu (Look to the Source)* (Honolulu: Hui Hanai, 1972), 2: 227.

41. Charmian London, *Jack London and Hawaii*, 238.

42. Ibid., 304.

43. London, "The Bones of Kahekili," *Stories of Hawaii*, 135–36.

Walsh: Historical Discourses

1. Earle Labor, Robert C. Leitz, III, and I. Milo Shepard, eds., *The Letters of Jack London*, 3 vols. (Stanford, Calif.: Stanford University Press, 1988), 3: 1435.

2. Jack London to J. T. Hamada, April 18, 1915, ibid., 1445.

3. David Mike Hamilton, *"The Tools of My Trade": The Annotated Books in Jack London's Library* (Seattle: University of Washington Press, 1986).

4. William Freeman Blackman, *The Making of Hawaii: A Study in Social Evolution* (New York: Macmillan, 1899), 65, 104, 230–31.

5. C. S. Stewart, *Journal of a Residence in the Sandwich Islands* (Honolulu: University of Hawaii Press, 1970 [1830]).

6. Katherine Fullerton Gerould, *Hawaii: Scenes and Impressions* (New York: Scribner's, 1916), 15.

7. Dale L. Walker and James E. Sisson III, *The Fiction of Jack London: A Chronological Bibliography* (El Paso: Texas Western Press, 1972), 31.

8. Jack London, "Shin Bones," in A. Grove Day, ed., *Stories of Hawaii by Jack London* (Honolulu: Mutual Publishing Paperback Series, 1968), 178–202.

9. Hamilton, *Annotated Books in London's Library*, 52.

10. Hayden White, "'Figuring the nature of the times deceased': Literary Theory

and Historical Writing," in Ralph Cohen, ed., *The Future of Literary Theory* (New York: Routledge, 1989), 25.

11. Stephen Greenblatt, "Shakespeare and the Exorcists," in Robert Con Davis and Ronald Schleifer, eds., *Contemporary Literary Criticism* (New York: Longman, 1989), 444.

12. Mikhail Bakhtin, *Problems of Dostoevsky's Poetics*, trans. Caryl Emerson, intro. Wayne C. Booth, Theory and History of Literature, vol. 8 (Minneapolis: University of Minnesota Press, 1983), 6.

13. Noel J. Kent, *Hawaii: Islands Under the Influence* (New York: Monthly Review Press, 1983), 14; Toni L. Han et al., *moe kau a ho ʻoilo: Hawaiian Mortuary Practices at Keopu, Kona, Hawaiʻi* (Honolulu: Bernice Pauahi Bishop Museum, 1986), 88. Kent observes that the history of white exploitation in Hawaii is a long one. As a direct result of European expansionism in the eighteenth century, Captain James Cook discovered what he named the Sandwich Islands in 1778. Native Hawaiians were introduced to European technology, fashion, and customs, and much bartering went on. In 1795, one English musket was worth nine large hogs. Han notes that guns were so valued by the Hawaiians that when they died, their guns would be buried with them, along with their other prized "native" possessions such as feathered caps, fish hooks, and tapa cloth. Other eighteenth- and nineteenth-century burial items included opium-smoking paraphernalia, medicine bottles, and buttons made from various metals and glass. Anglo influence in Hawaii is evident even in the graves of royalty.

14. Greenblatt, "Shakespeare," 429.

15. Kent, *Islands Under the Influence*, 16. The sandalwood trade in the eighteenth century brought Hawaii into the global economy. And with the aid of the British, who armed him, King Kamehameha, a pro-colonialist, united the eight islands, which had been sovereign states. However, not all Hawaiians approved. Kent quotes David Malo, a Hawaiian historian and a member of the *aliʻi*, who wrote in 1837: "If a big wave comes in, large fishes will come from the dark ocean which you never saw before, and when they see the small fishes they will eat them up. The ships of the white man have come, and smart people have arrived from the great countries which you have never seen before. They know our people are few in number and living in a small country. They will eat us up" (17). And the British feasted, exploiting the Islands until there was barely a sandalwood tree left.

16. Kent, *Islands Under the Influence*, 29, 43–60. Early in the nineteenth century, whaling became profitable in Hawaii, which marked the change to American dominance in the Islands. Also significant in this regard was the first sugar plantation, established in 1830, and American superiority in agriculture. Thus native Islanders wanting to hold on to their traditions had to fight two opposing forces. Subsequently, American agriculturalists and speculators flocked to Hawaii, buying up land and trading in sugar. By the middle of the nineteenth century, the politics of Hawaii were the rising bourgeoisie's. The Civil War created a sugar shortage in the United States,

and so sugar became Hawaii's major cash crop. By 1894, 92 percent of Hawaii's trade was with the United States. And because of laborers brought from the Orient and whites coming to the Islands, by 1890 only 45 percent of Hawaii's population was either Hawaiian or part Hawaiian.

17. Linda Hutcheon, *A Poetics of Postmodernism: History, Theory, Fiction* (New York: Routledge, 1988), 88, 96.

18. Earle Labor, *Jack London* (New York: Twayne, 1974), 129.

19. Han et al., *moe kau a ho 'oilo*, 17.

20. Ibid., 13.

21. Ibid.

22. Mikhail Bakhtin, *The Dialogic Imagination: Four Essays*, ed. and intro. Michael Holquist, trans. Caryl Emerson and Michael Holquist (Austin: University of Texas Press, 1981), 342–50. Bakhtin means by the term "authoritative discourse" the utterance that "demands that we acknowledge it, that we make it our own; it binds us, quite independent of any power it might have to persuade us internally; we encounter it with its authority already fused to it" (342).

23. Mikhail Bakhtin, "Discourse in Life and Discourse in Art (Concerning Sociological Poetics)," in Davis and Schleifer, *Contemporary Literary Criticism*, 397.

24. Edward Said, "The Politics of Knowledge," in David H. Richter, ed., *Falling into Theory: Conflicting Views on Reading Literature* (Boston: Bedford Books of St. Martin's Press, 1994), 202.

25. Bakhtin, "Discourse in Life," 403.

26. Jack London, "My Hawaiian Aloha," in King Hendricks and Irving Shepard, eds., *Jack London Reports: War Correspondence, Sports Articles, and Miscellaneous Writings* (New York: Doubleday, 1970 [1916]), 383.

27. Ibid., 398.

28. Bakhtin, *Dostoevsky's Poetics*, 63.

29. Bakhtin, "Discourse in Life," 403.

30. Hamilton, *Annotated Books in London's Library*, 264.

31. Charles Warren Stoddard, *The Island of Tranquil Delights* (London: Herbert B. Turner, 1904), 318.

32. Bakhtin, "Discourse in Life," 409.

Berkove: The Myth of Hope

1. According to information furnished me in private conversation with Earle Labor, London finished the story on May 20, 1916.

2. Earle Labor, Robert C. Leitz, III, and I. Milo Shepard, eds., "Introduction," *Short Stories of Jack London: Authorized One-Volume Edition* (New York: Macmillan, 1990), xxx. Theirs is the edition of "The Red One" cited in the text.

3. Recent useful studies include Thomas Clareson, *A Spectrum of Worlds* (Garden City, N.Y.: Doubleday, 1972), 87–90; Ellen Brown, "A Perfect Sphere: Jack London's 'The Red One,'" *Jack London Newsletter* 11 (1978): 81–85; Jeanne Campbell, "Fall-

ing Stars: Myth in 'The Red One,'" *Jack London Newsletter* 11 (1978): 87–96; Jens Peter Jørgenson, "Jack London's 'The Red One': A Freudian Approach," *Jack London Newsletter* 8 (1975): 101–3; Jørgen Riber, "Archetypal Patterns in 'The Red One,'" *Jack London Newsletter* 8 (1975): 104–6; James Kirsch, "Jack London's Quest: 'The Red One,'" *Psychological Perspectives* 2 (Fall 1980): 137–54; and Per Serritslev Petersen, "Science-Fictionalizing the Paradox of Living: Jack London's 'The Red One' and the Ecstasy of Regression," in Ib Johansen and Peter Ronnov-Jessen, eds., *Inventing the Future* (Aarhus, Denmark: Seklos, Department of English, University of Aarhus, 1985), 38–58. I also wish to thank Earle Labor for his gracious and unstinting assistance, including making available to me the manuscript of his unpublished talk, "From *Heart of Darkness* through *Modern Man in Search of a Soul* to *2001*: Jack London's Apocalyptic Vision in 'The Red One.'" Finally, I am deeply grateful to Professor Wilma Garcia, of Oakland University, for her invaluable advice and suggestions. A version of this study was presented at the American Literature Association Symposium on American Fiction in Cabo San Lucas, Mexico, on November 8, 1991.

4. Charmian London, *Book of Jack London*, 3 vols. (New York: Century, 1921), 2: 323.

5. The complete list of translations can be found in the *General Bibliography of C. G. Jung's Writing*, Bollingen Series 20 (Princeton: Princeton University Press, 1979). The two monographs by Carl Jung are *The Psychology of Dementia Praecox*, authorized trans. with an intro. by Frederick Peterson and A. A. Brill (New York: Journal of Nervous and Mental Disease Publishing Co., 1909); and *The Theory of Psychoanalysis* (New York: Journal of Nervous and Mental Disease Publishing Co., 1915).

6. Morton Prince, M.D., "The Mechanism and Interpretation of Dreams," *Journal of Abnormal Psychology* 5 (1910): 139–95.

7. David Mike Hamilton, *"The Tools of My Trade": The Annotated Books in Jack London's Library* (Seattle: University of Washington Press, 1986), 129.

8. In a letter of October 24, 1916, London remarked to a friend that he had "just recently subscribed to the *Psychoanalytic Review*." See Earle Labor, Robert C. Leitz, III, and I. Milo Shepard, eds., *The Letters of Jack London*, 3 vols. (Stanford, Calif.: Stanford University Press, 1988), 3: 1598. Unless the date the subscription began and the contents of the issues London received can be established, the late date of this letter prevents it from being conclusive evidence of London's earlier familiarity with Jung.

9. Labor, "Jack London's Pacific World," in Jacqueline Tavernier-Courbin, ed., *Critical Essays on Jack London* (Boston: G. K. Hall, 1983), 212. Details of torture and brutality from stories set in Melanesia, such as "Mauki" (1909), "The Terrible Solomons" (1910), "The Inevitable White Man" (1910), and *The Cruise of the Snark* (1911), are used again in "The Red One."

10. Apart from my uncertainty about London's having read Jung, I am reluctant to cast Ngurn as a "wise old man" archetype because, as my analysis shows, I do not find him wise. James I. McClintock maintains that in 1916, "Jung and Freud were

in substantial agreement about fundamental concepts so that it is, when discussing London's fiction, of little importance to distinguish what ideas he took from Freud and which from Jung. Subscribing to both men's views at this time would cause no intellectual contradictions that could lead to thematic or symbolic confusions in a work of fiction" (*White Logic: Jack London's Short Stories* [Grand Rapids, Mich.: Wolf House Books, 1975], 191 n. 289). This statement seems to me of doubtful accuracy with respect to the essential similarity of Freud and Jung, but even if it is given full weight, Ngurn does not function well as a representation of the superego. He is more principled, perhaps, than Bassett, but if tribal "whispered intrigue" is correct, he fathered Gngngn—the "addle-headed young chief" (585).

11. Just as Ngurn does not seem (from a Freudian perspective) an adequate superego figure, Balatta is not a convincing personification of libido, with all the wild energy that role demands. Her devotion to Bassett goes far beyond sexual satisfaction.

12. A comprehensive study of the development of London's attitudes toward women has yet to be written, but it is clear that Bassett in no way reflects his own position. London called his second wife, Charmian, "Mate Woman," and, as Jacqueline Tavernier-Courbin has shown, even in his earlier stories set in the Arctic, many native women are depicted as equals with their white mates. See, for example, "'The Wife of a King': A Defense," *Jack London Newsletter* 10 (1977): 34–38; "Jack London's Portrayal of the Natives in His First Four Collections of Arctic Tales," *Jack London Newsletter* 10 (1978 [1977]): 127–37; and "Social Myth as Parody in Jack London's Northern Tales," *Thalia* 9 (Fall-Winter 1987): 3–14.

13. The idea of intelligent life in outer space is not only a speculation by Bassett. It was part of the original germ of the story that London got from his friend, George Sterling. In his letter to Sterling of March 7, 1916, London asked if he remembered the "wonderful story you told me . . . of the meteoric message from Mars or some other world in space, that fell amongst isolated savages, that was recognized for what it was by the lost explorer, who died or was killed before he could gain access to the treasure in the heart of the apparent meteor?" (*Letters*, 3: 1542–43).

14. No comprehensive study of London's reading exists, although a valuable start has been made in Hamilton's *Annotated Books in London's Library*, which includes Otto Rank's *The Myth of the Birth of the Hero: A Psychological Interpretation of Mythology* (1914). It was likely that London was familiar with Norse myths, as interest in mythology burgeoned at the turn of the century. Those myths have long been second in popularity, in Western culture, only to those of Greece and Rome. In an 1899 letter, London used a learned allusion to Norse mythology when he described England as "the MitGart serpent of the nations" (*Letters*, 1: 99).

15. Kevin Crossley-Holland, *The Norse Myths* (New York: Pantheon, 1980), 8.

16. Campbell points out that decapitation "is an ancient archetype for castration" ("Falling Stars," 88). Insofar as this meaning may apply to the story, the heads in Ngurn's hut are, again, symbols not of wisdom so much as of humiliating defeat.

17. The reference to "supermen" may be yet another allusion—a negative one to Nietzschean philosophy. London began reading Nietzsche as early as 1904, but if we

can believe his later letters, though he found the philosopher stimulating, both *The Sea-Wolf* (1904) and *Martin Eden* (1909) were "indictments of the superman philosophy of Nietzsche and modern German ideas" (London to H. E. Kelsey, April 3, 1915, *Letters*, 3: 1439; see also London to J. H. Greer, August 4, 1915 (ibid., 1485), and to Mary Austin, November 5, 1915 (ibid., 1513). London's opposition in 1915 to Nietzsche's superman idea is another clue to his negative characterization of Bassett, who may be seen as embodying Nietzschean ideas and who hopes he will gain the intelligence of supermen from the Red One.

18. A useful contrast to Bassett's mind occurs at the end of London's "The Chinago" (1909). In both stories, the main character dies by decapitation. In "The Chinago," however, the lowly coolie who dies has been told that the guillotine's knife may even tickle him. But at the last instant he realized that "Cruchot was wrong. The knife did not tickle. That much he knew before he ceased to know" (338). The starkness of his simple honesty undercuts Bassett's fantasies.

19. Both Jørgensen ("London's 'The Red One'") and Riber ("Archetypal Patterns") recognized that Bassett's intended knife thrust is significant, and Jørgensen particularly sensed the masculine challenge the story poses. Both authors, however, wrote too briefly to develop these ideas, and their interpretations are very different from mine.

20. An additional evolutionary penalty applies to the main characters in "The Red One": they come to a genetic dead end. Bassett and Balatta have no progeny, and if Gngngn is Ngurn's son, he is substandard mentally and is forbidden contact with women.

21. In his discussion of the story, Clareson interprets Bassett's reflection on the stars, that "all must be comparatively alike, comparatively of the same substance, or substances, save for the freaks of the ferment. All must obey, or compose, the same laws that ran without infraction through the entire experience of man" (594), as signifying that the story is "the *cri de coeur* of a man appalled by a mechanistic universe governed by determinism" and that London "remains a product of his milieu, tortured by the dream of what man might be, the reality of what he is" (*Spectrum of Worlds*, 90). From somewhat different perspectives, we have arrived at seemingly similar views about the story. I do not find London either ultimately naturalistic or pessimistic, however, because of the change that occurred in his views one month later, after he read Jung's *Psychology of the Unconscious*.

22. McClintock, *White Logic*, 155–56. As indicated in the previous note, major swings in London's mood and outlook could occur within short periods of time, even a month.

23. Charmian London, *The Book of Jack London*, 2: 324, 334.

Labor: Afterword

1. See Earle Labor, *Jack London* (New York: Twayne, 1974), 117. For still further connections between London and Emerson, see Earle Labor, "From 'All Gold Canyon'

to *The Acorn-Planter*: Jack London's Agrarian Vision," *Western American Literature* 11 (Summer 1976): 83–84.

2. "Goethe," in *The Complete Writings of Ralph Waldo Emerson* (New York: Wm. H. Wise, 1929), 408–12.

3. Emerson, "The American Scholar," ibid., 30.

4. Quoted in Joan Sherman, *Jack London: A Reference Guide* (Boston: G. K. Hall, 1977), 119, 132, 136, 150.

5. Sam S. Baskett, "A Source for *The Iron Heel*," *American Literature* 27 (May 1955): 268–70; "Jack London on the Oakland Waterfront," *American Literature* 27 (Nov. 1955): 363–71; "Jack London's Heart of Darkness," *American Quarterly* 10 (Spring 1958): 66–77; "Introduction" and "Notes," *Martin Eden* (New York: Rinehart, 1956), v–xxvi, 383–84.

6. Gordon Mills, "Jack London's Quest for Salvation," *American Quarterly* 7 (Spring 1955): 3–14; "The Symbolic Wilderness: James Fenimore Cooper and Jack London," *Nineteenth-Century Fiction* 13 (Mar. 1959): 329–40. See also Earle Labor, "Jack London's Symbolic Wilderness: Four Versions," *Nineteenth-Century Fiction* 17 (Sept. 1962): 149–61, and the Author's Note to this essay reprinted in Ray Wilson Ownbey, ed., *Jack London: Essays in Criticism* (Santa Barbara, Calif.: Peregrine Smith, 1978), 41–42.

7. Maxwell Geismar, "Jack London: The Short Cut," in *Rebels and Ancestors: The American Novel, 1890–1915* (Boston: Houghton Mifflin, 1953), 139–216; Kenneth S. Lynn, "Jack London: The Brain Merchant," in *The Dream of Success: A Study of the Modern American Imagination* (Boston: Little, Brown, 1955), 75–118; Walter B. Rideout, *The Radical Novel in the United States, 1900–1954: Some Interrelations of Literature and Society* (Cambridge: Harvard University Press, 1956), 30, 38–47, 111; Charles Child Walcutt, "Jack London: Blond Beasts and Supermen," in *American Literary Naturalism: A Divided Stream* (Minneapolis: University of Minnesota Press, 1956), 87–113; Conway Zirkle, *Evolution, Marxian Biology, and the Social Scene* (Philadelphia: University of Pennsylvania Press, 1959), 301–4, 318–37, 349–50.

8. Clell T. Peterson, "The Jack London Legend," *American Book Collector* 8 (Jan. 1958): 13–17; "Jack London's Sonoma Novels," *ABC* 9 (Oct. 1958): 15–20; "Jack London's Alaskan Stories," *ABC* 9 (Apr. 1959): 15–22.

9. *The Bodley Head Jack London*, ed. Arthur Calder-Marshall, 4 vols. (London: Bodley Head Press, 1963–66); *The Call of the Wild and White Fang*, ed. Abraham Rothberg, Pathfinder ed. (New York: Bantam Books, 1963); Richard O'Connor, *Jack London: A Biography* (Boston: Little, Brown, 1964); *The Sea-Wolf*, ed. Matthew J. Bruccoli, Riverside ed. (Boston: Houghton Mifflin, 1964); *The Sea-Wolf and Selected Stories*, afterword and bibliography by Franklin Walker, Signet Classics ed. (New York: New American Library, 1964); *The Call of the Wild and Selected Stories*, foreword by Franklin Walker, Signet Classics ed. (New York: New American Library, 1964); King Hendricks and Irving Shepard, eds., *Letters from Jack London* (New York: Odyssey Press, 1965); *Great Short Works of Jack London*, ed. Earle Labor (New York: Harper and Row, 1965, 1970); Franklin Walker, *Jack London and the Klondike: The*

Genesis of an American Writer (San Marino, Calif.: Huntington Library, 1966); Hensley C. Woodbridge, John London, and George H. Tweney, *Jack London: A Bibliography* (Georgetown, Calif.: Talisman Press, 1966).

10. King Hendricks, ed., *Creator and Critic: A Controversy Between Jack London and Philo Buck, Jr.* (Logan: Utah State University Press, 1961); King Hendricks, *Jack London: Master Craftsman of the Short Story* (Logan: The Faculty Association, Utah State University, 1966); Charles Child Walcutt, *Jack London*, University of Minnesota Pamphlets on American Writers, No. 57 (Minneapolis: University of Minnesota Press, 1966); Joan London, *Jack London and His Times: An Unconventional Biography* (Seattle: University of Washington Press, 1968 [1939]).

11. King Hendricks and Irving Shepard, eds., *Jack London Reports: War Correspondence, Sports Articles, and Miscellaneous Writings* (New York: Doubleday, 1970).

12. James I. McClintock, *White Logic: Jack London's Short Stories* (Grand Rapids, Mich.: Wolf House Books, 1975).

13. Dale L. Walker and James E. Sisson III, *The Fiction of Jack London: A Chronological Bibliography* (El Paso: Texas Western Press, 1972); Hensley C. Woodbridge, John London, and George H. Tweney, *Jack London: A Bibliography*, enl. ed. (Millwood, N.Y.: Kraus Reprint Co., 1973); Sherman, *Reference Guide*.

14. Dale L. Walker, *The Alien Worlds of Jack London* (Grand Rapids, Mich.: Wolf House Books, 1973); Walker, ed., *Curious Fragments: Jack London's Tales of Fantasy Fiction*, with a preface by Philip José Farmer (Port Washington, N.Y.: Kennikat Press, 1975).

15. Franklin Walker, *The Seacoast of Bohemia*, enl. ed. (Santa Barbara, Calif.: Peregrine Smith, 1973 [1966]).

16. Lois Rather, *Jack London, 1905* (Oakland, Calif.: The Rather Press, 1974).

17. See Earle Labor, "Jack London, 1876–1976: A Centennial Recognition," *Modern Fiction Studies* 22 (Spring 1976): 3–7; this entire issue was dedicated to Jack London, as were *Western American Literature* 11 (Summer 1976), *Pacific Historian* 21 (Summer 1977), and *Europe: Revue Litteraire Mensuelle* 54 (Jan.-Feb. 1976). Also see Art Shields, "Why We Honor Jack London," *Political Affairs* 55 (Apr. 1976): 43–57.

18. Andrew Sinclair, *Jack: A Biography of Jack London* (New York: Harper and Row, 1977). I use the term "problematical" advisedly. Russ Kingman discovered more than 200 factual errors in this book. See also Dale L. Walker, "The Exhumation of Jack: Andrew Sinclair's Patho-Biography," *Jack London Newsletter* 10 (1977):119–26.

19. Ownbey, *Essays in Criticism*.

20. Richard W. Etulain, ed., *Jack London on the Road: The Tramp Diary and Other Hobo Writings* (Logan: Utah State University Press, 1979); Jack London, *No Mentor But Myself: A Collection of Articles, Essays, Reviews, and Letters on Writing and Writers*, ed. Dale L. Walker (Port Washington, N.Y.: Kennikat Press, 1979); Russ Kingman, *A Pictorial Life of Jack London* (New York: Crown, 1979), subsequently revised and reprinted for the Jack London Research Center as *A Pictorial Biography of Jack London* (Glen Ellen, Calif.: David Rejl, n.d.).

21. *The Call of the Wild by Jack London: A Casebook with Text, Background Sources, Reviews, Critical Essays, and Bibliography,* comp. Earl J. Wilcox (Chicago: Nelson-Hall, 1980); Jack London, *The People of the Abyss, with Jack London Photographs and Drawings by Gustave Doré,* foreword by Clarice Stasz (Malibu, Calif.: Joseph Simon, 1980); Howard Lachtman, ed., *Sporting Blood: Selections from Jack London's Greatest Sports Writing* (Novato, Calif.: Presidio Press, 1981), and *Young Wolf: The Early Adventure Stories of Jack London* (Santa Barbara, Calif.: Capra Press, 1984); Jack London, *Novels and Stories* and *Novels and Social Writings,* ed. Donald Pizer (New York: The Library of America, 1982); Stanley Wertheim and Sal Noto, eds., *Dearest Greek: Jack and Charmian London's Presentation Inscriptions to George Sterling* (Cupertino, Calif.: Eureka Publications, 1983); Jack London, *A Klondike Trilogy: Three Uncollected Stories,* ed. Earle Labor, illus. Jack Freas (Santa Barbara, Calif.: Neville, 1983); Sal Noto, ed., *Jack London's California: The Golden Poppy and Other Writings* (New York: Beaufort Books, 1986), and *With a Heart Full of Love: Jack London's Presentation Inscriptions to the Women in His Life* [Eliza London Shepard, Charmian London, Flora Wellman London, and Mabel Applegarth] (Berkeley, Calif.: Twowindows Press, 1986); Dale L. Walker, ed., *In a Far Country: Jack London's Tales of the West* (Ottawa, Ill.: Jameson Books, 1987); Earle Labor, Robert C. Leitz, III, and I. Milo Shepard, eds., *The Letters of Jack London,* 3 vols. (Stanford, Calif.: Stanford University Press, 1988). Cogent evidence of the recent rise in London's literary stature is the fact that the *Letters* received lead reviews in *New York Times Book Review, Times Literary Supplement,* and *American Literature;* a modified version of E. L. Doctorow's *New York Times* review has subsequently appeared in his *Jack London, Hemingway, and the Constitution: Selected Essays, 1977–1992* (New York: Random House, 1993), 1–13.

22. Joan D. Hedrick, *Solitary Comrade: Jack London and His Work* (Chapel Hill: University of North Carolina Press, 1982); I call this book "frustrating" because Hedrick undercuts her compelling thesis—that the central tension of London's career was his initiation into "the man's world of the working class" versus his subsequent initiation into "the woman's world of the middle class"—by dismissing those works produced during the last third of his career as "decadent extensions of patterns already established in London's life and art" (xviii). Clarice Stasz, *American Dreamers: Charmian and Jack London* (New York: St. Martin's Press, 1988).

23. Charles N. Watson, Jr., *The Novels of Jack London: A Reappraisal* (Madison: University of Wisconsin Press, 1983); Carolyn Johnston, *Jack London—An American Radical?* (Westport, Conn.: Greenwood Press, 1984).

24. David Mike Hamilton, *"The Tools of My Trade": The Annotated Books in Jack London's Library* (Seattle: University of Washington Press, 1986). London's personal library comprised more than 15,000 volumes, and Hamilton observes that it is "quite clear that London was not a book collector but an author with a professional library" (1).

25. Homer L. Haughey and Connie Kale Johnson, *Jack London Ranch Album,* fore-

word by Earle Labor (Stockton, Calif.: Heritage Publishing, in cooperation with the Valley of the Moon Natural History Association and the California Department of Parks and Recreation, 1985), and *Jack London Homes Album* (Stockton, Calif.: Heritage Publishing, 1987); Gorman Beauchamp, *Jack London* (Mercer Island, Wash.: Starmont House, 1984); James Lundquist, *Jack London: Adventures, Ideas, and Fiction* (New York: Ungar, 1987).

26. Special credit is due Earl Wilcox, Jeanne Campbell Reesman, Tony Williams, and Susan Nuernberg for organizing these multiple Jack London sessions for CEA, ALA, MLA, and PCA.

27. Russ Kingman was instrumental in winning the approval for this stamp and in organizing the Glen Ellen ceremony, attended by several hundred, including London's daughter, Becky London Fleming, and his great-nephew, I. Milo Shepard. San Francisco Mayor Dianne Feinstein officially proclaimed January 11, 1986, "Jack London Day in San Francisco." Another ceremony was held by U.S. Postal Service officials and London buffs at Jack London Square in Oakland on Monday, January 13. In 1988 the Jack London stamp became the first Great Americans Series number to be issued in booklet format.

28. Earle Labor, Robert C. Leitz, III, and I. Milo Shepard, eds., *Short Stories of Jack London: Authorized One-Volume Edition* (New York: Macmillan, 1990); Jack London, *John Barleycorn—Or, Alcoholic Memoirs*, intro. Clarice Stasz, Signet Classic (New York: Penguin Books, 1990); Jack London, *Stories of Boxing*, ed. James Bankes, preface by Becky London, foreword by Russ Kingman (Dubuque: William C. Brown, 1992); Jack London, *John Barleycorn: 'Alcoholic Memoirs,'* ed. John Sutherland (Oxford: Oxford University Press, 1989), Jack London, *The Call of the Wild, White Fang, and Other Stories*, ed. Earle Labor and Robert C. Leitz, III (Oxford: Oxford University Press, 1990), Jack London, *The Sea-Wolf*, ed. John Sutherland (Oxford: Oxford University Press, 1993), and Jack London, *The Son of the Wolf: Tales of the Far North*, ed. Charles N. Watson, Jr. (Oxford: Oxford University Press, 1996); Earle Labor, Robert C. Leitz, III, and I. Milo Shepard, eds., *The Complete Short Stories of Jack London*, 3 vols. (Stanford, Calif.: Stanford University Press, 1993); Jack London, *"To Build a Fire" and Other Stories*, ed. Earle Labor, The World's Best Reading series (Pleasantville, N.Y.: Reader's Digest, 1994); Earle Labor, ed., *The Portable Jack London* (New York: Penguin Books, 1994).

29. Mark E. Zamen, *Standing Room Only: Jack London's Controversial Career as a Public Speaker*, foreword by Earle Labor, American University Studies series (New York: Peter Lang, 1990); Eugene P. Lasartemay and Mary Rudge, *For Love of Jack London: His Life with Jennie Prentiss: A True Love Story* (New York: Vantage Press, 1991); Tony Williams, *Jack London and the Movies: An Historical Survey* (Los Angeles: David Rejl, 1992); Jacqueline Tavernier-Courbin, *The Call of the Wild: A Naturalistic Romance* (New York: Twayne, 1994); Earle Labor and Jeanne Campbell Reesman, *Jack London: Revised Edition* (New York: Twayne, 1994); Susan M. Nuernberg, ed., *The Critical Response to Jack London* (Westport, Conn.: Greenwood Press, 1995); *The Call*

of the Wild, by Jack London, with an *Illustrated Reader's Companion* by Daniel Dyer (Norman: University of Oklahma press, 1995).

30. Russ Kingman, *Jack London: A Definitive Chronology* (Middletown, Calif.: David Rejl, 1992).

31. Emerson, "The Poet," *Complete Writings*, 240–41.

32. Emerson, "Greatness," ibid., 824. London's works have now been translated into more than 80 languages, giving him legitimate claim to the title "America's Greatest World Author."

33. Emerson, "The Poet," 240.

INDEX

In this index "f" after a number indicates a separate reference on the next page, and "ff" indicates separate references on the next two pages. A continuous discussion over two or more pages is indicated by a span of numbers. *Passim* is used for a cluster of references in close but not consecutive sequence.

Adams, Brooks, 59, 63, 69, 72, 245 n.46
Adorno, Theodor, 61
Ahearn, Marie L., 244 n.33
Ainselee's, 22
Alger, Horatio, 62, 69
Anderson, Sherwood, 106
Apollodorus, 212
Applegarth, Mabel, 92f
Atlantic Monthly, 102, 232 n.28
Auerbach, Jonathan, 7, 257 n.26
Austin, Mary, 220

Baker, Ray Stannard, 20–21
Bakhtin, Mikhail, 194, 198, 201, 221
Bankes, James, 222
Bankes, Richard, 169
Barthes, Roland, 12, 229 n.4
Baskett, Sam S., 7f, 218f, 223, 253 n.2, 257 n.26
Bates, D. Michael, 221
Baudelaire, Charles, 59, 243 n.26

Beauchamp, Gorman, 221
Bellamy, Edward, 83, 87
Benediktsson, Thomas, 255 n.21
Berger, Victor, 58
Berkman, Alexander, 240 n.10
Bernays, Claude, 131, 138
Bernays, Mrs. Claude, 138
Bersani, Leo, 258 nn.34,38
Besant, Walter, 62
Beveridge, Albert, 72f, 247 n.58
Bhabha, Homi K., 69, 247 n.53
Bierce, Ambrose, 85, 92
Bilgrami, Akeel, 12–13, 230 n.13
Bishop, Jonathan, 9
Blackman, William Freeman, 192
Blaine, James, 192
Bonaparte, Napoleon, 4
Boone, Joseph, 101, 103, 108, 126, 258 n.33
Booth, Charles, 244 n.38
Booth, William, 65, 68, 70
Borus, Daniel, 6

Library of Congress Cataloging-in-Publication Data

Rereading Jack London / edited by Leonard Cassuto and Jeanne Campbell
Reesman : with an afterword by Earle Labor.
     p.   cm.
Includes bibliographical references (p.   ) and index.
ISBN 0-8047-2634-5 (cloth : alk. paper)
1. London, Jack, 1876–1916—Criticism and interpretation.
I. Cassuto, Leonard. II. Reesman, Jeanne Campbell.
PS3523.046Z8715   1996
813'.52—dc20   96-17052
                                                              CIP

∞ This book is printed on acid-free, recycled paper.

Original printing 1996

Last figure below indicates year of this printing

05   04   03   02   01   00   99   98   97   96